# The Cultural Roots of Violence in Malay Southern Thailand

# The Cultural Roots of Violence in Malay Southern Thailand

## Comparative Mythology: Soul of Rice

### Volume 1: The Tutelary Figures of Malay Political Heroism

**Jacques Ivanoff**

In collaboration with Igor Besson, Christopher Court and Azip Samuyana and the Narrators Useng Dereh and Samoh Paksuloh

**White Lotus Press**

Text and photos by Jacques Ivanoff (except Figs. 6, 7 copyright by Igor Besson)
Translated by Francine Nicolle
Drawings by Prince of Songkla University

White Lotus Co., Ltd
G.P.O. Box 1141
Bangkok 10501
Thailand

Tel. (66) 0-38239-883-4
Fax (66) 0-38239-885
E-mail ande@loxinfo.co.th
Website http://thailine.com/lotus

Printed in Thailand

ISBN 978-974-480-162-3 pbk. White Lotus Co., Ltd., Bangkok

The cow herders of Madru had brought the mother of wheat and placed her in the middle of the square. She was an enormous sheaf of ripened wheat of almost black straw but with hair that was still blonde. The ripened sheaf made of all the swathes which had just been cut in the fields was clothed with three women's skirts, and [with] a swirl of oats she had been made pregnant by men's labor. There she was, with her belly heavy with seeds, her straw breasts, her old head covered by corn husks. The harnessed cattle sniffed and stamped their hooves in the mud. They shook their bronze colored necks, causing their yokes to creak. They tried to turn around and escape, dragging their carts behind them.

Antonian stood still.

A cow herder had taken hold of a torch made of lavender. He raised the skirts of the mother of wheat. He started making love to her with his enflamed torch and she was quickly set ablaze. The roar of the flames, the crackling of the exploding corn husks, the moaning of the straw bundles inside the skirts drowned out the sound of the howling river. The light beneath the low sky spread out like a ripened harvest.

The men cried out:

"Wheat of fire! Wheat of fire!"

The woman of straw's belly was in flames and she writhed with pain.

Jean Giono, *Le Chant du Monde*, Gallimard, Folio, Paris, 1988, pp. 228–9

# Contents

# Acknowledgements

This book would not have been completed without the support of Georges Condominas, Jean-Claude Galey, Aliette Geistdoefer, Yves Goudineau and Patrick Williams from the School of High Studies in Social Sciences (EHESS Paris).

It was also made possible thanks to those who have also encouraged me to persevere and to finally unveil the fruits of several years of research, despite the data being too "old" at times (1990s). For this I am grateful to Igor Besson, Aliette Geistdoefer, Thierry Lejard, Odile Moreau and Olivier Ferrari for their support and for going over my work with such care.

While the afore-mentioned have played instrumental roles in this project, this book stems from my desire to keep a population's cultural values from disappearing. Here, I am striving to present to the Malays of southern Thailand all they have to offer to the world of research and politics.

It goes without saying that it is for the Malays of the region that I am publishing this work, so that I may give back the voice that was taken from them. Among the faithful and loyal people of south-eastern Thailand, this book is first and foremost dedicated to all those that made it all happen: Azip, Ruslan, Rusli, Jimé, Dilok.

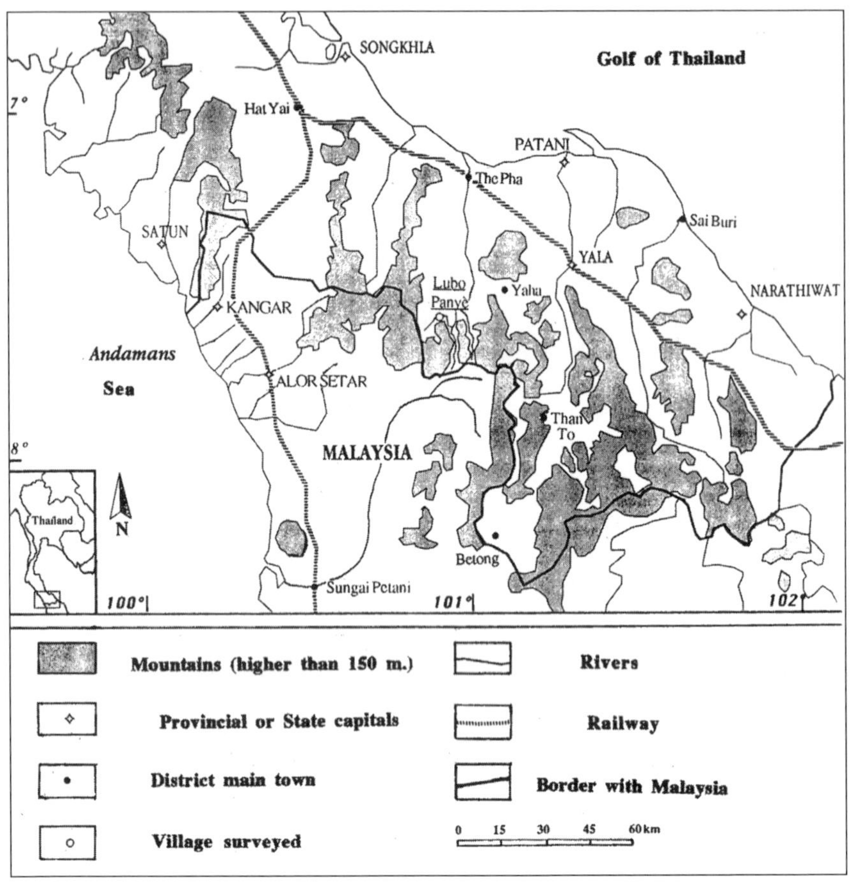
SONGKHLA
Golf of Thailand
7°
Hat Yai
PATANI
The Pha
Sai Buri
SATUN
YALA
Yala
NARATHIWAT
Lubo
Panyè
KANGAR
Andamans
Sea
ALOR SETAR
Than
To
8°
MALAYSIA
Thailand
N
Betong
Sungai Petani
100°
101°
102°
Mountains (higher than 150 m.)
Rivers
Provincial or State capitals
Railway
District main town
Border with Malaysia
Village surveyed
0 15 30 45 60 km

Map 1.

# Introduction

One day, when I had just begun my fieldwork among the Moken (the Austronesian and marine nomads of the Mergui archipelago), a group of Malays suddenly appeared at our campsite. After they had made some enquiries concerning alcohol and the consumption of turtles (prohibited by Islam), they decided to remain for a time in the camp. It would seem that cultural ties are much stronger than religious differences! Then, favored by a full moon, the Malay group gathered around my friend Madah, the Moken shaman, and asked him to narrate and sing a Malay tale in their language.[1] Madah did not need much urging! The Moken nomads and Malay fishermen seated themselves on the ground, or lay down, to listen to the story. This was a real surprise for me. There no longer seemed to be any doubt that the Moken were the guardians of Malay oral literature. I therefore decided to gather together all the texts which the Moken consider to be of Malay origin (Jacques Ivanoff, 2001a, 2004).

It was not long before I felt the need to visit the Malays themselves in order to penetrate their imaginary world and compare what I had discovered with the stories of the Moken and other populations of the region (Thais and Mons, for example) whose culture was beginning to become familiar to me because I had lived among them for several years. So I went to southeastern Thailand, to the so-called "Malay" provinces (Patani, Yala and Narathiwat—but not Satun[2] which is situated on the western coast and much more under Thai influence). It was there that I discovered an oral literature that was still alive but concealed in these areas where Islam has become rooted. The stories were different from those of the Moken but there were evident similarities, including those that had been imported from continental Southeast Asia.

Though anthropology no longer makes use of any notions of the functional archetypes of a group, a local proverb says that the Malays "die with their dreams".

They are also warriors who search for the lost link that once existed between the world and divinities; a quest that is expressed in magical rituals. That search explains how Chinese communities became established and why it has remained impossible for the Malays to build relationships with Thailand through an accord of principles because their identity, their way of thinking, their dreams and their quest have always been rejected. It is this dissociated way of thinking, between Islam's restrictive dogma and a tradition that is also restrictive, which has become the reality of the Malays' daily life. This explains their need to rediscover their spiritual values.

The magicians who travel from one village to another, those men of power who retain power even after their deaths, the saints whose tombs continue to grow with the growth of their skeletons, weapons that have a life of their own and that increase the power of the souls of their owners, warriors who search for unity and love, female plants that appear in order to help heroes to find their way in their quest, fabulous animals from local and Indian bestiaries, clear sparkling water surrounded by the monsters that one finds painted on the hulls of boats, these are the foundations of the Malay identity. But because they have been prevented from making the presence of these elements known, especially since the appearance of Muslim zealots and the domination of Koranic schools that were built after the collapse of the sultanates, and also because of the refusal of Thai people to recognize this "Malay soul", the Malays of southern Thailand have withdrawn into themselves.

These true adventurers are also farmers, fishermen and traders. But these two spheres, socio-economic and epic, are not exclusive. On the contrary, if one wishes to understand how Malay society functions, one must understood the motivations, desires and thoughts that define all their actions. It is the hero who ensures the balance and order of their world. He serves as a link between the two spheres. He makes use of what is already ordered, at least as regards the mythological representation of the world beyond and of nature (flora and fauna), and applies this to human society. Plants, for example, are the remains of an uncorrupted humanity and men and women who are pure and powerful are born from them. When associated with the heroes, an emanation of human disorder, they will put human society on the right path by re-establishing social ties but, more importantly, spiritual ties that unite men to the vegetal and animal reigns, thus re-opening the path leading to the world of the divinities.

The Malay territory of southern Thailand is reputed to be dangerous (as confirmed by the renewed conflict between government forces and communist, separatist or fundamentalist groups) and is closed to any form of research. Prince of Songkla University (Patani campus) was able to facilitate the present author's work because it was done in collaboration with French agronomists (from the French Research Institute on Rubber) who were investigating the supposed problem of rubber plantations that were considered to be too small (*cf.* Igor Besson, 2002). But difficulties in entering the rubber plantations and conducting their investigations had slowed down their work. The "developers" appreciated our knowledge of the milieu, the language and culture, so we worked with them to put in place a network of villagers in order to facilitate their investigations. This project of developing small rubber plantations required, in effect, the selection of a dozen villages having varying socio-agronomic characteristics (villages in the plains and mountains, isolated or open villages, Malay villages but also "Sakai" villages—and Chinese villages).

We then set up a network of villages in the region and obtained a reasonably accurate impression of the socio-economic conditions there. This work permitted me above all to lay down the bases of further ethnological research. I constantly tried to discover the reality of practices lying behind the discourse, to reveal what was hidden by Islam and to build close relations with the peasants, the imams, the chiefs of cantons. I had to be very persuasive since the Malays of southern Thailand like to talk, to discuss and to be convinced. I tried to show that it was impossible for the powerful men of the region, often respected hajis, to deny their ancestors simply because of the fairly recent but somewhat superficial movement in favor of Islamization. I was obliged to show them that I was well aware of the magical value of the *kerèh* (kris, a Malay knife with a curved blade) which was casually placed in "an old fashioned cupboard"; that I did not believe that the pottery that may be found in rice

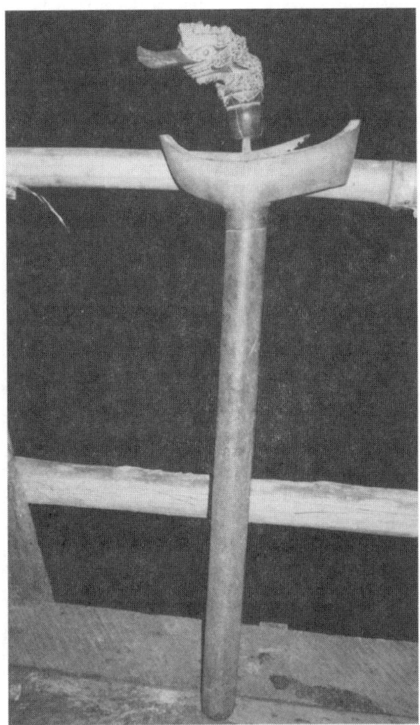

**Fig. 1.** Kris, typical of the Patani region, belonging to an old family of Yaha canton. (Ivanoff, 1990)

granaries had been left there, unused, for no reason; nor did I accept the reasons invoked in explanation of the presence of heteroclitic objects in rice fields (e.g. for tethering cattle to or for hanging hats on).

I was already aware that the region was culturally rich and that it had different codes and ideologies that the developers did not always understand very well and that the informants themselves were unable to explain.

When the rubber project was finally completed, the authorities respected their part of the contract whereby, in exchange for my help in facilitating their agronomic research in a region that everyone feared, I was given free access and administrative support for my fieldwork. This enabled me to put together a project,[3] and develop social science investigations in an area to which entrance had previously been forbidden. A long period of fieldwork permits an understanding of the many facets of different realities. This knowledge is made by brutal revelations, when small things that have been accumulated suddenly make sense. When I was touring the network of villages involved in the rubber project with my two assistants from Lubo Panyè (Jimé and Dilok),[4] I suddenly understood that all these strange things, that no questionnaire was able to quantify or explain, the eloquent silences that met my questions about traditions and all the contradictory practices (notably of the kinship system, the one "official" and patrilineal, the other "traditional" and uxorilocal) protected a system of unorthodox beliefs and rituals that proved to be the visible signs of an oral literature that was still in operation. From that time on, I tried unceasingly to find "something" which could lead me to the reality of local values even though none of my colleagues believed in the richness of the fieldwork we were undertaking. It was when one of my assistants returned with the first myth that had been told to him by Wo

**Fig. 2.** Heteroclitic vegetal material, scattered on the paddy fields, vegetal crosses, large protective bushes with *Borassus* palm trees. (Ivanoff, 1991)

**Fig.3.** Vegetal crosses are present in many rice, rubber, and forage areas and even in water holes. (Ivanoff, 1992)

**Fig.3.** Vegetal crosses are present in many rice, rubber, and forage areas and even in water holes. (Ivanoff, 1992)

Seng (Useng Dereh), whom I had suspected from the beginning was more than a malicious old man who was mocked by others, that I understood that I was right. Things began to accelerate and the hundreds of hours I had spent collecting such myths proved that my intuition had been well founded.

This is the first of two volumes covering the oral literature of the Malay people of southern Thailand. This volume is devoted to the oral corpus of these people within their social space. The aim of this first volume is to put into socio-political perspective the dynamics of the identity of the Malays of southern Thailand. I will present the framework of the whole subject in the first part of the second volume, where I will provide a much more detailed account of the history, political system and economic profile of the region and will give a full descriptive account of its inhabitants since, as we will see, oral literature is closely dependent on these socio-economic conditions.

The first part of the present volume outlines the general historical and socio-political background and the importance of the oral tradition in the region. The remainder of this volume comprises the oral texts that I collected and translated with the assistance and untiring work of my friend Azip Samuyana and the help of an exceptional phonetician, Christopher Court. These texts are illustrated by members of the staff of Prince of Songkla University, Patani campus. In this volume I present a comparative analysis and comprehensive catalogue of mythological narratives concerning the soul of rice throughout Southeast Asia in order to try to define the common influences and perhaps discover the mythological constants. The analogies I make here are not always structurally pertinent[5] and represent both an inventory[6] of traditions of rice culture and an exploration of possible directions for research based on different fieldwork.

The grouping of the texts within the subsequent parts of this volume was determined in accordance with their characteristics and the homogeneity of their forms and content. The narratives concerning rice occupy the central theme of Chapter 2, whether they be myths or epics.

Some of the epics make up a homogeneous whole, centered on the hero Hawè's quest, and in fact form a cycle. They have been grouped together in Chapter 3 (with the exception of the story of Hawè Jabut himself, who is interested in rice, and which I have put in chapter 2). This cycle should be analyzed separately, since the different stories are only episodes within the long epic framework that provides a cryptic outline of the Malay ideal of their world.

Chapter 4 brings together a variety of legends, mostly concerning animals, which are common to different cultures in the Insulindian world (for example, the story of the mouse-deer)[7] but also about the origin of rubber or certain activities that have a moral significance.

But beyond presenting these epic descriptions of a dreamed-of ideal, the aim of an analysis of oral literature is to establish comparisons, study the recurrence or absence of certain themes, define what has come from outside and bring to light, if not a definitive model, at least sub-sets. The aim of such an analysis is also to reconstruct certain obscure parts of local history, by the use of other supporting data. I am very much aware of both of these objectives,, but it would be premature for the moment to become attached to them since the work of reflection has not yet ended.

In a more modest way, one is able to make a sociological study of the texts by noting such matters of the terms of address, those designating kings, slaves, captives, warriors, etc. The appellation system is also full of data and throw light on the hierarchical structure of the society. Specific problem areas may be also noted, for example, that of exchange and gifts. The terms used for particular exchanges shed light on the social relations to which they refer. Thus, certain mythological themes reveal the social structure, and their sociological relevance will be discussed in Volume 2.

This study of the oral texts of the Malay world in southern Thailand exposes the richness of the local culture and the validity of the work conducted there. The links between the different groups become apparent and serve as a guide when one enters the labyrinth of installations, secessions, and social and cultural conflicts of the Austronesians.

The mythology and beliefs of the Malays of southern Thailand can be analyzed and compared with those of other Austronesian populations (notably the Moken and the Moklen); comparisons can also be made with the oral traditions of the Malays of Malaysia, using the rich ethnographic data and oral literature collected by other authors (e.g. Skeat, Skeat and Blagden, Clifford, Hill). A comprehensive analysis of all this material is beyond the scope of the present work. However I have decided to present here some comparisons (using certain texts collected by and analysis undertaken by Skeat among the Malays and Ivanoff among the Moken). It is necessary to link the oral tradition with the recurrent political violence in the south. The political reactions and violence are recorded in different oral traditions and serve as reminders of past acts of bravery, such as fights against tyrants whom heroes are called upon to destroy in order to recover the former unity of the Malays. The Malay identity in southern Thailand has developed both in pursuit of an ideal found in Malaysia that has faded with time and as a reaction to unacceptable Thai standards. The Malays are at the midpoint then between these two extremities and have developed very distinctive syncretic forms. It is in this way that their identity has developed. This is one of the reasons why traditions have developed and are transmitted more effectively here than in other places where national issues and Islam are dominant. Thus the Malays of southern Thailand have evolved in response to an interplay of events that constantly cause them to return to their own particular history, to epic narratives and even to their myths. The first narratives speak of the unity of men, an idea that permits Islam to be grafted on to customs (*adat*) without any problem since the values are the same. The unity of men implies the circulation of the vital elements that are constitutive of mankind and the universe; what the heroes accomplished in the epic narratives, the soul of rice accomplishes in the hearts of men and in their relations with their environment.

The quest of the Malays for unity is thus in a state of perpetual rediscovery each time their giant neighbors take action. Although these social movements have been suppressed by political parties or other organizations, not one of them has ever succeeded in totally subjugating the region, because they have been unable to capture the essence of these movements; nobody understands, or accepts, that they are rooted in a kind of millenarianist tendency (as Auesrivongse, 2005 understood), which proclaims the impossibility simultaneously of a return of the Malay identity and of the integration of the population into Thailand. The Malays of southern Thailand have a multiple identity that leans for support not only towards Islam but also to the Insulindian beliefs on to which other beliefs from continental Southeast Asia have been grafted. Torn between these two states they have built an identity on an epic base.

The question of Malay identity and multiple identity, as well as of the true foundation of that identity, remains unresolved. Apart from the issues briefly touched on above, international borders have continued to influence the question of multi-ethnicity (Herriman, 2005; Horstmann, 2005, etc.). The notion of Malay identity is itself complex and a constant subject of discussion (Reid, 2001), since it is recognized by Austronesian populations that one becomes a Malay by becoming a Muslim. It is much more difficult to establish differences between the Malay groups of the peninsula. Are the Malays of southern Thailand a group apart? It would seem that they are not, even though they have a different dialect and a tradition, long-since forgotten, emanating from elsewhere. The term *Jawi* utilized as an ethnonym inspires polemical reactions since it is not recognized by the authorities, the Thai people or even the Malays of the region ; the latter prefer to assimilate the Malays of the region as being *orè nayu*, "Malay men". However, the ethnonym *Jawi* appears to be endemic in certain communities with strong contacts with the Thais and who are therefore able to preserve their identity (as in Patani). Communities in other regions (e.g. Yala and Narathiwat) do not consider it to be a very strong identity marker. It is nonetheless quite evident that in a local context where Malays live alongside Thais, who are by definition Buddhists, the word *Jawi* refers to the Malays.

The term *Jawi* refers to all the Muslims of Southeast Asia, especially in the Insulindian world. It also refers to the local language (or dialect) and finally to Malay writing using the Arabic script. We can thus state that in some places, the word *Jawi* is considered as one ethnonym among others. Assimilation presents no problem since the Malays do not consider the co-existence of several ideas to be contradictory. For example, they may read a word in *Jawi*, in standard Malay written in Arabic script, but they will still pronounce the words in their local dialect.

Contemporary rebels, whether a tutelary epic figure like Haji Sulong or the youngsters who revolted in 2004 armed with machetes, convinced of their invincibility, have the mythical characteristics one comes across in oral texts and transmitted by the *bomoh* ("medium/traditional healer"). They are the modern heroes, avatars of their epic ancestors. This is how these rebels participate in the perpetuation of the Malay dream, one that the inhabitants of the region have incorporated so well in their sayings reflecting their opposition to the avidity of Chinese tradesmen and the pretentions of Thais or Western intruders (as a local proverb says). Malay identity has a solid base founded on continuing traditions and one that has been reaffirmed throughout contemporary history. No matter what political actions are taken to "pacify" the south, they have only succeeded in raising awareness of a southern Malay identity and justifying the search for an epic world. The particular characteristics of the region have then been reinforced by the search for references in oral literature that development has not yet been able to destroy, as has happened with their Malaysian neighbors. And with cultural information on the subject having acquired mythical status, and with the corpus of imaginary and epic references to which all inhabitants are attached, and with which they endlessly compare present-day actions, how is it possible for this Malay society, which remains so misunderstood, to find a place in Thailand? Like all traditional minorities, it feeds on this marginalization and lack of understanding.

The heroes of modern times resemble the heroes of their epics in their attempts to unify the Malay world and reunite the components of a universe that is in an explosive state and moving towards oblivion; present-day confrontations are simply pretexts that serve as an outlet and a means of expression of this desire. The modern world has a tendency to analyze modern conflicts erroneously. The result is that there is little interest in popular opinion and what it has to say about the reasons for such conflicts. This explains why such violence is recurrent and becomes a focal point. The objective of these manifestations escapes specialists. These forms of violence are the avatars of the epic adventures of the ancestors of the Malays. In this sense, the Malay dream, shaman trances, mythical unity transmuted into desires for modern Malay unity, make it possible for the soul of rice and Islam to co-exist, and to remain alive in the minds and hearts of the Malays.

It is because of the refusal of the Malays to conform to modern ideas (Islam as opposed to Buddhism, contemporary socio-economic development as opposed to underdevelopment) and their way of setting up new systems of regulation that are usually truncated that traditional Malay imagery remains alive in their hearts and minds, unaffected by the constraints imposed on them by present-day conditions. The people continue to live in conformity with their own rhythm and time. Scholars—political analysts, sociologists, ethnologists, historians and above all archaeologists and architects[8]—have produced reports about a field that remains largely unknown to them, justifying their own prejudices and their refusal to listen to the people. One has here an example of an area for fieldwork in which ideas that are totally out of context can be expressed in the certainty that there is no possibility that contradictory ethnographic data based on scientific fieldwork will be produced. And when the researchers utilize interpreters, interviews or spokesmen they simply explain the local tensions in terms of their preconceived notions. (For an example of this, one has only to look at the results of the French archaeological excavations in Patani in the 1990s, which were driven by economic considerations the aims of which were to develop museums in line with the ethnocentric ideas of the architects.)

A frequent, fundamental problem of much research in the Patani region is the absence of fieldwork, although some high-quality work has been done by European scholars (e.g. Horstmann, Roseman). One gains the impression that a direct study of the society concerned is unable to add to the data already reported by the most important investigators of the past (e.g. Skeat, Annandale, Endicott, Maxwell). Although researchers like Horstmann have opposed this tendency, research remains a prisoner of a postulate, that is, by refusing to accept a traditional society as an operational concept. There is a refusal to consider Malay society in southern Thailand as a living social body, dynamic and creative, a society whose relations with others is founded on very ancient imaginary, mythical and ritual influences. However, in spite of their attachment to this heritage, the Malays are still able to adapt themselves to present-day inter-relationships and to integration within the

Thai nation. But if one is continually searching to find answers on the basis of modern ideas concerning the manifestation of factors of identity, one forgets the broad meaning of the word tradition. Language, economy and history are considered a federation of sparse cultural elements. And the so-called absence of dynamic traditions and ethnological data (this volume shows that the oral tradition is still strong and contradicts the position of the researchers who make such claims) only reveals how impossible it is for scholars to accept the fact that populations still exist that continue to believe in and refer to very ancient oral traditions as being constituents of their identity. Such scholars refuse to accept the fact that oral texts could serve as models for them. And a refusal to familiarize oneself with these texts prevents, as we will see, not only any discussion of their content but also the development of a wider perspective on the situation in the south of Thailand. It leads one simply to forget that the people there possess ancient and powerful imagery that is deeply rooted in their traditions. To say that Islam and local customs are not in opposition to each other, while considering only Islam, is a scientific error that leads to a lack of understanding of the identity of the populations of the south and makes it impossible to analyze, from different angles, the tensions that continue to arise, without understanding why they take place.

I do not pretend here to undertake a cultural and comparative analysis of the texts, nor even a structural analysis of the narratives. I will simply present them as a counterpoint that will make it possible to acquire a better understanding of what I refer to as the multiple identity of the Malays of southern Thailand.

History is the cultural base of oral tradition in which the narratives are constructed and organized. Mythology provides the solution to the difficult alliance between Islam and customs. The Malays of southern Thailand have successfully won the challenge of unity, survival, transmission of values and regionalization. Therefore this history is an integral part of this book and I will try to define its most important contours. I am well aware that more than ten years have passed since the material published here was written. There have been the events of 2004 and the endless analyses by political scientists and anthropologists, who continue to ask why outbursts of violence that lack any real "political" elements (i.e. the involvement of communists, separatists or fundamentalists) remain endemic . The answer they seek remains elusive because it is cultural.

During these ten years works worthy of interest have been published that I mention in here in an effort to link together today's violence with episodes from the past. We will, of course, refer to the investigations by Horstmann (2002b and 2004) because he understood that representations of the problems of the nation, particularly those of the borders, are essential in processes of rebellion and integration. He also began to understand the "Robin Hood-type" behaviour of young people during the events of 2004, thus enabling him to avoid any preconceptions in his political analysis. Herriman (2005) also had a clear understanding that political explanations and the failure of most interventions over the period of a century have more profound roots than one might think and that they are deeply embedded in the cultural heritage. However he understood cultural elements as referring to known data and did not consider them as operative. Without a knowledge of what causes the souls of the Malays to vibrate, without an understanding of the role ancestors play in their memory and the constitution of a model, socio-economic explanations continue to prevail. We will also refer to the very good work by Thai scholars (e.g. Satha-Anand, Chaiwat, 1983, 2005; Surin Pitsuwan, 1985) but our more detailed discussion of their work is deferred to Volume 2.

It is thanks to the work and support of my colleague and friend Igor Besson, agronomist,[9] that I am able to present a socio-economic synthesis. The disappearance of the elites as a result of the rise of religious factors, the appropriation of territory by the Siamese at the beginning of the 20th century, the resistance and penetration that resulted, the separation from the Malay matrix, the introduction of rubber plantations that replaced the traditional paddy fields, all these are indispensable factors for understanding the survival or disappearance of myths and rituals. The presentation of economic, sociological and technical profiles of the region makes it possible to understand relations existing between, on the one hand, symbolic aspects or rituals and social or technical rules on the other. I will study their interactions in order to gain a better understanding of how the Malay society of southern Thailand was built.

I do not claim to have translated the Malay texts in as rigorous a manner as those of the Moken whose language I have spoken for many years. Many of the concepts escape me and it is only thanks to the efforts of my assistant, Azip Samuyama, that I have been able to write this book. But, even if I have made every effort to understand the meaning of the framework and the vocabulary of these tales, I was further handicapped by the disappearance of the tapes. Nonetheless, I was obliged to study traditional texts and local exegesis in order to try to understand the rich language contained in the narratives if not always that concerning events of daily life. The numerous footnotes are necessary to alert the reader to the choices I made in translation.

Thus, although the geographical field is restricted to enable comparisons to be made, the work is arduous and I do not pretend to have made an exhaustive or an objective study. It is impossible to guarantee a successful outcome for any form of collaborative investigation in the very particular world of French ethnological research. The road is a long one for Sir Perceval and I simply consider the objectives as a Holy Grail to try to attain!

**Fig. 5.** The drawings illustrating this book are the work of various members of staff of Prince of Songkla University, Patani campus.

**Map 2.** Peninsular Thailand

# Chapter 1

# Epic literature in Peninsular Thailand: A coveted isthmus

## 1.1 Oral texts

The Malay texts presented in this volume include some comparisons with Moken texts and certain themes that derive from continental Southeast Asia. A more detailed comparative analysis that takes into consideration several levels (Moken, Malay, continental and insular Southeast Asia, India and China) but to different degrees will be presented in Volume 2. This will enable me to define more precisely how these different populations think of themselves, and explain their differences and origins, the formation of their identity and their history.

This in-depth study is based on the fertile creative imagination of the Austronesians of peninsular Thailand compared to the Malaysian matrix predominating in the region. My aim is to extend this work to observe the interaction of this great matrix not only with the Thai, Mon and Lao populations but also with the Indians and the Chinese. This is a vast project and I plan to present here only the preliminary results that will serve as groundwork for future studies.

This rigorous and systematic collection of Malay oral literature reveals traces of the contours of models of identity claimed by local ethnic groups. These models have been forged by the rich common Austronesian background, influenced by Siamese and Mon-Khmer elements. Parallel to this revelation of the ideological foundation of social structure[1] proposed by oral literature this study aims, of course, both to preserve "traditional" cultures that are beginning to fade, and to facilitate a linguistic and ethnological literary analysis. To gather these texts among the different Austronesian[2] populations and to compare them with the oral narrative of the Thais and Mons of Peninsular Malay Thailand enables us to obtain a significant series of variants, outside influences and points of comparison enabling us to elaborate a synthesis about the formation of the different identities of the south.

The ideal would be to compare the literature of the Moken seafarers and the Malays of southern Thailand, a comparison that would permit a reconstruction of the mythological corpus which evolved from the history of each group (*cf.* Appendix 1). My task would then be to detect the patterns of migration which had conditioned the cultural affirmations of the Austronesian population of southern Thailand and more especially their relations with the peoples of continental Southeast Asia. Nonetheless, convergences, divergences and syncretism have appeared and reveal the common backgrounds of these groups. Such an analysis would, of course, require one to take into account the surrounding population: the Mons, the Thais and even the Burmese. This would be difficult if undertaken purely as an ethnographic study, but other approaches are possible, even if they appear at times to be only approximate. Thus, I also consulted relevant texts in Thai and in western languages, as well as my own notes on my missions, translations from *The Cultural Encyclopaedia of Southern Thailand*, 1986[3] and records of interviews.

Much work still remains to be accomplished in the domain of comparative oral literature among other Austronesian populations of Southern Thailand, like the Urak Lawoi, the people of Lonta or the people of Sireh; also we must not forget the Moken whose oral narratives include many "Malay" texts that still remain to be collected and translated and of course those still existing among the Malays and which are found in this volume. To collect such a large number of texts among the two million Malays who live in southern Thailand proved to be a hazardous undertaking and very different from doing fieldwork among several thousand sea nomads. So I decided to develop a methodology that could be incorporated into a wider scientific project in which each participant, with a different field of study, would contribute data to a much larger corpus of knowledge. This work was undertaken but the hazards of life made it impossible to achieve our goals, and so the dream remains incomplete. I nonetheless decided to present everything I had already collected and translated, with my assistant Azip Samuyama. The work took several years, but enabled me to test my own theories. I was well aware that the translations would present great difficulties (of language, poetic expression, imagery, context and so on). I then added (*see* Volume 2) the work on which I had collaborated with Igor Besson, an agronomist, covering history, geography, archaeology and the economy. The data we collected is far from complete, but outlines the cultural background of the Malay identity which is neglected by other scholars and which may explain certain peculiarities of local violence and political misunderstandings.

It is clearly impossible to offer a complete panorama of the geographical and human environment of such a historically rich and diverse region. However, I considered it important to present our findings despite our lack of formal training in history and archaeology. Our aim was to offer readers a more accurate picture of the region than the "official" Anglo-Saxon view advanced by historians and archaeologists whose interest lay in what were seen as the "important" problems like Islamization, relations between the "Indian" Langkasuka and the "Moslem" Patani people, fundamentalism and so on. Lack of fieldwork prevented previous researchers from giving any credit to cultural identity, the richness of the tradition which makes it possible to better understand the so-called "southern problem." None of these researchers had any interest in the reality of the daily life of the people here (mostly because of the dangers involved). Their vision was inevitably distorted by the deeply ingrained moral and cultural constructs of the dominant political and scientific position. However, some investigators were aware that local traditions were only slowly disappearing and that the work that had been done in Malaysia had been badly conducted and had misled researchers into thinking that everything had disappeared.

Researchers who refused to listen or to do any fieldwork claimed that the problem was the confrontation of two belief systems, a question of economic development. They believed that it was necessary simply to re-contextualize the question of Malay identity, based on a representative system, which in itself was rooted in an oral tradition that had remained alive even after the official spokesmen of the local royal courts had disappeared with the annexation of the provinces by Siam at the beginning of the twentieth century. The annexation permitted the fishermen, peasants, adventurers, warriors, bandits and pirates to re-appropriate their history and stories and build their own vision of the world. No researchers were interested in trying to understand this vision or in either listening to or accepting what the storytellers had to say; they regarded these new purveyors of tradition as ill-educated and refused to recognize the evident identity dynamics of the region. Nevertheless, the particular features and demands of the population are evident, including language, culture, traditional paddy rice cultivation that respects the social balance, the dominance of community interests rather than an imposed form of Thai clientelism, respect for a system of credit and distribution of wealth, the teaching of the society's moral, religious and cultural values to children.

The Kru Sé mosque, where protestors were massacred in 2004 and was the cause of significant conflict with Bangkok, symbolizes the people's new outlook. A Chinese temple had been built on a hillside nearby many years previously and was a destination for pilgrims. The Chinese and Malay communities there co-existed peaceably, aware of the benefits that stemmed from their mutual exchanges and the respect for their separate traditions; on all levels (kinship relations, economic, political and technical) their association was satisfactory. The cultural values of this mosque, which was never completed (see below), will be explained in this book. Nonetheless, it shows that Islamization did not destroy the Malay cultural identity, and that relations with other communities can work well.

But the authorities in Bangkok, in their blindness, planned to reconstruct it, or what is much worse, considered it an integral part of Thai national patrimony (see the efforts of the Fine Art Department in 1990 to integrate the mosque against the will of the local population, or Thaksin's gift of millions of baht to rebuild it against the will of the local Muslims). This mosque shows the vitality of Islamic, pre-Islamic, Austronesian and Austro-Asiatic beliefs. It also symbolizes the local inhabitants' vision of the world. This syncretism is expressed almost everywhere in the region and is one of the characteristics of the multiple identity of the Malays in southern Thailand and not only in those provinces with a strong Thai influence.

> "In contrast, in Thai-speaking provinces of Southern Thailand, the world of ancestor-spirits is a powerful culture in which the hybridization of local cosmologies takes place in a fascinating manner: Some of the oldest Buddhist monasteries can be found in the region around Lake Songkla which co-exist with Islamic mosques in mixed neighbourhoods. In the Lake Songkla region, rituals with mixed religious elements can be observed as Buddhists and Muslims believe in common ancestors (taa jai). In the Patani region, pre-Islamic Hindu beliefs and Malay popular culture are reproduced among the Malay group, while Malays are careful not to blend Malay-Muslim and Buddhist traditions." (Horstmann, 2007, p. 3)

Nonetheless, rather than listening to these Malays of southern Thailand, rules about Islamic observance, education, and economic matters were imposed while their traditions, myths, technical know-how and cultural habits were ignored. Thus, the essential features of these southern Malays continued to remain unrecognized and Bangkok, influenced by the "scholars" of the western world, in effect created a war in which the fundamentalists became active. (I witnessed the arrival of the first Mujahidins at the beginning of the 1990s.) They are now present in large numbers, thanks to this "dialogue of the deaf" and have replaced the marginal communists and separatists, profiting from the long-established structure for the regional diffusion of the Islamic doctrine.

What I propose here is a vision of the Malay world of southern Thailand that I learned from the Malays themselves.

**Fig. 6.** The mosque of Kru Sé and the temple of Lim Ko Nyao, symbols of cohabitation and of a syncretism that are the characteristics of Malay cultures. (Besson, 1990)

## 1.2. Comparative analysis

My intention here is to offer our readers a brief and general picture of the mythology of rice in southern Thailand and among a population mainly composed of Malays. I will use a method that may be defined as one of "decreasing circles."[4] The first circle will be a comparative analysis of the inner intermediate social space[5] of the Malays in the south of Thailand (in the provinces of Patani, Yala, Narathiwat);[6] the second offers a comparison of data contained in the first circle with those collected in the Austronesian periphery (among the Malays of Malaysia and the Moken and Moklen found in the provinces of Ranong, Phang Nga, Phuket); the third circle is for illustrative purposes and not in order to draw up a complete comparative chart of local mythology and its links with the rest of continental and insular Southeast Asia. For this reason other items of Austronesian oral literature are placed in the appendices.

One example is the story of *The shellfish king* (see Chapter 3), in which the poor youngest daughter is rejected by her family but, being chosen by the gods, marries a man who is a divinity and so is able to overcome all the obstacles which lead to her acceptance into the royalty. This theme is also present in the Moken "Malay" narratives (the tale of *Awang the Frog*, *cf.* J. Ivanoff, 2001, pp. 71–89 ; the tale of *Sangthong* in Thailand, *see* Nathalang Siraporn, 2004, pp. 9–10). The same themes are found, almost word for word, in these tales. The Malay tale is presented in its original perspective, responding to more precise social and mythological objectives than the Moken epic narrative. But the nomads take as much pleasure in and feel as much intimacy with the divine hero as their Malay cousins every time the tale is told. Thus, it is possible to envisage making a comparative analysis. Even more so because the epic narratives contain mythological themes common to continental and insular Southeast Asia, although their way of utilizing mythological themes is different (examples are the father's lies, the jealousy of the sisters-in-law and so on). The Moken draw their images and themes from Malay oral literature (*cf.* J. Ivanoff, 2001), but these oral narratives are also a means by which Malay history is kept alive, and the geographic contours of which are difficult to identify precisely. But the continental world of Southeast Asia is ever present (including India and China). These two cultural matrixes are always present in our oral recitations, but rather than simply imposing their mark, they have given form to the expressive framework of the legends. This is why some themes are common to the Malay, Moken and Thai stock of oral literature (*The shellfish king*, *Awang the Frog* and *Sangthong* for instance) which in fact reflects the common socio-cultural patterns, like uxorilocality and matrilinearity (which is still strong in the Malay Muslim population).

Peninsular Thailand is the point of contact between the two worlds of Southeast Asia and is therefore the expression of cultural choices that indicate either syncretic models or a significant rejection of them. Is the south a cultural frontier, or does it reveal the existence of a fundamental unity that exists in Southeast Asia? Since we are here at the confluence of several different civilizations, we feel that we must first of all describe the beliefs of each one: the Thai, the Mon (including the Sakai sub-group), the Malay (with the Moken and Moklen sub-groups). Though the predominant culture is that of Malaysia and Islam, the region has been under the direct influence not only of Srivijaya and the Hinduization of Southeast Asia for almost seven centuries but also of Thailand.

These influence are perhaps more strongly rooted here than elsewhere, because the southern region remained underpopulated for a long period after its decline. This is particularly true of the eastern coast where the alluvial plains favoured agriculture and the development of small coastal states which engaged in trading activities with the great powers of the time. The western coastlines are rugged and do not favour human settlements or the development of towns. Nevertheless markets (mainly Indian) were established there (e.g. at Takkola, the actual site of Takuapa, for example). The weight of history is, therefore, much stronger along the eastern coast which underwent many changes during the third century[7] because of the development of different states. The region is also situated along the important historical trading routes of Southeast Asia, China and India. In the southern peninsula there were many production and diffusion centres engaged in important trading activities and exchanges from the Indian period (3rd–5th centuries), the Khmer period (10th–13th centuries) up to modern times (as revealed by archaeological investigations at Chaiya, Sathing Phra, Takuapa-Takkola, Nakhon Sri Thammarat-Ligor, Yarang-Langasuka).

The geographical position and strategic military and commercial importance of Patani have always made it a place of interest to its neighbours: on the one side the Malay world and its various kingdoms (Srivijaya, Mojopahit, Malacca) and on the other, the kingdom of Siam, which has long wanted to annex the southern states of its peninsula over which it considered it had held sovereignty since the 13th century (Hall, 1968, p. 174). Patani was able to retain its independence and prosperity from the 14th to the 20th century by skilfully playing these two powers off against one another. But after the administrative reform of 1902 by the Siamese king, Chulalongkorn, followed by the Anglo-Siamese treaty of 1909, Thailand put an end to such vague inclinations for liberty. Since then, the problem for the Malay Muslims in the south of Thailand has been to participate in the political life of a country where the State is rooted in Buddhist cosmology.

The Malay peninsula is the point of transition par excellence between the Indo-Chinese peninsula in the north and northeast and the Insulindian archipelago in the south and southeast. There are of course differences, geographic and also religious and agricultural, between the five countries of continental Southeast Asia (Burma, Thailand, Vietnam, Laos and Cambodia) the five countries of insular Southeast Asia (Indonesia, Malaysia, the Philippines, Brunei and Singapore). Schematically, Theravada Buddhism and wet rice cultivation have dominated the cultures and agricultural economy of the continental countries for centuries. Islam (and also the Catholicism of the Philippines) is widely present in the archipelago, where farming is today clearly oriented towards production for export, especially the crops of natural rubber, palm oil and spices, as it was during the period named "the age of Southeast Asian commerce" by the Australian historian Anthony Reid (1993).

But all of these influences, Hindu, Buddhist and Muslim, have followed the same routes, not only maritime, across the Malacca Straits but also on land, notably covering the Malay peninsula. Furthermore, the countries of Southeast Asia, because of their common origins, form a physical unity, in particular in terms of climate and botany.

Southeast Thailand is a storehouse of traditions. The political and ethnic situation of the Malays of southern Thailand has allowed the recognition and maintenance of a foreign tradition destroyed by economic development elsewhere (e.g. in Malaysia). An area where economic development is slow often retains many of its old traditions and can be of great interest to anthropologists. However this region, ignored by Bangkok for decades, is now undergoing rapid development, to the satisfaction of the Thai authorities who have been investing in the area to suppress the separatists and revolutionary groups, and watching with approval the social integration of a population that for centuries they have wanted to subdue.

The Malays who have lived in southern Thailand since the Anglo-Siamese treaty of 1909 (the populations of Narathiwat, Yala and Patani) are culturally part of the Malay sphere and more particularly, that of Kelantan (notably from a linguistic point of view) but have broken free of it. Though they depend on two countries and two cultures and are subject to two influences (one cultural, the other political), these people have been able to create an intermediate cultural space and retain their specific character.

The region was the crossroads for Indo-Chinese commerce. An appreciation of the role of India and China is essential in order to understand the development of local cultural material which was adapted through their oral literature. The

Chinese, who often visited the region over the centuries to develop their contacts with the trading powers, mostly served a technical role (in such areas as rice culture, forging, pottery).[8] The role of the Indians, however, was limited to keeping alive the traditions they had brought with them.

Not far from the ancient city of Patani is *kota cina*, "the town of the Chinese" where ceramic ovens were discovered. There is a canal beside this site that leads to the city of Langasuka, a religious city, where excavations have revealed monuments built in the 12th century. A ship's mast discovered in the lower reaches of the canal is probably a relict of the tradition whereby successful ship-owners cut off and threw away their masts to mark their success, thus affirming that they no longer needed to go to sea (*cf.* the story of *Chémè Chéwè* in Chapter 3). The local ceramics at this site were generally imported from China. More than half the shards collected at the site of Kru Sé, the historical heart of Patani, seem to have been imported after the 15th century; history has confirmed this fact (*cf. The true story of the Kru Sé mosque* in Chapter 4). The Chinese themselves lived not far from the city, of course, and made ceramics and pottery for the population; the imports were for the aristocracy. The Indian influence was essentially spiritual and has affected local beliefs, whereas the Chinese influence was a more material one.

It is possible to compare the strong influence of Indian traditions with those of the Cambodians and the Mon-Khmers generally. A question that remains is the extent to which influences from continental Southeast Asia, with its Austronesian cultural traditions, mostly imported from the Mon-Khmers, India and China, affected the population of this region. It should be noted that the images found in the tales discussed here are to be found all over the world and that the influence of the Mon-Khmers of Southeast Asia serves as an epic canon.

> "A study of Khmer tales, their 'constants' and 'variations', to employ the language of folklorists, leads one first to the recognition of the universality of popular tales. In effect, one encounters animals with the gift of speech, the themes of Cinderella and Tom Thumb, treasures guarded by the jinns and fairies who work miracles in such tales. But their specific characteristics are well affirmed and the fruit of cultural inspiration, inherited for the most part, from India and collective representations, aboriginal archetypes of the Mon-Khmers or Austro-Asians." (S. Thierry, 1988, p. 6)

The problems of influence are found in linguistic studies and offer interesting comparative data. For this reason I include in this volume extracts of the transcripts of oral texts (*see* Appendix 1). Comparisons of such material raise many questions, particularly as far as the Moken are concerned. For example the Mon-Khmer influence in their language is slight compared with that of the Malays and more recently that of the Thais who have adapted and "detonalized"[9] it. A comparative analysis of the Austronesian languages in the south of Thailand provides more details about the movements of populations. One can follow the course of Malay influences along the coast thanks to a detailed analysis of local dialects that follow the direction southwest to northeast; for the *Jawi* language there is an east-west difference (littoral/pioneer front), as it passes from standard Malay to the Malay of Kelantan. Establishing itself in a Thai geopolitical context, *Jawi* appears and is slowly tonalized.[10] This seems only logical in the evolution of the Malay-*Jawi* languages. The situation is different for the Moken since they are remote from the important centres of cultural diffusion and have guarded their own language, which varies according from one sub-group to another and is subject to Burmese, Thai and Mon influences. Since they are not a central Austronesian sub-group, the Moken have developed their own linguistic characteristics quite easily since language, for them, is less of an identity reference than it is for the Malays of the eastern coast. A linguistic study of other Austronesian sub-groups should also be made but in the absence of any such a study, we offer our readers, for comparative purposes, some suggestions.

### 1.3. Collecting the texts

The gathering of oral texts was inspired by a scientific ideal which was at first based on regional comparisons. I became interested in Moken oral texts in 1982, during my first fieldwork investigations among them. Since then, I have collected and recorded[11] almost one hundred and fifty hours of narratives, most of which have also been translated. It took me many years to collect and translate a corpus of Moken oral literature and though considerable, it is not exhaustive (*cf.* J. Ivanoff, 2001, 2004), because the texts are always being adapted to external realities. The Moken have always been considered to have no oral tradition, like the Malays of southern Thailand, even though their cultural specificity is founded on it. With patience and intuition and by freeing myself from the preconceived notions and reductive themes that the Anglo-Saxons wished to impose on the French school (as far as immersion—in terms of language, culture, custom—in the field is concerned) I discovered an inexhaustible source of traditional values, reference texts, tales, songs (both magical and non-magical). But in order to discover these riches one must be firmly convinced that the search is well founded and that the investigator is capable of extracting these hidden ethnological jewels, in spite of the time lost in dealing with bureaucratic constraints and the lack of material means. The task of collecting, translating, recovering and even safeguarding a tradition is an arduous and solitary undertaking.

I collected the texts in different regions of southern Thailand inhabited by the Malays (namely, the provinces of Patani, Yala, Narathiwat, Phang Nga, Ranong) and compared them with the oral fragments of the Thais and Mons of the south, thus obtaining a significant series of variants and sufficient comparisons to develop a synthesis. However, I would first of all like to present and compare the Malay corpus of southern Thailand within the social space of the Malays of southern Thailand, sometimes defined as *Jawi*, one of the local ethnonyms. Southeast Thailand is a storehouse of traditions. In spite of the particular political and ethnic situation of the Malays of southern Thailand they are able to recognize and maintain a tradition which has been destroyed elsewhere because of economic development (in Malaysia, for example).

I made several hundred hours of recordings, thanks to a network of connections we had established with the villagers, supervised by our assistant Azip Samuyama. It was first necessary to locate the reputed storytellers as well as the centres where traditions are still very much alive. Once this had been established, some villagers offered to help us to collect the stories. These were then transcribed, according to a model adapted by the international Grand Sud project, to the local language.[12] Then the work of translation could take place. The tales were collected in particular in two of the dozen villages (chosen according to their socio-agronomic characteristics) that had already participated in an ethno-agricultural investigation.[13] Once the network was organized, we made more detailed enquiries in the villages where we had personal contacts; there was also a scientific interest to these investigations, once the project's ethnological research base was established. These villages were: Samoh[14] (Rangé district, Narathiwat province), Sudé[16] (Kalapo district, Patani province), Lubo Panyé[16] (Yaha district, Yala province), Bené Dalé[17] (Yarang district, Patani province) and Tanoh Meroh (Yaring district, Patani province). Once a village had been selected and the storytellers chosen, the work developed in the surrounding area. Our corpus took on a more substantial form thanks to the occasional storytellers we met and also because of other unexpected encounters (e.g. in Peté,[18] Yalta district, Yala province; the Karo quarter in Patani; and Bangpu (municipal district, Patani province).

## 1.4. The storytellers

I will mention the Moken storytellers only briefly since their tales are the subject of another book. I should simply like to point out that all the narrators of stories are elders, *potao*, more often sacred men, *olang puti*.[19] Certain storytellers are able to spend entire nights narrating epic tales before a breathless public, avid for adventures, even though they are not officiants. Thus, the epic tales are more often the property of storytellers who have no religious status, while the tales (which have a moral message) and the myths (with a religious message) tend to be the property of sacred men.

I shall first outline the development of the Malay corpus of the village of Samoh, which is fairly homogenous and serves as a good introduction to a particular and specific literature which until now has been little known, if not entirely unknown.

The village of Samoh, where most of the stories come from, is situated in the southernmost province of Thailand, Narathiwat, which is divided into twelve districts, including Rangé, which itself is divided into six cantons, including Bongo. There are five hundred inhabitants and seventy houses in the village, which is divided into four hamlets (Plong, Samoh, Lubo Beranyé, Lubo Tapu), all of which share a mosque and a school. It is also the home village of my assistant Azip Samuyama. The village is isolated, being about one hundred kilometres from Patani, at the foot of the Kalakiri mountain chain that protects Malaysia, not far away, and diverse groups who, for a number of reasons (both political and criminal), remain there in hiding, under the benevolent eyes of a population conscious of its force and determination. The village is not far from the border; it is in the sphere of influence (mainly linguistic) of the northern Malaysian state of Kelantan, with which they make numerous exchanges.

The cultivation of rice, associated with fruit growing and, to a lesser degree, rubber production, is the major economic activity of this relatively inaccessible village.[20] Its four hamlets house family groups. The officials are an imam, a *kotep*, a *bilal*[21] and the village chief. There are also several ritual specialists, and a medium and a traditional healer (*bomoh*, locally pronounced *bohmo*). These people have an important place in rituals and performances. Our two[22] principal narrators belong to these fraternities (Wo Seng[23] and Po' Suloh[24]). These two elders, who were formerly very strong and vigorous men, have gone through life without repudiating either magic nor violence and they are not averse, when the occasion arises, to add a little religion to their knowledge. They are known for their savoir-faire, their magical power and the force of their characters. In 1993, Wo Seng was more than 90 years

Fig. 7. Hunting for wild pigs is tolerated even in Islamic areas and with the complicity of rebels. (Besson, 1991)

old and Po' Suloh was about 60. The villagers are more inclined to listen to Po' Suloh, whose single eye flashes when he tells epic tales to a captivated audience in his tumbledown shack, situated just outside the village. His words and their power are respected by everyone. He is the one who decided what tale he would relate on different occasions. Magician, reputed *bomoh*, he goes off for many days into the forest to engage in activities unknown to others, but he pretends that he goes "hunting."

As for Wo Seng, "Old Seng", he lives in the centre of the village and offers his knowledge to whoever shows any interest and a desire to hear him tell a story. Listeners ask questions, make noisy signs of approval or remain in respectful silence. He is a malicious old man and rather deaf but his words are convincing. He is a reputed magician, who participates in all the village ceremonies and festivals (*kenduri*),[25] but also takes part in rituals (Moyong)[26] and Teri.[27] He thinks nothing of walking several kilometres to join his companions, who are all musicians: he also plays in the orchestra that participates in performances. As a fiddle (*rebab*) player he is the one who is in contact with the spirits.

These performances can last for one or up to forty days (for the Moyong performance).[28] Wo Seng is an experienced traveller, having covered hundreds, if not thousands of kilometres and crossed several borders; he has been married several times and has worked in many trades, including the socially recognized one of highwayman, aided by his knowledge as a fortune teller. He has had a full life and now remains in the village where he was born without any feelings of nostalgia.

Wo Seng became one of my principal storytellers. His stories are long and follow a fairly classical pattern. The poor hero or one who has been banished, his quest and its outcome when he becomes a rich man and marries several women, all of whom are the daughters of the gods or nagas[29] or magicians. The social ideal is

**Fig. 8.** Wo Seng playing the *rebab* in a Moyong performance. (Ivanoff, 1995)

present in all these stories, namely, the one who is poor and has been banished by the blind authorities finally reigns supreme, assisted by his wives who have been chosen by the gods. Without these women, who are often a pretext for the stories, the hero would have no power. He is only a puppet in the hands of these sweetly tyrannical women who know how to rule the world.

### 1.5. The beautiful things of the south

Oral literature in southeast Thailand is still alive, though not always apparent. This is due to the conflict between the moral values found in the tales and epics and the precepts of Islam. Nonetheless, oral literature is found everywhere, remains a spontaneous form of expression, is listened to, is very much present and is solidly rooted in the hearts of the people. Though the recitation of the stories may be less brilliant than in the past, oral literature is still as effective as ever. It serves as a model and reference of an idealized society and speaks of an epic dream. Thus, the present is judged by comparison to a glorified past where daily events included not only wars, tyranny and violence but also heroic adventures and love.

Is oral literature really still alive or is this only the wishful thinking of an ethnologist who wants, at all costs, to bring back to life a bygone age? I do not think so: one has only to read the myth *The origin of the soul of rice* (in Chapter 2), which speaks of the sacrifice of a daughter by one of her parents to ensure the growth of rice and reveal its soul, to appreciate its continuity with the past. This myth is widespread in the Austronesian world and resembles, almost word for word, the ones mentioned by Skeat at the beginning of the twentieth century (1900, rep. 1965) and Hill, somewhat later (1951). Southern Thailand has become a cultural storehouse with a very precious comparative ethnological potential.

The model that emerges in oral literature can be used as a political instrument since it brings back to life the past of the Patani region, which since the seventh century has seen a succession of protests against its assimilation, not only by the Malays (in Malacca, then in Srivijaya) but also by the Siamese (first in Sukhothai, then in Ayuthaya). With the disappearance of the sultanates and aristocrats, political warnings were issued by religious factions who rejected oral literature, even though it supported

**Fig. 9.** Porcelain bowls, traditional clay vessels, dammar (resin from the dammara tree), necessary for the betel ritual, and in the white face powder used by young girls. This is how the presence of the soul of rice is revealed. (Ivanoff, 1989)

**Fig. 10.** Not far from the swaths are the "old things" to watch over the soul of rice: traditional blades (in the form of a leaf or saw), a container for the young girl who is the soul of rice. (Ivanoff, 1989)

socio-political aspirations, since they felt that the stories retained traces of animism and idolatry. Oral literature is thus not as socially important now as it once was but it is more than just a pleasant relict of the past, *bahri*,[30] as contemporary students of folklore and even the Malays themselves term most of the local tales. These "things of the past", with their fine words, enriched by the strong personalities of the narrators, bring to the surface the memories that each one carries within himself and with which he is identified. Unfortunately, fewer and fewer people listen to these stories and they have become sterile in the minds of the older people.

Some of these stories are known and legitimized by those in power today in Bangkok; they have been freed of the law of silence imposed in the south for many decades. But certain epics passed into folklore when they crossed the cultural borders imposed on them by the Thais; this transformation occurred in order to safeguard a patrimony that until now has been negated.

These prefabricated clichés are sold to "collectors" of culture in the capital, whether journalists or students of folklore within the universities, who (because of their desire for personal recognition) depoliticize oral expression. In reviewing these stories one must always keep in mind the socio-political dimension present here.

## 1.6. Malay heroes, political instruments

The storytellers often have very strong personalities; they are travellers, bandits, mediums, fortune tellers and musicians. They have neither a religious nor a political status but they serve as an anti-establishment force. The menacing waves of development and the occasional rise of fundamentalism are only accidents of

**Fig. 11.** The history of a syncretism is painted on the hulls of the boats. The fabulous figures of a Chinese naga and an Indian garuda are placed beside real animals. They guarantee survival at sea, recognition of the past and the surrounding paradise. (Ivanoff, 1989)

**Fig. 12.** The bird-elephant, *burong gajoh*, on the *banga* that ploughs through the waters, protects sailors and guarantees that the boat will be able to break through the waves and that the fishermen will catch many fish. (Ivanoff, 1989)

history; while the oral texts, their creation and the message they convey remain and will only come to an end with the disappearance or the complete alienation of society. The storytellers are greatly respected in the different communities. They are the elements of an epic dream and serve as instruments to broaden the vision of local populations since, like their heroes, they travel a great deal. The stories told by Wo Seng speak of an ideal and adventurous life which resonates in the hearts of all men. The adventure is, more often than not, a sea-going one, a memory of the social characteristics of the Austronesians who were traders and travellers, always on the move and prepared to make new conquests.

I have already evoked the socio-political aspects of the stories which glorify the past, so that the desire for independence remains alive in the region. The very negation of these stories by the central authorities is proof of their awareness of the danger oral traditions may pose politically, since the stories offer the legitimation of an identity and provide memories of rebellious kingdoms. These "beautiful things of the past" have, or have had, potentially political motivations and influences for a past which they honour. They also provide clues for students of human geography since they offer precise information about the establishment of villages, the founding of royal kingdoms and so on, which is confirmed by the study of toponyms. One may also discover epic traces of the animal and human landscape in the original oral texts: the names of villages, sacred sources, magic mountains still exist and are part of the landscape. The history of Patani,[31] Yaring[32] and the Kru Sé mosque (the centre of the ancient capital razed during the eighteenth century) is concealed in the epic poems, tales and myths. It is in this way that their memory is kept alive and conserved and resists the cultural erosion that is at times imposed by the capital.

Orality itself has become the expression of social and political claims. The men of knowledge, whether bandits or members of parliament, are responsible for the diffusion of some form of knowledge. Although at times only partial, this knowledge is always important and impossible to neglect from an historical point of view. (Let us not forget that the aristocracy and monarchies were destroyed and consequently there are no longer any annals.)

Such people describe the history of the region, the revolts, the resistance movements, the ideals and the daily life of the inhabitants, and in this way, generate a discrete but just as important a model as the one offered by the national education system. Thus, present-day Malays accept two systems of knowledge, and in this lies their power. The Thai schools are integrated and respected (in spite of some bombs) but so are the Koranic schools. Both are necessary even though the children are consequently overworked, causing a remarkable absence of life in the villages. They are obliged to study official history, as it is considered important for ensuring one's success in life but the one the people listen to and remember comes from the Koranic schools, from public story telling, reunions, electoral manifestos, pilgrims, itinerant storytellers, actors and so on.

No matter what the objectives may be, reading historical texts is not only possible but desirable. The histories constantly tell of kings being dethroned, nominated, assassinated and defended. Kings appear to have been constantly threatened by their enemies and would-be conquerors. In effect, the migrations in this part of the world of the Austronesians who were constantly searching for new land, provoked conflicts, since they wanted to take over local territories. Every advance on the part of the Austronesians had repercussions in the local principalities. These conflicts are proof of a population constantly moving and expanding.

In order to give some sort of legitimacy and to justify their power, the monarchies resorted to epic stories in which are found a royal elephant, an epic event like the arrival of a king or a miraculous royal hunt; all such events then become fixed within the tangible world: beaches, forests, roads. The epic rejoins history. Underlying the official discourse and legitimation are the messages contained in the epics; they are very important for an understanding of the rearrangement of the human landscape.

The Malays consider themselves as living "at the end of the world"; they are willing to accept certain cultural practices like wet rice cultivation. They have the same attitude to forged iron and masonry, which are produced by techniques controlled by the Chinese. The Malays appear to be a people whose only problems are their fights against autocratic rulers, the discovery of new lands, usually in boats, and sea-going adventures that are combined with trading activities. For example, there is not one text in the Hawè Cycle that does not mention the Chinese who possess the technical knowledge necessary for construction and forging. Each time someone wants a fine instrument, he goes to see a Chinese man (the tale of *The man with the big knife and the lazy man* in Chapter 3, for example), or even goes alone to look for the object he covets in the "country of the Chinese". This will be the framework of the story and of the quest (the tale of *Hawè Sada* in Chapter 3, for example). The Malays do not seem very interested in themselves developing techniques other than those of war. In this respect, though, they show great inventiveness and imagination; for example, they have extensive knowledge of making canons.

As well as being interested in Chinese technology, they also had a desire for Chinese women, who were supplied by the Chinese community. The Chinese were also responsible for the methods of rice cultivation, and the inevitable *taukays* (traders, intermediaries and money-lenders). The Malays, by contrast, seemed to be dreamers, lazy, adventurous, discoverers and lovers, in a perpetual quest to surpass themselves and in conflict with the authorities. The Chinese had no difficulty becoming assimilated in such a milieu and the local proverb itself echoes this ideal distribution of roles:

> "The White Men die because of their self-importance.
> The Chinese die because of their commerce.
> The Malay die because of their daydreams."

The Chinese then "cooked" the Malays of southern Thailand by introducing techniques of rice cultivation, construction and trading. They then ensured the Malays' fidelity through intermarriage and in this way reinforced their economic hold over them. This guaranteed them an incomparable place at the heart of Malay society. We will see that they have an important place in oral narratives, a role confirmed by archaeologists since the discovery of *kota cina* (Chinatowns) surrounding Malay towns, especially in Patani (*cf.* Ivanoff and Sawang Lertrit, 1995).

Let us now return to our epic tales and the quest for the absolute. All forms of social breakdown lead to contact with the natural, supernatural and divine. The man who has been banished or chased away, an abandoned child or one who is lost, will find along his road a spark of the divine to help him accomplish his quest because social clashes become the hero's call to celestial powers; having been chosen by the gods, the hero, in his flight, becomes the historical agent of these gods whose task is to bring order back into the world of men. His principal duty is to remove barriers that exist in the world and reunite the different fragments of humanity that have become dispersed because of aggression and Man's greed. These human tendencies cause them to slowly lose their identity. The hero then is the divine link unifying groups of people with the same cultural identity but who no longer have the means to safeguard it. The hero's ideal inspires him to strengthen identity references.

Union is force; it is the hero who is able to achieve unity; his task then is to remove the barriers existing in the Malay world and reunite all the specific characteristics of each kingdom in order for unity to appear. This unity is at first geographic, then psychological, and symbolizes the Malay world in construction. The hero then becomes the instrument by which ethnic unity is realized, the one capable of ensuring a harmonious union between the different kingdoms and re-establishing their lost unity with the divine world. The epic affirms itself historically because it stands between myth and public affairs. After the construction of this ideal union in the Malay world, history continues—as do identity references. The Malays of southern Thailand will then continue to define their distinctive features in the heart of modern Insulindian life and become a distinctive world.

**Fig. 13.** Slash-and-burn cultivation is still practised. It permitted the development of pioneer fronts and the conquest of territories but also self-sufficiency and mobility. (Ivanoff, 1989)

# Chapter 2

# Myths and epics

## 2.1. The origin of the soul of rice (version 1)

***(Village of Samoh, Province of Narathiwat, November 1991*[1]**
***Narrator: Wo Seng***
***Type of story:*[2]*bahri*)**

The Lord wants to transmit something. Adam wants to make a rai.[3] But no one knows what he wants to plant. No one knows what he wants to eat. Rice doesn't exist yet and before doing anything else it will be necessary to clear the land.

He already has many children[4] but he still doesn't know what he wants to plant. So the Lord[5] sends his divine breath on him. He transmits a sign to Master Adam. He must chop up one of his daughters. So Adam chops without stopping and scatters her in the rai that had already been prepared. This is what he did!

Seven days later the rice started to grow. Then Eve said:

"Where is our other child, Adam?"

He answered:

"She is in the rai."

"How is it that I didn't encounter her when I went there?"

"Ah! But how did you expect to find her if you didn't call out to her?"

"Oh! Little girl."

"Yes?"

"Oh! Little girl!"

"Yes."

This is how she became our rice!

In order to have rice, it was necessary to chop up a child.[6] But the rice also comes from the Lord's sweat. In effect, rice is good when it is salted. One grinds shrimps and fish together. But if no salt is added it doesn't have a very good taste, if no salt is added, it is not good.

## 2.2. The origin of the soul of rice (version 2)
***(Village of Samoh, Province of Narathiwat, June 1995***
***Narrator: Wo Seng***
***Type of story: bahri)***

Before, nobody existed. Then someone appeared. They were the lords Adam and Eve. Eve gave birth to twins and God told Adam to make a rai. But there were no seeds and nothing could be planted. Adam wanted to plant trees but he was unable to. So he went to clear the field and prepare the soil. He burnt everything there. Then he received a sign in a dream. Someone commanded lord Adam to chop up his child. He was to chop up his daughter and scatter the pieces. Yes, he had to scatter them. Then all these pieces began to grow and became rice. Ah! Adam was then able to eat rice and no longer had to eat *Sali* flour. Before rice appeared they had to eat *Sali* flour. Ha!

Adam's wife, Eve, asked him where their child was. So Adam answered:

"Our child lives in the rai, over there where rice was planted and which is now growing very well!"

"So why didn't I find her when I went looking for her? I called her, but she didn't answer and I couldn't find her. I didn't meet her."

Adam said:

"You must go and call her like this: 'Oh, little daughter, come back!' if you want her to answer."

So, she went and called out: "come back!"

She called out like that so that her daughter would come back; but there was no answer. She could not see her.

"She is dead! She is dead!"

Then they were able to eat the rice. The rice ripened and they could eat its fruits. Since then one can eat rice.

Ah! This is how rice is. Ah, hahaha. . . God made rice. He gave us rice so we would have something to eat and this, just until today. Long ago, there was no rice, no, there wasn't any but today there are great quantities of rice and there are also many people. Eh, a great deal of people! Adam had many children. He has had just until our generation and we all come from the prophet Adam. Hahaha, the prophet Adam. Ah, Adam. Ah, the prophet Adam! He had children and grandchildren, lord Adam, and all of them became a part of humanity and now there are many people in the world. But there is something else, because Eve, the wife of lord Adam, gave birth to twins. Every time she gave birth she had twins and they married each other: this one with that one, hahaha, because there was not any humans yet.

Ah, people even today can eat this thing, rice. Ah, yes, that's how it was. Adam only had to speak and it appeared; hahaha.

Ah! Long ago, everything people ate wasn't good. No matter what they ate, it wasn't good. But people learned to plant this thing, this one, this thing. I plant this and I eat.

And it is very tasty. But long ago, there wasn't any of this and we ate everything grilled. Then we tasted it with brine, we ate, hahaha, it was delicious. But in the past there wasn't any of this, neither onions nor chilli and we didn't even know about the acid taste. The only thing we knew how to do was to grill. But today, we eat with brine, hahaha, just until this very day. And this is all I have to say.

## 2.3. The ritual of transplanting *mula paddy*[7]

***(Village of Samoh, Province of Narathiwat, November 1991***
***Narrator: Bèlé (bomoh)***
***Type of story: ilmung "magical knowledge")***

[Description of preparations] [8]

The *bomoh* takes some of the leaves of the *sépuleh*[9] tree and plants of paddy. He goes down to the paddy field and pulls down the leaves. He turns towards the west and reads a chapter of the Koran. When he has finished he turns towards the south[10] and recites some verses[11] of the Koran. Then he does some magic[12] in the *Jawi* language. The invocation is recited in one stretch and the flow of words is rapid.

"Auzubilloh[13] mina saito[14] ni ro[15]jim
May Allah protect us from the demon.

Bismilah[16] biroh mani rohim[17]
In the name of Allah, may he be good and have some pity on us."

Hey! Demon of the soil,[18] evil demon of the paddy fields, I am asking you to open the way to us and go away, today, now. I am asking you to do this because I am going to transplant the rice of the old Suhèng, today, now.

May no one come here to abuse us. May no one be jealous and may no one come to wreak havoc here.

Hey! Demon of the soil, demon of the small dikes, I am asking you to open the way and go away, today, now. And I am not only speaking to the demon of the paddy field but to everyone to leave the road. Demon of the small dikes, I am asking you to leave the road, today, now. I am asking you, so listen, all of you listen, today, now.

May nobody act badly, nobody show any bad humour, today, now.

I am performing this ceremony for the four roads of the sky,[19] for the four roads of the earth, for anyone who finds himself confined between the earth and the sky[20] and for those who live on the earth.

I am asking each one of you, I am asking all of you to open the way, today, now.

To those who destroy and turn their back to the sky and whose chest is offered to the earth,[21] to all of them, I am asking them to open the way, today, now.

I am asking the Lord: *ya ji mu ya rohim aloh*. Ah! Allah, Lord.

[When the invocation ends, the *bomoh*, who is facing south, plants the rice stalks which he held in his hands during the recitation. He plants near his feet, two or three blades of rice, nine times, in three rows of three. When he reaches the ninth plant, he takes a leaf of *sepulèh* and plants it next to the paddy plant. He does the same thing for the first, third, seventh and ninth blades. When he arrives at the ninth plant there is more paddy for this one than for the others. Then he takes some rattan canes[22] which he plants around the nine plants.]

## 2.4. Ritual for different stages of rice culture
***(Village of Samoh, Province of Narathiwat, November 1993 Narrator: Bèlé (bomoh))***

Salutations to the king of the paddy fields.

I greet you and all the others, I greet you, too. Lords, earth and guardians who are here and look after everything and inside everything. You who watch over the paddy fields.

[He gives the name of the owner.] Eh! Jémalè of the small barriers and paddy plants, it is the end for all this, we will now return to what is sacred.[23] The midwives of Samo are sacred, this one [proper name] is also a magician[24] and that other one also and this one, too [proper names]. I greet all of you.

Don't play at being ghosts and don't frighten the owner or the others who will go and harvest the rice. If they go one day here and another day over there, you must bring along with you seven stalks and say:

"Hey! Noseri, Noroning, Nomaning, return to the palace where one eats well, sleeps well, bathes oneself and sleeps profoundly. Don't be worried, chickens, ducks, cows, buffaloes, goats and sheep. Don't be afraid of the mortar because there are good machines used today even though we continue to speak of the mortar."

And the *bola*[25] offerings? [the assistant asks].

We put them in our mouth, eat them and then spit them out, while we go three times to look for the seven stalks. We cut them and then leave. One must not speak when one cuts and when one returns. One can only speak when the rice has been harvested.

If the *bomoh* goes alone, it is more difficult. He needs bananas, sugar cane, a lamp for the rice granary. In the past, it was the people who put the bananas, sugar cane, rice (an upper layer of cooked rice), water, and a lamp there. It is the *bomoh* who does the harvesting, it takes three days. Formerly, if the *bomoh* didn't go by himself to the paddy fields, there were problems. Here is what the *bomoh* says when he is alone:

"Asalamualaikum alai kumusale
I am speaking to you, lord of the rice
I greet you and all the others.
Lord of the earth, guardian of the room to the place,
Who takes care of the doors and the interior.
Jémalè, since I am going to harvest the
Rice, I am asking you[26] to leave us in peace and leave.
Jémalè, if you belong to the small barriers,
Then return to he small barriers
I ask all of you, all the magicians of the
Cardinal points, all the magicians who have
Power, come and look for what belongs to you.[27]
Ghost of the earth, Jémalè of the earth.
Ghost of the world, Jémalè of the world.
I am asking you to leave
Hey! Jémalè Saga, I am asking you to go away.
Because I am going to harvest the rice today.
Let nobody come and disturb me and no one become angry.
May there be no sadness nor anger.
Hey! Noseri, Noroning, Noramaning,
Come to the room of the palace.
One eats there until one is full, one
Sleeps with closed fists, one bathes oneself with pleasure.
Don't be worried you chickens, ducks, cows, buffaloes
Goats, sheep and mortar."

Now we will go and harvest seven stalks and come back and put them in the granary, on the tallest grindstone. One must not speak when one carries this rice back. One can speak after the rice has been installed.

Three days or seven days later, one can go and harvest the rice. During these three days or seven days we must light the lamp in the granary.

**Fig. 14.** The rice granaries lined up in front of the houses. (Ivanoff, 1989)

## 2.5. Aso paddy, The knowledge of rice
***(Village of Samoh, Province of Narathiwat***
***Narrator: Mali)***

This is what my older one told me. When we go to the paddy fields, we must walk around it and say:

"Hey! Little girl,[28] little boy.[29]
*Seri*[30] May you be you bath, my child
Grow up quickly, girl[31] or boy![32]
Grow up very quickly!
Here is the water which will drown you!"

You must sprinkle water in the paddy field while you are turning around it. You must do this as many times as you want to. My elder one didn't tell me how many turns one should make.

It we don't want the rodents to come and destroy our rice, we must come to an agreement with them. We must give them some rice which has been cooked after the harvest. We must do this every year. The prophet Selèmé[33] will be the witness So you must give them one or two sacks of harvested rice so that they will leave the rice in peace. But this doesn't mean that we shouldn't do everything we can to keep them from coming: by flooding the paddy field, for example.[34]

### 2.6. The nine souls of rice

***(Village of Samoh, Province of Narathiwat, December 1993***
***Narrator: Bèlé (bomoh)***
***Collected by: Abdullwaheb Samuyana***
***Type of story: kèché "to speak")***

First of all, they left their country, China. The nine young brothers left their country, China. They were nine young boys, nine brothers and where did they go? To a country where two of them stayed. Two boys remained in this country. But what country? In India, the country of the *rotis*.[35]

"Ho! You are going to stay here, older ones, but we are going to leave."

"Go then, younger ones."

So, they left and went to India. There were now seven brothers who remained. They travelled for a long time, for a very long time and finally arrived in the country of Henu:[36] the country Heni where people also eat *rotis*. Two other brothers remained there and the five others left and finally arrived in Kedah.[37] Two brothers remained in this country where the people ate rice and the three others took to the road again until they met an old man. They met an old man who raised cows, buffaloes, goats, sheep and who knows what else. I don't remember. But we will speak of something else now. The brothers said:

"Ho! what are you doing, old man?"

"Nothing special, young men. I raise goats and cows."

"Ho! Is your house far away, old man?"

"If I tell you that it is far away, I am afraid that you will think it is close by and if I tell you that it is close by, you will think it is far away."

"But it will soon be night and we would like to know if we can sleep in your house."

"Ah! That's no problem but about eating rice that's another story."

This is what the old man said, that there was no rice left.

"Hum! It doesn't matter. We would like to sleep there."

So they went off and stayed in the house of the old man. Their beds were prepared and the old man said to his wife:

"Can they eat some rice?"

"Ah! I don't know."

She got ready to cook the rice and opened the container where the rice was stored.[38]

It was full.

"What has happened, old man? A few minutes ago, there was not even one spoonful left and now the container is full. How did this happen?" she asked.

They cooked the rice and then ate it. The next day, the brothers were still there. They stayed for a long time, the next day and the day after. And there was still rice in the container every day. There was always some rice and before long it was time to plant in the paddy field. The young men took care of this. When the rice grains had been set in the ground they decide to leave.

"We are going to leave now," they said, "but don't worry, old man, you will be able to eat. Take good care of your cows and your ducks. Pay attention to the grains of rice which have not been husked.[39] And don't forget to put back the grains of rice which have fallen down from the mortar."

So they planted the grains of rice, but in the enclosure for buffaloes.

"But how many measures[40] of rice are there in the enclosure for buffaloes?"

"Wait a minute, old man."

They began to transplant the rice. The young men did this, They transplanted the rice.

"Old man, you must go and look for some branches of the *sépulèh* tree and the leaves of the *setawah*[41] tree."

"There are many of them in the forest," said the old man.

So, they went off to look for them.

"We will also need seven lianas of rattan[42] in order to cover up the first ones we transplanted, the first nine ones because we are nine brothers who have come here."

"Ah! Alright."

The old man then began to transplant.

"Ah! Have you finished, old man?"

"Oh! Yes, I have."

"Now your wife can transplant the rice". She transplanted the rice all over the enclosure.

"This enclosure is very small. How can I transplant the rice in it?"

But the enclosure was full of rice plants and there was a very rich harvest. It was very tiring for her to gather together all the rice, the old man was also very tired and couldn't imagine when all this hard work would be finished. He had a hard time carrying the rice to the granary.[43] The granary was full of rice.

"Ah! Eat as much as you want, old man but be careful not to abandon the unhusked rice. You must collect it as we told you to do. The unhusked rice should not fall down. The chickens and all the other animals should not come into the rice granary before you collect the rice, you should take some bananas, sugar cane and a lamp with a wick long enough to last for three days. It is only after doing this that you can blow it out. This is what you must dȯ when you gather the rice. One cuts a little rice and stores it in the granary. Then one stops for three days. It is only after that one can collect. But you must wait three days before you do this, when anyone goes to gather the first paddy's plants, he must be careful not to meet anyone. If you meet someone, don't speak to him because you will be carrying the rice."

The soul of the rice spoke like this and explained everything to the three brothers who were there, Noseri, Noroni and Normani. The eldest's name is Noseri and the younger ones are Noroni and Normani. They told the old man what their names were. One must plant nine rice plants since they were nine brothers and these three brothers had come to our place.

In our country, Jawo, is that it? [audience]

Yes, yes Hindustani[?], India and our country, Jawo.

And the rattan?

The rattan is used to cover up the first planting to protect the plants from intruders; the animals who have their backs facing the sky and their chest facing the ground are a menace for them. These also include birds, cows, buffaloes, sheep and goats.

## 2.7. The soul of rice: the Chinese sisters[44]

**(*Village of Samoh, Province of Narathiwat, October 1993*
*Narrator: Bèlé (bomoh)*)**

In the beginning were the souls of rice. They came from China. They travelled for a long time, a very long time, until they reached the earth. They docked their boat. At that time, one had to use sailing boats. When they reached the land, they began to walk. They walked for a long time, a very long time in the country of India.[45] The soul of the rice was triple,[46] one was called Noseri,[47] the second Nosewi and the third Nomani. This was the soul of rice. They had been walking for a long time when they met an old man[48] who raised buffaloes. Yes, this old man raised buffaloes. Night fell, it must have been about five o'clock in the evening.

"Eh! where are we going to sleep?"

It had been a long time that they had been walking before they met the old man.

"Oh! Old man! We want to sleep at your place. Is it far away?"

"No, it's not," said the old man. "If you only want to sleep there, that's no problem. But as for the rice, I don't know," he said.

The rice is always a problem. They had come from their country and had been here for quite a while The three young girls were in the first room of the house and did not move. The old man's wife went to cook the rice. There wasn't any; nevertheless, when she opened the container[49] it was full. It was full of rice! So, they all ate the rice. When the next day came, the young girls were still there, they were still at the old man's house, they remained for a long time until the day arrived when the rice had to be prepared again.

"Eh! We must prepare the rice. Is this possible?"

"It's not difficult to prepare the rice," they said. "Go and dig up the earth in the enclosure for the buffaloes."

"Dig in the enclosure for the buffaloes? How is that?"

"How! Go there and then come back."

When the time came for the harvest, the enclosure was full of rice. The small enclosure was full of rice. He harvested it but the work never ended.

"I have been harvesting for two days now in the enclosure for the buffaloes and I can't do anymore," the old man said.

The work seemed to last for a long time, for the old man but it was the time for harvesting. At the moment of the harvest, the youngsters said:

"If you want to harvest, old man, you need bananas, sugar cane, cooked rice, water and light, a lamp for three days; you will also need a coconut. Then put everything in the rice granary."

The old man did everything they told him to do. Then he went to harvest the rice. It took him three days to do this. He never stopped cutting the panicles but there was still rice in the enclosure for buffaloes. His work really never ended in the enclosure for buffaloes.

But it was now a long time since the young girls had arrived. One said to him:

"I am going to leave with my sisters. We must resume our travels again."

"Where do you want to go, youngsters?"

"Hum! Wherever fortune takes us; in the large open fields; at the crossroads of the routes, we must take one of three roads. If we arrive at a mountain, well then, we will go up the mountain; if we arrive at the bank of a river, we will go on the river, if we arrive on a hill, we will go up the hill."

"Don't leave, youngsters."

"We cannot remain here, the time has now arrived for us to leave."

So, they took to the road once again and walked for a long time until they reached[50] the country of the Jawis, our country. They met men there; one of them once again was an old man. They stayed there for a long time and told him the same thing that they had told the first old man. They told him to transplant the rice in the enclosure for buffaloes but he didn't believe them.

"Don't be angry, and wait until the time for the harvest arrives."

They told him to do the same thing that they had told the other old man to do.

"Take some bananas, sugar can, rice, water, a lamp and a coconut, put all these things in the granary for rice. When you go off to look for rice, you mustn't meet anyone on the way. If you do come across someone don't bother about him and don't speak to him."

The old man went to look for the rice and then returned. It took him three days. When he went to harvest the rice, the inside of the granary was full. They stayed there for a long time in our country, Jawi. They are still there today. This is the end of our story.

## 2.8. What one must do to satisfy the soul of rice
**(*Village of Samoh, Province of Narathiwat, February 1993*
*Narrator: Mer Keci*)**

This is the story of the first sheaf of rice. The time for harvesting arrives and one must put the crop in a clay vase with a rounded bottom. This is where one finds the soul of rice and this is what one does before harvesting. One must also plant a tree[51] in the paddy field to protect the rice from diseases.[52] There is also a tree called *riyong*[53] which is used to take care of it. The girls, as well as boys, can harvest the rice. First one must blow[54] over the husk.[55]

One does this while making an invocation.[56] One brings the chaff and makes an invocation. One makes an invocation with the chaff. It is the men who do this. They harvest the rice and make invocations to chase away Jémalè. Jémalè is the evil spirit of rice. One must use magic for this.[57] One must pronounce magic words to make the spirit *pari*[58] go away. This must be accomplished before the harvest. This must be done before the rice is harvested. After the harvesting is over, one must prepare everything so that it will not be necessary to use the magical chaff.

But one must not forget the oil, the comb [for hair], flour, cooked rice and above all, the first spoonful of cooked rice. The chaff is still used. If one uses it, it is then no longer necessary to make offerings of cooked rice, bananas and flour. Before harvesting, one must rub one's hands over the chaff to make it easier to grab hold of the panicles of rice which will be cut and then say *killualoh*.

Does one have to wait seven days after this before harvesting the rice? [the assistant asked].

Ho! yes, one must wait, wait until the evening before putting the cooked rice in the granary and change this rice the next morning, one must wait seven days but it is also possible to wait only for three days. After three days, one can then harvest the rice.

## 2.9. Naséri and Naséwi: the two souls of rice

**(*Village of Samoh, Province of Narathiwat, February 1993*
*Narrator: Tohé*)**

One must put water and cooked rice in the granary if one wants to have a harvest. This is what the elders say, they learned this from their ancestors. This is what they teach and this is how we learned about this, except if one is a teacher;[59] then one doesn't accept this method. The ancestors took hold of an armful of rice to chase away Jémalè. We respect this way of doing [it]. During the time of rice, we do not eat in the evening, one must also avoid talking too loud or shout because the rodents will come in the evening to the paddy field to eat. Those who know about rodents say this but we don't know very much about them. One recites verses of the Koran, says prayers and recites verses of *kursi,*[60] one prays for god's blessing and that of the prophet,[61] *too pah aazutarim,*[62] *ate loh hitamaatu*[63] *muso,*[64] *akima kho,*[65] go and repeat this three times. We respect this. One must not breathe or open one's mouth. One does the same thing when one transplants.

Should one plant trees in the rice paddies? [my assistant asked].

Yes, because it is a way of taking care of it. One must put in it a plant or *riyong* to chase and a plant called *ngedèng*[66] to ward off the spirit. There is also the *jenuru*[67] tree to chase away the spirits but I have never used it. The bamboo *godèng*[68] is also a remedy used to protect the rice when it turns red.

The soul of the rice listens. It is said that it is double: Nasari and Nasewi, the soul of rice. One formerly used flour and other things which were placed in the granary. A comb and some flour were put there. The soul of the rice is a girl. When one harvests, it is necessary to wait three days. This rule must be absolutely respected. One must also do as the ancients used to do, pick up armfuls of rice. If there is any shadow one must stop harvesting. If one sees two shadows, one must do the same thing. This means that Jémalè[69] is present and if one sees two people at that time, well that means that one will not have enough to eat (because the rice has been left in the granary). Ha Ha Ha! But the teachers don't like what we have just said today. One sees people stepping on the rice in their houses. One never did this before.

### 2.10. Paddy: the soul of rice

***(Tanoh Meroh, Province of Patani, March 1993***
***Narrator: Méa***
***Type of Story: siloh)***

The paddy is the soul of rice. She is the same as men. Her name is Seven. When one calls her, one says only: "little girl, little boy." And when one wants to collect her and put her in the granary, one must say:

"Hey! Little girl, little boy, come here. I want to take you back with me. I want to harvest you because you must be very hot in this heat."

But no one knows exactly what this soul of rice looks like. She doesn't speak but she is with us. One sees her here. You simply have to call her. You have to call the soul of rice if you want to take her home with you. In order to do this, one must say:

"Hey! Little girl, little boy, come, because I want you to go back home with me. I want to make you happy in a place where there is wind and waves."

This is what one must do during the season when one transplants. One must speak of the wind and the waves. Ah, yes! One must speak like this, like the elders did before us. We have to speak about all this. This is the news about rice. But one cannot see the soul as one sees others things. Before labouring, one must choose where one wants to begin and look for the day that will be beneficial. For example, one can't work on Wednesday. One has to look for another day.

The old people of the past spoke of the soul of rice as if she was a human being. One cannot do anything bad to her; it's not possible. One must act towards her as one does with men. One cannot see her but there is no doubt that she is the rice. Even though the elders taught us all this, we don't know how to speak very well about this.

A long time ago, the soul of rice was a woman. A man spoke to another one who was younger than he was:

"Eh! Let's go and make a paddy field."

The young man lived with his adopted mother. He lived with her and went one day to transplant the rice. He transplanted the rice, all the plants in the seed nursery. This was the soul of rice. He transplanted and continued to transplant but he took pieces of the cut plants that the men had abandoned! He transplanted like this but this rice man is really the soul of rice. He continued to transplant and the rice became very lovely.

When the rice is beautiful, one holds ceremonies.[70] And soon the rice is ripe and he goes to put it in the granary. But he doesn't have very much.[71] We are talking about the husband of the soul of rice. He stores the rice and goes back home. His mother notices something. He goes back carrying water and flour with him. His father had prepared the granary. He goes in with the water and other things. But the mother sees them and begins asking questions.

"Ooh! There must be someone there, otherwise why do they go in with water and other things? There must be a young girl in this house. Yes, there certainly is a girl there."

So, she hit the soul of rice. She hit her so hard that the soul of rice ran away. And soon there were no longer any big rice stacks in the house. This is why one brings water and other things. One must go in with flour, oil, with something. This is how one must go into the house of rice and follow the example of the elders.

This is rice, this is the origin of rice, the soul of rice. The woman made her run away and there was then no more rice in the house. This is the story.[72] The soul left and that's the end. This is how it was with the rice a long time ago and this is why we can tell the story.

One knows that one must enter with oil, flour and other things. It is the same thing for the harvest or for storing [rice]. This is why we can begin to store [rice] today. One saw [what happened] this time when the boy entered with offerings. It is said that there was a young girl there. Hoo! So, one must go with sugar cane and other things. But when the mother saw the young girl, she beat her. Hoo! She beat her, so the soul of rice ran away. There was no more rice in the house. She had struck the soul of rice. This is all we know about this story.[73] This is how it is with the rice. This is why people of today call out "little girl, little boy", when they store the rice. But we don't know anything more about this. One must also call to the rice when one goes back home. One must say:

"Come here. You must come home, little boy, little girl. Come and take pleasure from the wind and the waves."

And when one harvests the rice, one must leave before dawn, before the others see.

## 2.11. Little girl, the soul of rice

***(Village of Tanoh Meroh, Province of Patani***
***Narrator: Méa***
***Type of Story: kéchè "to speak')***

She has a name and she has a master. The soul of rice has a name but we don't know what it is. But she is a girl. When men want to call her they say:

"Little girl! Little girl!"

People are afraid of her, so they call her "little girl." No one knows what her name is, but this is how people call her. She plants the rice that the men abandoned in the nursery. Everything she does is right. She is there at the start of rice. She transplants whatever the men have abandoned. This is rice.

This story is about a couple and the husband's mother. They are going to transplant and gather. The rice granary is still full. Some people saw this. One must buy bananas and other things. When one harvests the rice one needs bananas, flour, oil and other things as well. The day comes when the rice will be put into the granary and one sees:

"Oh! That's why the young man goes into the rice granary with bananas and flour; it's because there is a young girl there."

The mother strikes the soul of rice in the house, so she runs away. It is when one stores the rice that one can see her. This is why we can tell this story. And when one stores the rice, one must say:

"Little girl, little boy, come here, here where there is wind and waves."

Then she appeared. But since she had been beaten, she ran away. I don't know much about this soul of rice except that she had been beaten and ran away. The son of the one who had struck her told us this story.

Can young girls harvest the rice? [asks the assistant].

They can, so can boys because the women don't dare go there early in the morning. It is the moment when one should not meet anyone, nor even speak.

## 2.12. The soul of rice and the jealousy of the mother-in-law

***(Village of Petè, Province of Yala, November 1992***
***Narrator: Po' Chi Petè)***

She has gone away!

She left and that's how things are. There was once two people, a man and a woman. The husband never stopped going and coming. In the afternoon, he carried water and other things to the rice granary. He came and went without stopping. So his wife started asking herself questions and decided to follow him to see what was happening. She opened the door of the rice granary and saw a very pretty young girl. She went home and was very angry and said:

"Haa! This is why he keeps going and coming from the granary to the house with all sorts of things. He wants the girl who is there."

The husband and wife quarrelled and so the soul of rice, who was afraid of both of them, ran away. Where did she go? She went to the Chinese[74] country. But later on, they called her again and she returned. But she didn't come back completely. This is all I know.

She went away and the rice was harvested. In the past, one took a string that was tied from the house to the paddy field and the rice came all by itself; it was not necessary to do any harvesting. But when the soul of rice left and only half came back, harvesting was necessary. She was angry and didn't want to return. She was afraid of the husband. Since that time, women are not allowed to enter the rice granary. And this is also why one has to lie today, when one calls to the soul of rice.[75] But she comes back slowly, very slowly.

It is also thanks to her return that there are grains in the rice. It wasn't like that before. One planted rice but couldn't eat it. That was how it was during that time. There was no soul of rice! Everything had been broken and destroyed and so how could we eat? There was a great deal of rice but no grains in it because there was no longer any master of rice due to the fact that the soul of rice had run away to the country of the Chinese. Then the men called her:

"Don't stay too long in the Chinese country. Don't stay in the house of others."

They called her so that she would come back. If there is rice in the paddy field, one must call the soul to come to the house:

"Little girl, little boy! Come back completely."

She is difficult, the soul of rice. If one believes what happened, the women can no longer enter the rice granaries! They are really prohibited from going into the granaries, otherwise the soul of rice will be very angry.

### 2.13. Wind and waves for the soul of rice
***(Bangpu, Province of Patani, November 1992***
***Narrator: To Khimoh and others)***

This is what one must say when one harvests the rice:

"Come little girl, come little boy! Come and play with the wind and waves. It is very hot and the wind blows in the centre of the parcels. The rice must be transported when it is ripe. One must harvest it and bring it home."

"Come little girl! Come little boy! Come and take pleasure from the wind and waves. You must go back and play with the wind and the waves. Come to the house."

When people begin [to plant rice], they plant seven stalks. And when we transplant the rice, we must say:

"Come little girl! Come little boy! Come and play with the wind and the waves."

That's the way things are. Ask the elders, they know. This is what they say. But there are others who say something else.

[Assistant]: Why do you need seven stalks? Isn't it possible with two?

No. One needs seven.

[Assistant]: And why seven?

If there are two, well then, there are two! But seven is a great deal.

[Another person intervenes]: When one stores the rice, the seeds, the prophet must be invoked. The rice must be well stored otherwise the domestic animals will destroy it. The invocation must be made in *Jawi*.

[Assistant]: And when one transplants?

One has to choose the day when one transplants. If it is the second day of the month, you have to wait and find a favourable day for the earth during the thirty days of the month. There are days for earth, fire and wind. You are not able to do any harvesting on the day of fire. You have to choose the day of earth, water or wind and make invocations. You have to invoke the name of god. We are Muslims and so, we don't abandon the prayers.

[Assistant]: Are there any stories?

Yes! There are. It is the elders who know them. For example, To Khimoh knows. He is a man who knows about rice.

One has to find a good day when one stores the rice and only do it on that day. It is the same if one wants to transplant or to sow.

### *The story of To Khimoh*

When one ploughs the earth, one has to choose a day of the earth; the rice will then grow very well. You have to choose one day of the month, for example, and then start transplanting. When you transplant, you must say:

"Come,[76] soul of rice! Come and take your pleasures from the rain and the heat; come and play with the waves and wind!"

[Assistant]: And when one stores the rice?

You store it but first you must stamp on it and then go away. You can begin to harvest the rice the next day. [You must say]:

"Come, soul of rice. Come and live there where there is neither wind nor waves."

This is the way it is, but I myself don't know anything about it. One must be very polite to the rice and shelter it from the wind. One puts four or five stalks, even ten, in the place where the mother stack[77] is found. Then you must put down some water, bananas and cane sugar near them.

[Assistant]: Why?

I don't know. This is the way the elders used to do things. They put out some water and a cup. I have no knowledge of these things. If one wants to transplant, one first has to go and get the rice from the nursery. First you have to plant the stalks all together and say:

"Eh! Stop breathing, all you animals and everything else." If one wants to protect oneself from rodents and other things, one must stop breathing and plant the rice stalks, four or five of them.

[Assistant]: Do we speak inside ourselves [silently]?

Yes, that's what you do.[78] One says: "Everything that has wings, everything that has teeth." During this time, you mustn't open your mouth: all the animals and everything else. Also, you must plant without breathing and close your teeth tightly together so that the rodents won't come and eat the rice. Sometimes, they eat everything. But if one does what I just said, they eat less.

[Assistant]: How many stalks should one plant?

That depends. Four or five according to how long it takes to breathe again. But if some plants of rice remain, one plants them. It isn't important.

We can choose any day for planting, a day that we want to, any day, whether it is Friday, Sunday or Thursday, any day except Wednesday.

[Assistant]: Has the soul of rice a master?

Can we live if we don't have a god? It is god that takes care of us. The soul of rice is like this, she helps the rice . . . .

The wind makes the rice plants bend but there is always one that is straighter than the others. An elder said that the same is true with men. Something happens and everything bends. We pull out[79] the stalk that is the straightest and transplant it. It will be the first one that is cut.

How does one begin when one transplants the rice? This should be done on a windy day so that it goes more quickly. Then, yes, it is rapid.

It is the same for all work. If a good day arrives, even if you don't want to, you must work. When you store the rice you have to move everything and put everything in order so as to chase away all the animals. You have to make salutations and pray: "May peace be upon you." You have to do this so that the animals who destroy and eat the rice will go away. You have to invoke the name of God when you transplant but with your mouth closed. All the animals, the cruel animals then will not open their mouths.

[Another assistant]: Why is there always a piece of wood planted in the centre of the paddy field?

People say that it is an umbrella.[80] It is a parasol because it is really very hot and serves as a shelter for the soul of rice.

People tell a story about a man and his wife who were quarrelling. Their quarrel made the soul of rice run away. But this is not good and we don't like this. All of us ask Ni[81] to help us when we start the rice. Before the first prayer, you must take hold of the soul of rice and not meet anyone. One day, the man met someone who had a gun. [The man with the gun] didn't want to say anything and looked like a robber.

When you [plant] rice, there must be a beginning and if you want more rice, something else is needed. It is To Mudeng, who circumcises, who takes care of this. When you begin, you have to face the mountain. [The man] had to turn towards the mountain and say:

"I want rice, a stack of rice as big as this mountain."

**Fig. 15.** Harvesting the soul of rice.

It is the same for the animals as it is for robbers. Those who know go far from the robbers who then go towards other people.

Then when the rice has been harvested and there still remains some after it has been stamped on, you cannot give any to the ducks. After the rice has been stamped on, you have to hit it so that the grains come out.

And when you boil it, you mustn't move or go far from the cooking pot, otherwise it suffers. You mustn't move until the rice is dry. It is just like our breathing.

[Another assistant]: Does the soul of rice look like a human being? Does it look like a girl?

A girl? That's not certain. We, we speak about the soul. If you make many paddy fields without knowing, it will never be sufficient. But if you make a small number, that's good. As for myself, I don't have a paddy field. It is a long time now since I stopped.

### 2.14. The soul of rice or the paddy that is lying down
***(Bang Pu, Province of Patani, October 1992***
***Collected by Rusli Weyeng***
***Narrator: Unknown)***

Men of long ago remember. As for myself, I am an old man and I remember. It is about the soul. The soul is a woman. A woman! Who is she? She is the queen of rice! We are going to speak quite simply. Haa! It is about a time long ago; but one still does it today. This is one of our beliefs.[82] When one finishes gathering the rice, one must make offerings[83] and puts them in the house. We are talking about rice. Will the Lord let us see her? We can see her human appearance in the rice granary. Men of long ago were really very nice: a woman? Ha! A woman! We are still talking about this soul of rice. But time passes, generations also. One continues to make offerings, offerings to the soul of rice. Otherwise the rice is not good and one cannot eat husked rice. But today, haa! There is the mortar [for pounding] betel. It costs one hundred rien[84] and since that time it is difficult to eat. Haa! That's the way it is. Those who make paddy fields can no longer eat. Why? Hooo? But of course, because of the offerings made to the soul of rice. Hooo, this is the way it is. One is no longer able to eat since that rich man there bought a mortar for betel. Do you know about the mortar for betel? It is worth one hundred baht today. Before, it was called rien. Hoo! Yes, he could buy this because he was a very rich man. He was richer than Haji Teh and even Haji Daut, the two rich men of today. But there is something to do after harvesting the rice.

[Assistant]: What then?

But, the soul!

[Assistant]: The soul?

Yes, the soul, after the harvest. In effect, after the harvest one must lay down the rice plants. One must lay them down and then do other things, too. This is what the elders say. Haa! You must make a party and tell all the people of the village to come. As for you, go into my house and as for me, I will go into yours. We will call each other to eat and make a party. There are many things. People come to eat.

[Assistant]: Did people do this in the paddy fields also?

No, not in the paddy fields. When the harvest ended one ground the rice for the meal. Haa! One crushed the rice and stamped on the grains with the feet. We grind it with our feet here, but over there, in Kedah, they use a big straight sifter and strike the stalks of rice with it. In Bangkok, they hit the rice on the ground. It goes faster that way. People of long ago tell this story. The platform was filled with people who listened. But no one wants to tell stories today. There are no longer old people. We, we are young people who like to eat and listen to stories, like the one about the king who had a dog's head. . .

## 2.15. Why rice has become small

***(Village of Seno, Province of Patani, November 1992
Narrator: Ché O)***

During that time, the rice was big. One had to really grind it. In order to eat the bones of husked rice, one had to grind, grind, grind. . .

Then it was gathered together and boiled. But before doing this, one had to throw away what we call today, the pod. In the past, it was only the bones of rice that were put to boil. Why did the rice become small? Well, I am going to tell you: it was because of an iguana. She climbed on to the rice stalks, the grains fell down and she let herself fall over them. So, the iguana said:

"Rice, I want you to be as small as the end of my tail."

And the rice became as small as the end of her tail, because she had fallen over the rice and it suffered. Before, it was as big as a coconut. Yes, the rice suffered. The men of the past say that the soul of rice is a woman! But in order to store the rice and transplant the first plants, it is better that it is a man who does this. A man must store it and go and look for rice in the granary. It is the men who must do all this. Yes, it is the men because women should not take care of things like that. They stamp on the rice because the soul of rice prefers the company of men; it is like a woman who loves a man. That doesn't make her angry. But if a woman goes into the granary, then the soul of rice doesn't love so much. Is this the way you think, you other men? One doesn't know whether what the elders say is true or not. The soul of rice will be a woman. They also say that it is men who should harvest the first stalks, as well as the first storage of the rice that has been harvested. When you go to get some rice to eat, it is also a man who should do this. The women only stamp on the rice. But if a man goes in to look for rice to eat, he must know what the desires of the soul of rice are. If you don't know the nice words to speak to her, you cannot take any rice. She won't allow you to take any rice. You must treat her well and be clever. You go in to see:

"Ooo! No one is allowed to take the rice; it is not authorized!"

So you go out, smoke one or two cigarettes and do some thinking. Then you go in again, in order to see. You enter:

"Still no one can take any rice!"

So, you go out again. Yes, you really must know how to treat this soul of rice. How can you know whether to take the rice or not? You must know what she desires. The next day, you take a basket to put the rice into but, above all, you must not think about how much to put in it, or the soul of rice will not permit you to take any. She won't give you any of it. You go back in the afternoon. She finally authorizes the men to take the rice. So then, you have to take a great deal all at once, or if not you break the stack and change the order. You have to take a great deal and put it all in other baskets. Then you can stamp on the rice and there will be enough. If you

**Fig. 16.** Living ouside the village.

have several baskets in advance, it won't be necessary then to go back to the rice granary and you only have to go and look for it.

The elders don't often eat rice because you have to come and go to the rice granary. One day, a married man saw the soul of rice in the granary: she greatly resembled a woman, except that you can't sleep with her. He saw a very pretty young girl there; she was perfect. You must really dream[85] in order to desire such beautiful things.[86] But what to do to obtain them? How to take the soul of rice? She is a beautiful young girl; she knows our desires but you can't sleep with her. This is what people of long ago say: they told us what to do in order to take the rice from the granary. You cannot play when you go looking for rice.

## 2.16. Hawè Jabut, the soul of rice

***(Village of Samoh, Province of Narathiwat, May 1992***
***Narrator: Po' Suloh***
***Type of Story: hikaya')***

There was once an angel[87] who threw seven grains of rice into a waterhole.

He sent them there for Adam and Eve.

Adam and Eve had children but they had nothing to eat.

So, Adam went to look for the angel:

"Eh, Angel! What are my children going to eat? They are starving and continually crying. Milk is no longer enough for them."

"That's no problem. I will go up above and ask the Lord to send down seven grains of rice."

"Will seven grains of rice be enough to take care of human beings?"

The angel answered:

"Don't do any harm to the rice because if you do anything bad against it, even if you ate one hundred full sacks[88] it would not be enough to feed you. This is how the Lord wants things to be with the seven grains of rice. The seven grains of rice is the wisdom of the Lord."

"Where will we go with these grains? We don't know."

Adam then left to gather the seven grains of rice that were lying in the waterhole.[89] They would become seven stalks. But Adam and Eve had no idea what they were supposed to do and, above all, how to plant the rice. So, they went back and asked the angel:

"Eh Angel! I gathered the grains but what should I do now in order to feed my children?"

The Angel said:

"First, you must pull out the weeds; then you must clear the land before making little seed holes. This is how the seven stalks of rice can grow. But nothing will grow if someone behaves badly."

So, making the seed holes Adam and Eve pulled out the weeds and cleared the land. But a bird came and ate all the seeds.

"Eh, bird! Don't eat our seeds."

At that time animals were able to speak, so the bird said:

"Eh! Then what will I eat?"

"In that case, you have only to take seven grains and eat them."

They then shared all the food with the chickens, ducks and the other animals.

Eve soon finished making the seed holes and after that the rice was harvested.

When the harvest was over she brought seven handfuls of rice to her house and left them there.[90] But during the night, the rice filled the entire house, from top to bottom.

**Fig. 17.** A happy soul of rice make the granary full.

The animals had already eaten since they had shared the rice with one another. It is from this time that the [giving of] gifts to the poor started.[91] The rice was left on the ground and the rodents didn't even come to eat it.

Then Adam said:

"But this rice, all this rice must have a master and if it does have a master he must be able to speak."

But the soul of rice was still not able to remain there. This is why Adam called it Hawè[92] Jabut, "the one that one pulls." Hawè Jabut then appeared and spoke:

"A master does exist and he is myself."

Eve said:

"If a master does exist he must have an appearance. Is it possible to know him?"

At this time, Adam and Eve had only one child. Eve wanted other children but was unable to conceive.

The master of rice soon appeared.

"You wanted to see Hawè Jabut? Well, here he is."

"Eh! How can he have such repulsive appearance?"[93]

"That's how things are. You wanted to see what I look like. But I am now going to become even more white than the husked rice."

"Can we see him one more time?" said Adam's child.

Hawè Jabut then split open his chest with his hand; he tore it open and everything became white. His stomach was transparent and there was nothing cleaner or more beautiful than this.

Eve asked:

"Do you have a wife?"

Hawè Jabut said:

"I don't have a wife but if you seek a young girl you must first make some glutinous rice."

But there was no glutinous rice in those days. Adam then went up to see the angel, who asked him:

"Why have you come here again, Adam?"

"Eh! Things are still not finished. The paddy is a man but there is not yet a woman there."

"But, nevertheless, she exists, the mistress of rice. The first thing you must do is to gather some glutinous rice, one grain to the left and one grain to the right. Then you must take the two grains and crush them between your fingers so that they become united. There will then be a woman."

Adam then went back to his house. He met Hawè Jabut there and he asked:

"What did the angel say?"

"He told me to take a grain of rice to the left and then one to the right and to crush them so that they become united."

"Then pick them up," said Hawè Jabut.

Adam did what the angel had told him to do and crushed the grains of rice between his fingers. Then he heard someone weeping, so he said to Hawè Jabut:

"That is a woman who is weeping."

Hawè Jabut said:

"You have just started to come out, we have a glimpse of you and you are crying. But as for me, I didn't say anything."

She then appeared and it could be seen that she had a magnificent appearance, like those of nymphs, as our master had said she would. The son of Eve then fell madly in love with the mistress of glutinous rice, of the soul of rice. He said to Hawè Jabut:

"Eh! I am unable to make a woman since my skin only belongs to me and so, I cannot make a woman."

This is why human beings went to ask the angel who had given to men. This is why it was now Adam's turn to give.

Hawè Jabut said:

"We are going to transform this girl."

Eve said:

"But no! You must not transform her because my son would like to eat glutinous rice from time to time."

This is the reason why she has remained like glutinous rice until today. She stayed for a long time and was able to speak. Eve soon became pregnant and brought a girl into the world. She had nine children in all and all of them married among each other. What Adam had authorized was then possible but today it is impossible.

All the animals saw that human beings married between brothers and sisters. So they said that all men were crazy and did so well with Adam that the angel came down to see what was happening. Hawè Jabut said:

"Eh! You human beings, you already have families! But you must think about raising me at the same time. If you don't take care of me, who will do so after you?"

So, Adam's children accepted him and welcomed Hawè Jabut, who put on his sarong and vanished. But it would be well to remember this.

"I still have something to say to all of you. From next month on, I will no longer speak to human beings; but the animals will still be able to talk to you."

He went back into the paddy fields and stopped speaking to human beings. Adam's children took the soul of rice and placed it at the top of the rice granary. This is the reason why one must take seven stalks of rice and put them on the top of the rice granary. But the soul of rice came out one more time and expressed the desire to say something else to them during one hour.

"What do you still want to tell us?" Adam's children asked.

"If you want to take me again, you must first say some prayers. You must confess your faith seven times, invoke the name of God seven times, call everyone to pray seven times, you must also take hold of the rice by the armful. Then you must first of all refrain from leaving the pestle in the mortar when you go with me to the granary. Secondly, when you separate the pods from the grain you must not gather up the grains of rice that fall over the side of the mortar. Thirdly, during the time when the women have their periods, they must not enter the rice granary because the first time we gathered the rice we prayed and my first phrases were made so that I would be clean and beautiful. It is the Lord that sent us all this. One cannot gather the rice in the granary on Friday or on Monday either. In effect, on Friday, we read and learn. We learn that I shared things with the rodents and other animals. You must remember all this. You must preserve what has been transmitted to you."

"We will remember," said Adam's children.

"Very well then. You must transmit all this to your descendants."

As soon as he finished speaking Hawè Jabut went back into the paddy fields. Some of the people passed on Hawè Jabut's words and others didn't. There is something else you must remember: if a leech bites one of the animals, then you can crush the rice but you must ask its pardon in this world and in the next one too.[94] There is still something else that Hawè Jabut told us: when anyone enters a paddy field, he should not whistle or otherwise the rice will be dry. Tears appear and blood flows from his nostrils.

But you cannot see his soul. If someone goes out into the field, it is better to read and recite prayers. When the harvest is over, then one can whistle. One must respect this when the rice becomes pregnant and until it blooms.

Now, here is what Adam's grandchildren said:

"What are we going to do now? Our parents are dead but the animals and trees are still able to speak."

Adam's descendants sculpted an image made of earth and it soon looked like an animal. But they didn't know what the thing they had just created was called. Then one night, they had a dream.[95]

"This thing is called a buffalo. You will see him eating herbs tomorrow because I[96] gave him life."[97]

This is what the soul of rice, who had gone to the Lord to ask for life, said.

The grandchildren then saw the buffalo which was eating herbs. It was just as they had seen in their dreams. He possessed life and was eating some herbs. They then asked themselves what colour he would be. What would his reflection be? They gathered together and asked again how to give him a colour.

"This is not difficult. You only have to take some of the grease," one of them said.

"What grease?" said another one.

"It is enough just to take the envelope that covers the pods of rice grains after they have been thrashed. This is the membrane of the rice. You must take it and then crush it between the hands until it becomes oil which can be rubbed on to the buffalo's body and then it will shine," said another one.

"Eh! But white is not at all beautiful!"

"How can we make it black then?"

"It is enough just to take some of the earth where we planted the seedlings. We will rub it on his body and he will become black," said another one.

So this is what they all did.

This is why since that time albino buffaloes have existed, and also black buffaloes.

"There is still something else. We must create cows."

So, all Adam's grandchildren helped one another. This is why there are now buffaloes and cows. In the past, cows and buffaloes didn't eat rice because they had come from the earth and rice. They can eat rice today because men committed a fault. The soul of rice had pity for human beings since they had made an error. So, she[98] was then transformed.

"Eh, men! Now you can see me."

In effect, he had just come out of the rice. He was ugly due to his skin disease; moreover, he smelled bad. During this time, Adam's grandchildren cooked the rice. Hawè Jabut arrived and asked for some rice. He said:

"I am very hungry and would like some rice."

"You can eat some but we will serve it to you in a coconut and you will eat over there since we have no wish to eat with you."

The grandchildren gave him some rice but it was not very good because they had served him as if he was a cat.

Hawè Jabut had a heavy heart.

"I will keep this appearance for nine seasons. I wanted to see human beings but look how they treat me and the animals!"

Adam's grandchildren had children of their own. They had many children. One of them went away to work in a far-off place. During the work season, the buffalo only laboured until the afternoon. He excused himself and said:

"Eh! Excuse me, man, but it is very hot."

"Ha! You are lazy. You don't want to keep working even though we have only just started."

They stopped working from time to time in order to pray. The man said:

"It is now time to stop since the birds have stopped singing (because of the afternoon heat)."

Then the buffalo's master tied him to a stake so that he could eat some herbs. He left the buffalo there and went to eat. But the buffalo was exposed to terrible heat and began to cry. The cow approached him and said:

"Hey, buffalo! Why are you so hot? And how is it that your master still hasn't come back?"

"Ah! I am almost dead with sorrow and suffering waiting for my master. But when he returns, I will pronounce a judgement. Since he doesn't take care of me during the day, I will never speak to human beings again."

His master came back when he had finished eating and approached the buffalo, who was so hot that he was foaming at the mouth. It was so hot that the skin on his back was cracking.

"Eh! Look what you human beings have done to me."

"You are not going to tell me what to do because I am more intelligent than you are."

**Fig. 18.** Playing and designing the buffalos.

The buffalo said:

"Alright then. You are cleverer than I am. I was able to speak to you until this season but from now on I will remain silent. I don't want to speak to you anymore."

The soul of rice was there and heard what the buffalo said. She thought in her heart:

"But what are men doing? I am going to continue to do many things for them but they will have to do the same for me. And now, I am going to pronounce a judgement[99] against men; they have committed a fault. The buffaloes, cows, chickens and canaries are all crying. And I see the errors men have made."

This is what the soul of rice thought.

"I will raise the goats from now on."

She wanted to give men a good lesson. Then she went towards the houses to look for the goats.

"Who then owns many goats that I can raise?"

One of the inhabitants answered:

"Someone like you wants to raise goats? You are too lazy to even wash yourself. You are not a human being and so you can't take care of the goats. You are not like other men and, moreover, your skin is oozing pus and you smell bad."

Hawè Jabut said:

"Maybe I smell bad but do you know who I am? Do you know what you eat everyday? Who does this come from?"

The man answered:

"I don't know about all that. We must not speak too much and we are still young and don't think too much yet."

"Very well! Then listen to me, all of you who are capable of any reflection. How many goats do you have?"

"I have forty and if you want them, then take them. But will you have the strength to take care of them?"

Hawè Jabut said:

"Forty goats? Even if you had a hundred of them, I could still take care of them."

"And what will you give them to eat? Even if you take only two of them, they will surely die."

"Give all of them to me."

"Very well then. Go and take them."

Hawè Jabut climbed up to the house and asked:

"Where are the goats?"

"I don't know."

"You must call them and they will come back."

"You call them then. If they come back, you must take hold of them if you are able to catch them."

Hawè Jabut went down the staircase until he reached the last step.

Then he said:

"Come here, all your animals and goats, all forty of them. Come here."

So, the forty goats came to the house and kissed Hawè Jabut's feet and the rest of his body. The goats all surrounded Hawè Jabut. He said:

"Are you really going to give me the goats now that they have come to me?"

The man responded:

"No, I won't. I will give you only half of them and you will give me half of the small ones when they are born."[100]

"Why then? You yourself saw how they came to me. We made an agreement and you promised to give me all of them because you were sure that I wouldn't be capable of taking care of them."

The master of the house said:

"But no! It isn't like this. If I give you all of them, I will get bored."

"So you lied to me when you said that you would give me forty goats!"

This is the reason why from this time on the goats are blessed.[101]

"But no! You will leave twenty goats with me and you will take twenty for yourself and we will see if they die."

So Hawè Jabut took twenty goats.

"Hey, you twenty goats! Follow me."

The goats followed Hawè Jabut and he took them into the paddy field. He sat down under a tree and stayed there with his goats day and night. But one day, the king's daughter saw him there. She asked him:

"Hey, young man! Are you crazy to take care of your goats so far from men? Is it because they would eat all the plants in their gardens? Is this why you do not want to raise them near the houses?"

Hawè Jabut answered:

"Did they eat your plants?"

"Not yet! This is because you have taken them so far away. But be very careful."

Hawè Jabut said:

"If by chance my goats eat your plants, even if it is only one tree, I will give you two goats."

"Very well then," said the king's daughter.

"Hey, goats! Don't go into men's gardens," said Hawè Jabut.

So, the goats did not go away but stayed close to Hawè Jabut. When they had finished eating in one place, they went to another one. During this time, all the goats that had stayed with the master of the house died.

**Fig. 19.** Harvesting the rice and keeping the goats, main activities of the Malay peasants.

"You were right, Hawè Jabut," he said. "I should have given you all the goats instead of only twenty."

He went to see Hawè Jabut.

"Eh, horrible young man! Can you give me back half of my goats? All the ones I kept died from sickness like stomach pains and many other things."

"They didn't die because they were sick but because you had made a promise to me."

"Are you a magician?"[102] asked the master of the house.

"No, I am only a poor man; but if, for example, I tell you that you will be hungry, then you really will be hungry."

The master of the goats said:

"Very well then! Do it. Make me hungry. Go ahead! Pronounce some magic words[103] so I will believe you."

The master of the goats went home. The next night, the rice left the granary. Not even one grain of rice remained, not even one pod. The rice left and went to meet Hawè Jabut. The rice asked him:

"Where will we live now?"

"First, hide in the termites' nest. As for myself, I will go and speak to the master of the rice granary."

The master of the house then felt very hungry and went to look for some husked rice. He saw that there was none left. He then went to the rice granary, but there was none there either and he became worried.

"Who then has come to take my rice?"

He asked everyone all over the village. They all went to the rice granary and saw that it was true; there was nothing left. They all began to be very worried and no one could say what had happened. During this time, Hawè Jabut's goats went into the king's daughter's garden. They began bleating under the king's house.

"Eh subjects! Go and hit the goats; they are keeping me from sleeping," he said.

The king's daughter said:

"Hey, father! Don't hit the young man's goats. I will go and speak to him."

"Who is this young man?"

"The horrible young man is in the paddy field."

The king left to look for the young man. He went to the master of the goats, Hawè Jabut, who woke up and found himself face to face with the king, who saw the horrible features and purulent body of Hawè Jabut. The king said:

"Don't send your goats to me anymore, otherwise I will beat them and tell my servants to throw them all over the place."

"Don't do that to my goats, lord."

This is how the king spoke. Hawè Jabut stayed with his goats. He started singing and dancing in the paddy field. He was happy and ran from one stalk of rice to another. But the king's daughter soon heard Hawè Jabut singing and the song was really beautiful.

"Men, do you know where this song is coming from?" the king's daughter asked.

She went down from the house and left to look for the singer that she had sometimes heard over the rice stalks and at times under them. The king's daughter left the paddy field where there were several stalks of rice.

"I really did hear someone singing here!"

Hawè Jabut heard what she said.

"What's the matter? Who is looking for me?"

"I came here to see who was singing because his song was really magnificent."

"It was myself," said Hawè Jabut.

"It's not possible that it was you who sang so well. I don't believe you."

The king's daughter went home to sleep and Hawè Jabut started singing in the paddy field again. Then the king's daughter left again to look for the singer and finally saw him. Hawè Jabut was sitting on a rice leaf.

"It's really beautiful; your song and your white color are really magnificent."

The king's daughter fell madly in love with Hawè Jabut and could not bring herself to leave. She asked:

"Eh, older one! Can you sing again once more?"

"I can no longer do so since those with such a horrible appearance cannot sing well. Moreover, what will people say if they see us talking together?"

The king's daughter went home and told everything to her father. But he didn't believe her and called Hawè Jabut.

"Eh, young man! I want to ask you something."

"Of course," Hawè Jabut answered. "But please wait a minute because I first have to take care of the goats."

"Go then," the king said.

Hawè Jabut left to find his goats.

"Hey, goats! Don't go anywhere. Stay where you are because I have to go and speak to the king."

Hawè Jabut went to see the king.

"I greet you a thousand times, lord."

"Who is it then who is singing in the paddy field?" asked the king.

"I am, lord."

"And why do you sing?"

"I get bored with my goats."

"Why doesn't your song resemble those of other men? Can you sing again?"

"I cannot. It is not possible if I am not accompanied by my goats. It is not possible."

"And why then?" asked the king.

"The goats help me by responding to my song."

So the king let Hawè Jabut go and find his goats because he wanted to hear him sing once more.

"My servants, who would like to hear him sing?"

"I will go," said the guardian.

"Very well then."

The guardian want to the paddy field where Hawè Jabut lived and heard his song. When he heard it, he fainted.

The king was in this house and waited for the guardian to return so that he could tell him about this song. He waited for days and days but the guardian did not return. So, he sent someone else who returned and told him the following:

"Lord, the guardian was killed by the young man."

So, the king called Hawè Jabut.

"You killed my servant!"

"I did not kill him."

"He is dead, though, in the paddy field."

"But, no! If I had killed him there would be some traces left."

"Can you go and get him since you say that you did not kill him?"

"Of course."

He went back to the paddy field, took a leaf of paddy and passed it across the guardian's mouth, and he woke up.[104] The guardian went back to the king.

"Hey, lord! His song was so magnificent that I fainted."

"How many songs did you hear?" asked the king.

"I only heard one and even then, not entirely. If you do not believe me, lord, you can go and see for yourself."

So the king called Hawè Jabut so that he would sing in front of the door of the palace. But Hawè Jabut said:

"I cannot because my goats are in the paddy field."

"Call them and tell them they can all come into the palace."

"That is not possible, lord. They would eat all the plants. They do not understand anything."

"This is of no importance. If they eat everything I won't be angry."

So, Hawè Jabut called his goats and told them to go into the palace. Hawè Jabut planted a paddy stalk and sat on top of it.[105] He sang and the king fell asleep; his daughter was crazy about Hawè Jabut.

**Fig. 20.** The soul of rice.

"Hey, older one! Wake up my father. Help me and if you do this I will marry you and you won't have to pay anything."[106]

"But I don't want to marry yet."

"If necessary, I will ask you ten times, older one and I will still want you."

"If you ask me ten times, your father will be angry."

"Even if my father beats me, I will still continue to want to marry you."

Hawè Jabut didn't want to make any difficulties so he climbed up and woke up the king who was about to faint. When he woke up, the king said:

"But what's the problem? Of course my daughter can marry the young man even if he is covered with a skin disease and is ugly. There is no problem, little girl. Then take him as a husband."

"Eh! Do you mean it, father? But I have no wish to marry yet. I want to take care of my goats. I am afraid they will eat all men's plants."

Hawè Jabut came down from the king's house and his daughter started to cry. She had remained near Hawè Jabut and became pregnant without being married. She gave birth one month later. When Hawè Jabut heard this he returned to the king's house.

"Don't think too much about all this. There won't be any problem if you give me something."

"What kind of thing?" said the king.

"There mustn't be any party; I don't want one. I want a simple marriage."

"This is not possible. I have to let my servants assist at the festivities and the marriage."

"But after the marriage, I will not be able to stay in the house because I must first think of my goats and also, I am not like you; I really cannot marry and I am not truly like other men."

Everyone was astonished by his words. What does he mean, not a man? He can speak, though, like everyone else.

"When will the marriage take place?"

The king wanted a real marriage and for many people to come to it. Hawè Jabut said:

"Don't be worried about the husked rice."

"But I am not worried."

"Where will you get it, father?" Hawè Jabut asked.

"I will buy it. I am very rich."

"But I would like to help you."

"How can you? Where will you get the money? Even if you sell your seventy goats it will not be sufficient."

"Don't be worried about this, father. Invite all the people and take care of the dishes but don't think any more about the rice because I will bring three million sacks tonight."

"Alright," said the king.

The next day, there was a great quantity of rice lying on the ground. Everyone had the impression of being on a sandy beach. The king held a celebration which lasted for seven days and seven nights but the mound of rice didn't get any smaller, no matter how much of it was used for the feast. The other kings who had been invited wanted to see the new son-in-law but the king said:

"My son-in-law is in the paddy field. You must not go to see him because he smells bad and he is very ugly."

Hawè Jabut was in the paddy field and his heart was heavy when he learned what the king had said. People behaved badly towards him. But soon everything was finished and Hawè Jabut asked the father:

"Father, is there any rice left?"

"There is still a great quantity left."

"Will you keep it?" If you don't want to, I will take it away since it does not belong to me."

"Where do you want to take it?"

"I will wait until tomorrow and then come and take it away."

The next day, there was no more rice left and the king was astonished.

"My son-in-law must really be a magician!"

"Little girl! You will go to sleep in the chamber and I will sleep outside."

So, the king's daughter slept inside and Hawè Jabut stayed outside. But the mother came and didn't want her son-in-law to sleep in the house. She told him to go and sleep near the ladder. Hawè Jabut did this because he didn't want to cause any problems. The two old people went to sleep, but just as they were falling asleep they saw a light of many colours near the roof.

"Hey! But what is happening with the young man? What a surprise! What kind of magic is this?[107] What is that light?"

The king's daughter was sleeping and soon had a dream. She was very hungry in her dream. She woke up and went to see Hawè Jabut.

"Hey, older one! I am hungry."

"Yes, I am too," said Hawè Jabut.

His wife went to cook some rice in the middle of the night. When she had finished she called Hawè Jabut. She took some chilli, three chillies, and added them to the brine *budu*.[108]

"Hey, younger one! I cannot eat chilli."

She waited until her older one had finished eating but she could not see that he swallowed anything. She was astonished.

"Hey, older one! Aren't you going to eat? I didn't see you swallow anything."

"Then you didn't see me eat?"

"No, I didn't see anything."

There was a king there who wanted to see the son-in-law. He had heard that he was very ugly. He went to see Hawè Jabut and said [to the king]:

"I would like very much to see your son-in-law, king."

"You only have to go over there where the goats are."

"He doesn't seem to look so bad. If he is really your son-in-law he cannot take care of goats. If he has become your son-in-law, he should have a dagger, whether it is a small or a big one and be armed like a warrior. King, your son-in-law is only a sick man and not an ugly one."

The king's daughter was cooking some rice. She made a chilli[109] sauce since the king liked it. He ate, took the chilli sauce and poured it over the rice.

Hawè Jabut was seated on the ground and felt a great heat; his skin burned him.[110] He went to see the father and said:

"Father, I don't like the way you eat, either on this earth or in the other world. You all eat like that but I don't like it."

"Why then are you telling me all this?"

"Men do not understand anything. They are like the cows and buffaloes, neither more nor less. And it is really true that the Lord doesn't like chillies, especially when they are mixed with rice. If you eat some, you must put seven grains of rice on the edge of the plate and leave a place for me to stay. It is true that rice nourishes and fills one but if one adds chillies, they take up all the space."

Then the king spoke:

"I don't believe what you are saying."

Some men believed him and others did not.

"Do as you see best if you do not believe me," said Hawè Jabut. "But if you don't believe me you will see that it won't be long before you will be hungry after each meal."

The soul of rice no longer helps men because in the past, or in other words, before there were machines to shell the rice, it was necessary to leave the unhusked rice to dry. In effect, when the rice dries, the soul of rice cannot come out. But today, things are not done in the same way. One takes the rice directly to the factory. The soul of rice runs away and comes back when the rice has been cooked. Then one eats and is full. But the soul of rice is no longer there and the ghosts[111] have arrived. This is why one must recite the name of the Lord each time.

The soul of rice said:

"Long ago, when the planting of the seedlings began one planted seven stalks of rice. Everyone today does the same thing. Why then do people eat chillies? In the past, when one began to plant the seedlings one prayed[112] seven times and it was over. Now there are lectures[113] for the rodents and all kinds of other things. In the north, on the north side of the parcel of land, there was the female mistress of glutinous rice. But now the soul of rice no longer has a house and she cries."

The people took some cake made of cane sugar to arrest the soul of rice during seven days. They put her in a braided basket. Why did they arrest her? It was because the elders had said:

"Hey, soul of rice! You are really very beautiful and you should go into my basket where there are many good things to eat. You can eat as much as you want."

This is one of the invocations used to retain the soul of rice. So she remained there, in that place, for one week.

But let's go back to the goats. They were at the house of Hawè Jabut's wife. The goats were worried about Hawè Jabut because they saw how he was waiting and crying in the braided basket which was soon filled with tears. Then his wife gave birth and all the goats started bleating, all seventy of them. Hawè Jabut wanted to leave, so he made a dream for the master of the house.

"I must leave since I have to go and see my wife and child."

Did his wife gave birth to a boy or girl? One hundred and forty people came to visit the child but no one saw him and could not say if it was a boy or a girl. The soul of rice took some glutinous rice that she gave to the goats.

"Hey goats! Come and take some glutinous rice."

There were seventy goats. They brought the glutinous rice to the child, who ate it. He ate seven grains and stopped crying.[114] The mother wanted to take the child but there was no body to be seen. Hawè Jabut took him to the paddy field and stayed there with him. The child played in the paddy and the soul of rice didn't get angry. The soul of rice (Hawè Jabut) reflected and asked herself what she was going to do with his wife. She wanted to transform herself and become a man in order to remain with his wife, become very ugly and go to his father-in-law's house.

"Hey, father! I want to stay with my wife."

"As you wish," said the king who was happy about this.

He (Hawè Jabut) went then to meet the king and his wife. He was going to see his mother-in-law but she refused to greet him or even touch him.

"Don't come to see me any more."

Hawè Jabut was sad. So he transformed himself and became very handsome so that his mother-in-law could see him. She fainted.

"Why have you fainted, mother? Father! Mother has fainted."

The king came running and he too fainted. Only Hawè Jabut's wife remained conscious. The king's servants arrived.

"Horrible man, did you give the king some poison to drink?"

"Not at all. I didn't give him anything to drink. He fainted when he saw me."

There was a king visiting who said:

"What kind of appearance do you have to make these two faint? Can one see?"

"If you want to see me you must look at the rice."

"But the rice is still not beautiful."

"Yes, but here is his master. You must remember this, you human beings, I am really like other human beings."

"You are not the same. You are so ugly that there must be some magic under all this."

Hawè Jabut was sad when he heard this and became transformed and handsome once again. The king saw him and so did all the others. Everyone except the king fainted. He said:

"You are really splendid and no one can equal you."

But there were many people who were jealous and the king gave orders to kill him. The servants came to kill him. Hawè Jabut said:

"It will please me if you kill me."

He then took on his ugly appearance. The servants said:

"Lord, we are going to kill this horrible person."

So the servants beat him but each time Hawè Jabut disappeared and then reappeared a short time afterwards. The men then said that he was a magician.[115] Today, people speak more of Jémalè[116] than of Hawè Jabut but I think that he is rather a ghost.

### 2.17. The origin of the grains of the rubber tree

***(Village of Samoh, Province of Narathiwat, September 1992***
***Narrator: Domè Sao***
***Type of Story: bahri)***

We are going to tell a story tonight. What story is it? We will tell the story of the grains of the rubber tree.

There was once a teacher.[117] He opened a big religious school.[118] He had many disciples,[119] thousands of disciples. This teacher was a holy man. He taught year by year, day after day, week after week, month after month. Years passed, dozens of years went by. And then one day a spirit[120] arrived. He had the appearance of a human being. The spirit arrived and asked to follow the teaching. He was welcomed and started to study. He studied for a very long time. The teacher ate, slept, got up and defecated. But only men can do this; as for the spirit, he did not eat, did not sleep and did not defecate; in fact, he did nothing at all. This was astonishing. Then a day came when the teacher and his disciples asked him:

"Why then don't you eat nor sleep, wake up nor defecate? You don't do anything as we do. Nonetheless, one must sleep, get up, eat and defecate."

Ha! The teacher found all this really very strange. But the spirit remained quiet and didn't answer.

"Eeh! He remains very quiet."

The next morning, the teacher gathered his disciples together and asked them what to do. Is he a man, an angel,[121] a human being, a spirit?[122] He told his disciples to watch over him. So, they watched over him night after night, week after week, month after month. No one did anything else but look after him. Finally, one night, one of the disciples went to see the teacher and told him that he was some kind of spirit.

"He came in order to mislead us. He came in order to transform the sacred[123] books."

It was then that the teacher was sure that he was a spirit. He called all his disciples together to try and catch him. But the spirit was already aware of what they were planning to do (in effect, the Lord had warned him). The spirit knew that the men would try to catch him. So he ran away. The men ran after him and clasped him on his side. He ran, ran and kept running but the men did not stop running after him. Haaa! The spirit was finally caught by one of the disciples who grabbed hold of his testicles and pulled on them. He succeeded in tearing one off. Haaa! The spirit ran away and the disciples went back to the teacher with the testicle. They found him and said:

"What are we going to do with this testicle that no longer has an owner? Where will we keep it?"

"Go in front of the house, in the field and plant the testicle there. Bury it."

The disciples were sure that this would not be difficult. They took a shovel, dug a hole and left the testicle there. Days passed, week after week, month after month. Time flowed and the testicle started to grow. Ha! It was growing. The teacher then went to look at it.

"Hoo! it is growing."

Many more months passed and one season after another. Two, then three years passed like this. The thing grew until a leaf appeared. Ha! Yes, a leaf. The teacher went to see it.

"Hoo! There are now leaves."

One season passed after another and many months passed too. Haa! The tree was not big. The tree was the testicle of a spirit.

"Haa!" said the teacher. "This trunk is really beautiful. We will try to cut it."

So, he struck the tree and blood started to flow from it. Haaa! It was latex.

"What are we going to do with this tree that is full of latex?" the teacher asked.

There was now a rubber tree. The disciples followed the teaching one year after another until one day, the tree had fruits. Haa! The tree had fruit. The teacher went to see.

"Haa!" he said. "There are fruit on this thing."

Time passed and the fruit split open and fell from the tree. They became seeds. So the teacher came back to see them.

"Haa!" he said. "There are our seeds now."

He thought about what he could do to develop his school and make it become known. He would have to inform one hundred countries that there was a rubber tree here. So he sent the seeds outside and the people there had never seen anything like it. They planted them since the teacher had sent them the seeds. And the people struck the tree with the rounded point of a knife[124] and saw the rubber. Then they said:

"It is profitable to have such a tree."

They went to see the teacher and asked him for more seeds of the rubber tree. They met him and told him that they wanted to buy the seeds.

The teacher was satisfied with all this. One could do something with these seeds. One could make some money with them. The people in the other countries also planted the seeds. Haa! This was all fine because [the story] became known everywhere and reached people outside the country and even those farther away. It really went far. Everyone came to see the rubber tree and bought the seeds. Days passed; the teaching was slow. Of the ten courses that he taught, there was soon only eight left; the next year only seven; a year after only six. All the problems came from the seeds. Soon there was nothing more to teach at all because everyone was engaged in trading. There were so many people who had come to buy the seeds of the rubber tree! So, the teacher started trading too and opened a shop where he could sell his seeds. All his time was taken up by this activity. Though he had a turban and keffiyeh in the beginning, he now only had the turban. There was no longer time to do anything since the people kept coming to buy the seeds.[125] Still today, we know about the seeds of the rubber tree. They are known as the seeds of the rubber tree today, but in fact they are really the testicle of a spirit. Haa! It is just as we have told you.

## 2.18. The origin of the Moyong[126]

***(Village of Sanoh, Province of Narathiwat, November 1991***
***Narrator: Wo Seng***
***Type of history: torèh)***

It was during the time of limpidity. But the angels existed long before Adam. There were thousands of millions of angels. All the rest are of no importance. The chiefs were Jebrael, Jibrael, Mikael, Asrapel. They declared that Adam had to be created since they were bored. Jibrael said:

"What must be done in order to achieve this?"

They went to ask the Lord.

"What must one do to create Adam, Lord?

The Lord spoke:

"You must go and look for the earth."

"Where can we find this earth?"

"The earth is found in the world, there where the waters are mixed. Everywhere where one finds these waters that are mixed, there is power."

"Where then, Lord?"

"At the bottom of the Muhatahat[127] sea; at the bottom of the Terga[128] sea. But it is very difficult to take hold of this earth. You must stand upright and be alone. You must take three steps. You must raise your arms three times at the same time that you take three steps. You must toss your head up three times. You must move your head from the right to the left and then from the left to the right, three times. No one must see you when you take hold of the earth."

This has become a spectacle. The Lord taught him all this. Jibrael went back to the angels.

"Well then, Jibrael, what did you find out?"

"It is possible but the earth must be taken over there."

So, they went to take hold of the earth. Mikael said:

"Jibrael, go and gather a handful of earth."

But the earth was crying.

"You must not take me, Jibrael! You want to create Adam but you haven't even made any prayers. It's not as easy as that. I will ask you then for a delay so I can make my devotions. You cannot take me without feeling some compassion and pity."

Jibrael spoke to her:

"No one must see and no one must hear."

It was Jibrael who created our parents all by himself. He went to take the earth in the Mustaha sea. He went there with thirty religious/moral obligations [in mind]. Then he saw the soil. He climbed over it with his three prayers and true desires. He crossed his arms over his chest and confessed his faith in Islam thirty times. The [traditional Malay] martial art *silat* remembered everything. No matter how big a problem is, it is of no importance. So, Jibrael took a handful of earth in order to create Adam. A handful of earth to create Adam is as important as the entire earth.

"Why take so much?"

"We must think about cleaning it."

They washed and cleaned the earth in order to create Adam. The earth that they possessed had sixty different shades. After having created Adam, they waited for forty years.

The angels had accomplished their task. It had been necessary to look for life with the Lord.

The Lord put something formless in Jibrael's hand.

"Don't open our hand[129] while you are on the road."

But he didn't listen to this warning and opened the finger of the spirits.[130] It had become a spirit. So, it was necessary to search once more for life.

### 2.19. The search for the Moyong

***(Village of Samoh, Province of Narathiwat, September 1992***
***Narrator: Wo Seng***
***Type of story: bahri)***

What was there in the beginning? I am going to help you to discover this now. We are going to speak about a great king who lived in the country called Banarélamo.[131] His wife's name was Pemahsuri.[132] They had many children, three or four girls.

"Eh! I am going to talk to you, my servants. I have not been lucky because I only have daughters. Every time a child is born it is a girl and I do not have a boy. Who is going to succeed me then?"

"Listen all of you, my beloved Pemahsuri, my servants, my warriors. If I have a boy I will have him circumcised so that he will become a Muslim. And during the ceremony I will have the Moyong performed. But we do not have this here. We have an orchestra and all the instruments, the fiddle[133] and all the musicians but we do not know the Moyong. We don't know how it is performed."

That's all I have to say for the moment. We will now speak of something else.

During this same month, Pemahsuri became pregnant. She became pregnant during the same month when the king spoke. She now has been pregnant for almost seven months. The eighth and ninth months approached. She gave birth and it was a boy. Yes, it was a boy. So the cannons were sounded since it was the custom to announce that the king had a son. Haa! Until that day, the cannons had never been sounded since the king had only had girls. The cannons are never sounded for girls, only for boys. The sound was very loud. Haa! The king was very happy to have a son.

Masses of people came to the pavilion for the reception. There were many people and there was no king greater than this one. He was the most powerful in the country of Banarélamo. The child grew and soon was nine years old. The warriors were told to go and invite everyone to come to the ceremony of circumcision. A great number of people arrived, accompanied by buffaloes and cows. There were also chickens and ducks. Someone also brought a great quantity of rice. People came from all over the country. A shelter was prepared in a big field where the ceremony would take place since it was impossible to do this in a house.[134] It was necessary to hold the ceremony in a vast field. It lasted three days and three nights. The third day arrived and everyone, the people and the kings, including their wives, all fainted.

Now we are going to speak of something else.

Three old people with broken backs[135] approached. They had come to pay a visit to Pemahsuri who was sleeping. She was still in a faint and dreaming.

"Eh! Why have you forgotten the promise you made?"

"Aa!" she answered. "What did I forget?"

Even though she was still sleeping, she talked in her sleep.

"The king promised to play the Moyong if he had a son and could circumcise him. That is why you must receive us now, young girl. When everyone wakes up, the people, warriors, those in power and the king, you must go and look for the Moyong, young girl, or you will never wake up again. You must rectify the fault committed."

"We are going to look for the Moyong, but where, old men? Who will look for him?"

"Very few people can go and search for the Moyong. It must be an old servant, a younger and the youngest one. These three can go and search for the Moyong. They must be close to the king, like his lieutenants. An old lieutenant, one younger and the youngest one. They must go."

**Fig. 21.** Resting and dreaming on a *salah*.

Then, when their mouths and hearts were liberated, the people woke up. Everyone woke up.

"Come here and see, warrior. Go and look for your older brother because I think that this dream is a true one."

"What is the matter, beloved?" the king asked.

"You once made a promise. You said you would play the Moyong when your son is circumcised."

"Oh! That is true. And we have a son. We must play the Moyong but where is it?" he asked.

"I don't know. It is really difficult," she said.

"Who then will go and search for the Moyong?" the king asked.

"It is said that this is possible. It is said that people can find the Moyong, but it must be your lieutenants, an old one, a younger one and the youngest one. These three can find the Moyong and not the others."

"Aa! Call my lieutenants, warriors!" the king said.

The warriors went to look for the lieutenants, the old one, the younger one and the youngest one and brought them to the king."

"This is the way things are, my lieutenants. You must go and search for the Moyong. You three, the old lieutenant, the younger one and the youngest one must go and look for the Moyong together. If you do not learn [how to play] the Moyong, I will not be able to complete the ceremony. I don't care how long it takes but I forbid you to return without the Moyong. Otherwise, I will kill you. If you come back, it will be with the Moyong."

"But lord, where will we look for him?"

"That is up to you."

Aa! The three of them started crying, and went on the road. They walked for a long time and continued to cry. They cried while they were walking. They continued along the road and finally left the country of the king of Banarélamo. They walked and walked and finally arrived somewhere. They arrived at a crossroads. They talked things over in order to decide what to do with the three roads that were unknown to them.

"Where will we go?" said the eldest one. "As for myself, I will go to the right," he said. "And you, the younger one?"

"I will go to the left and the youngest one will take the one in the middle."

"Alright. But if we don't find anything, we will come back here."

"Aa! Very well," said the youngest one. "I am going now, older ones." So he left the other two.

We will now speak of the youngest one who has gone off. He walked for a long time up hill and down dale, by long roads. He reached a vast field, narrow or wide, one couldn't tell. It was not possible to see the sides of it. It was very big. There was not one tree there but he nonetheless kept walking and soon found himself in the middle of the field. He noticed something that resembled a root but could not yet see it very well. In any case, it was very dark.

"No matter what it is, I will go and see. I am going to see what kind of thing it is."

He went into the field and approached the thing. It was a man.

"Aa! This is a black man," he said. "He is as black as the bottom of a cooking pot. Aa! Very well then I will go and see him and ask this old man for news. I will ask him if he knows the Moyong."

The man remained upright.

"Well then, young man, what bay do you come from? From what island? From what place? What do you want, young man? From what island do you come? From what sea? From what beach?"

"Hey! This is a long story."

"What do you want?"

"It would be too long to tell you, old man. But what is your name?"

"Aa! I am old and my name is Kadé Hité."[136]

"Aa! I can then ask you some questions, old man."

"Well then, ask!"

"What I am doing would take too long to explain, old man, but I have come to look for the Moyong."

"The Moyong? What is the Moyong?"

"I don't know, old man. People call it the Moyong. Did you ever hear anyone speak about it?"

"Ah! There is no such thing as a Moyong. I never heard anyone speak of it. You are the first one who has ever spoken to me about it. I never heard anyone else speak of it and I don't have any idea where you should go to look for this Moyong."

"Then where will I go?"

"Keep walking and you will surely find what you are looking for."

"Ah! Very well then, goodbye."

"Not at all. Go."

So, he continued walking and then found himself once again in a vast field. It was really a very big one since it was impossible to see where it ended. There was not a single tree there. It looked like the sea. The old man could no longer be seen; the black thing had disappeared. Even if one turned one's head to right or left, nothing could be seen. Nevertheless, there was something white, like cotton, there. But he couldn't see what it was because it was too far away. So, he went closer to it.

"I will go to see it no matter what this white thing is."

He soon found himself in front of it.

"Ah! But this is also a man. He is all white, like cotton, and so is his reflection. Aa! I am going to see."

So, he went nearer to him.

"Eh! Young man, what bay do you come from? What island? From what place? I see that you are very tired and sweating. Why have you come?"

"It is a long story, old man. What is your name?"

"I am called the old man, young man."

"Ho!"

"My name, given by those who call me day and night, is Kado Puteh. But what do you want? Where are you going? What do you have to do, young man?"

"Aa! That is a long story, old man. I only want one thing, not two or three. I want to ask you for news of the Moyong."

"Oo! I, an old man, have never heard anything about it. What does the Moyong look like? I myself don't know. I don't know and this is the first time I heard anyone speak of it. I don't know. I don't know what it resembles and don't understand anything."

"Aa! You don't know either, old man."

"I don't know. I can't tell you anything."

"Then where should I go?"

"Keep walking and you will end by encountering him."

So, he continued on the road. He walked for a very long time and entered a vast field in which was a platform.

"Eh! That was a good idea to have made a platform since I can now go to sleep. I am going to stop there. I am exhausted."

He climbed up the platform and went to sleep. He slept for three days and three nights, seven days and seven nights[137] and didn't wake up.

But now we are going to speak of something else.

There was a pagoda named Seven and it was made of gold. The name of the venerable abbot was Masiyong Putong Api. There were also novices there called Neng[138] and Pong.

"Eh! Pong," said the venerable.

"What do you want?"

"You must put the goat near the platform."

"Aa! Go there, Pong."

"Where?"

Both Neng and Pong went there; each one followed the other. They led the ghost.

"Aa! But someone is sleeping, Pong."

"Where, Neng?"

"Over there."

"Eh! Wake up or else our abbot will be very angry. In this place, we cut our hair in order to be ordained. He will be very angry. Let's go! Let's wake him up."

They tried with wooden sticks but he did not wake up. They rolled him over but he still did not awaken. So, they went back to see the abbot and Neng and Pong told him everything that had happened.

"Venerable, venerable! There is someone sleeping on the platform."

"Oo! Well then, go and wake him up, Neng and Pong. It is not good that there is someone over there," he said.

"He doesn't want to wake up. We have already tried."

"Alright then. I will go to see myself."

**Fig. 22.** Platform for travellers and paddy field workers. (Ivanoff, 1989)

The abbot tried to wake him up with a wooden stick but he kept on sleeping. He turned him over but he still didn't wake up. He was facing the sky with his head thrown back and his mouth wide open.

"Eh, eh! So, he doesn't want to wake up, Neng and Pong. Then let's leave him alone. Let him sleep."

His mouth was wide open and the abbot spat into it: *tuh tuh*. He spat into it three times.

"Don't bother him any more. Let him sleep. He will wake up when he wants to."

So, they went back. Neng and Pong stopped bothering him because they were afraid of the abbot's anger.

The man suddenly woke up and was surprised.[139] He woke up at once and looked to the right and to the left, to the front and to the back, but he could see nothing.

"I did, nonetheless, feel some danger. I felt something enter my breast. However, there is no one here."

But a song echoed in his ears, the sound of a fiddle, the sound of a drum.

"I feel something in my heart and in my breast. What is taking place, then, young man Minung? There is nobody in the surroundings. But nonetheless, I feel something in my heart and in my breast. It would be best if I call my servant, the young Minung."[140]

He forgot everything. But there had been a song and the young Minung.

"If this is how it is, young boy, you must come out. I am calling you."

He answered:

"He!"

"Aa! Come here, young Minung."

"Aa!" The king heard the song, woke up with a start and his servant came.

"Aa! If this is the way things are, go and look for one or two of your friends. We need to have other people so that we can think. If there are only the two of us, we will not be able to."

**Fig. 23.** Discovering the Moyong.

Aa! He is singing, he sings a song of war in order to call his two servants. They arrive. He calls to them and they both come. He sings another song.[141] This is another scene, the story of King Soléhong, whose mother is named Soléhé. The eldest daughter's name is Sehsena and the youngest one, the young princess, is named Dame Benjamin.[142]

He woke up after this story.

"Eh! I am really crazy."

And the group laughed. All three of them were amused. They laughed so much that they began to urinate. Are the three of them conscious now? Yes, they are.

"But why are things like this? We play the Moyong while we are like this. Let's go back home."

They took to the road, one behind the other and arrived in the very vast field, the one they had already gone through.

"Ah! What's going on?" said the old man.

"Aa! Kadoh Puteh, come here. I want to ask you something."

He came closer.

"Well then, young man. Where do you come from?"

"Aa! That is a long story, old man."

"Aa! Have you found the Moyong, young man?"

"Eh! Not yet, old man."

"Aa! You have nevertheless been gone a long time."

"I went to sleep on the platform and woke up with a start. There was no one around, neither to the right nor to the left. But there was something in my heart and in my breast. A servant heard me. I called him and he came."

"Ah, yes? Then you are the Moyong."

"Ah! Good. Is this true, old man?"

"Yes, it is the Moyong. You call two lieutenants and they arrive. There is a song. This makes a story, the one about King Soléhong, his mother Soléhé, the eldest daughter and the young princess Dame Benjamin."

"Aa! So that is the story of the Moyong!"

"Yes, that's how it is."

He left but did not go back to the platform but to the crossroads.

He soon encountered Kadé Hité and told him his story.

"Ha! That is the Moyong, young man."

He left. The three of them went home together and went to see the king, in the country of Banarélamo. They met some warriors at the door of the citadel; they were keeping guard. They were afraid, afraid that the king would kill them if they didn't have the Moyong.

"Aa! Well then," said the warriors, "do you have the Moyong or not?"

"Yes, but we cannot play it, warrior."

"Ah! Why not?"

"There aren't any musicians, nor a drum. But the Moyong, yes."

"Then wait a minute, I will inform the king."

"They have come back, lord."

"Do they have the Moyong?"

"Yes, they brought it back."

"That's good."

"But they don't have any musician or a drum, or a gong."

"But I have many of them."

He had everything but the Moyong. So, the warriors went to inform the three companions.

"Haa! The king said that he had everything you need."

"Haa! Then we can play now."

They told the warriors to make a shelter in the vast field so that everyone could come there. It was filled with people and there were so many that it was impossible to say how many were there.

They played then at night. It was a good spectacle and everyone assisted. There were all the instruments for the music and everyone was able to play on them. Then they performed the Moyong. The ceremony ended with the circumcision. The performance ended and the old people who were playing said that the shelter should now be destroyed. But the king said:

"No! We will not take away the shelter because it will now be necessary to teach the others."

Ha! So then the people learned the Moyong. They learned the Moyong in the country of Banarélamo. It was always filled with many people who were learning the Moyong. All the cooks and the servants of the king were so captivated by the Moyong that the king has nothing to eat, even his wife spent all her time there.

The king said, "They are all crazy about the Moyong. That's enough now! I am going to put fire to the shelter, even if it is solid."

**Fig. 24.** Danger and destruction of the Moyong.

Here then is another story. The king set fire to the shelter intended for the Moyong and the fire destroyed everything. There were flames for three days and three nights and everyone died. Aa! The fire went out and we are now going to speak about princess Dame Benjamin in the country of Dereda[143] Mudo.

"Eh! Older one."

"What is it?"

"I hear your song and everyone is playing the Moyong in the country of Banarélamo. Get the boat ready and we will go and see."

It was far away and they had to put up the sail.

"Aa! Let's go now."

They put on their trousers, sarongs and shirts and went there. They finally reached the country of Banarélamo.

"What is the Moyong?"

"Hum! One can no longer see the Moyong."

"Why?"

The king had set fire to the shelter for the Moyong and no one survived.

"Aa! That is bad luck, older one."

"Then let's go back."

"We cannot go back. Let's first go to the shelter for the Moyong."

The fire had just gone out.

"Ha! That is the Moyong."

Dame Benjamin took a towel which she unfolded and ran to the centre of the shelter to take some ashes which she put in her towel. They went home with the ashes, to the country of Dereda Mudo. They attached the towel to the beam of the roof.

This is why one can become a Moyong thanks to the ashes from the shelter of the Moyong that the king had burned. If a small quantity of ashes is found on our road and if someone steps over it, then he is possessed[144] by the Moyong.

So, princess Dame Benjamin brought the ashes to her country, Dereda Muso. And three months later the princess had learned the Moyong. She knew the Moyong. And this is how the Moyong is until today. It is the princess Dame Benjamin who teaches the Moyong because since that time, she has played the Moyong and everything we know about the Moyong comes from her.[145]

# Chapter 3

# The cycle of Hawè

### 3.1. The man with the big knife and the lazy man[1]

*(Village of Samoh, Province of Narathiwat, November 1991*
*Narrator: Po' Suloh*
*Type of story: hikaya')*

Here is the tale of the man with the big knife.

His father died when his mother was in her seventh month of pregnancy. It was during the seventh month that she gave birth all by herself. The brother of the father took care of the new-born child but it was not long before he began to hate him. The uncle hated his nephew. There was a man standing near the young mother's bamboo bed[2] who wished to marry her. He said:

"Ah! You are now a young girl."[3]

"Yes, it is true."

"Is your child a boy or a girl?"

"A boy?"

The mother's name was Kemalo.[4]

"Can we get married?"

"We can get married but there is the problem of the child. Are you willing to raise him?"

"Ah! that's no problem. We will keep him. He is your son and we must take care of him."

The future husband spoke well because he wanted to marry the young mother. They spoke together for a while and then got married. Two or three seasons went by. The child was then at the age to go to work.[5] His mother (mothers were formerly called *mo* and not *me* as they are today) said to him:

"You must go and work with your stepfather now. He is like a real father for you. But you are so lazy!"

"No matter what kind of work I do, I[6] will be lazy."

"Even if you are lazy, you must work. You shouldn't be like this otherwise it won't be long before you are filled with regret.

"But this is the way I am, mother. I have no desire whatsoever to work. The only thing I want is to do nothing."

In the past, those who were lazy went to play in the forest where they caught birds. It was not long before the adopted father hated his son. The day came when he asked his son to help him clear the land.

"Let's go! Let's go and clear the land."

"I don't want to."

He answered in the same way when it came to doing any kind of work like turning over the earth, which his stepfather asked him to do. His name of lazy man really fitted him well since he refused to do anything at all for anyone. This is why he was called lazy man by everyone in the village.

"Hey! What are we going to do with someone who is so lazy? I no longer have any desire to take care of him."

The father was very angry and tired.

"But you promised me to take care of my child and you have now changed your mind."

"How could I have known that he would be so lazy?"

"Well, do as you wish, elder one."[7]

"If that's the way things are, then I think we will have to kill him. We must abandon him in any way possible."

Then the mother spoke and said:

"As you like, elder one. I will respect your wish."

She was confused and didn't know what to think since the people of former times never thought about abandoning their children. It was not long afterwards that the father decided to play a trick on his son in order to kill him. But when the moment came to cut off his head, he didn't have the courage to do so. Nor did he have the courage to cut him into little pieces. so the stepfather went to look for someone to help him.

"Eh! Is there anyone among you who has the courage to kill my son?"

In the older times, there was never anyone who would be willing to kill someone else. People had pity and there would not have been one among a hundred who would agree to do such a thing. People would more easily accept deliberately tricking someone than killing them, in the past.

"You really are too lazy. I am going to kill you."

The child said:

"As you wish, father.[8] If you want to kill me, then do so."

"What are we going to do with you? I really don't know what to do. Your friends ask you to help them but you are so lazy that you refuse."

So, he sat down on a ladder and thought about the matter.

"Ah! What shall I do? Does the mother really love her son?"

"Do as you wish but don't ask me such a question."

"Listen my son, you are going to follow me today."

"I don't want to go with you. That's the way things are. I don't want to leave."

"Then what do you want?"

"I want a knife. This is what I want, a knife."

"This is possible. But if you want a knife, you must first go with me for three days. It is only afterwards that I will give you a knife. If you want one, you must go to work. So you must go with me and I will need your help."

The lazy man thought about this and said to himself that it was probable that his father wanted to assassinate him. He nevertheless decided to go with him for three days.

"Alright then, we will go off together into the mountains."

"I asked you to go into these mountains to work but, in fact, I am going to kill you," the father said.

"Do as you wish, father. If you want to kill me, that's no problem. No one can do anything for me since I am so lazy."

"Lie down here. In this way, you will see your father in a dream."

He lay down on the side of a stone. Then he took hold of a piece of wood in order to raise the stone. He did so and then made a space and slid into it. His stepfather thought that his son had been crushed by the stone. So he went home. The mother cried bitterly until night fell. She refused to eat.

"You must not cry for your son. We can live happily together now that he is dead. It is all over now."

But the son soon returned. He was carrying the stone on his shoulder. He put it down near the foot of the ladder.

"I have brought you the stone you wanted, father."

The father turned around to see what this was all about.

"Isn't this child dead then? I will play another trick on him in that case."

He then asked his son to go with him into the mountain.

"Wait for me here and watch me cut down this tree.[9] Pay attention and watch how it falls down," he said.

The tree was three arms wide. The father took the axe and cut down the tree. When he had almost finished, he struck the other side of the trunk and said:

"Wait for me on that side!"

"Aye! Why should I wait on that side of the tree if it is going to fall down there?"

"The tree will fall on the other side. I am going to strike the other side so it will fall down on that side."

"But no! You are trying to trick me." He thought to himself: He tells me to go on that side but the tree will fall there and hit me on my neck. But he said: "Alright, father, if you want me to go over there I will do so."

The father then struck the tree from the other side and it fell down. The son was lying down on his stomach under the tree but the earth opened and protected him. The tree came crashing down, the branches hit him and everyone in the village heard the noise of its fall. They were sure that the lazy one was dead.

"Your son is dead. It is finished. The noise the tree made when it fell down proves that he was crushed under it."

The mother started crying. Her husband returned shortly afterwards and told her what had happened.

"Ah! The lazy man is really dead. He died under the tree that is really very large and heavy."

But while the father was speaking, the son returned carrying the tree on his shoulder. "Nga, Nga, Nga," was the sound of the leaves. He soon found himself at the foot of the ladder.

"Do you want it, father? You can build a new house with it. Go and find some men to help you cut the tree because now that I have brought back the tree we don't have to go to the mountain any more. I also brought back the stone and we can make mortar with it."

The father was furious.

"What must we do now in order to kill your son?"

"Elder one, do as you wish if you want to kill him."

"Listen to me carefully, father. I am aware of everything you have done in order to kill me. That is not very nice of you. I know that you wanted to kill me and I would be dead now if the Lord had not protected me. What did you try to do to me? You have broken my heart."

The son climbed up to the house and lay down. The inhabitants of the village all hated him again because he went to eat his food in a different house every day. He profited very well from these meals. The people of the village soon hated him because he ate whenever he wanted and as much as be wanted.[10]

"I can't help you any longer; it is no longer possible. I want a knife. My heart is broken, mother, because I have not repaid you for all you have given to me.[11] I want to repay you for everything but tell me why you continue to try to kill me?"

"It is because you are so lazy."

"If I am so lazy, mother, there is a reason."

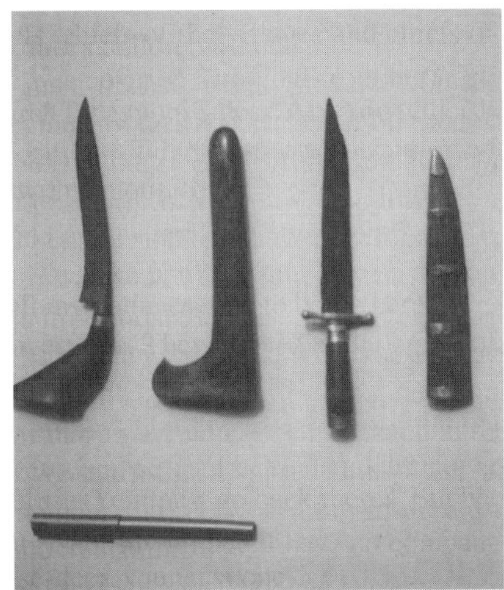

**Fig. 25.** Malay knives are numerous and varied. (Ivanoff, 1991)

"What is it?"

"My desires have never been satisfied because all of you asked me to go to work as soon as I was of the age to do so. I had hardly opened my eyes when I was told to go to work. You should have allowed me to do some of the things I wanted to do. But instead, you asked me to go to work even though I know nothing about trees, stones, water or rivers."

"Well, it doesn't matter. If you want a knife I will get one for you."

So, the father went off to make a knife and then went home. The knife was as big as the palm of a hand.

"What will I be able to do with a knife of this size? It will break as soon as I strike something with it two times."

"It's not an axe; it's a knife. What do you know about such things, lazy one?"

"Hey! I want a knife much bigger than this one."

So, the father went off again to make another knife, even though it was against his will to do so. He worked on more than five kilos of iron which cost him four hundred[12] coins since he had to pay everyone. Then he went home.

"What can I do with a knife of this size? I don't want it."

The knife was so heavy that the father had to carry it on his shoulder. But his son was able to pick it up with only two fingers."

"You must know what you are doing. First you want a knife like this and then you want a knife like that. Well then, take the money and go and make one by yourself."

The father gave the son nine hundred coins. He took the money and went off. He met a Chinese man on the way and asked him:

"Eh, *taukay*![13] Do you have a good supply of iron in your reserves?"

"Yes, I have a great deal. What do you want it for?"

"I want to make a knife."

"What size do you want the knife to be?"

"I will need all the iron you have and even more."

So, the Chinese man took all the iron he had, loaded one piece on top of the other until there was a pile which almost reached the platform.

"Is that enough?"

"It's too little, *taukay*."

"Don't worry! There is still some more left."

He went to see another *taukay* to get more iron and piled it up too.

"Do you have enough now for your knife?"

"I still need more, *taukay*."

"Don't worry. I can get some more."

He went to see three other *taukays* who had iron and there was finally enough. The son went home but there was not enough space under the house, so he had to put the iron behind it. But the ironmonger refused to make the knife for him.

"Well, if that's how things are, I will make it by myself. But I will need seven forges."

"I will look for them for you and if you still need more iron I will find it so that you can put it into the seven forges."

The Chinese *taukay* arrived with one hundred people to help him but there weren't enough of them to raise the knife.

"Don't worry, *taukay*. You can leave now and I will manage everything by myself."

He took the iron and put it into the fire in order to melt it. He didn't stop talking until the work was finished. The knife was as big as a car when it had been made. He carried it with only one hand and went home. All the people of the village were astonished when they saw him. He put the knife down on to the veranda but it collapsed because of the weight. So he put it upright against the wall of the house but it collapsed too.

"There you are, father. You were once going to kill me but I am going to help you anyway today. I am going to pay back all my debts today."

He had given the nine hundred [coins] to the Chinese who had refused [them] at first. The lazy man took hold of his knife and split the wood of the tree.

"You wanted a new house, father. Here is the wood to make one with."

He took hold of it again and hit the stone with it until it broke into little pieces and resembled water. He hit it as if a train was passing over it.

"Here is the stone, father. It has now been completely destroyed. Please forgive me but I wanted to make a new house for my mother. I will make it all by myself. You don't have to help me."

His mother and all his ancestors had shed many tears because of his laziness but now that he was so strong, they loved him again. He went to wash himself and people came to help him soap his body. Everyone took care of him. He cried when he thought of his former life. He worked and cried. His heart was broken when he thought about what his stepfather had done to him. He finished making the house anyway. It took him seven days and seven nights to build it.

"There, mother! Today I am paying back the nine hundred coins you gave me. Here is your new house. You can climb up and go inside."

It was then that the king, who had been informed, came to see it.

"Hey! This young man will soon have more than myself. He will end up by taking my place."

The king was afraid and wanted to kill him. He wanted to kill the lazy man.

"Go ahead and kill me; it doesn't matter. I had no idea that I was doing something wrong. I only wanted to pay back my debts to my parents. Now I would like a sack of seeds. I will give you some rice so that both of you can eat. You can now live happily. In the past, I was not able to work but I can now do so and I want to pay back my debts."

His mother then went off to look for the seeds. But her son didn't want the ones she brought back with her. She went to look for others in the house but her son refused these also. He refused them because the soul of the rice was absent from them.

"Since you are so difficult, go and look for the seeds yourself. What kind of rice do you want then?"

So he climbed up into a rice granary and then came down. The people asked him:

"Why did you go to the rice granary?"

"I went to see the rice because I need some seeds. If I find what I am looking for, I will buy what I need."

He went to another house and climbed up to the granary and then descended. Then he went to seven other granaries and finally found what he was looking for in the last one.

"This is the only place where I have found what I was looking for."

"Hey, elder sister[14]! How much do you want for this sheaf of rice?"

"Take it if you want. You don't have to buy it from me. I will give it to you."[15]

She gave the sheaf of rice to the lazy man who then went home. He asked his mother to stamp on the rice.

"Can you husk this rice for me, mother?"

"Oh! But it's the same rice as before. It is exactly the same."

"No, it is really very different. While you are stamping on it you mustn't think about how many sacks there will be, you must count with the measures.[16] I am going into the forest now, to the mountains, in order to clear the land."

He then left and laboured for seven days and seven nights clearing the land, without stopping. This is how he discovered three mountains. Seven days later, he lit a fire and the three mountains became enflamed. The light was seen as far away as the village. It resembled burning oil lamps. They continued burning for seven days and seven nights. The king came back again to see what was happening.

"Hey! What is that light on the mountains? It resembles the light of oil lamps."

"It is my son who has made the fire. He set fire to the mountains so as to make a ray of light."

When the king heard this, he called his men and said:

"Who among you has power over the animals?"

"Me![17] I have. All the animals of the forest are my friends and they serve me."

"I want you to go and tell them to destroy everything that the lazy man is doing. I am jealous of this man. Stop him from making seed holes because if this continues, we will become his servants."

The man who had said that he was a friend of the animals went and called them to come out of the forest.

"What is it that you want? Why have you called us to leave the mountains, forest and our marshland?"

"I want all of you to go and destroy the lazy man's rice. He is on the mountain."

The lazy man returned home after he had finished with the fire. He asked his mother:

"Have you stamped on the rice? How many measures are there?"

"There are four measures."

"Four measures means four sacks."

For him, one measure was a sackful. His mother poured the rice into the baskets made of leaves.

"Hey, mother! When one fries the rice, it bursts open. Fry seven grains of rice so that they will burst open."

So, the mother made seven grains of rice burst open and put them into a basket. The lazy man left and went to the mountain. When he arrived, he called for all the animals to come.

"Hey! Listen, all you animals. There is something I want from this mountain and I will tell you what to do."

All the animals came and went to see him. The three mountains were full of animals and there were even scorpions. They put the seeds in the seed holes, using their claws. The elephants and tigers made the seed holes but the lazy man didn't make any effort to help them. The work was finished after three days and three nights.

"The work is finished but I would like all of you to be repaid for your work."

All the animals came and gathered around him, just as one does for a king.

"I cannot pay all of you since I am a poor man, who has problems because my stepfather wanted to kill me and I became desperate, I have seven grains of puffed rice which I will give you as payment. Even if we only have one hair we must share it with each other."

The owl said:

"Hey! We don't want the young man to pay us. We have to think on the matter first."

It is well known that the owl is an animal who thinks for himself. The other animals followed his advice and there was not one among them that asked for payment. The man whom the king had sent to find some animals to destroy the lazy man's fields called out to them. But when he called out to them, he saw that they were crying. He asked:

"Why do you come out crying? I am asking you to do what I asked you to do and in the way I explained to you."

The white elephant who had nine tusks said:

"We don't want to do anything wrong to the lazy man since we have worked on the rice for him."

So, they didn't do what the king had asked them to do since the lazy man spoke better than he did. [The king] said:

"Hey! If that's how things are, it is because I don't have the lazy man's magic power."

The lazy main said to the animals: "Hey! All of you animals including the chickens, ducks and mouse-deer, I need your help to look after the rice because I am going home."

So, all the animals agreed to help and made a circle around the rice. Even the bees looked after the rice.

The lazy man went home and remained there for about three months. He was waiting for the rice to ripen.

"Hey, father! Can you build a silo for me?"

"Don't worry, I will do everything necessary."

The stepfather spoke to his son as if he loved him.

"Yes, do so."

The father built a silo of thirty arm's lengths. The lazy man came to see it.

"Hey! But it's not big enough. There isn't enough room inside to put the rice there."

"Perhaps you are right, but it's the best I can do."

The man with the big knife then cut the poles, tore down the old ones and made a new silo. He drove the four new poles into the ground but there was still no roof or door. He asked his mother to make braids for the walls.

"Can you help me, mother? Ask some people to help you make braids for the walls since I must leave now and harvest the rice. I will go off very soon now."

His mother went to look for some people to help her but no one wanted to do so. They were all too lazy. Nobody was willing to help the lazy man. His mother returned and said to her son:

"Hey! Nobody wanted to come back with me. I asked everyone but they are all lazy. No one wants to help the lazy man." His mother went home and said to her son:

"Hey! There was no one who was willing to come back with me. I asked everyone but they are all too lazy. No one wants to help you because you are the lazy man."

"Well, that's the way things are. Don't think about it and don't cry."

He went to speak to his father:

"Eh, father! I would like you to help me to carry the rice. Is this possible?"

"No, it is not possible because the rice is on the three mountains and we will need at least one entire season to carry it. And even then, the work will not be finished."

"Alright then. In that case, wait for me here both of you. Prepare the silo for the rice."

"Don't worry. Everything will be ready."

The lazy man went off to the mountain and called all the animals.

"Hey! I would like for all of your animals to come here one more time."

The animals arrived and asked him:

"What do you still want us to do, lazy man? Is something broken? Is your rice broken?"

"No. Nothing has happened to my rice."

"Then why have you asked us to come?"

"I want all of you to help me harvest and carry the rice to my house."

The owl then spoke:

"I will take care of everything. Don't worry."

So the animals began to harvest the rice. Each one brought a small quantity of rice to the elephant, the tiger, the rhinoceros and the bear. They all helped to transport the rice. But when they reached the village, the people there were afraid. They were afraid during the day but they continued to work during the night. The silo was full the next day. Even though the mother and the father had prepared the silo, they did not really understand where the rice came from. It took seven days and seven nights for all the rice to be collected. Then the lazy man came and said:

"Mother, I would like you to stamp on the rice and fill one sack."

"Why?"

"So that I can pay all those who helped me. I want to repay them for having harvested my rice."

"But one sack is not enough. You will need at least one hundred sacks."

"No, one will be sufficient."

So, his mother stamped on the rice until she had enough to fill one sack. She gave it to the lazy man who carried it away and shared it with the others. He gave each one seven grains of rice. There was enough for each of the animals. Seven grains for each one was ample. He said:

"Listen, all you animals. Don't be sad when I leave you. We will soon separate because I will no longer live here in this country."

All the animals cried and suddenly felt pity for him. What happened then? All the animals got together and complained about the departure of the man with the big knife, who was a good man. He went home and said:

"Mother, I no longer wish to remain here. I don't want to stay here with you any longer, my parents. I no longer wish to live in this country."

His mother asked him:

"Where do you want to go then? You shouldn't go away and live with other people at your age. You don't even know the people of your own village very well."

"Maybe you are right but don't give me any problems. If a person is lucky, he can stay alive. If a person dies, he will do so, no matter where he lives."

His mother cried bitterly. She cried so much that she finally fainted. Her son then took his knife and brushed his mother with the blade. He caressed her with the flat side of the blade and she regained consciousness. He said:

"Mother, I would like some husked rice. Give me one measure for the voyage. I am going to leave soon."

His mother prepared three sacks of husked rice for him. But he said:

"I don't want a sack of rice, mother, a small quantity will be sufficient, one measure. I explained to you that I wanted to pay back my debts."

So his mother gave him one measure of husked rice.

"I want to pay back my debts,[18] mother. If I had any knowledge I could reimburse you thanks to it but I don't have any. I would be able to reimburse you thanks to my daily labour, but I don't know how to work. Therefore, I will repay you with this rice."

The son was able to repay his parents for the time he had lived in the house with the rice gathered after the harvest from the first mountain. He paid back the price of his milk[19] with the harvest of the second mountain. This was the best he could do since he didn't have any money. He could only pay back what he owed them with the rice.

His mother no longer said anything.

"As for the third mountain, mother and father, the harvest is destined to feed you for the rest of your lives and the next one,[20] as well. You mustn't be afraid of doing anything wrong since there will be no problems with all this. I will be sad if mother refuses to eat what I offer her in this world and in the other. "

His adopted father also started crying, "ho, ho, ho". He cried because he was beginning to love his son. The son climbed down the ladder and prepared to leave his parents. He said:

"Hey, father! I am going to give you something to repay you. I will give you seven grains of husked rice to pay back my debt to you."

He put the seven grains of rice between his fingers and his father put them aside. He put them on his bed, took a piece of yellow cloth and covered them with it.

"Now you will always have a full stomach, father. You will never again lack something to eat."

It wasn't long before his father became very fat and sound but he didn't eat all of the seven grains of rice that his son had given him.

"Now you will always have something to eat. The rice contains everything necessary. It is good and complete."

The lazy man took some husked [grains of] rice and wrapped them in a piece of cloth.[21] He went up into the house and made a salutation to his mother.

"Pardon me for having made you suffer so much,[22] mother."

But the mother fainted and no longer was able to say anything.

"Pardon me, father, for all the bad things I did. You have been like a real father to me since you raised me since the day I was born."

The father no longer understood anything and was so astonished that he fainted and defecated.

When his son had asked pardon for everything, he took his knife and left. He travelled at night and slept during the day. This journey lasted for a long time. He finally reached the Berenè[23] mountain where he saw some men who had been pulling on a rattan tree for seven days and seven nights, "haaa do." They pulled on the rattan. How many hundreds of kilos[24] did it weigh? No one knows. He went to meet the three men who were pulling the rattan.

"Hey! It is now seven days and seven nights that we have been trying to pull this rattan."

"Hey! What are you going to do with it?"

"Nothing at all. We only want to know how long it is."

"In that case, let me help you. I will help you pull on the rattan."

"Hey! We don't need your help since we have already tried everything we could to carry away the rattan. We even pruned the trees surrounding it during seven days and seven nights. But the more we pull, the more of them there are."

"Ha! Ho! I will help you anyway. But you must give me something in exchange. I will help you and you will cook some rice; a pinch of rice will be enough. Then we can all eat together."

The three men agreed. They took a pinch of husked rice.

"Go and cook this rice."

"Hey! Will there be enough for the four of us? There are only seven pinches of rice."

"Ha! First cook it and don't be worried because if there is not enough, there will still be more left."

They lit a fire and cooked the rice. They cooked seven pinches of rice but since the cooking pan was so small, it wasn't long before the rice spilled over. It swelled up until it reached the cover of the pan and spilled over. The three men who had been pulling on the rattan started thinking.

**Fig. 26.** The long rattan, wonder of the forest and link with the gods.

"What kind of rice is this that we are eating?"

They all ate together and when they had finished he said:

"Ha! Now we can separate. But first, I want you all to move away because I am going to pull down the rattan. Don't worry. Go and hide in a quiet spot. I am going to pull down the rattan."

The three men went to hide and the young man was now alone. He grabbed hold of the rattan and pulled it only once. A million branches of the tree[25] fell down. He pulled at it a second time and the rattan tree fell down. Then he removed the bark. When everything was finished, he called out to the three men:

"I helped you, so now it's your turn."

"Ha! Do you want us to pay you?"

"Ha! I don't want you to pay me. I want you to help me with sincerity since we don't know each other. We have never seen each other before."

The three men still wanted to reward him for his work, so they gave him a ring with a black stone on it. The man with the big knife took the ring and looked at it.

"Eh! You shouldn't give me this ring. It is really a magic one. There is not one that exists which is more powerful. If someone were to encounter the animals with this ring, they would all join their hands above their heads. If a fly were to get too close to it, it would die."

"Take it then because we don't want it."

So, he took the ring and put it inside the pocket of his shirt. But as soon as he did this, the blade of the knife changed colour and became dark and luminous. He himself was transformed. At one moment he was handsome and at another, he was very ugly.

"Ah! It really is a magic stone."

They all took to the road and separated shortly afterwards. The young man walked for a long time and finally reached a place where there were a group of people who were trying to stretch some leather over a drum which came from a mosque. It was a drum from a small place where prayers were made.[26] No one in the group was able to put the leather in place. They tried to attach it to the drum but without success. The lazy man asked them:

"Hey! What are all of you doing?"

"We want to put this piece of leather over the drum."

"What is the drum used for?"

"It is used to awaken people along the road. When we strike the drum everyone goes off to war."

"Ha! And who is able to do this?"

"Nobody can do this."

"Well then, I am going to help you fix up your war drum. I will put the leather over it."

One of the men started talking for no rhyme or reason. He said:

"Hey! There is nobody who exists who is as handsome as you are. You are not the sort of person who is able to work. You give one the impression of being a very lazy person."

The young man took hold of his knife and then put it down.

Ninety people tried to raise it but failed to do so.

"Hey! This is really very strange.[27] It is truly very heavy."

Forty or fifty people would be unable to raise it while this man is able to do so with one hand.

They became frightened and gave up.[28] They allowed him to put the leather over the drum. He did this with the point of his knife. He drove in little pieces of wood in order to fix the leather in place. When he had finished, he struck the drum. Everyone fell asleep when they heard the noise. The sound the drum made was truly marvellous. Everyone fell asleep.

"Eh! I am going to wake you all up since we need to decree some laws."

If the lazy man is present, the sound of the drum is really wonderful but if he is not, the sound is not a very pleasant one.

"Don't be angry with me."

"Ah! Don't worry. It will be fine no matter what kind of sound the drum makes."

He soon went away and left the drum. He went far away, covering a distance of one hundred *lanyuk* (or *languk*[29]). It really was true that the sound of the drum was not a very nice one during his absence. No one knew why this was so. The truth of the matter was that the magnificent sound the drum had made was due to the stone of the ring. They then wanted to transport the drum as far as the intersection of four roads but no one was strong enough to carry it.

"If this is the way things are, we must find the young man who was here. He must come back and help us one more time. If he wants to become king in exchange for this service, well then, so be it. We are in accord."

This is what they said during their meeting. They then went off again to look for the lazy man.

"Why have you come back to see me?"

"We want you to come back with us because we need your help."

"We need someone to carry the drum. Nobody here is capable of doing so. The one who can do this, who is able to carry the drum as far as the intersection of the four roads, will become the new king."

"Ah! Well, I can always try."

So, he went back with them. He struck on the drum with the point of his knife and pulled at it until he reached the intersection of the four roads. When he arrived there, the lazy man said:

"Can I strike on the drum one more time?"

"Ah! Of course you can "

"What is it that you still need?"

So, he struck on the drum three times and a couple of garuda birds flew down. The people wanted war because of the drum and the garuda birds descended from the sky.

"Hey! How dare you strike the drum! Who do you think you are? We can't sleep in peace. This is why we will have to take flight now."

"With me? But you mustn't eat me because I am a stranger. I only struck the drum. That's all I did."

After he had spoken in this way, the male garuda took flight and then swooped down on his prey. He started to seize him with his claws but since he was so high and the knife shone, he thought it was the man. He rushed on to the knife and wanted to tear it to pieces but the knife turned over and as it fell, it cut off the male garuda's head. The garuda died and his wife said:

"Eh! young human being! Why do you resemble the light of the moon and that of the stars? Are you a human being?"

"I am unable to say. I cannot speak of everything that is in me."

"Why? What country do you come from?"

"I come from my country."

"Which one?"

He was not able to answer since there were many countries where he had never been. This is what he said. The female garuda then said:

"Do you have a wife?"

"No, I don't have one."

While they were speaking, the garuda gave birth to a little girl.[30] When the girl saw the man with the big knife, she fell madly in love with him. The mother said:

"If you don't take my daughter for your wife, I will eat you."

"Well then, eat me because I do not want a wife."

The garuda opened her mouth to eat him but blood came out of her mouth and nose.

"Do you want to die or to do you want to live?"

"If you want your mother to live, don't marry me."

"Alright then. I won't marry you."

He then took hold of the stone on his ring and stuffed it into the nostrils of the garuda who returned to life and left. She said to him:

"Please forgive me. We are now going to separate but we are going to give you something of great value."

**Fig. 27.** Man fighting a garuda with a magic knife.

But he didn't want anything and then left. He walked day and night for several days until he finally reached the sea. The king who lived there called to his subjects and said:

"Who among you is able to empty the water of the sea? The one who can do this will marry my daughter even if he does not have anything to give me in return. I will also give him half of my territory and he will become the new king."

All the subjects began to dry up the sea. It is impossible to say how many millions of men he had. They had been working like this for seventy years but the sea was far from being dried up. Then the lazy man said:

"What are you doing here, my friends? Are you trying to make the sea dry?"

The king answered:

"My people want to dry the sea and the one who succeeds in doing so will be able to marry my daughter even if he has nothing to give me in exchange. He will obtain half of my territory and become the new king."

"Can I try?"

"Go ahead. He who wants to do something must do it."

"In that case, I want everyone to move away from the level if the sea because I will enter the water alone."

One man said:

"Hm! People who speak a great deal often come back with empty hands."

But everyone drew back and the lazy man descended into the water by himself. He plunged in and plunged his knife into the water. This prevented the sea from passing. It was not long before the sand became as solid as the earth because he had removed the water which remained by striking it with seven blows of his knife. All the white fish could then be seen and there was even one which was enormous. It weighed several hundred kilos. One could not really say how many kilos it weighed. The king saw it and said:

"Hey! The one who brings me this fish will be rewarded with a piece of gold."

All the men then tried to catch hold of the fish while the lazy man just sat and did nothing. Two men tried to take hold of it but without success. Then three other men tried, then four and then five but they also failed. Even one hundred men were unable to raise it.

"Come out of there," said the lazy man.

"I am going to see what can be done."

He caught the fish with one hand and brought it on to the land. The king then gave him his reward.

"Take this gold, my friend."

"I don't want it. I don't want any gold."

"Then what do you want?"

"I want the head of the fish."

"Well then, if that's what you want, take it."

The king gave it to him and the lazy man cut it and threw it so far away that it fell into another country. It fell into the country of King Sanyanyo.[31] Before long, the country of that king was invaded by a terrible stench. The lazy man became the king of the dried lands and he could have had a palace there but he said to the king:

"Hey! I don't want to become the new king of this land. I must continue my travels once again."

"Where do you want to go?"

"I cannot tell you since it is a long story. In the beginning I made a promise to my parents while I was living with them and since then, I must be continually travelling. I have no country. I am a man who travels. If I were to remain here I would break my promise and become a liar to my parents."

So he took to the road again and travelled day and night.

Here is another story about what happened in the country of Sanyanyo. The king gathered together all the people who lived there and said:

"We must find out what it is that smells like rotten fish at the doors of the city."

They all went off to see what it was and found the head of the fish there. They went back to the king and said:

"Lord, we have discovered what it is that smells so bad."

"What is it?"

"It is the head of a fish, lord. It is bigger than your house."

"Why didn't you throw it away?"

"Hey! It was impossible to do so since it is so big. It is bigger that two or three men standing upright with raised hands. The head of this fish is bigger than your house."

He called all his men once again to decide how to throw away the head of this fish. The men tried to raise it but it would not move. So the king said:

"If this is the way things are, all of you must go and find someone who is capable of raising the head of this fish. I will give my daughter in marriage to the one who succeeds, even if he has nothing to offer in return. I will give him half my territory and he will become the king."

All of them then went off in different directions to find someone who would be able to raise the head of the fish. They found many men but not one of them was able to raise the head. As soon as they arrived and saw what the trouble was they refused to try. Then the lazy man arrived and said:

"Lord, will you permit me to enter the city?"

"Yes, I will."

The lazy man entered and the king said:

"Hey, young man! Are you able to raise the head of this fish?"

"But where would I find the strength to do so, lord? I am only a young boy."

The king continued speaking, then he said:

"You can either look for someone else or try to raise the head of this fish by yourself. I will give my daughter to you to marry even if you have nothing to give in exchange. I will give you half of my territory and you will become the king."

The man with the big knife said:

"I will try."

He went and put the fish head between his fingers and then threw it. The king saw this and said:

"Hey! You are really very strong, young man. All the men of my kingdom have come and tried to raise the head. You arrive now and are able to lift it with one hand!"

The king thought and was afraid of this man but he gave him what he had promised. Shortly after, the man married his daughter.

"Hey, young man! What is your real name?"

"I don't have a name. They gave me a name so as to make fun of me. They call me the lazy man."

"Ah! I never before heard of such a name. What a curious name they gave you, lazy man! Where does this name come from?"

"I used to be very lazy and refused to do anything."

"Ho! Then you must not be very well accepted by your parents."

"They didn't chase me away. It was I, myself, who wanted to know about the countries."

"Little daughter, come and see what your future husband is like. Does he please you?"

The king called his daughter. The lazy man took the ring with the black stone and breathed in deeply. He changed and became magnificent to see; he was white and handsome. When the girl came out and saw him, she immediately kissed him, without saying one word.

"What is happening, lazy man? You don't have a very nice name but there is no one on earth who can equal you."

"It doesn't matter to me if he is lazy or not. I don't care. He is really very handsome," said the king's daughter.

So, the young man married her and became a prince. Then he said:
"I am really married now but I cannot remain here in this country."
"Why?"
"Because that's how thing are. I spoke to my parents and told them that I was going to leave in order to discover other countries."
"And when will you return?"
"I can't say. I could tell you next month or maybe even next year but I really don't know when."
"Ah! What will you do now, my daughter?" the king asked.
"If my elder one leaves, well then I will also leave."
"Very well. If you want to go with him, then do so."
The man with the big knife said:
"No, you must not leave. Stay with your father. I will go alone."
"I don't want to. If you leave so will I. If you die at the right, I will die at the left."
So they left and walked for a long time. They arrived in the middle of a road where the fish head was beginning to rot. They reached the country of a king. I don't remember very well but he was the captain of a boat.[32] This king was very rich because he was engaged in trading activities. But it really smelled very bad in the place where he was to be found. The smell was so bad that his boat was unable to move. He couldn't put it in the water. Even when he finally was able to do so, the boat could still not move because the head of the fish was blocking the sea. The king said:
"Who is able to raise this fish head? I will give him a boat and he won't have to pay[33] anything."
"Alright," said the captain of the boat.
"Hey! There is no one who can raise this thing."
"Then go and find someone who can. I will give him a boat."
They went off to look for someone but no one was able to raise the fish head. One after another tried but without success. During this time, the man with the big knife and his wife arrived. Those who were there looking after the boat wanted the woman of the man with the big knife. They thought about what would be the best strategy they could employ for this and said:
"We must let him look for the head of the fish. He will be given a boat but we will take it away from him and engage in trading activities with it. But before doing this, we will take away his wife."
The man with the big knife was also thinking.
"Eh! Can you go and look for the fish head? Can you answer me?"

"Yes I can. It's not very difficult to do. Stay here and watch."

"Be careful, elder one. I am worried. If you go into the sea, you will die. What is there in the sea? Nobody knows. There are sharks and other dangerous beings there, elder one."

"Don't be worried, younger one. I forbid you to be worried since I am putting myself in the hands of the Lord. It is he who will take care of us and protect our lives."

He went and dived into the sea. The group who remained on the land spoke to the woman:

"What are you doing with the man with the big knife? He is ugly. It would be better for you to remain with us and help us with our trading activities. Our boat is full of many goods and profitable things which we can sell.[34] The only thing you have to do will be to remain quiet, eat and drink. You will not have to do any work."

They deliberately tried to deceive the wife of the man with the big knife who went into the sea. He took his knife and removed the impurities from it which had been caused by the head of the fish that was now in a state of decomposition. When he had finished doing this he returned to the land and said:

"You can go and see if your boat moves now."

He put the boat into the sea and it moved without any problem. There was no longer anything which caused it to be blocked.

"I am very happy that you are not dead, elder one. How would I ever have known what had happened if you were dead?"

"You shouldn't be troubled, younger one. As long as I have my knife in my hand, I will not die. This knife is my heart and my body."

"That's good."

"I would like to give you something, younger one."

"What do you want to give me, elder one?"

"I want to give you the stone of my ring. It is the one which was given to me by the men who were pulling on the rattan. Take it and use it."

The man with the big knife took the ring out of the pocket of his shirt and gave it to her. The younger one hung it on her barrette [hairclip].

All the men on the boat ceased looking at the sea and started looking at the woman, who was very beautiful. How lovely she was!

"What should we do in order to take away this girl? Who is clever enough to do it? A brain that eats?"[35]

"Of course. We will do the following."

"What will we do?"

"We will go back to the land."

"And what will we do after that?"

"We will go back to the land and offer everything he wants to the man with the big knife if he agrees to help us dig a well."

"And then?"

"When he goes down into the well, we will cover it up."

"Good idea!"

So they went back on to the land and said to the man with the big knife:

"Hey, young man who is so ugly (they didn't know his name), we want to ask you to do something for us. Can you come with us?"

"Yes I can. What is it that you want me to do?"

"We want to dig a well. It mustn't reach the water but it has to be as deep as three people standing upright with raised hands. Is this possible?"

"I would like to say yes but maybe I won't be capable of doing it. But I will try. However, you will have to give me three days before I try to do it."

"Ah! It doesn't matter. Take three days if you want and then come back."

His wife said:

"Hey, elder one! Are you aware of how difficult it is to dig a well? It is not your role to do such a thing."

"What do you mean, younger one?"

"They don't want you to dig a well. What they really want is to kill you and take me as a wife!"

"Oh! But things will take place as they are meant to."

"Oh! But don't be worried, elder one."

"What do you mean, younger one?"

"How many days did you ask for?"

"Three days."

"Good! You will go down to the well and I will call the white rats to come and make a hole so that they can join you."

"That seems to be a good idea."

So, his wife called all the white rats, seven of them. She called out to them and seven white rats appeared.

"I want all of you to go down into the well where my elder one is digging. Help me to make a hole which will reach him."

"When?"

"Today."

The white rats went to join the man with the big knife and they descended before he did. Then the group arrived.

"Is it possible to go down today?"

"Yes, it's possible."

So, they went down. The man with the big knife got ready and jumped down into the hole while the others rushed to the spot to cover it up. But the seven white rats dug another hole so that they could reach him. The group surrounded the wife of the man with the big knife. Each of them asked her if she wanted him. But she didn't want any of them. Then they said:

"If that's the way things are, we are going to kill you."

"Kill me if you want to. Go ahead and kill me."

During this time, the white rats had made a hole where the man with the big knife could see what was happening. Then he jumped in with a loud "boo" and came outside on to the earth.

"What are you doing here?"

They all ran away.

"How are you, younger one? What did they say to you?"

"They came to trick us. They wanted me but I refused because I am your wife."

"Why didn't you accept?"

"Why do you speak to me like that? I wouldn't have followed you if I had decided to accept them."

"Alright, younger one. But we are going to play a trick on them now in order to kill them and I will become the king here. We will go off now."

"What are you going to do?"

"It's not difficult but you must go and ask them to search for the black stone in the sea. You will tell them that the one who finds it will be your husband."

"But you must not be there, otherwise no one will believe me."

"Alright then, I am going to leave now. I will return when they are all dead."

"Where are you going?"

"I am going over there, to the Sohmaliki country."

"But it must be far away, elder one."

"No it isn't, younger one."

"If you want to take another wife, it doesn't matter. But don't leave me."

He left for the Sohmaliki country. The men on the boat arrived and the woman said to them:

"Come here. I want to talk to you and ask you to find something for me. The one who succeeds will become my husband."

"What do you want?"

"I want the black stone which is to be found in the sea. Who is able to find it for me?"

They all went to look for the stone because each of them wanted this beautiful woman. They went into the sea and they all died, one after the other. The only one who remained was the *taukay*, who said:

"This stone does not exist. What are we going to do now?"

"Maybe it doesn't exist but I cannot be certain."

So, the *taukay* went into the sea and died (there are many bad things in the sea that wish to harm us). But in the country of Sohmaliki the people there saw the man with the big knife.

"You look like someone I know," said a girl.

"Who?"

"This happened a long time ago when we were in the country of Jawo."

"Did you live there?"

The girl of the country of Sohmaliki knew that he was a magician because they were close to each other.

"Elder one, why were you thrown outside?"

"But I was not thrown outside."

"You planted rice on three mountains, elder one and we had pity on you since you could neither eat nor drink and had to go and visit all kinds of different countries."

"Who told you this, younger one?"

"Don't try to hide anything from me." She was a magician and much stronger than he was. She was the king's daughter and she always got everything she wanted. They spoke together like this for a time and then finally got married.

"I don't want to remain here. I want to go home."

"If you want to leave, I will go with you."

"No, it is not possible, there is nothing at all where I am going. Life is very hard there. There isn't enough to eat or to drink and I won't be able to clothe you."

"But you mustn't be so sad, older, one since it is I, myself, who will take care of all that and I will accept what you are able to offer me. I will see to it that you have everything you want."

"If that is so, then there are no longer any problems."

They went off and before long came upon the first wife.

"How did things go, younger one?"

"They are all dead, elder one."

"Who is that behind you?" the second wife asked.

"My wife."

"Forgive me for having taken your husband, younger sister."

"It doesn't matter. I am willing to share him with you and I ask your pardon in this world and in the other one because we must not separate and both of us must be very careful."

The youngest one said:

"That is very fine, older one, since all three of us will live here together. We will live in peace. Two of the boats are full."

"Very well, younger one, but what will we do now? We are going to need a house."

The youngest one said:

"I will take care of this. I ask your permission to use my knowledge to build a house."

"Ha! If this is so, younger one, you will take care of the house and your older sister will take care of the bowls, plates and mortar."

The younger wife took a deep breath and made an invocation.[36] Through her prayers and power[37] she called the Lord to build a house. And it wasn't long before a house, which resembled a palace, appeared. The first wife did the same thing and plates, wells, bathroom and many other things appeared. It was the first wife who was responsible for finding things to drink and eat.

Then the boat left so they could do some trading. They gained a profit of millions and millions. They became kings in the palace where they lived. So the young man became a king and shortly was crowned and made laws. Later on, the younger wife said:

"Older one, now we can go and look for your mother."

"Ho! I don't want her to come. Father and mother can now eat and drink. I paid back my debts to them. I no longer have any debts and we can live happily here. We will be happy and go sailing. We will soon reign over the people." He actually did become a king in this place, a king of the sea. There was never again another country like this one.

### 3.2. Hawè the lazy man

***(Village of Samoh, Province of Narathiwat, November 1993***
***Narrator: Wo Seng***
***Type of story: Hikaya')***

Long ago, at the beginning of time, lived the parents of the lazy one. They did not have any children for a long time when a child was finally born to them. The lazy ones' parents were rich. When the child was fourteen years old, his father, who was old, said to his wife:

"Hey! We have only one child but he refuses to do anything. He is very lazy. We own many rice fields but our child is lazy and doesn't want to work."

When the child was fifteen years old, his father became sick. He was very old. He was sick for two months and finally died. His mother then said:

"Hawè the lazy one!"

"What do you want mother?"

"Your father is dead, so you will have to go to work."

"Hum! I have no desire to do so, mother."

"Ah! What will become of us if you refuse to do anything?"

"We will always have something to eat because there are people who work our land."

Then the mother died. At that moment, there was five hundred handfuls of rice in the house.

"I really don't have the courage to stamp on the rice."

Nonetheless, if he wanted to eat he would be obliged to stamp on the rice. Though he had everything else he needed he was unable to eat correctly. He had rice but it was unhusked. He asked someone to help him to crush it and this is how he obtained two or three sacks full. He gave some of it to those who had helped him.

"I now have some rice."

He lived alone since he no longer had a father or mother. He lived in a big house covered with tiles.

"Eh! There seem to be many fish in the sea. I must go and find some fish-hooks."

He searched for some copper and went to ask the blacksmith for help.

"Eh! One can't just make fish-hooks like that, lazy one! If you had a knife,[38] we would be able to work the copper. It would then be easy to work on it."

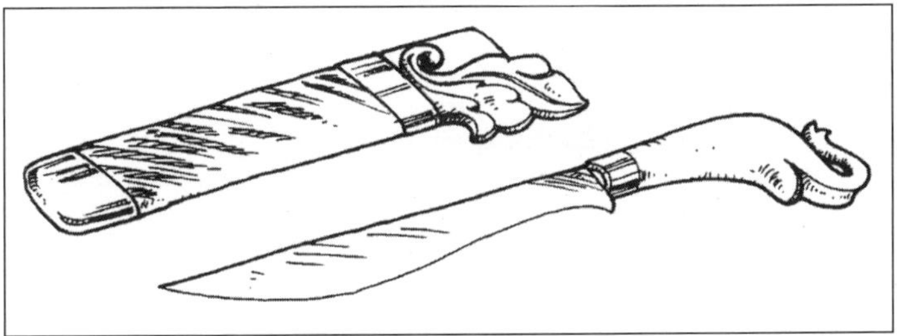

**Fig. 28.** A traditional knife from Patani.

"That's no problem, older one. I am going to buy a knife, so we can work the copper."

"Ah! Very well then."

When they had the knife, they worked the copper and then attached a string to the fish hook. Hawè the lazy one looked for some bamboo to make a fishing pole. He would now be able to go fishing and sell the fish he caught. People buy fish when it is fresh; they also buy fish that have been cleaned and salted or put in brine.[39]

This is how one can get rice without asking any help from others to thrash it.

"I no longer need anyone to help me to stamp on the rice. "

He was able to find some money and some rice but not enough. He left early in the morning and returned in the afternoon with his fish strung over his shoulder. He cleaned the fish and took out their eyes, which he placed in a small jar.[40] He prepared all his fish in this way and put their eyes into small black jars.[41]

**Fig. 29.** Fillling jars with treasurse, eyes of fish/precious stones.

When one of the jars was completely full, he took some clay in order to seal it. In this way, the jar was hermetically closed. He then filled another jar with the eyes of the fish, took some more clay and sealed it, too. People came to buy his fish which had been pickled in brine. One day, someone came and bought half a jar.[42] He had quite a lot of money.

**Fig. 30.** Brine jar.

But now we are going to talk about something else.

Hawè the lazy one earned a great deal of money with his fish that had been pickled in brine. Someone even came one day and bought half a jar from him. He was a ship-owner[43] and also a trader. He said to his wife:

"Wife! You will go to see Hawè the lazy one and buy half a jar of brine fish because we will soon be leaving and will have need of some provisions."

"Ha! Alright!"

She went off and arrived at the house of Hawè the lazy one at midday.

"Ah! Where do you come from?"

"From the house of the ship-owner."

"Why did you come?"

"I want to buy half a jar of brine fish."

"Ah! Yes I have some. Why do you want it?"

"Ah! The ship-owner needs some provisions for his sea voyage."

"Oh! Ah! Can I leave something in your care?"

"The ship-owner is going out to sea, so you can entrust him with anything you want."

"Ah! Very well then, take this. They are fish eyes and I want to send them to the country where the Chinese king lives and exchange them for a knife that I need in order to work the copper and make fish-hooks."

"Ah! Can you bring them to us?"

"Ah! Don't worry. I will bring them to you."

It is like this that one can see if a person is lazy or not. There were effectively half a jar of brine fish and two jars of fish eyes but instead of making something to carry them,[44] he put one of the jars on his shoulder and another one under his armpit. He put the last one over his forearm like this but he finally reached the ship-owner, who said:

"One can see that he is a lazy person. He didn't even take the trouble to make something to carry them with. He is really very lazy and that's why people call him the lazy one."

"Well then, lazy one, what do you want?"

"I would like you to give these jars with the fish eyes inside to the Chinese king in exchange for a knife which I need in order to work the copper."

"Ah! Leave it here. We will soon be leaving. Go home then and don't be worried."

"I will go home but I want to go fishing before."

He left in the middle of the day and returned home in the afternoon. He went fishing but didn't catch much of anything. He only caught enough to fill a vase.[45] During this time, the ship-owner left with two of his sailors. He had taken the jars with the fish eyes with him. After having sailed for one night, he arrived at the Chinese king's place. It was half-past three.[46] The cannon resounded at his arrival; it was a very big one. This is how things were done a long time ago, in order to announce the arrival of someone to the king. The Chinese king said:

"Guardian!"

"Yes!"

"Go and see who it is who has just arrived."

The guardian left.

"Ah! Where do you come from, ship-owner?"

"From my place."

"What does that mean?"

"We want to ask your permission to sleep here."

"Ah! That's no problem."

So they slept in the meeting hall. They spoke without stopping until they went to bed. The next day, the ship-owner greeted the king and said:

"I will leave now, lord. Goodbye."

"Ah! Then go, but wait a little. We are going to cook the rice."

"Don't bother. We will eat once we are out at sea. Here is something which we have been asked to entrust to you."

"What is it?" asked the king.

"Hawè the lazy one would like to entrust you with two jars filled with eyes."[47]

"He wants to leave two jars full of eyes with me?"

"Ah! Yes, here they are."

The ship-owner told his sailors to bring the two jars and put them in front of the door. They brought one of the jars into the meeting hall.

"When will you come back, ship-owner?"

"The man who has entrusted these jars to you would like to have a knife in order to be able to work on some copper."

"That's no problem. We know how to do this. We are blacksmiths."

"I will return in about three months."

"Very well," said the king.

The ship-owner went out to sea, towards unknown countries. He engaged in all kinds of commerce. One day, the Chinese king said:

"Eh! Servant!"

"What is the matter, father?" asked Dame Benjamin.

"What is in these jars? What kind of eyes did Hawè the lazy one leave us?"

"What eyes, father?"

"I don't know. The ship-owner spoke of eyes. We must open the jars."

He told his daughter to go and open one of the jars which was filled with precious stones.

"Eh! How is this possible, chiefs?"

He had called the chiefs. Maybe they were the chiefs of the district or of the villages.

"How is this possible? Women,[48] how is this possible?"

"The one who left these two jars with us is called Hawè the lazy one. He wants a knife which he can use to work copper with. What do you women, chiefs of the district and chiefs of the villages, think about all this?"

"Ah! We really don't know."

Dame Benjamin remained quiet. One of the chiefs, the one of the palace, made a salutation and said:

"Lord, maybe this story about a knife is a lie. Is it really a knife that he wants to work copper with?"

"Ah! Yes, he truly wants a knife."

Everyone discussed the matter and they had a meeting, but no one really knew what it was all about. The king didn't know nor did the chiefs.

"Tell the carpenters to come here. Tell them to make a chest as deep as one breast-stroke."

**Fig. 31.** The Chinese Princess travels in the wooden box to follow her lover..

The chest was about one metre square and one could put two people into it. They also filled it with provisions. The carpenters were the only ones who knew about it. They went to work and the chest was finished in three days. It was waterproof, which meant that if it fell into the sea it wouldn't sink. It was now two months since the ship-owner had left. He had said that he would return in three months. It was now two months and ten days since he had left. The king said:

"Come here, servants!"

"What is it, father?"

"Prepare some cakes, food and other provisions. We must find out the country Hawè the lazy one comes from. We must go and see what it is like. He wants a knife and he offers us two jars filled with precious stones, in exchange. I have been a king now for thirty years and I have never before seen one precious stone. Servants, prepare the food and cakes."

Who were the servants? Well, they were old ones. So, seven days went by. The ship-owner would soon return. The king awakened at dawn and during the morning he got some iron and went to forge it. It was the king himself who did this. He made a knife which took him one entire day to finish. It really was a very beautiful knife. It had not been made for just anyone, or was it made to inspire laughter? When he had finished, he spent two days sharpening it. He finally finished but it took him seven days. Only four days remained before the ship-owner would return.

"I finished sharpening the knife," he told his daughter.

"And how is it?"

"It still has to be soaked in water."

The next morning, after he had eaten some cakes, he took the piece of copper and went to forge it. But the knife refused to "eat" the copper.

"Ah! I never saw anything like this. Yet, I have made thousands of them. But this one refuses to work the copper."

Dame Benjamin said:

"Father, come and eat."

The king was full of sweat after having worked for so long at the forge. He went up into the house. He dragged the knife behind him. It made a noise like "gang gang, gung." He put it on the ground.

"Why are you so angry, father," Dame Benjamin asked.

"Do you have any idea about what has happened?"

"Why, father?"

"I have been forging this knife since this morning but it refuses to work the copper."

He went inside the house to eat. Dame Benjamin took the knife and the copper and "kruh," it ate the copper, "puh."

"Now then father, it is done. How did you think it [the knife] could want to eat the copper?"

He ate his rice, made a quid of betel and went outside.

"Where are you going now, father?"

"I am going to do some forging again."

"Father, you are going to forge once again but how do you think that the knife is able to work the copper all by itself?"

"The knife is here, the copper is over there and yet nothing happens."

"What do you mean?"

"It will not eat the copper."

"Ah! Really father, are you sick?"

"What do you mean? Do you think that I am crazy? What do you know about such things?"

"Look, father."

She took hold of the knife and "bruh"!"

"Ah! Now you see what one calls eating the copper with the knife. You wanted the knife to eat the copper all by itself; it is not alive!"

"Ah! So that's how it is!" said the king.

"Ho! This is the way the knife eats the copper."

"Ah! Very well then, I agree."

The ship-owner returned three days later. The cannon resounded "gung" when he arrived.

"Ah! The ship-owner is here. Servants, prepare something to eat and drink and put everything into the chest."

They put everything into the chest: rice, cooking pans to cook the rice with the accompaniments. The chest was full of all kinds of different things.

"Ah! You have returned, ship-owner," said the king.

"You knew I would, lord."

"Yes, and tomorrow you will be leaving."

"We will give you something to take to Hawè the lazy one; we will give him something in exchange for what he has given us."

"Ah! Very well, lord."

They went to sleep. The chest was closed and it was not possible to see anything from the outside. It was as deep as one breast-stroke.

"Hah!" said the ship-owner. "I come to you with my greetings, lord and I am going to leave now."

"Wait a minute," said the king. "Tell your two sailors to come here."

The two sailors would have to carry the chest. It was very heavy. But it took four men to carry it and put it in the prow of the boat.[49] They didn't put it in the hold but on the plank and attached it so that it would not fall into the sea. Then the ship-owner left the port. But suddenly he said:

"Ah! Wait a minute! Turn the boat around. We are going back to the port."

"Why did you come back, ship-owner?"

"Where is the opening of the chest?"

"Don't worry! It will open all by itself when you reach Semalah's place."

"Ah! That's good then."

Then they left. They sailed during one night and one day. It was still dark since the king's daughter was really a magician.

"They will all go to sleep now, servant."

"Yes, they will go to sleep and we will remain at the helm."

"Ah!" said the servant. "That's good, mother."

The helmsman, the ship-owner and all the others were asleep. The two women did the navigating. It took them only one day and one night to arrive at their destination. Yes, these two women were really very rapid and knew what they were doing! And "jah"! They reached the jetty. The helmsman, the man at the prow and the ship-owner all woke up. The two women ran until they reached the chest, even before the sail had been lowered.

"Ah! Where are we? How did we get here?"

"I don't know, lord. I was sleeping."

"Oh! But what country is this?"

"Do you hear that noise "totoh totoh," chief?"

"Ah! What is it ?"

"Chuh, chuh." They were afraid it was a ghost. They heard a noise like a kind of murmuring "sosèh sosèh."

"Aah!"

Everyone on the land heard the noise.

"Don't go too far away. I will go and see what country this is." The ship-owner took a sarong, put a skirt on his shoulder and went off. He walked until he reached his own house.

"Ah! But we have arrived home! If this is the way things are, we must tell the people to come and help to carry the chest."

"Four people won't be enough. We need six."

They untied the ropes and brought the chest on to the land.

"Be careful!" said the ship-owner.

He was afraid that a ghost had been placed in the chest.

They arrived at their destination in the afternoon. Semalah had gone fishing and at seven o'clock he had still not returned home. Once they reached Semalah's house, they called out to him:

"Semalah, Semalah, Semalah!"

But he wasn't there.

"Ah! What are we going to do? We are very frightened."

So, they carried the chest to the top of the ladder because they were afraid there was a ghost in it.

"We will put the chest here, between the veranda and the ladder and hide it under the earth so that no one can see it."

Once the chest had been taken up and installed, they ran away, "dung deng," since they were truly filled with fear. Oh! People were easily frightened in those days. The servant and Dame Benjamin hid inside the chest. Semalah returned walking quickly and put his fishing pole against a tree. He held a fish in his hands, "geng geng geng" and went up to his house.

"Aye! I still haven't prepared the fish," he said.

The two women in the chest remained quiet. What fish was he talking about?

"Ah! I still haven't cooked the rice."

He lit a fire, cooked the rice and prepared the fish.

"If I let this fish rot, it will smell bad when I mix it with leaves and not be good."

After he had prepared the fish, he tied them to the wall which was made of interlaced bamboo strips. Ah! it was really a beautiful house! He did all this but still had to salt the fish. He went inside to eat, chewed on a quid of betel, smoked a cigarette and went to bed. He woke up the next morning.

"Oh! It is almost afternoon!"

He was worried about the fish so he went to get them.

"Ah! There he is," said Dame Benjamin. "Get up," she said to the servant.

They both got up and opened the door.

"Come into the house. How should the fish be salted?"

They then salted them.

"They are now salted, mother."

"Go and get the cakes that are in the chest and put them on a tray over his bed, near his head.

They saw the cakes, some food, dates and other good things in the chest.

"Mother, you should also put a glass on the tray and leave it on his bed. I will go and cook the rice."

So, the servant cooked the rice. Dame Benjamin broke open a coconut and grated the meat in it, so that it would serve as an accompaniment for the fish. She grilled the fish with a great amount of oil which came from the Chinese king. She prepared the fish and other things to eat. Everything was really very well cooked. Soon everything had been prepared.

"Eat, mother. I will serve you."

Dame Benjamin served the rice and ate it. But she wasn't very hungry. When Semalah came home, the sun had reached its zenith so the two women remained in the chest. They suddenly heard a noise, "greba, greba." It was the noise of Semalah's footsteps. He was carrying the fish.

"Ah! I caught many fish today but I do not have any water to cook the rice."

So, he went off with a bowl and opened the water jar.

"It is full. Who put water into it? There was hardly any left yesterday. Ah! I will prepare a fire for the rice." He took a bowl so he could wash the rice in it but it was already full of rice. He served himself some of the cooked rice.

"Who is it? Who has done all this? The fish are still not grilled but the tray with all the accompaniments has already been prepared. There are vegetables. Who then prepared them? No matter, I am going to eat them."

He ate and the food was really very tasty.

He ate a great quantity since he had never before eaten such tasty food. And all of it was for him! Who then had prepared his food?

The lazy man really didn't care! There were fish fried in oil and all sorts of other good things to eat. He ate until he was full.

"I still haven't prepared the fish," he said.

He spoke to himself. Then he went outside, lay down and chewed some betel. Suddenly, he saw something.

"What is that under the bell jar?"

He raised it.

"Who then prepared the food? There are still some cakes left to eat. Is someone trying to poison me? It doesn't matter. I am going to eat them anyway."

He ate and drank some tea. Then he served himself again.

"Maybe someone wants to poison me. But I will die lying down." So, he lay down. He was no longer hungry. Then he fell asleep. The women came out of the chest in order to prepare the fish. After they had done this, they strung them on a string and attached them to the wall of interlaced bamboo strips. They salted them and put them into a large container. There were many of them and it took them all morning to do all this. When everything had been prepared, they returned to the chest and went inside it. Semalah woke up late in the afternoon.

"Ah! I still haven't prepared the fish. They are going to rot."

So, he went quickly to the pot.

"Ah! But they have already been prepared! The fish are hanging on the wall of the veranda. Who has done all this? Ah! It really is not difficult to go fishing if there is someone who prepares the fish for you."

Night fell, so he went to bed. The next morning, he took his fishing line "gredung, gredung" and went fishing. He spent the entire day doing this. When he returned home in the evening he saw that someone had prepared everything for him, just as they had done before. The same thing took place during three days. When he returned home, everything was already prepared. We now arrive at the fourth day.

"Eh! Who is it then who prepares everything I need in the kitchen?"

He went fishing that day and came back with about twenty fish.

"Who then is it who does all the cooking?"

He had returned home about nine o'clock in the evening. The fish he was carrying made a sound like "juweh, juweh." He went to the well and leaned his fishing line against it. It was just at that moment that he heard a noise coming from the kitchen of his house.

"It's him! I will see who he is today."

After a short moment, he went inside his house. He was unaware of the existence of the chest; he had never seen it. He quietly entered. Dame Benjamin was serving some rice and eating. He was on the veranda and "gung, gung, gung", he rushed into the kitchen. Ah! He saw Dame Benjamin there.

"Do you want some rice?" Dame Benjamin asked.

"You eat first," he answered.

He went outside and was speechless for a time because Dame Benjamin was really very beautiful.

"Ah! Why aren't you preparing the rice now that he has returned?" the old servant said.

"Come and eat," said Dame Benjamin.

Semalah got up and went into the kitchen to eat.

Dame Benjamin went into the chest. Semalah served himself three times and when he came back, Dame Benjamin had disappeared. He ran around looking for her. He called to the old servant and asked her:

"Where is she?"

"She is over there."

He looked for her but couldn't find her.

"Over there, near the ladder is a chest."

"Ha! Where does this chest come from?"

It would have taken six people to carry it. But he was able to carry it all by himself, "bruuh."

"I will break it open. I will take an axe and break open this wooden chest."

"Ah! Don't do that, I will open it."

She opened the chest and Dame Benjamin came out of it with a big smile on her face. He put his arms around her and put her on his bed. Then they spoke to each other.

"I have been here for several days now."

"Ah! Why didn't you tell me? Where do you come from?"

"From over there."

"Ah! And to think that I didn't even see the chest!"

They spoke together for a time. He looked at Dame Benjamin's fingers and saw that she had a ring with a precious stone on one of them.

"That's a pretty stone."

"It's from one of the men that you left with us the other day."

"Ah! And why didn't you make one for me?"

They remained like this for a time. Ah! He would no longer go fishing any more because of Dame Benjamin.

"Why go fishing, older one? It is not worth the trouble."

"Ah! But I must find something to eat."

She prepared some food.

Some time afterwards, a midwife was asked to come and also the imam because he was going to marry Dame Benjamin and she would have to become a Muslim. She was the daughter of the Chinese king and she was going to marry Semalah. As for Semalah, he no longer did anything. He stopped working because Dame Benjamin did everything herself.

"What do you want to do?" said Dame Benjamin.

"We have to eat."

"But there is everything we need here if you want to eat", said the Chinese king's daughter. She was the daughter of a rich man, so they would to be able to live for a long time, be happy and not have any problems.

Now we are going to speak about King Sanyanyo and the one who went hunting for birds for him. He left to go hunting with his bird.[50]

"I didn't catch anything today. Eh! But what is that noise?"

"There is someone at Semalah's house. Semalah lives in his father's house. He lives alone now since his parents died. And he is lazy. Ah! Well, that's the way things are. But I am thirsty, so I will go and pay him a visit. "

"Ah! Is the master of the house at home?"

"Ah! Yes, he is."

Dame Benjamin was in the house. She was looking at Semalah who was asleep.

"Come up, old man."

"I only want some water."

"Ah! First come up into the house. We will give you some cakes, water and other things to eat."

"Ah!" He saw Dame Benjamin and shook his head.

"Have you been here for a long time?"

"Yes, I have been here for some time now."

"Where is your husband?"

"Oh! He is over there. He is sleeping."

"What is his name?"

"Ah! His name is Semalah, the elder."

"Oh! Are you Semalah's wife?"

"Yes."

"Very well then, I am going to leave now."

"Come back whenever you want, old man. Come back here whenever you go hunting for birds."

The hunter ran to see the king.

"What has happened?" the king asked.

"Ah!. . .! Yes. . . Really. . ."

"What then? Are there birds over there?"

"Ah! Yes. . . There is one and it is lovely. Yes, it is really beautiful."

"Ah! What bird are you talking about?"

"It is in the house of Semalah."

"What kind of bird is it? Is it in the house?"

"Yes, lord, I am speaking about the wife of Hawè Semalah. Ah, she is also lovely! One cannot even compare her to your wife, lord. She also speaks very well."

"Hum! Is she as pretty as all that?"

"Hum! Yes, she really is."

"Alright then. I will go and see for myself tomorrow."

The king put on a shirt and a sarong the next day, put a piece of cloth on his shoulder and left.

"Prepare the cakes and the tray," said Dame Benjamin.

"Why, mother?"

"Because the king will soon arrive."

She had hardly finished preparing everything when the king arrived.

"Ah! Is the head of the house here?"

She greeted him and said:

"Yes lord, he is here."

"Ah! That must be the woman," he said to himself.

"Please come up into the house."

She served him some cakes and water.

"Where do you come from?"

He went up into the house to eat the cakes and drink some water. Semalah was asleep. They talked together for a time. The king provoked her a little.

"Ah! This is a nice house but something is missing. It has tiles but the columns are made of bamboo."

Dame Benjamin made a salutation and said:

"Lord, the insects don't eat the bamboo columns."

"Oh! They don't want to lose Semalah's wife."

They continued talking together for a while and then the king got up to leave.

"I am going to leave now."

She made a salutation and said:

"Lord, you can come back here whenever you want to."

He went home and called the bird hunter:

"Well then, lord! Did I tell you the truth?"

"Yes you did. But now we must tell the chiefs of the villages and districts and the other chiefs to come here. I must have Semalah's wife."

"And how will you be able to take her away?"

"That's none of your business. Don't ask such questions. I have to bring back Semalah's wife with me."

The chiefs came and he told them everything.

"Eh! Lord, There is something strange which exists that may help us."

"What do you mean strange?"

"There is a jasmine flower[51] that exists on Mount Seven but no one is able to pick it. There are magic[52] flies surrounding it and an enormous, cruel and venomous serpent lives there. If anyone gets too close to it, it jumps on to you. Nobody is able to pick this flower. If we send Semalah to look for it he will not return and will die."

"Ah! very well. Guardian, tell Semalah to come here."

The guardian went to Semalah's house.

"What do you want, guardian?" said Dame Benjamin.

"My lord wants Semalah to come and see him."

"Very well. Wake up, older one!"

"What's the matter?"

"The king wants you to go and see him right away."

"Ah! Alright, I will go there."

He went off on the road.

"Ah! Here you are, Semalah."

"Yes, I am here."

"Eh! Semalah, I eat but I am never full; I sleep with covers but I am still cold. I bathe myself but I am never clean. This is because I can't stop thinking about the jasmine flower."

"If someone is endowed with magic powers lord, he could go and look for that flower, lord."

"Ah! Very well. When can you go and look for it?"

He made a salutation and said:

"Whenever you want, lord."

"Then go tomorrow."

"I will go the day after tomorrow."

He went home.

"Well then, elder one?"

"I will have to go and look for the jasmine flower."

"Ah! That's good, older one. Did the king ask you to go?"

"Yes, the king asked me to go."

"No matter then. When do you have to go?"

"If I am not mistaken, it is the day after tomorrow."

"Ah! Very well. Go then and don't be worried. You can go there."

The day after:

"Ah! Cook the rice, servant, because Hawè Semalah is going off to the mountain."

She prepared the rice and everything else, cut some leaves so that he could roll the cigarettes, prepared the provisions and three quids of betel.

"Ah! But how will I get there, younger one?"

"Older one, you must go straight ahead towards the setting sun. Don't go in any other direction because there are no other roads leading there. When you reach the high mountain and you see running water, you will stop and chew the betel. Here is the ring which I am going to put on your third finger. When you hear any noise at the foot of the mountain, put your hand on your head."

He left and walked all afternoon before he reached the foot of the mountain. He stopped there and washed his face. He chewed on a quid of betel and smoked a cigarette. He suddenly heard a strange noise, "gruu gruu gruu".

"Ah! That's the noise the younger one spoke about."

He put his hand on his head and it wasn't long before everything became dark.

"Ah, lord!"

The serpent greeted him.

"Where do you come from, master?"

"From over there. I have come to pick the jasmine flower."

"The jasmine flower? But why do you want it?"

"Eh! It is the king who wants it."

"Ah! That's no problem. I will go and look for it, master."

"There is no need for you to climb up."

He went to look for it.

"Ha! Here it is. You can leave now, master. I am tired of looking after this flower."

He took the flower and left in the afternoon. He arrived home at three o'clock.

"Ah!" said the servant, "Semalah, the older one, has returned."

**Fig. 32.** Naga stays still in front the magical stone hold by the hero.

"Prepare a piece of cloth and put it near the ladder because we are now going to receive the jasmine flower. We will also wash Semalah's feet."

She washed Semalah's feet and then he went up to the house carrying the flower. He put it on his bed.

"Prepare a fire in the hearth, servant."

The servant took the hearth and put the flower near it. Dame Benjamin put it over the fire.

"Ah! Go outside, younger one. Some friends are there."

She went out, "choh." The mistress, Dame Flower of Jasmine,[53] was there. She was even more beautiful than Dame Benjamin.

"Ah! Now go to the king's house, older one," said Dame Benjamin.

He took the flower and went to the king's house.

"Ah! The flower is much lighter than it was yesterday."

Yesterday, it possessed something but nothing is left today.

"Well then, Hawè Semalah, you have finally arrived."

He took the flower and carried it into the palace. Then he did the same thing that Dame Benjamin had already done.

"I will leave now," said Semalah.

Two days later, the king called his guardian.

"Go to Semalah's house and see if he is there."

"Ah! And why wouldn't he be there?"

The guardian went there and saw two women who were massaging Semalah. He ran back to inform the king who decided to go and see for himself. But at that moment a message arrived from prince Kereso Forty. Semalah's wife, Dame Benjamin, is engaged to him, the message said. The king was very surprised when he learned this. The people wanted to engage in a battle in order to recover the woman. But there is nothing to be worried about because Semalah had been born of the sperm of his father and the belly of his mother and he held a Malay dagger in his hand and had a spear inside his sarong. Seven days went by and another message arrived saying that at three o'clock prince Kereso Forty's men would arrive. This king had only military men with him. There were thirty-nine of them, and including the prince that made forty.

"Ah! Servant," said Dame Benjamin.

"Yes?"

"Ah! Prepare some underpants and undershirts."

"They are ready."

"Very well then. People will soon arrive and go close to our ladder. The older one must go inside the chest and close the top."

The moment arrived. "Yaa yaa." The warriors came inside so that they could take Semalah's wife away with them.

"Well then, servant."

"I have done what you asked me to do."

Dame Benjamin then struck out with her hands, "peng" and leaped up, "dung" and started to fight.

All of prince Kereso Forty's men were killed very quickly.

The old servant also struck the warriors. Only the prince remained; all the others had perished. Their hands had been cut off, as well as their heads. Yes, they were all dead and cut up. When everything had ended, Dame Benjamin leaped up.

"Well then, servant?"

"It's finished but there still remains gold against gold."[54]

Dame Benjamin put her feet down on the ground at the place where prince Kereso Forty was.

"Well then, older one, what do you think?"

"There is nothing to say."

"Ah! Well then, you will no doubt appreciate the knife of my servant."

"Ah! This woman talks too much."

"No, older one. You have come from far away and arrived at my house and in my village. We serve betel in my house and we will serve you well, also. But you must come inside. I beg you, older one, come inside and chew some betel in my house."

"I have my own provisions. Ah, this girl talks too much!"

"No, I don't, older one. But if you are thirsty then come in and drink and if you wish, you can chew some betel. I, myself, will serve you some cakes. But you must come inside the house."

"Ah! Don't tire yourself. I don't think you are so strong."

"If I don't invite you to climb up to my house I will be ashamed. This is how things are. If you have something else to say, go ahead and speak."

"Ah! You really talk too much, woman."

He rushed forward with the intention of thrusting his sword into Dame Benjamin but she took a step backwards and dodged away. He tried to catch her but she jumped in the air. He kept on striking out but nothing happened. This lasted for quite a while. Finally, Dame Benjamin said:

"You keep on striking out, older one, but if you want to rest for a while come and eat some cakes and drink some water. You must be thirsty. Come!"

"Ah! This girl never stops talking!"

He became even more angry and struck out again but still nothing happened. Dame Benjamin drew back, took the knife which she had hidden in her chignon, a knife which was folded up seven times. She grabbed hold of it and with one clean stroke, she opened it. The noise was heard as far away as the house of her father.

"Ah! What is going on, younger one?" her father asked his wife.

"What to you mean, elder one?"

"Ah! Dame Benjamin must have some problems. I heard the noise of her knife."

"Don't worry. Not one hair has fallen yet, not one hair."

The fight continued at Dame Benjamin's place. She sliced around the prince's waist, with her knife, two times.

"I am going to strike now, older one."

"Ah! Then go ahead, woman."

She struck out and cut his body into three pieces.

"Are you tired, older one?"

But he was dead. She ran to Semalah who was hiding in the chest. The chest was full of excrement because Semalah had been very much afraid. The servant cleaned everything and emptied the chest.

"Mother!"

"What do you want, servant?"

"There are so many dead here! It is not good."

"It doesn't matter since we ourselves are still alive."

Night fell and they went home. She took a leaf of betel, wrote a message, called to the sacred flies and sent her message to the sky, to Mani Telmu, asking him to make it rain holy water[55] so that the bodies would come together again. The dismembered bodies came together again and the dead returned to life, thanks to the perfumed rain water, which fell down during the whole night. The next day, Dame Benjamin went to see prince Kereso Forty, who greeted Semalah.

"Well now, Semalah, if you have any problems one day, you only have to call us in the morning and we will arrive the next morning. We are no longer enemies. We won't speak any more about battles and enemies."

We will now speak about King Sanyanyo. The king called Semalah to him:

"I have only one daughter and I will leave her to you since we don't want to remain here any longer."

The king left the country. Dame Benjamin married Semalah seven days later and so did the king's daughter. Ah! He had three wives now. Dame Benjamin made Semalah the king since the king had run away because he was afraid. Dame Benjamin did not go away but stayed in Semalah's house. They made a large living room in their house, a meeting hall where everyone could come and talk about their problems. The problems and other questions were studied with Semalah but it was Dame Benjamin who took decisions. Semalah was the prince and the king was Dame Benjamin. As for Semalah, he now had three wives. Hahaha. This is the end of the story.

### 3.3. The man who abandoned his children

***(Village of Samoh, Province of Narathiwat, November 1991***
***Narrator: Po' Suloh,***
***Type of story: bahri)***

A woman had two children, a boy and a girl. She decided to take a new husband and remarried. She had a little girl who was almost six years old and a boy three years old. The new husband said:

"Eh! Why don't you stop crying, young children?"

He hated his adopted children. The stepfather and the mother had a child together. The stepfather's name was Mamu and the mother was Esoh. Mamu said:

"We are both happy. Why should we take care of your first children?"

When the children heard this they started crying but were already thinking of their vengeance. The mother also cried a great deal. She had two children, a girl about six years old and a boy about three years old. The stepfather thought about how he could create problems for his children. He then ordered them to go and wash the clothes and blankets. But one of the cloths was carried away by the current. They anxiously went back home and said to their mother:

"Mother, one of the cloths was taken away by the current."

But the stepfather heard this and said:

"And how did it fall? Why didn't you catch hold of it?"

"It didn't fall, it was carried away by the current. I wanted to go and look for it but I was afraid that my brother would fall into the water."

The father then beat her. He beat her so heavily that the marks of two fingers soon appeared on her back; two fingers as thick as a thumb. He hit with a rattan stick and the girl soon fainted. The brother didn't stop crying. Then the stepfather said:

"If you don't recover the cloths, I will beat your brother too. I will hit him even harder."

Then the mother said:

"This is the way things are, older one. If you love the cloths more than myself we had better separate."

The stepfather answered:

"So, this is how you love your children!"

The mother wanted to separate but Manu didn't want to.

"No matter what happens, I will not separate from you until death. You must no longer speak to me like this since it is I who am the king. Moreover, I am going to kill your children since I cannot keep them any longer. They have not been issued from my seed. I want to kill them since they do not come from my seed. And this is how things are. It won't be long before they eat my head.[56] They aren't even able to keep the clothes."

The mother was incapable of thinking about anything. She wanted to leave him but it was impossible. Some time later, she went to harvest the rice; it was a rai.[57] She continued the harvest until the stepfather built a raft with the trunks of the banana trees. He took four trunks of banana trees and tied them together, like the children when they play. He puts three half-coconuts full of paddy on them. The mother said:

"You can't remain here. This is my land and it has never belonged to you. Everything here belongs to me."

**Fig. 33.** Abandonning the child on a raft.

He put the rice on to the raft and took the little boy and put him on top of it. The raft followed the current and continued to move along until the little boy's sister saw him and said:

"That's my brother who is going down!"

She followed the raft, caught it and climbed aboard.

"Eh! What our stepfather is doing is really not very nice."

She spoke and thought all alone while the raft continued to follow the course of water. It was not long before they were lacking rice and the three coconuts were empty. Then she said:

"What are we going to do now?"

Time passed and where did they arrive? They came close to rapids that carried them away. The water spun the brother and sister this way and that and they were unable to see any longer. But the sister saw some aquatic plants near the river. They were creeping plants and were lying over the cloth that had been lost.

"Younger one!"

"What is it?"

He was able to speak. It was very strange[58] but since they had been following the course of water he could speak.

"Younger one, I am going to get the cloth that is near the white spot over there. Stay here! I am going to take hold of a long stick to catch the cloth with."

But she couldn't reach it and the flow of water carried the cloth away again.

"Hum! The cloth has been carried away."

They began to descend the river and encountered White Mother Crocodile[59] who grabbed hold of the boy and carried him in her mouth as far as her cave.[60] She carried him into her cave, to the place where there were cloths of all colours, pendants and necklaces. The sister spoke:

"Hey! Don't devour my little brother, Mother Crocodile. Ask for whatever you wish and I will give it to you."

Sweat ran from the crocodile's skin. The crocodiles were once able to speak.

"Eh! But no, little girl. I[61] will not eat him. I won't eat him but I would like you to instead admire all the things that belong to human beings that are here."

**Fig. 34.** Discovering the crocodile's cave full of riches.

He [the crocodile] called his sister, not to eat her.

"If you want to go to the shore and climb up to the earth there, you will do so by yourself. Your brother cannot do this because if he did, someone would kill him."

So, Mother Crocodile caught her and guarded her in her lair. She covered her with gold and dressed her from head to foot.

"Eh! I would like to go home and see my mother."

"You want to return home? Why then? What do you want to do there?"

"I want to go back home and I would like you to give me this jewel. I want to take it to my parents to pay for the clothes that got lost."

"But you can't do that! Those do not have the same values as these clothes. Then take this precious stone and go home."

"Mother, here I am. I have come back."

When her mother saw her, she fainted. She remained unconscious for seven days and seven nights and none of the traditional healers that came to see her could wake her up. The White Crocodile then called the younger child from her cave and said to him:

"Hey! Your mother has fainted in her house. Yes, she fainted when she saw [your sister]. And moreover, you wanted to pay her back for the lost clothes."

"What are we going to do now, older one?"[62]

"Well, you will remain here and I will go. I will go in my form of a crocodile."

The crocodile soon arrived at the house that was near the river on the shore and the elder sister saw her. She saw the crocodile who had a wide-open mouth and made noise. But since she was far away she thought that maybe someone was hitting something with a piece of wood. The crocodile said:

"Eh, little girl! Come here."

The young girl came and said:

"What is the matter, grandmother?[63] I have come."

"Come and take this. It is magic[64] and one can heal with it. In any case, there is not one traditional healer in the village who can do anything. But don't be worried, your mother won't die."

The crocodile spit and a bezoar[65] came out of her stomach. The young girl put it on her mother's forehead and she began to feel better.

"Hey, little girl. How long has it been since you left?"

"I didn't go anywhere, mother. I left because father was not happy about the clothes that were lost. But maybe now he will change his attitude. He has raised us during our childhood and we would like everything to be in good order with our stepfather. We would like to pay him back."

The father arrived at this moment and said:

"Ha! This child is not dead and perhaps her brother that I do not see is here?"

"This is the way things are, father. We have come back to live with our parents. But we would like to give you this precious stone to pay you back for the lost clothes. You can sell it and we will not take anything in exchange for it."

The father then saw the stone surmounted on a ring. He examined it well and noticed twelve lights since the stone had a divinity in it. There really was a divinity in the stone of the ring. He went to sell it to a Chinese man. The man looked at it but didn't want it. Why then? Because he didn't have enough money to buy a stone of such value. Today, one would need not a million but tens of millions for a stone like that one. It did not have its equivalent in this world.

"Eh! Why don't you want my stone, *taukay*?"

"I don't have the means myself to offer for such a stone and if I bought it now with the money I have, you would be angry with me when you discovered its real value. This is why I don't want it."

He went to other shops but still had no success. He finally went back home.

"What am I going to do with this stone? I must test it but I don't know how."

It was because he was so cruel that he didn't know what to do. This stone is really magic but he could do nothing because he was very cruel. About ten years went by and he was unable to obtain anything because he did not know how to use the ring. Time passed and he said:

"Eh! I am going to call the children since I don't know what to do with this precious stone."

But that night, he had a dream.

"You, Mamu! You are really cruel to your adopted children. This ring that was given to you would serve you if you would listen to your desires and follow your cravings. Even if someone bought it for a million, it would not be enough for you. What do you really want?"

"I don't know what I want. What do I want? I want a house."

He suddenly had a desire for a house.

"If you want a house, nothing is easier. You only have to take seven pieces of paper[66] and rub them on the stone of the ring."

He woke up the next day. He woke up and rubbed like he had been told to do. He took seven pieces of paper and rubbed them on the ring. And seventy million appeared!

"It was true then," he said.

He really believed in this stone of the ring since he now had seventy million. He called to the labourers to build a house and each one started to work. If there was not enough money, he only had to rub the ring again. This precious stone really made magic with no matter what. The house was finally finished and it was prettier than that of a king.

But let's go back to the children now. The younger child was six[67] years old and he wanted to ask Mother Crocodile something. He was old enough now to go and visit other countries[68] and speak to men. His sister was fifteen years old.

"Elder sister!"

"What is it, younger one?"

"We must ask grandmother something since we now have to go out into the world. We must go and see the countries of men."

In effect, until now, they had been staying in the crocodile's cave and weren't able to know about anything.

"Alright, younger one. If you think that we must really go and see the countries of men, alright then. But why? You don't even know yourself."

"Because we will have friends and we can find out who we both are. We can't know ourselves all alone. The others will reveal this to us."

"Come out of there, grandmother. We want to ask you something today. We want to say something to you."

The crocodile came out and said:

"What do you want to tell me?"

"We want to ask your permission to go and visit the world. Is this possible, grandmother?"

"It is possible, young girl. But wait a little because the way you think is not mature enough yet. If you go out, there will be suffering and bad things will happen. You mustn't have any bad encounters. In order to avoid this, you have to go and see Mother Tiger."

"That's no problem."

"You must think very well about all this. Younger one, you have to help your sister and teach her perfectly well about everything."

"Why then?"

"Because your sister is not a magician."

So they went on to the land and soon found Mother Tiger.

"Eh! Why are you sitting down and thinking, you two young people? Why are you sitting and crying?"

"It's nothing. We are crying because we want to go and discover the world and we don't know how to do it."

"Oh! Is that the problem? You mustn't talk so much, little sister, since it is the younger brother who is responsible for you, elder sister."

"One can see that you don't have a younger one to look after."

"But this is how things are and if you want to leave, it is possible. I am going to give you something that will makes this possible."

"What do you want to give us, Mother Tiger?" the younger one said.

"I am going to tell White Mother Mare to come and take you since you certainly cannot make the voyage on foot. There are too many dangers."

The Mother Tiger called and the White Mare appeared and asked:

"Mother Tiger, why have you called me by waving your hand like this?"

"Can you take care of these two young people and watch over them? See to it that nothing bad happens to them. If anything bad happens to them, you will die."

"That's no problem. I will put them under my protection and life will be guaranteed for them."

When they had stopped talking, the mare told the young people to jump on to her back.

"Climb on, young people," she ordered them.

They climbed on to her back and the mare ran off with a leap. She ran for days and nights, nights and days. Seven days and seven nights passed. They finally reached the place where the mare was to take them and in this place she was no longer held to her promise.

"Come down, youngsters. I still have something to tell you. You are going to travel over these mountains but pay attention, after the second mountain, you will be in danger.

"What kind of danger?"

"Someone is going to capture your elder sister and take her for his wife."

In fact, when they had gone over the mountains, some men came and jumped on them and captured the elder sister. The younger one fought with great vigour but had no success and he ran away to the ogres. But he didn't know how to get there. When he arrived, he leaned against a tree[69] and had an idea. He said:

"I am going to call Mother Tiger and tell her to come."

So he called and the Mother Tiger arrived.

"Eh! Why then are you crying?"

"My sister was just captured."

"Where do the people come from who captured her?"

"I don't know where they came from."

"What is their name?"

"I don't know."

He couldn't answer anything. The Mother Tiger kept on asking, again and again, but she had no answer. No one knew them. She finally found herself in a village and Mother Tiger roared and bit everybody there. She finally reached the king who said to her:

"Hey! Why have you come here to my country, Mother Tiger? And why are you roaring like that?"

"I am roaring in your country because I am looking for a young girl that someone has taken in order to make her his wife. And if you do not give me back my young girl, I will break all those responsible into little bits. I will keep roaring and devouring all the chickens, ducks, cows and sheep."

"Hey! It is all the same to me. I am not afraid. I have many subjects, millions of them and none of them will send your girl back to you."

"Who then captured her?"

"It was my son. He has taken her for his wife. Will you permit this?"

"I am not able to say anything, you must ask the younger one. If he accepts, then I will say nothing."

Then the king asked the young brother to come and they spoke and kept speaking together. The younger one refused to authorize the capture of his sister. He was now 13 years old and said:

"I cannot authorize such an action. We are relatives[70] in Islam and each one of us is able to speak and to think. People must not fight each other, quarrel or get angry. Listen carefully to my words. Open wide your ears. What you have done is not good."

The younger one spoke to the king like this. And the king could say nothing and remained silent. He then called for his son:

"Do you know the elder sister of this young man?"

"I know her."

Then the king told him to leave and "ung!" the elder sister appeared. The brother and sister embraced each other and cried together for a long time. Tears fell and covered the ground. The younger one said:

"You must not cry since I have come back to help you. Don't cry any more."

"And what are you going to do?" said the king.

"I want my sister to go back with me."

"Very well! But does your sister want to leave? She is pregnant."

They spoke for a long time together and the younger one was given a kingdom by the king. He would be the only head of half of his lands and responsible for everything. As for his sister, she would become the queen of his son's country. This is what the king said. But he had two children, a boy and a girl so he proposed:

"Do you want to marry my daughter? Your sister will be with my son and you with my daughter."

The younger one answered:

"I don't want a wife."

This is what he said but the king's daughter fell madly in love with him the minute she saw him. She was unable to either eat or drink. The younger one left and the king's daughter went to the door of the palace. She stayed standing there for a long time, all alone, without even seeing the people who passed by and greeted her.

"Eh! People come by and greet her, but she doesn't even notice them. She doesn't want anything."

So the younger one called for his father. He called his sister's father-in-law father.

"Father, I am going to leave you now. You must consider me as your son but don't ask me to become your son-in-law."

The king answered:

"Where will you go?"

"I want to see other countries. Until now I only know one country and I would like to see other ones. Why? Because I don't know either my father or my mother."

He went on speaking and soon he became engaged to the king's daughter who said:

"Where are you going, older one?"

"This is how things are, younger one. It would be too long to tell you everything. I still have life before me and strength in my body and I want to discover other countries and meet other Muslims."

"And when will you come back?"

"I don't know. I don't know either when or how I will come back. I want to discover the world while I am still alive. Perhaps I will have to face some dangers. I really don't know."

"And is there no way in which you can let me know if everything is going well for you?"

"This is not difficult, younger one. If you really want to know what is going to happen, I will make you a promise. But I can't stay here too long now since I must leave by myself to discover the world. Why must I do this? If we marry and I die, you will have problems while for the moment there aren't any since we are only engaged."

"But how will I know what is happening to you?"

"Here is how, younger one. You must go and look for a tree[71] and plant it at the foot of the ladder. You will look after this tree; it is exactly like my heart."

"Only if it grows! But if it does not, you will have problems. Perhaps it will die."

"But no! It won't die. Even if you plant that tree upside down, it will grow."

"Alright then."

They did as they had decided to do. The younger one broke a branch of the tree and planted it at the foot of the ladder.

"And how will you know what is happening with the tree? I will have a small problem if one of its leaves dries. If the branch dries then I will have problems in one of the countries and if the tree becomes completely dry, I will have problems in three countries. This is how it will be, younger one."

"Alright then. And what will you take with you?"

"I don't need anything."

His sister came running up to him.

"When are you leaving?"

"I will leave during the day."

He exchanged some words with his sister and then left. He walked for a long time, entered a forest and then left it to continue on the plains. He went to the forest again and came out on to the plains until he met White Mother Elephant. This female elephant with nine tusks exists in the shadow[-puppet] theatre.

"Eh! Why have you come alone into this country, grandchild? What is your problem? What are your parents' names?" asked the elephant, who could speak.

"Hey! But you can't fight, grandmother; it would not be right. I have not come to make any trouble nor to shout at you, grandmother. But I want to ask you something. I would like to take hold of your tusks, grandmother."

"Go ahead. If you want to touch them with your fingers, then do so." So he reached out with his hand and caught hold of the nine tusks. The elephant immediately started to urinate and tremble all over, including her tendons and bones.

"Eh, grandchild! Why do I start trembling when you take hold of my tusk? I am trembling all over. I cannot confront you. Why is this?"

The elephant didn't know that he was a magician.

"There is a reason why. I have wanted to touch the elephant's tusks for a long time now."

"What do you want, grandson? And where do you want to go?"

"I don't want anything at all. I only want to discover the world."

He continued on his way and walked for a very very long time towards a place where there was a garuda who said:

"Unless I am wrong, I smell a human odour. Why have you come here, young man?"

This garuda had a daughter who was very beautiful and he was the king of this country, the country of the garudas.

"Hey! I never saw a such thing before! Since I was very little, even a fly has never passed in front of me. And now here is a man who is walking under my eyes. No one can come here."

He didn't open his mouth or stick out his claws but he was thinking. During that time, a girl appeared; she came out of his hair.[72] She came out of his hair: she came out of the hair of the garuda and was really of an incomparable beauty. She was much more beautiful than the king's daughter, the one he was engaged to.[73]

"Eh! Father!" said the girl to the garuda. "Go away. This is none of your business. This concerns me."

So, the garuda started running and flew away. Forty of his hairs fell down.

"Eh, grandchild! Speak to this man and take him for your husband. Why? My hair has never fallen down since I was born; I have just lost 70 of them. You must absolutely deceive this young man."

He then left. He did this just as all people do when they don't want to hear something.

"Hey! Where do you come from, older one?"

"I come from behind."

"Where are you going?"

"I'm going ahead."

"Why then have you come to my country?"

"For no particular reason."

"Then why are you here?"

"For no reason. I simply want to travel over the world and meet other people."

"Maybe you are looking for a wife?"

"No, I don't want a wife."

"Well then! Even if you don't want one, you must nevertheless take one: myself."

"But no! We are too different and I cannot marry you because I am a poor man, one who is thrown into the river like rubbish so that he will be killed."

"You don't have to tell me all that; I already know all about it. Don't tell me anything since I really already know everything about you. You came with one of your sisters who found a husband over there. Her husband is the king's son, who moreover has another girl who is your fiancée. Why then have you come?"

"For no particular reason. It is true what I am going to tell you: I have come to discover the world and I don't think of anything else. In effect, I have never known human beings since I was small and now I want to see some other countries. But I am not at all looking for a wife."

"But this is the way things are, my older one; you are obliged to take me and even if you refuse ten times, I will continue to want to marry you."

"Well, if that's the way things are, then I can only welcome you with open arms. But I want something in exchange. I want seven flowers with seven different colours. If you are able to get them for me, then I will marry you."

"Here you have your seven flowers of seven different colours. Take them. If you want forty, I will find forty for you."

The garuda child then carried out an act of magic and the seven flowers appeared, in seven different colours. She gave them to him.

"Eh! What does a flower correspond to, younger one? And to what do the colours correspond? What are their names?"

"It is like this, older one: you will carry these seven flowers and you will discover seven countries, each one, thanks to a colour: yellow, white, red, black, grey . . . You will take the one with the grey colour and when you go out to sea, you won't have any more worries if you carry this grey flower out to sea. When, then, are we going to get married?"

"Don't worry about the steps it will be necessary to take for the marriage.[74] But there is still a problem since I want to leave. I still desire to travel and I still haven't seen all the countries, nor the place where there is no longer a king."

"But are you going to take me or not?"

"I will take you when I return."

"I would like to have a way of knowing when you are in any difficulty. How will I know?"

"Don't worry about this. I will give you a way of knowing."

He then took the tree and did the same thing he had already done before. He stuck it in the ground and "perèt!" He then declared:

"When a leaf falls, this means that I have reached a different country and when there is any problem, a branch will become dry. And when I have a really big problem, it will be like over there, the tree will dry up completely. I am going to go now."

"You must meet my father before you leave. You must talk to him for a little while."

The child called her father and the garuda arrived.

"Eh, father! Come here and see. My older one is going to leave us."

The garuda then jumped and came in and asked:

"What did you say, little girl? Does he want you or not?"

"He will take[75] me when he returns."

"And what kind of engagement[76] has he made with you?"

"I took seven flowers of seven different colours as a witness[77] and gave them to him."

"That's fine then; it's a good promise and so now you are engaged to be married. With these exchanges,[78] you are married."

He had already taken a test[79] before becoming engaged and offered the price of the fiancée. He had first of all followed the religious rules very well. He left the girl and continued his travels. He was on the road for a very long time. He walked and walked and walked by following a colour. Which one? The yellow colour. And where did he arrive? He arrived at the navel of the world.[80] He found the country to be very strange since there was no one there. There was a country but no subjects. He asked himself what kind of country this was. He visited all the villages and went everywhere. A king had nonetheless existed but everything had been devoured by the ogre.[81] He said:

"Eh! Is there still anyone in this country? If yes, come out or show yourself."

He spoke like this three times but not one person had the courage to show himself. Only the king was able to do this.

"Hooo! I am afraid of the old ogress."

The young man went into a small mosque.[82] He went up to the small mosque and hit the drum.

"Eh! Don't hit the drum or you will make the ogress come."

She arrives without any warning.

"What does she look like, the old ogress?"

"Eh! She is fat. She is seven *gah*[83] high and seven *lèdè*[84] fat."

"I don't know what these measures *gah* and *lègè* are. I know nothing about the *lèdè*. What is she like? Let her come and then I will see her."

"If you want to see her, you must simply strike the drum three times."

"Dung! Dung! Dung!" He struck it three times and it became darker little by little, because the female arrived. She was truly very cruel but was not able to either think or speak.

"Hey! Why are you striking the drum, young man? Don't you know that I cut off the heads of all the inhabitants and killed them without exception?"[85]

"And why did you do this?"[86]

"This is not a bad action; I simply want to become the king here."

"Haa! But this is not possible. This was possible before I arrived but now, it is I who want to become the new king."

**Fig. 35.** Beating the drum calls the fighting garudas.

The female garuda[87] then called her male who arrived immediately. He didn't even take the time to speak but rushed at the young man in order to devour him. The young man stuffed the flower in his mouth and the garuda vomited; all his hair, his mouth, his feet and his nose, as well as his entire body, were oozing blood. He collapsed. He had lost.

"Eh, solitary young man! What do you want in this world and in the other one? I will never again act as I just did. What kind of magic does this flower have?[88] It entered my body very strongly and touched me from the feet to the hands. Why then have you come?"

"For no particular reason. I left to discover humanity so that I would have some companions, some friends."

He moved away then and after a moment made a promise.

"How then is all this possible? You are really the most powerful, the strongest[89] in the villages of men."

"I am not the most powerful and I have not come here to show my force but simply to discover the country and find some companions since we all come from the same country and are all issued from the same blood and matter. Don't we all come from Adam and Eve?"

Haa! When he heard that, the garuda remained speechless. To have spoken of Adam and Eve caused him to remain silent. The other garuda then said:

"Alright then, companion. You can go and take seven arms[90] and then kill us. It is not worthwhile for us to remain here."

"I am still going to speak of this common blood and matter."

The king of the garudas wanted the young man to kill him. But the young man did not have the heart to do such a thing. He said:

"Alright then, grandfather, go somewhere else then. Go away! I want to work alone here."

He worked here and was still working when the king came out of the drum where he had taken refuge.

"Eh! It is very well that you came here. As for myself, I didn't want to leave and hid in the drum."

"Haa! But this has no importance, lord.[91] There will still be life and I will help you until I am totally exhausted," said the young man.

"But my friend, don't you want to be the head of the country? Don't you want to become the king?"

"No, I don't want to. I don't want to be the king here. I am not made for this since I am still young. I don't know how to think very well and it is not for me. And, moreover, lord, you are the king here."

"But we must go and find subjects. We must fill the country with them."

The king then started to think.

"And where will you find these subjects? Where we will find them, companions? And you want to fill my country with them!"

"It is not difficult though. We only have to find a woman. You will have children who will have grandchildren and they will have great grandchildren. In this way, the country will be full of people."

But there was no woman.

"Where will you go, companion?"

"Eh, companions! I still have six flowers to follow and so, I still have six countries to discover."

"Eh! It is fine to be able to travel like this. It is good that people travel."

"I do what has to be done. I am alone and I do what has to be done. But I still have to continue on my way until I reach the six other countries. So I must leave now."

So he followed the yellow flower and found himself in the country of the yellow flower.[92] One cannot speak of the people of this country. They never stopped climbing up and down the ladders since there was no longer enough space and all the houses touched each other.[93] This was the way it was in the country of the yellow flower, the country of ceremonies. Moreover, today's ceremonies come from there. The people have followed the example of this country. All the ceremonies existed there, but those who took part in them had to have a really very strong relationship with the ceremonies.[94] It was the yellow flower that had brought him here. And it is because he found himself in this place of the Teri[95] ceremony that the traditional healers of today have to speak of the flowers, as in the shadow[-puppet] theatre also. He entered the country; the inhabitants were all gathered in the centre of the village and they were amusing themselves. Loud noises[96] were heard and cries of surprise and encouragement. He went in and said:

"Hey! What then is this country? Why are you so happy, companions? I want to know what is happening.[97] Why are you amusing yourselves like that?"

The king said:

"Where do you come from? Who are you that you disturb us with words?"

"I have no country."

"Where do your parents come from then?"

"I don't have any parents."

"Ha! Why then did you come here?"

"There is no reason. I am going to discover foreign countries."

The king then became angry because he only wanted to amuse himself.

"Hoo! Don't be angry."

"And why not since I can no longer do what I like to do?"

"Hey! You my children, all my companions and all my coolies, all my subjects, go and kill this young man."

They arrived, one hundred and forty people, with sabres. They came one by one and soon raised their weapons in order to kill the young man. The young man took out his green flower and said:

"Hey, don't kill me yet. I first want to ask you something."

"What do you want?"

"I first want [you] to smell this flower."

"Haa! The people of this country like to smell flowers. That's nice."

They came and all of them smelled the flower. Then they fainted. The only one who remained was the king.

"Hey! Why has everybody fainted? What kind of flower is this?"

"This is how it is, father. I can't tell you anything. I cannot speak of these flowers that I gathered along the road. I didn't want them but my hands moved by themselves and picked them up."

"Hey! That's strange, young man."

The king's daughter then appeared. She was covered with gold from her neck to her navel. Then she saw the young man.

"Hey, father! Where does this young man come from? I find him very attractive, father."

"Hey! You can't have him. We don't even know where he comes from."

"So what! I will accept him, no matter where he comes from. Where do you come from, older one?"

"I come from behind."

"And where are you going?"

"I am going ahead."

"Why do you speak like this, older one? You come from behind and are going ahead!"

"I can't say since I don't know my country, nor my village. I have no companions."

"Hey! I really love you very much, older one. Will you accept me?"

"I don't want a wife."

"But I want you and no matter what you say, I will follow you, even if you beat me, kick me with your feet, hit me. I would still want you."

"If that is so, younger one, you must wait until I return for us to marry."

"Where are you going?"

"I cannot tell you but since I still have five flowers, I still have five countries to visit."

"What flowers are you talking about, older one? I would like to see them."

"Haa! You can see them."

She then wanted to take hold of the flowers but they flew away. The girl who had given the flowers knew what was happening and called the flowers that the other girl wanted to take. She didn't want anyone else to touch them. And from then on, this is how it is for those who have two wives who are continually quarrelling because of their unfaithful husband. Hoo! He could be sure that he would have descendants since he has two wives.[98] One can have descendants and two wives who quarrel with each other. This [story] comes from those times.

"Eh, younger one!"

"I want to know, older one, but your flowers avoid me, they jump and curl up as if it was night-time."

So, there was a problem and the tree felt it. One of its leaves dried up since this was the signal that had been decided on. A leaf fell. Then she said:

"I am going to give something in exchange, older one."

"And what are you going to give me, younger one?"

"I am going to give you this. It is a magic ring."

She took the ring off her finger and offered it to him.

"What's so special about this ring? How does one use it?"

"My ring, older one, listens to the desires of the one who wears it. Why is it so? Because you have seven flowers, seven different flowers. And my ring will respect your wishes. Give me your hand. I am going to put the ring on it."

He put out his hand and she put the ring on his finger. Now she could call him her fiancé. Haa!

"When are you going to leave?"

"I am going to leave today."

"Eh, father! He wants to leave today."

"Haa! But you run the risk of dying if you go into other villages. I won't let you leave."

"You can't prevent him from leaving. Even if you try ten times, you won't be able to prevent him from leaving."

"Haa! What a nice son-in-law!"

"That's the way things are, father. But it's very easy to die. And why? Because we have life in ourselves and when the Lord wants to take us away, well then, we will die on that very day."

"Hey! You are cunning, young man. Go then! I won't retain you any longer."

So he left and walked for a very long time, until he reached the third country where he met another girl who said:

"Hey! Where do you come from?"

"From behind."

"And where are you going?"

"I am going ahead."

"Come up to my place."

"But I am not of this sort. I will remain in the puddle of waste water and we will speak together."

"Don't talk like this, older one! I am aware that you don't speak well but that's no reason for you to be so rude. You now have women everywhere, older one, but I still want to talk to you. You seem to be very tired. If you don't accept me for your wife I will no longer be able to live."

She was the king's daughter so he took her for his wife. This was the third wife. He continued his travels and walked for a long time again. We are going to tell the story more quickly now since I am beginning to have a pain in my jaws. He walked until he reached the country where the people emptied the sea.[99] They had been doing this for seven years, seven months, seven days. But they couldn't dry it up completely and there were still fish on the surface. It was far from being dry. He came near the men who were emptying the water and said:

"Hey! Why then are you all gathered around the sea? Hey! Stop, my friends."

"Haa!" The king answered. "Don't stop and don't speak to this young man. He is going to deceive us because if we stop emptying the water, it will come back. Where do you come from?"

"I cannot tell you where I come from. I don't know what country I come from. The lower part of the back of my mother gave birth to me. But since I was three years old, I don't know anything about my life. For how long have you been emptying the sea water, lord?"

"For seven years, seven months and seven days we have been trying to empty the sea but there are still fish swimming on this surface."

"I understand, lord, but let me help you. I will only ask you for one thing and I will empty the sea by myself."

"But you will not be able to do that."

"If I don't succeed you can kill me, if not I will ask for something. When we are able to see a big fish, I will take his head."

"Haa! Alright then, this will be your reward."

So, he went into the water of the sea and dipped his ring two times into it . . . and the sea water dried. The fish were wriggling on the sand. Then he said:

"Hey! Do you have a big knife here?"

"Hey! Why wouldn't there be one? Of course we have one. We have many of them."

"Hey! It won't be enough to cut off the head of the fish, lord. I want a knife that is equivalent to yourself."

"Ha! But that is difficult."

"It doesn't matter."

So, the king took out his knife which was as wide as two fingers and as long as two fingers. The young man then went to cut off the head of the fish. He sawed it and "pah"! it broke. Then he brought it on to the ground and the king turned it over with his foot and tried to raise it, but without success. The young man said:

"Hey! Who among all of you is able to raise the head of this fish? I will give him anything he wants."

He possessed the magic ring. The men tried, one after the other, to raise the head but without success. The king then declared that he would give all his land to the one who was able to raise the head of the fish.

"Hey, young man! If you are not able to raise the head of this fish we will no longer be able to remain here. It really smells very bad. But if you are successful, I will give you half of my kingdom. I want you to become the king here."

"Is that true, lord?"

"Yes, it is true."

The king gathered his subjects together.

"Hey! Come here all of you, my million subjects. You must welcome the young man who is going to raise the head of this fish."

And for what reason? Because a promise had been made. Everyone greeted him and he took hold of the head of the fish and threw it. In exchange, he received the letter that gave him the territory that was promised to him.

"Hey, lord! Can you look after my territory for a while?"

"Why?"

"I still have to go to four[100] more countries."

He went on his way and walked for a long time, not one or two days but for entire years before he reached a country. He arrived among a population. Who was the king? Was it King Muso[101]? I am not sure. This king's land smelled very bad because of the head of the fish and the people were unable to remain in their houses. But no one knew what kind of animal it was that smelled so bad.

"We can no longer live here. We can neither eat nor drink nor swallow anything. We will die here if this continues."

They went to look for what it was that smelled so bad and finally found the head of the fish. Only half of the head remained since the rest had been eaten. For six months, then six years they tried to cover it with earth.[102]

"Eh! What are we going to do if we are not able to cover the head of this fish, even though there are so many of us?"

At this moment, the young man arrived and saw the men digging the earth.

"Hey! What are you doing?"

"We don't know why, but half a fish head has come to our country and since then everything has gone wrong. We can neither eat nor drink because of the bad smell."

"Ah! Well then!"

"The one who is able to cover the head of this fish with the earth will be given my daughter to marry and half of my country. And this without having to pay anything in return."

"Let me try."

"Hey! But you won't be able to do it."

The king called his subjects and told them to try. They did but without any success.

"Let me try. Is it true that you will give me part of your land, lord?"

"Yes, it's true."

"Well then, you are committed to your word."

It is like we do now but we don't have any papers and contracts.[103] He caught hold of the head of the fish and threw it. Everyone was then very happy and the king called to his subjects and told them to play before the young man so as to thank him. He became king of the lands and was crowned. When everything had ended, the king asked:

"Where do you come from?"

"I can't say but I must leave now because I still have three[104] countries to visit."

He went off on the road and walked for a long time until he met a king who said:

"Eh! Who are you? Where do you come from, young man?"

This young king was his older brother. He did not know him because his father had taken him away when his parents divorced. They met and it was not long before they began to quarrel.

"Where do you come from?"

He spoke in a loud voice.[105]

"I come from behind."

"Haaa! And where are you going?"

"I am going ahead."

"Eh! You really don't speak well, young man. You are being spiteful.[106] You didn't come here to take a walk. You came to cause me problems with your words."[107]

They quarrelled like this for a long time. They took turns to respond. The stone of the ring suddenly fell out and the two brothers rushed over to take hold of it. They began fighting with their hands and feet and almost broke their legs to obtain it. But it was the younger one who recovered the ring. He put it into the pocket of his shirt.

"You should not take the ring. It belongs to me," said the king.

"If you are talking about your belongings, you can have them. I will not take them."

He threw the ring on to the ground and didn't pick it up. So the king then called to his subjects:

"Who is going to pick up this ring? The one who brings it to me will become a king."

But no one was able to pick it up.

"Take your ring. I don't want it any more," said the king.

So, he picked up the ring and put it in his pocket. Then he said:

"Where do you come from? Answer me frankly, companion."

"Even if I wanted to tell you the truth, I could not. And why can't I? For this reason: my mother abandoned me and this story began when I was three years old. I was thrown into the river and since then I have been travelling to discover different countries, so I could have companions."

After he had said all this, the young king started crying. He bent down on his knees and made a salutation to him, with his hands joined over his head. Finally, he said:

"Pardon me, younger one. I am really your older brother and not your half-brother on your father's side. I come from the same mother as yourself.[108] If you want to, you can ask mother. Don't you have an older sister?"

They spoke together for a long time and told each other everything.

"That's how it was, younger one."

The older one had become a king here since he was different from the others.

"That's how it was, older one. But as for myself, I am not a king. I cannot be equal to you since you are the king. But I don't want any quarrels between brothers."

"It is good that you speak like this. But where will you go now?"

"I still have to discover two countries."

So, he went to the country of Soh Progi. There were only women there and they were all beautiful. Everyone was beautiful in this country. All the women were crazy about him because his features had changed when he arrived in this country and he was more handsome than anyone else. Everyone came to see him and cried and implored him. They came from everywhere and surrounded him and took hold of his feet and tore apart his shirt. Then three girls came and the queen of Soh Progi said:

"Be careful of these girls. Go away from them. Which one are you going to choose?"

"But I don't want any of them. I didn't come here looking for a woman but I came to find friends and companions. I only want to discover the country."

"It's not possible. You must choose one of the girls and if you don't you will be responsible for many problems."[109]

"Very well then. I will take one of them and do everything I must do. But I have something to say. I cannot marry now since I still have to go to another country."

He spoke for some time with the three girls and the queen and then went off. He walked for a long time and finally reached the country Pereda' Mudo.

There was much fighting in this country and it was in this very place that the ring lost its magic powers. His ring lost its magic because he had had everything he wanted, four women.[110] He had visited the seven[111] countries and the last one was Pereda' Mudo.

"Eh! Solitary human being, young man. Can you explain why you have come here?"

The one who had just spoken called Hanuman,[112] the white monkey. He called Hanuman, the white monkey, to kill the young man. But it is a delicate task to wake up the white monkey and once he is awake one must run off in all haste. He arrived and "kèng!", he hit him with a stick and struck his feet and hands with his fists. They fought together and the battle lasted for some time like this. The young man fell down and like him a tree fell down, in fact three trees fell down. The entire trunk of the tree, up to the top, broke and fell down.

"Hey!" he said.

Since it was the first woman who had pity on him, she said:

"He is in danger, father. The older one is in danger. He made the signal we had decided upon together."

"Eh! But who is in danger? In what country? We don't know anything."

So, she thought about this since she knew as well as her husband what was happening. Then the third wife said:

"Hey, mother!"

The queen answered:

"Does your husband have a problem then? What are we going to do?"

"I don't know, lord. What can one do?"

"All of you, go over there. Clear the road because I am going to call an animal," said the third wife.

All the subjects cleared the road and she called an animal.

"Who then knows this young man, the one who was three years old? He is my grandchild."

The girl said:

"Who can give us some information then? In what far distant place is he?"

The garuda answered:

"Someone must go and find him. He must go to the country of the Jangi[113] tree. There is a crossroad there. The people are fighting and trying to capture the young man."

They then went off together and went towards a house where there were many subjects who were coming out to meet them and follow them. The garuda said:

"Eh, father! I am going to fly and look for your son-in-law. He has fainted on the beach. But where? I am going to look for him."

He flew away and soared for many days and nights. He went straight towards the young man since it was his ring that was leading him.

"Eh! Perhaps he is over there."

He went down, "gerraaak!" He descended but was hit by an arrow before he reached the ground. It was Hanuman with his bow. The father of the garuda waited for a long time for his return. He thought that maybe he was dead.

"Eh! And how will we be able to look for him?"

He searched for a solution. He wanted to go to the country of the Jangi tree. He would have gone there if he hadn't had a family. He wanted to know. But let's go back to the queen. The three girls went off and walked for a long time. They finally encountered the older brother.

"What then is this country?" he asked.

"We don't remember."

"How did you come here?"

"Like this: we have just resolved a very serious problem, a big one like a mountain, big like a hill and bigger than our heart."

"What is the matter?"

"We came here to find a member of our family, an older one or one who is younger. We are looking for a young man but we don't know what has happened to him. We don't even know what country he is in."

The older one thought and said to himself:

"Eh! But they are speaking about my brother."

He said to the girls:

"If you want to know where he died, go and ask the young king and he will make a promise for you. Why then? Because he comes from the same mother as the one you are looking for."

They went to find the king who said:

"Eh! Where do you come from?"

"I have come to look for someone close to me."[114]

"He is the one who was raised by a crocodile."

"That's my young brother. Oh! He is my brother and he has many problems in this country of the navel of the world, the country of the Jangi tree."

"He wants to go and look for him."

"Don't bother. I myself will go."

He left and walked and walked and continued walking and said.

"With the head I have I will surely be killed. I am going to make myself become older."

His body became bent like those of old people.[115] He continued walking and met White Horse.

"Where are you going?"

"I am going to the navel of the world, to the country of the Jangi tree."

"And what will you look for there?"

"I simply want to take a walk."

"If this is what you want, old man, climb on my back and I will help you to travel through one or two countries."

"That is nice of you to want to help me like this."

He climbed on the back of the horse who started running and soon left two countries. Finally he descended.

"You can stop here. I will continue my route. But how does one go to the navel of the world, where the Jangi tree is?"

"It is not difficult," said White Horse. "You just have to call[116] the sharks."

So he called the sharks; the one who was forty years old and lived in the sea. But nothing is known about this. He went towards the river, towards the prince's country and called. Forty-eight sharks responded to his call. He climbed on to the back[117] of one of them who asked:

"Eh! Where are you going, old man?"

"I am going to the navel of the world where the Jangi tree is found."

"And what do you want to do there?"

"I want to see if the young man is dead."

"Eeeh!" said the shark. "He isn't dead. He has been attacked and suffers a great deal. He is very hot and has no protection from the rain."

The young king started to cry. He cried with all the tears of his body.

"Why are you crying, old man?"

"I am crying for my younger brother."

"Ho! So he is your brother!"

"Ho! He is my brother."

"You mustn't cry because he is not dead. You need to have some magical assistance. You must go and wash yourself seven times and your brother will become what he was before."

The fish gave him a small bezoar and climbed on to the shore. The old man climbed up too and saw the garuda take the magic stone, put some water in his hand, place the stone inside it and shake it. He rubbed the face of the garuda with his hand who suddenly got up and returned to life. He came back to life and flew away. The younger one said:

"Hey, old man! How did you get here?"

"Oh! It was easy. I came with White Horse."

"And how did you jump up here?"

"The sharks helped me. And one of them gave me a magic stone so that I could become transformed."

"Eh! And how will I be able to pay you back for what you did? You have really performed a good action but I don't know what to give you as I am poor."

The old man said:

"I don't want anything."

"How was it possible for you to come here without anything bad happening?"

"For a simple reason. I have only pity for others."

At that moment the sharks arrived looking for the old man.

"There is no longer any problem, old man. We will now go back, old man!" They went back and once they were on the ground, the girl said:

"Hey! Did you come back, older one, because you remembered me? You first have to take me."

"I don't want to."

The old man answered:

"But no! If the people want you, you must accept them. You must give in if only for one morning or one day, so that the marriage will take place. So they got married and when everything was over, they called the sharks who rose to the surface to take them away. They soon came to the shore. And there, one person then two came to welcome them. They got married again here. Then they went to see King Bujè[118] where the man got married once more. He asked pardon for everything and especially for his absence. The king of the country of Bujè said:

"This is how things are. You mustn't hide anything from me since I know everything. You are talking about your older brother, are you not?"

"Hey! No, it is not him."

"It is him."

"But no!"

"No? Then I am going to do something magic."

"It's not worth the trouble since I want to remain in the skin of this old man."

The young man's wives arrived in this country and said:

"You already have two wives, older one."

"Yes, it's true."

"You have many wives," said the third wife. "We must get married here."

They came to the young man's house, to the house of his stepfather who possessed a big and beautiful house.

"Ha! You hid from us the fact that you are rich. One only has to see your house that is much more beautiful than mine."

The stepfather noticed them:

"Who is it? Who has come here with four women?"

The mother answered:

"I don't know. I do not know him."

He went up into the house and said:

"I ask your pardon, inhabitants of this village. But I would like to ask you something. What is going on here? How have these lands been divided up? What country is this?"

"It is the country of the prince."

"Are my parents here?"

"Who then are your parents?"

"My parents? My mother's name is Esoh and my father, Mamu."

They immediately fainted when they heard what he said. The youngest one said:

"Why have they fainted?"

"Ha! They were once very cruel towards me."

"How?"

"I don't know," said the older brother. "But in any case, they are really your mother and stepfather. Whatever he did that was bad has now turned back against himself. He abandoned the younger one, aged three years, in the river and it was White Mother Crocodile who raised him."

"Ah! So this is what happened."

"And what are we going to do to the mother who has fainted?"

"Move away, older brother. I will take care of her with my four wives."

One of them caressed her face, the other her stomach, another one her backside and the last one, her feet. They massaged her all over and the mother finally became conscious again.

"Eh, mother! I am your son, your true son, the son that the stepfather threw into the water. Do you remember that time?"

"Oooh! I remember and I ask your pardon, a thousand times. But what was I supposes to do since my husband had taken such a decision? He is much stronger that I am and I could do nothing."

"What are we going to do now?"

"It is not difficult, older one; this is what we are going to do. We are going to deceive him and he won't be able to do anything."

"How are we going to deceive him?"

"That's no problem, older one. It's true isn't it that one must not be unfaithful? We are going to use this unfaithfulness against him."

The girls and the boys heard that and understood.

"Let's go and amuse ourselves."

They amused themselves for a long time. The stepfather and his son soon arrived.

"Eh! He really has a bad heart, your father. That is why he abandoned his child in the river, when he was three years old."

"We are going to kill him, older one. We want to kill him and this is the truth."

All the people of the village and even those in the surrounding villages came to see how the old man was going to do this. He was going to make an example. He wanted everyone to see and listen to the truth. "When I was three years old, I was abandoned in the river. How could you have done such a thing, father? You are really very cruel. Look how he has behaved with his own daughter-in-law that he doesn't even know. He has truly dishonoured my wives and doesn't recognize them. A man like this is an animal. What judgement[119] shall we pronounce for him? He doesn't even deserve the fate reserved for the Sakai."[120]

A long time ago, there were the Sakai. He killed him and the blood flowed into the forest and was transformed into Sakai. Another jet of blood transformed him into a monkey.[121] The blood that came out of his brain and fell on the top of a tree became another species of monkey.[122] This is why the monkeys who are issued from the blood of the brain are much more cunning. These transformations took place because this man had magic powers. And all this happened because the stepfather had acted badly. But there was still magic in his blood that transformed itself. This is how it is. How he was killed. He killed Mamu. Hooo! Yes, he killed Mamu.

### 3.4. The shellfish king[123]

***(Village of Samoh, Province of Narathiwat, September 1992***
***Narrator: Wo Seng***
***Type of Story: hikaya')***

Long ago, at the beginning of time, in the country of Senoh Paga Riyoh,[124] there lived a great king. Who were his servants? Sema and Turah.[125]

"Our king is truly the great king of the country. No one is as rich but, nevertheless, he has no wife."

One night the great king had a dream. He had a dream and when he woke up he said:

"I must find the woman who has two names," he said. "Her name is Dame Rotero and I don't know where she lives."

So he called his two faithful servants.

"You are the only ones who can go there."

"How will we able to make a search?"

"I don't want to know how, but go and search. If you don't leave I will kill both of you. Don't come back without her."

"Ah! You have no pity, lord. Where will we go to find her?"

The servants went off with heavy hearts. They walked for a long time and finally reached the Seven Gold Pagoda. The Buddhist monk Jeli was there. The two servants hid themselves. Jeli's aunt passed by. She was carrying some cakes on her head made of glutinous rice flour mixed with coconut.

She was going to give them to her chief; Jeli grabbed hold of one of the cakes as the aunt went by but he was caught, and attached to a tree near the well used for waste water.

"Ah! But I didn't do anything very serious. I just took one cake."

The two servants of the great king soon arrived and went to the well because they wanted to defecate.

"Ah! How are things done here?" said one of them. "How can one wash oneself?"

"Can we wash ourselves with the water of the pagoda?"

"Yes, of course you can. There is a well over there."

"Ah! Well then, we will defecate here and get some water from there."

This is what they did and only pulled up their pants when they arrived at the well, in front of Jeli.

"Come here," Jeli said. "Why are you washing your backsides on my head?"

"What is happening?" the servants asked. They were astonished.

"What? What is happening, you ask? You are cleaning your backsides over my head!"

"And why are you here?"

"I committed an error when I took one of my aunt's cakes. It was destined for the king. And now I have been condemned. Don't abandon me. Help me to untie myself from this tree."

"But if we do this, the king will be very angry."

"Let him be angry! I can't stay here in this cesspool."

"If we free you, will you help us?"

"In what way?"

"Ah! We are asking you whether or not you will help us. If you don't help us, we will not untie you."

"I will help you. I really will do so, even if I must die in doing so."

"Ah! Alright then."

And the servants untied him.

"Ah! Now tell me what you want."

"We want you to take us to Dame Rotero."

"Hula! That will be an enormous task. It will really be very difficult; but no one but myself can go to her place."

"That is why we are asking you to help us. It is your duty to do so. You promised us."

"Ah! Very well then, servants."

"We cannot return to our king or he will kill us."

"Don't be worried. Let's go."

He walked for a long time and finally arrived not far from the shore, after having gone through the forest.

"Ah! I am really exhausted. I am going to sleep here."

He fell asleep under a wild cotton tree. He was sleeping profoundly when a fruit spirit[126] spoke to him.

"Eh! Young man."

"What is it, young girl?"

"Where are you going, Jeli? You are all alone and you have only clothed yourself with a sarong which is tied around your waist."

"I can't speak here since the trees listen to us in the middle of the day."

"But there is no one here. Who will then be able to listen to us?"

"Young girl, I am looking for Dame Rotero who lives on the seashore. She lives in the belly of the naga, the lord of the sea, the navel of the sea, near the Jangi tree."

"And how to go there? Climb up!"

He was very hungry, so he took one of the leaves from the cotton tree and turned it over on his hand and crushed it. Then he spread all of it on his belly. He was no longer hungry!

"How can one go into the sea?"

He took another leaf of the kapok tree and crushed it, then he rubbed it on the soles of his feet. He was then able to walk on the sea water. The novice monk Jeli was a child of the divinities.[127] He soon woke up.

"People spoke while I was sleeping. They spoke a great deal."

"Ah! I really am very hungry."

So, he did what he had done in his dream. He crushed a leaf from the kapok tree and rubbed it on his belly, then belched. He was then no longer hungry.

"I am really full now. I will go now and take to the sea thanks to a leaf of the kapok tree."

He crushed one of the leaves and rubbed it on the soles of his feet. He was then able to sail for a very long time.

We are now going to speak about the Chinese king.

The Chinese king was also looking for Dame Rotero. He went in the direction of the navel of the world where the Jangi tree is. But he was in a boat. It was not long before the novice monk Jeli saw the boat. He raised his hand to attract his attention.

"Lower the ladder so I can climb up."

The Chinese king lowered the ladder.

"Where do you come from?"

"And you?"

"I am looking for Dame Rotero in the navel of the sea, where one finds the magical mango tree. And you?"

"I am also looking for her. Perhaps we can go there together."

**Fig. 36.** The seven headed naga.

"Alright then."

"You will go under the water with the rattan basket."

"Alright," said the novice monk Jeli.

"If you can do this, it would be good. Climb aboard."

The boat was not able to come closer to the spot as it would sink.

There was a whirlpool there, like a well. They tied the ropes to each other and Jeli went down in the basket. He went lower and lower, the novice monk Jeli. He went down in the basket. When he arrived, there was no more water left. He stood still for a time without moving.

"Well, here I am. I have come down into the country of the naga. But how will I be able to go ahead? I heard it said that if one takes the road to the right, the naga devours you even without asking any questions. But if one takes the road to the left, he will not eat you."

So, he took the road to the left.

"Oh! Where do you come from, Jeli?"

"I came here to find you."

"Oh! As for myself, I have been keeping a flower for you for a long time now."

"Ah! But I haven't come looking for a flower!"

"Then what do you want?"

"I came to get Dame Rotero."

"Who do you want to give her to? To the great king?"

"I don't want to give her to the great king. I will give her only to you. She is your flower. But I will never give her to the great king. That's the way things are."

"I will tell him that I want Dame Rotero for myself," he said to himself.

"Ah! Alright then, I will take her."

"Ah! Here is Dame Pako Biru.[128] She is coming out of my body."

It was really true; she lived in his belly and came out of it.[129]

"Go and take your beloved Dame Rotero."

The novice monk Jeli then went to take her. The naga had guarded her just for himself. He put her in the basket. Then he pulled on the rope three times, as they had agreed on. The Chinese king was up above and pulled the basket up and took it out of the navel of the world. Dame Rotero was soon on the bridge of the Chinese king's boat. He let down the basket once more and Jeli climbed up after having pulled on the rope three times. But the Chinese king cut the rope and Jeli was carried away by the current. He drifted towards the west, then towards the east. Many sharks, lobsters and crabs came to help him go to the shore where a swarm of birds were flying over him. They gave him some shade and stopped looking for food for the moment. Jeli had his head in the sand and his feet in the water.

But we are now going to speak of something else.

We are going to speak about the warrior, White Monkey, the one who lives alone on the Anero Biry hill.

"What is happening? I never before felt anything like this," said Jeli.

He took to the road and walked for a long time. He was tired but at the same time, he was attracted to the shore. He had taken the magic[130] stick with him and walked for a long time. Then he noticed the birds.

"What is happening? I will go and see. Ah! Where do you come from, Jeli?" It was one of his relatives.

"Where has he come from to be in such state?" the monkey asked himself.

He took his stick and pointed it towards Jeli who woke up.

"Ha! The Chinese king! The Chinese king!" he said.

"No, my younger one, it is me."

"Where are you, older one? The Chinese king played a trick on me. He took Dame Rotero away."

"Ah! You took a wife?"

**Fig. 37.** The fabulous animals of the sea protect men. (Ivanoff, 1989)

"But who are you?"

"I am your elder one, the warrior White Monkey."

"Then where is your tail?"

He took the tail and pulled at it in all directions.

"What are you doing? You are hurting me!"

"Go and look for Dame Rotero for me."

"Ah! Very well. This Chinese king! When I had gone on the sea and was half-way there, the king cut the rope and I was never able to reach the boat again. And the Chinese king left with his boat and took the woman with him."

"How can we find him again, elder one?"

"Take the magic stick."

He caught hold of the magic stick and sent it flying over the water in pursuit of the Chinese king, until it reached his country.

"Ha! There we are! But what will we do now?"

They fought against the Chinese king's men. There were many people in this country. They fought without stopping, one after another or all together, but they finally got very tired.

"This Chinese king really played a dirty trick on me."

He took the stick and threw the end[131] of it towards the men, who all fell down. Then he took the other end of the stick and turned towards them and they all got up again. The battle started once more. The men continued to flight with each other, without stopping and they soon got tired. The stick hit all the men. The operation was repeated three times and the Chinese king's men were exhausted. They finally had had enough.

"We can't bear your stick any longer, younger one."

"Well, in that case, tell me where the Chinese king has taken Dame Rotero."

"She is in the kingdom of Gano[132] with the seven doors. But pay attention since there are many guards there."

"It is all the same to me."

The battle started again. And the men fell down three times in succession and got up again. They finally gave up and Jeli was then able to go and fight with the Chinese king himself. The Chinese king fell down three times and raised himself three times before giving up.

"Take her. I don't want her."

This is how he was able to recover Dame Rotero. But there were other men who came to take away the women of this country. He helped the men to protect them and take them away. He only had to raise his stick and everyone found themselves on the ground.

The naga had warned him that if he wanted to return home, Dame Rotero would have to be transformed into a flower. This is what happened. He slid the flower[133] into the pocket of his shirt and flew away. He stopped when he came to the place of his elder, the monkey, who was praying at the base of the ladder.

"Ah! Jeli, you have found your woman again and you no longer need my stick."

Jeli went from house to house.

"Eh! Elder one, I, Jeli the novice monk, want to go home."

"And where do you live, younger one?"

"I don't know. They say that it is in a house near the hill."

"Come with me, younger one. We will go and look for it."

She soon became pregnant but not from the king who had gone to look for her. It was no doubt Jeli who had made her pregnant. He was alone and took out the flower since he was bored. But his elder one soon come looking for him.

"You broke your promise."

"But I couldn't help it, venerable one."[134]

"But you got her?"

"Yes."

"Where is she?"

"She is here."

"You lied. You should have given her to the king. Leave her with me and I will take her to the king."

"I couldn't help it. That's the way things are. Alright then, take her." And Jeli rose up to the sky.[135] He went up until he reached the place where the divinities live. He went there with his magic stick but he soon returned because he wanted to see the king.

"Well then, servants?"

"Here we are," they said.

"Eh! You tricked me, servants. I don't want a flower to keep me company but a woman, Dame Rotero."

"But it is she, lord."

"Ah! You are laughing at me."

The king became very angry and the servants ran away.

"Ha! Younger one."

"What?"

"Take the woman. Go and see the king and tell him that she is your wife."

"I agree, but why should I do this?"

"We are going to lie and tell him that she is your wife."

Turah then brought Rotero.

"And where does she come from, servant?"

"She is my wife. She is my[136] wife."

"Give her to me."

They both began to quarrel and the two servants arrived.

"This woman is Dame Rotero, the one you asked us for."

And the king married her. She was pregnant three months later but her big belly was really the fruit of her adventures with Jeli. Hahaha! She was pregnant and someone called the fortune teller who came from the same family as the servants. He was the fortune teller[137] Seven. He came to see if the Dame was carrying a son or a daughter. The fortune teller made an invocation and declared that it was a boy and that he would bring all of them good fortune. Yes, he would really have good luck and the country would be able to go beyond its frontiers.

"And what will he mount later on, our son?"

"On a white elephant.[138] A white elephant with black tusks."

Then the king went to hunt for the elephant in the depths of the forest. The woman was pregnant and remained in the house. She had been pregnant now for seven months. She stayed in the house and her husband had gone into the deep forest to hunt. He drove the game into the traps and captured a white elephant with black tusks. Then the king had a dream. He dreamed that the elephant had got free and that his dagger had broken into two.

"The king's wife is going to give birth," said one of the servants.

"The elephant has run away. He has gone," said another servant.

The king then understood that his wife was going to give birth and asked his servants to go to the market and buy everything necessary: bananas, cane sugar, sticky rice flour and cakes. They came back with full sacks and the wife gave birth to a shellfish. The king's wife gave birth to a shellfish and someone took some cloth to tie it with. He used many pieces of cloth.

"Ah! Why then is our son a shellfish?"

"It is too soon to know."

They quarrelled and ripped the cloths with their hands. One of the servants gave them to the king who opened one cloth after another. He discovered a shell in the form of a spiral and threw it away. But a servant caught it since it was the queen's son. The king chased her away and hit her forty times. She took a container made of broken clay and ran away. She put her son inside the container made of clay.

"The father of my wife must have been a shellfish," the king said.

The wife cried and refused to see anyone. She took the container with the shellfish inside and went off. Where did she go? She went to the wise[139] old man's house, whose name was Jenèng.[140] He was a man that the king had once chased away from his land.

"Where are you going, young Dame?"

"I don't know. I don't have any family."

"You can stay in this house but there is not always something to eat here."

"It is not important, old man. I will look for some firewood that I can sell in order to get some rice."

"Ah! Yes, that's a good idea."

"But you will help me and watch the level of the water in the container made of clay."

"Ah! Don't be worried. I will take care of this."

So she went to look for some firewood and sold it for some rice. Then she went back to the house.

"Have you eaten, old man. Did you cook the rice?"

"Yes, it is cooked."

"Did you eat?"

"No, not yet."

"Then why is there only half left?"

Half of the rice had disappeared.

"Liar," she said.

"What to you mean, liar?"

"You said that you had eaten nothing but half the rice is missing."

"No, young girl! I didn't eat anything."

"Haa? And where is the fried fish? Did you eat some of it?"

"It was ready. But someone had eaten it."

"Ah! It is just like the rice. Are you sure that you ate nothing, old man?"

"I am sure."

Then he raised his voice to the one who had eaten their food.

"May the person who ate our food be devoured by the tigers!"

The shellfish, who was in the container, became very agitated. He was crying.

"Why does my mother speak to me in this way?"

"Ah! I didn't know. Forgive me."

"There is nothing else to eat in this country."

"Yes, it's true."

The mother then went away and was no longer seen. The old man remained with the child.

"Old man, old man, I would very much like to play."

"Go ahead, but be quiet."

The old man had left a piece of rattan trailing on the ground. He was unable to make a rope with it.

"Don't you know how to make a rope, old man?"

"Why? Do you know how to do it?"

"Of course. Give me a knife."

He took a knife,[141] crushed the rattan and hit it with the knife. Ah, yes! He knew what to do.

"Stay here and amuse yourself. Don't worry about the Dame who abandoned her child. I don't know where she went."

"But I am a good boy, old man."

"That's fine, that's fine."

"But what will we do if you get hungry?"

"There is not a grain of rice in the house."

**Fig. 38.** Jars containing local brine. (Ivanoff, 1989)

"Old man, I am hungry."

"But there isn't a grain of the rice left!"

"Of course there is!"

"Where?"

"In the container for rice,[142] up there."

"Ah! But no, I am guarding this rice in case of famine or sickness."

A pinch of rice remained and he went and cooked it.

"What will we eat the rice with?"

"With the *budu*."[143]

"I don't want any."

"Then what will you eat?"

"Some dried fish[144] that is hanging over the rice."

But when did he see it? The old man cut a slice of fish as large as the palm of one's hand and as long as two spread-out fingers.

"We are going to grill it?"

"No. I won't eat it if you do that."

"Don't you want to eat it?"

"Yes, but fried in oil."

"But there is no oil."

"Yes there is some in the corner of the pillar near the rice."

"But when then did this child go and see all that?"

So, he fried the fish in oil and put it on a plate. But the child was not happy. The son of a king cannot eat from the shell of a coconut!

"I don't want any. I want the plate that is near the rice."

"Ah! But when did he go to see all that?"

And he went to take the plate.

"I want you to eat enough so you will be full," said the old man.

"When I am no longer hungry, I will go and play in the field."

"You are a good boy, my child. And now you are full."

"Yes. But I want to defecate now. I want to defecate, old man."

"Alright. Take out a plank from the floor and go."

"I don't want to."

"How will you defecate then?"

"On your knees."

"What to you mean, on my knees?"

"Because I am still too young."

"It's not very funny," said the old man to himself, "but kings' sons are like that."

"Come then."

And he took off his pants.

"I don't want to. I don't want to."

"But how will you defecate then?"

"On your pants," he said.

"Hola!"

So, he raised his pants and also put up his head so he wouldn't be able to smell the odour. Then he got up.

"Don't get up, otherwise the excrement will be lost."

"What to you want to do with it?"

"Taste it."

"But what's the matter with the kings' sons. They ask us to eat their excrement."

"This is the way you will know whether I am sick or not."

The old man dipped his finger into the excrement and tasted it.

"Ah! It has sugar in it. Do you still want to defecate?"

"No, it's finished."

And he went to wash himself.

"Why is there so much noise outside?"

The young rascals have gone into the field. Forty children of the servants of the divinities had gone to play in the field. They played in the field and in the enclosure for the cows and goats. Ya! They didn't know whether it was day or night and destroyed the plants, the herbs for the animals, the saffron and the citronella.

"If that's the way things are I will go and see them. I will go and meet them."

Yoyoyoyo! The children were making a lot of noise while they played.

"And you, where do you come from?"

The one who asked the question thought that he was going to hit him.

"Why? I live in the house over there."

"And where are you going?"

"Straight ahead."

He entered the enclosure where the band of youngsters were gathered and received some blows.

"Ah! But you cannot hit me. And he returned the blows."

They fought together like this. There were thirty-nine in all and with the other one, that made forty. They built houses and meeting halls then decided to choose a king. There were girls as well as boys there. There was a real mixture of divinities among the children. They chose a king but at the moment they made salutations to him, they had headaches and stomach pains. Things kept on like this and no one among then could become the king.

"And this handsome boy over there?"

They chose him, made salutations and didn't become sick.

Ah! From then on they had a king.

We are now going to speak about something else. About a man who captured pheasants for the king. That day, he hadn't caught anything. He suddenly heard a noise and came nearer.

"But why then are there so many children in this field?"

The children arrived.

"Ha! There is the old man without any teeth."

And they made fun of the toothless old man.

"Ah! But what's the matter with these children?"

"Is this tamed pheasant yours, old man?"

The children took hold of the pheasant and asked the old man for a knife.

"Give us your knife, old man."

"Ah! But no," he said.

"Then we will go ourselves to take it, old man."

The king's son went to take it.

"Aye! Old man, come quickly, come quickly! I have a thorn stuck on me. Come and help me."

And the old man came.

"Let's see your knife, old man."

"No. I am going to take it out myself."

"No, I don't want you to. It hurts too much."

"Ah! But what's the matter with these children? Here, take it."

He took the knife, struck the earth and cut out the pheasant's throat. He cut it into small pieces and destroyed the snares. Ah! The old man was really very angry.

"Ah! All of you are really very bad."

They continued to mock at the toothless old man.

"That one is going to have problems."

But the children continued to make fun of him.

"Do you want a woman, old man?"

"I don't know."

"But she wants you. You do, don't you?"

"Yes."

"He does want one. So what shall we do?"

"If she agrees, that's fine. Haahaahaa!"

"Don't be worried. We are going to prepare some nice clothes for you and you will meet each other so that you can get married."

To marry a daughter of the divinities,[145] such a pretty girl of the divinities! But the children caught hold of the old man and cut a cross in his hair. The old man started crying. They took a knife but they didn't just cut off the end, they cut off all of it! Then they let him go home. As soon as he arrived, he ran to see the king and told him about all his misfortunes. The king told him that they would have to catch these rascals, especially the handsome young man. But the forty children of the servants of the divinities had gone back to the domain of the divinities. The kings' men said they would kill all those they could catch. And they were able to catch the handsome boy in the field. At the moment they were about to kill him, he said:

"Wait a minute. Let me say my two prayers[146] first."

And he recited them.

"Ah! Come here so that I can kill you now."

One of them men cut the body with his spear but instead of blood, rice cakes appeared.

"They are there for you to eat. If you cut me up, you will soon be tired. So, go ahead and eat."

The old man became angry because he had not been able to kill him. He returned to see the king to tell him. The inhabitants were told to collect some wood to make a stake on which they were to pour some oil from the lamp.

"You want to make a fire?"

"Yes."

"Wait and let me say my two prayers first."

He addressed his mother.

"Go ahead. You can make a fire now."

And hop! There was a fire but it didn't devour the body. A pool of water appeared with the cakes and everything else that one needed for food. Then the fire died down and only the pool of water remained.

"Ha! You wanted to burn me, old man. You must be tired."

The old man went back to see the king.

"Even though we burn him, he doesn't die; we cut him up and he doesn't die either."

So the king gave the order to prepare a big cannon and a sack full of gunpowder. He told the young man to come and clean the cannon.

"Do you want to kill me, father?"

"Of course not."

"Wait a minute so I can recite my two prayers."

The cannon thundered and the young man, who was transformed into a projectile, found himself on the Beting Timo[147] beach. He lay there unconscious.

And now let's speak of something else.

There were a woman and a naga. The Dame lived in the naga's belly. She came out of it.

"Grandfather, I am going to wash myself at Beting Timo."

"Ah! Go then but come back quickly to me."

"Don't be worried."

She left with her servants and met the young man. She washed herself and went back, rowing, with the young man.

"Where does this child come from?"

"I found him at Beting Timo."

"Put him over there until he becomes conscious again."

And the ancestor naga breathed in and spit out some glistening water on the young man, who got up.

"Hum! Where do you come from, young man?"

"I come from the country of Cenoh Paga Riyo."

"You are the son of whom?"

"I am the son of the great king."

"And your mother?"

"Dame Rotero."

"Oh! Then you are truly one of my grandchildren. That's good. I can raise you since I have many servants."

He remained there for seven days but nonetheless, he had to start thinking about leaving. There were many women there. The naga had a vast number of descendants and everyone fell in love with the young man since he was so handsome.

"You will have to leave. You will go and study farther away because the women are crazy about you. You will go to the country of Relobekaso."

"How will I get there? I don't know where it is. But it doesn't matter, I will go anyway. "

The naga king slipped a missive into the prow of his boat.[148] He blew once and the boat arrived in the country of Relobekeso. He didn't use the missive even once. And here is what the ogre then said:

"Ha! We are going to be able to eat human beings. No one has ever come here before."

He ran and jumped into the water until it reached his waist. Then he quickly started to pull the boat towards the beach. It was then that he saw the missive.

"Ah! It is one of our grandchildren. Since he is one of our own family, we must take care of him."

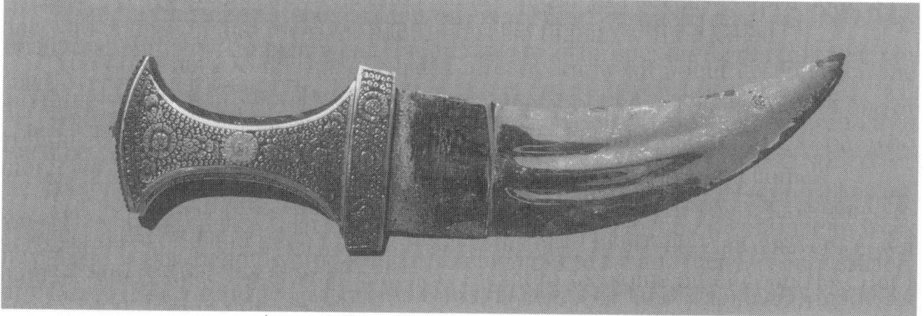

**Fig. 39.** Local knife. (J. Ivanoff, 1989)

"You are going to study here but be careful not to play with the knife. Don't go too far away either since you have come here to study. You must not go either to the west or to the north. We are between the two. You must not go behind the house and not into the kitchen either. Stay here. I am going to look for some food. I won't be long."

And he left for one week. The young man went to see what was behind the house and went into the kitchen. He saw the heads of dead human beings there.

"Ha! My ancestors eat men."

He went to look for some food also. On the way, he saw a well with a golden red colour. A well of gold. He dipped his finger into it.

"Ah! I am caught."

He rolled his hurt finger in a small piece of cloth.

His ancestor returned.

"I am hurt. I am hurt. I hurt myself with a knife."

"Show me."

"No. It is better and hardly hurts any more."

"Stay quietly here and don't play with knives any more otherwise you will hurt yourself. As for me, I am going to look for something to eat. I won't be long."

So, the young man went towards the west and encountered Dame Pako Hija.[149]

"Ah! This young girl is really very pretty."

"How long have you been here, older one?"

"For several days now. "

"Come up then, younger one."

He climbed up and they spoke together for a long time. Ah! She was really very pretty! They spoke together and took much pleasure in each other's company. They cooked some rice and ate together. Then they went into the house and lay down. But he didn't close his eyes and looked up.

"What is that, that resembles a big sack of rice."

"That? it's the sarong of the ogre,[150] my ancestor."

"Ah! And how is it?"

"If one goes inside it one becomes an ogre."

"And over there? Is that a fishing pole?"

"It is a magic stick."

"What do you mean, a magic stick?"

"Ah! Put on the sarong, take the stick and you can fly."

"Ha! And what is in this bottle that is moving?"

"It is the water of the hill of the bamboos. If one is followed, one breaks the bottle and a hill of bamboos appears."

"And over there? What is it that thing with a reddish colour?"

"It is a sea of fire. If one breaks it, a sea of fire appears."

"Holala! And that bottle full of fog on the flower of the column?"[151]

"It is the life[152] of my ancestor."

They went to sleep. Dame Pako immediately fell profoundly asleep. He quickly got up and took the bottle full of the ancestor's life and put it in his pocket. Then he took the bottle of the hill of bamboos and the one of the sea of fire and put them into his pocket. He seized the stick and went off, neither to the north nor to the west, but to the centre. He went until he reached the golden well. But the ancestor arrived at that moment.

"The young boy has run away."

He was in the forest and ran after him. He came closer and closer. The young man then broke the bottle of the hill of bamboos.

"Ah! You are cunning, young man."

His pursuer lost time in creeping through the forest but he was soon able to run again. He came dangerously closer. The young man then broke the bottle of the sea of fire.

"Ah! Here we are," the other one said.

And it took him even longer because he had to go through the sea of fire. But as soon as he did, he continued his pursuit. The young man found himself on the top of a mountain; his pursuer was at the foot of the mountain.

"Ah! Come down, grandchild. I am not angry and I am all alone."

"No. I don't want to come down. I am afraid."

"I am not angry, grandchild. I want to give you a formula for untying."[153]

"If this is so, write it on the stone. It's finished?"

"Not yet."

"Now?"

"Yes. It's finished."

"Is it really finished?"

"Yes, it really is. You can come now, grandchild."

But the young boy took the bottle with the life of the ogre in it, spit and broke it. The ogre died. The young man then rolled himself in the ashes so that no one could see that he was covered with gold. He took to the road and where did he go? He went to the country of the great king who had seven daughters who were about to marry. The eldest one with the guardian of the dogs, the second one with the guardian of buffaloes, the third one with the guardian of the cows, the fourth with the guardian of goats, the fifth with the guardian of horses, the sixth with the son of king Kereso Forty and the last declared:

"As for myself, I will marry the one who is covered with ashes."

"And why are you speaking like this?" her sisters asked.

"I don't know. It just came out like that."

Ah! The great king married his daughters. He invited all the chiefs of the villages and districts, all the chiefs to come. There was no one as rich as the king but his son-in-law was covered with ashes.

"Ah! How can I make my daughter renounce him?"

"That won't be difficult."

After the ceremony, the king told his youngest daughter and her husband to go and live in the forest. He hoped she would become bored there and return. The king's men went there and made a fire under the house in order to get warm. This is how the young man was able to cover himself with ashes. The king's men tried everything but nothing worked; the youngest daughter did not got bored.

"In that case, lord, ask your sons-in-law to go and look for some fish[154] so you can eat some. In fact, the young man has neither a square net, nor a dipping net, nor a casting net and no one to help him. If he doesn't bring back anything, you will kill him."

"Oh, yes! That's a good idea."

The guardians called to the youngest daughter.

"Your husband must go with your brother-in-law to look for fish. The one who brings some back will be king."

"Ah! Alright then. That will be easy."

But she went into the house and started crying.

"What's the matter?"

"It is really horrible, elder one."

"What?"

"My father wants some fish and he asks you to go and get some. We don't have a net, nor a snare,[155] nor a square net."

"But we can go fishing with the others and profit by their instruments."

The six brother-in-laws left and went to catch some fish by attracting them into the nets in the freshwater current. But not one of them was able to catch any. The young man sat down on a rock and remained upright.

"Ho! Why are you taking my fish? Who did you ask permission to do this?"

"Holala! Where does this child of the divinities come from? Who is he who shines like that?"

"Why, if you have come to catch fish, do you make so much noise? You will not be able to catch any if you continue like that."

"We are looking for fish. Excuse us."

"What are you going to do?"

"Our father-in-law wants to eat some fish."

"Why don't you ask him if you want some fish?"

"Ah! We are asking you, lord. One fish for each one."

"Ah! This is possible but you must give me something in exchange."[156]

"If you want money, we have a hundred coins."

"I don't want money. I want to make an exchange: the ends of your noses in exchange for the fish. Each of you cut off the end of your nose."

They did what he had asked and he put all of them into his pocket. Then he caught the fish with his hands, six fish, all of the same size. The six brother-in-laws hung them on their sticks by their gills. They went back in single file. The young man returned to his house and put a fish in the jar at the entrance to his house.

"Well then, have you a fish?"

"I had neither a net nor a trap.[157] How could I have caught any?"

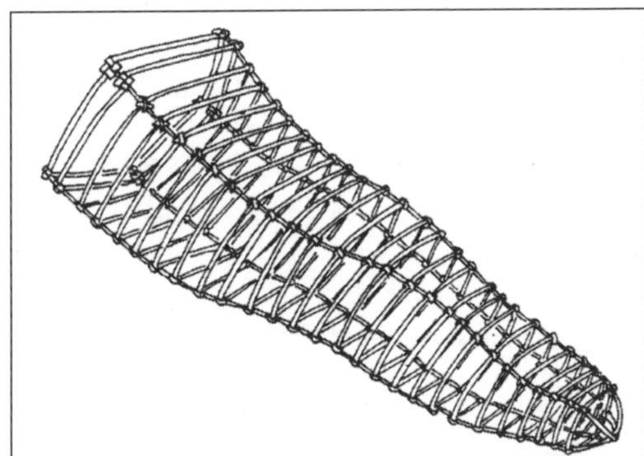

**Fig. 40. and Fig. 41.** Local traps to catch fish.

"My father will kill you, then!"

"We will see. Maybe there is a fish in the jar."

"What do you mean, in the jar?"

"Near the house."

"Eh! There is a big fish inside."

"I don't know. What fish are you talking about?"

"People call it *belano*."[158]

"Yes, that's what it is."

"Is it you who put it inside?"

"No, I didn't."

She got dressed and washed herself. She was going to take the fish to her father. He would either eat it or raise it according to his wish.

"Should I put a stick in his gills?"

"Put it in your hand. It won't move."

So she did this and took it to her father.

"What are you going to do with it, father? Will you keep it?"

"No, I am not going to keep it, I am going to eat it. I want seven different dishes with seven different fish. It will be delicious."

So, she went back to prepare the fish.

"What are we going to prepare it with? We don't have any onions, nor citronella, nor ginger."

"Hum! I will have to use the magic stick."

He commanded the stick to make seven different dishes with the same fish. Then he hit with the stick so that seven bowls would appear. Her sisters had almost finished while she had only just begun.

"Ha! You are going to die," said the chiefs of the village. "The others have almost finished."

She took the fish and went to the back where no one could see her. She hit the fish with the magic stick and seven dishes appeared, each one with seven different bowls. She went to serve the king.

"Ah! Come here all of you, chiefs of the villages, chiefs of the districts because I want you to taste the dishes my children have prepared."

He took a mouthful from each. He tasted all the dishes which his children had prepared.

"Among all of these dishes not one is worth the one my youngest daughter has prepared. And if you don't believe me, come and taste them yourselves. If you don't do this, I will be accused of favouring my youngest child."

So they all came to taste all the dishes, the chiefs of the villages and the chiefs of the districts to taste all the dishes.

"Yes, lord. The dish of your youngest one is really the best."

"Come back here tonight and the night after. I want to speak to all of you about something."

"Ah, yes. You still have a problem. You are rich and have many subjects. You have everything you want but you have a son-in-law who is covered with ashes."

"What must we do to mislead him, chiefs, chiefs of the villages and chiefs of the districts?"

"In this way, lord. Tell him to go and search for a mouse-deer. Ah! You will ask him for a mouse-deer because you want to eat one. Tell him that you want seven plates with seven different dishes all made with a mouse-deer."

"Ah! Yes, that's a good idea."

The next day arrived.

"Come here, guardians and servants. Tell my youngest one to come here."

So, the guards went to look for the youngest one. They arrived at the house of the ogre.

"What do you want, Benu?"

"Your father wants you to come."

"If your father orders this, you cannot refuse. You must go back there." But he, himself, did not go there.

"Ah! I now have the desire to eat a mouse-deer, youngest one."

"Ah! What do you mean, father?"

"Hey! Can the man who is covered with ashes go and get one for me?"

"He has no servants to help him catch one. He has nothing to make snares[159] with and he doesn't know how to make them."[160]

"If he doesn't succeed, I will kill him. I will kill both of you."

She went back crying. Her tears flowed without stopping.

"What is the matter? Are they asking us to separate?"

"No, elder one."

"Then why are you crying?"

"My father wants a mouse-deer, elder one. How will we be able to find one? We have no snares,[161] no servants to catch the animal. Who then will be able to do this for us?"

"Hum! You mustn't cry. We don't have anything but I will go with those who do and we will share it. When does he wants this mouse-deer?"

"Tomorrow. You must go and hunt for it tomorrow.

"Ha! We will leave before," said his six brothers-in-law.

They took some dogs with them, some traps[162] to catch the animal and kill him. They went deep into the forest and cried out: "woweh, woweh", in order to catch the animal. The mouse-deer was panic-stricken and ran into the traps.[163] The young man sat down at the door to the traps. The ogre remained quiet at the door of the trap. But he had taken off his dirty shirt and was now radiant.

"Ah! Who is this king at the entrance to the trap?"

"Eh! You over there! What are you doing?"

"Ah! We offer you our salutations. We are going to hunt mouse-deer."

"Ha! But if you do this, you will catch all the mouse-deer and then what kind of food will remain for me?"

"Pardon, but our father-in-law wants to eat some mouse-deer."

"Ha! So that's what it is. Do you have one or not?"

"No, they all escaped."

"How many do you need?"

"We need one for each of us."

"Oh! But I don't sell them. I exchange them."

"What do you want in exchange, lord?"

"I want a piece of your ears in exchange."

They made a sign to show him that they had understood.

"What do you think?"

The son of Kereso Forty said:

"Very well. He can take a piece of our ears. We are going to cut them off and in this way we will have our mouse-deer. And moreover, we won't tire ourselves."

"Ah! We agree."

"Well then, so be it. Take them and carry them on your shoulders."

The servants came to seize the mouse-deer and carry them on their shoulders. Each one carried one with their paws attached to a stick. They caught the mouse-deer easily, without any effort. Then they went home. They went home one behind the other and each one carried a mouse-deer. They passed in front of the house of the youngest one.

"Ho! Each of you has a mouse-deer?"

"Ho! We are hunters, the brother-in-laws," they said to the youngest one.

But her husband had not yet returned. Did he also have a mouse-deer? They all left.

"Come mouse-deer. Come with me," said the young man.

And the mouse-deer came frisking about.

"Come to my house."

He didn't have to carry it. He simply walked and the mouse-deer followed him. They arrived and the youngest one was sleeping. He went to the back of the house.

"You stay here."

The six others had mouse-deer of the same size. He went home.

"Ah! You have come back, elder one."

"Yes."

"Did you catch a mouse-deer?"

"How could I without a snare? They are wild animals and they run away."

"Hum! Then my father will kill us if we have no mouse-deer."

"Hum! Well then, let him kill us, the king causes us many problems."

"Ha! We don't have a mouse-deer."

"Maybe there is one behind the house? Do you hear the noise? We must go and see."

"Ha! It's a mouse-deer. Go quickly and catch it."

"Why catch it? It's not necessary. He will remain here."

"He will run away."

"No, he won't. He is going to stay here."

"Then, what can we do?"

"Ah! We are going to wash ourselves and get dressed because you must go with the mouse-deer to see the king."

"And how will I take hold of him? I am a woman and this is an animal."

"Hey! But you don't need to carry him. He will walk there."

She finished preparing herself and went down to see.

"Ah! Come here, mouse-deer. Come with me to my father's house."

The mouse-deer followed her and went with her into the royal chamber. He climbed up the stairs all by himself.

"I will follow you whether you go into the palace or into the kitchen."

There were many people there. The others had already cut the throats of their mouse-deer. They had removed the flesh and washed the animals then went and cooked them slowly. They prepared the dishes that the father wanted to eat. But the youngest one had only just arrived.

"Ah! You won't have any time to prepare anything, younger one," said the chiefs of the villages and the chiefs of the districts. "The others have already cut their mouse-deer into little pieces and it won't be long before they present their dishes. As for you, you haven't even cut the throat of your mouse-deer yet. You are going to die."

But, nonetheless, she climbed up to the king's house.

"Come with me into the house."

The mouse-deer jumped up into the royal house and met the king.

"Father, here is the mouse-deer that you ordered. Do you want to keep it?"

"Eh! No, younger one, I want to eat it. Have them bring it to me. I want to eat seven plates with seven dishes on them. Seven plates with seven dishes on each one. All the others are ready except you who is the last one."

"Go and cut its throat," said the chief of the district. "You will no doubt be beaten, younger one, because you still haven't cut this animal's throat while all the others have already done so."

She went back to see the ogre.

"What are we going to do, elder one?"

"What do you mean?"

"My father wants to eat. All the others have finished and are ready but as for myself, I still haven't cut the mouse-deer's throat."

"Take, the magic stick, pull the mouse-deer as far as the kitchen and hit him with the stick. Seven plates will appear."

She left with the stick.

"Ha! The youngest one doesn't do anything the way she should," said the chiefs of the villages and the chiefs of the districts.

She went to the back of the house and went into the kitchen while the others were carrying the dishes. They had already gone in and there were dishes everywhere. But she went into the kitchen and hit the mouse-deer, "peng, peng!", and seven plates with seven dishes appeared. Ah! She called the servants.

"Come and help me, servants."

"Ah! When did you do this, younger one? When did you cut the mouse-deer's throat? When did you prepare the flesh."

She arranged the seven plates.

"Ha! Here you are, youngest me. We are all gathered together again, the son-in-laws and sisters."

Only the ogre wasn't there. The youngest one remained quiet, immobile.

The king tasted what was on each plate, one mouthful for each plate. But there were many of them, seven plates of the meat of the mouse-deer. Ho! But there were so many of them! Seven plates of mouse-deer meat. Seven mouse-deer in all.

"Ah, I don't want to eat any more."

The chiefs of the villages and of the districts said:

"Which one is the best, lord?"

"Eh, the one of the youngest one was the best of all. And if you don't believe me, taste it yourself. Taste what I have just tasted."

So, they tasted it and shook their heads. They tasted the dish of the youngest one and shook their heads. It was really delicious. But where did she get these instruments of the kitchen, they asked themselves? They finished the meal. Some days went by. Three days went by before the guardian went to tell the youngest one that she must return. So she went back.

"What do you want, father?"

"Ah! I am going to reunite all the people of this royal house in order to choose[164] the best man and make him a king."

They built a new house[165] for the new king. The labourers were told to build this new house in front of the old one. The son of King Kereso Forty was chosen to become king. All the people made a salutation to him but since he had a stomach ache, he fell down and was rolling on the ground. It had not been a good choice. The ogre had still not come. They had to wait one more day since there were seven brothers-in-law. There were many people in the king's house. They tried to choose four kings but this didn't work. There still remained three so an appointment was made for the following day.

"You must get washed, younger one, because we are going to see the new king."

So, the younger one washed herself.

"I am going to wash myself, also."

He was covered with ashes. He changed his trousers and shirt and combed his hair. Finally, he was ready.

But we are now going to speak of something else. We are going to speak of the white buffalo who had thousands of stars marked on him.

"I cannot stay in this enclosure. My skin is full of prickles and they are scratching me. I have the impression that someone is sticking the points of a sword into me. I cannot remain here in this enclosure."

So he destroyed the enclosure, jumped out and went off. He reached the house of the ogre, "krudung, krudung."

"Hey! Where are you going, buffalo, "krudung, krudung?"

Shortly afterwards, the guardian of the buffaloes went running after him.

"Oh! The buffalo is being followed!"

The guardian turned his head.

"Ha! Do you live here, lord?"

"Where are you going?"

"I am going after the buffalo."

"Come here first. Your buffalo is going to come back."

"What is it, lord?"

"It is not worthwhile following it."

"And the buffalo?"

"He is going to come back."

"Then what do you want, lord?"

"Don't go away. Go instead to see the men who are choosing the new king. Wash yourself. You are sweating."

So, the guardian of the buffalo washed himself completely and changed his clothes.

"Come. We are going to go there."

They went on the road, one behind the other. The people over there had tried all the kings and the only one left was the husband of Dame of the Neck, the guardian of the horses. He was made king and everyone offered him their salutations but he suddenly fell backwards. The guardian of the horses fell down. Ho! He fell down because the older people had made salutations to him. And here he was now, with a headache and stomach ache. Ha! it was finished. He would not be king.

"The only one who remains is you, the husband of the youngest one. You who are covered with ashes. Is it a good thing to choose you?"

"Eh! Climb up, guardian of the buffalos."

The guardian of the buffaloes climbed up. To the left was the husband, the guardian of the buffaloes and to the right, Dame Benjamin. Everyone offered him their salutations since he was the new king.

"Do you have a stomach ache?"

"No."

"Don't you have a headache?"

"No."

So he became the king.

"Ha! There is no one else but him. What can we do to change him? Just imagine! A man covered with ashes becomes king!"

But the new king went down into the royal chamber.

"Ah! Listen all of you! Listen to what I have to say to you, I the ogre who is covered with ashes. Listen and try to understand. This is how things will be from now on, all you subjects, friends, servants, companions of my father-in-law. From now on, the kings will be the guardians of the buffaloes and Dame Benjamin. They will be the great kings of this earth. I married Dame Benjamin but I will leave her with you because I didn't want to marry someone from a far away country. But she had such a strong desire to do this that I accepted."

And he went away. He walked for a long time before he came to the country Gua Batu Singo Maneng.[166] There he met Dame Pemasu. But he also met Dame Mahsuri[167] and married her. She became pregnant. She had been pregnant for three months, Dame Mahsuri and prepared the dishes for the meal. They were made with the bird Gago'Sure Lekapo.[168]

"Eh! Where did you find such a bird, younger one?"

"What, older one? If you don't know how to find these Gago'Suro Lekapo birds, we will divorce."

"Ah! If that's what you want, younger one," he said.

"Yes."

So he thought for a while. He didn't have his sarong on since it had been put away.

"Good. I will go there but I don't know what one must do or even where to search. I have never heard anyone speak of this thing and I don't even know what this bird looks like."

"Ah! That's fine, elder one."

He took a warm[169] shirt and a sarong and put them over his shoulder before going into the big field. When he arrived there he saw the bird Gago'Suro Lekapo.[170] He tried to catch it but the bird Gago'Suro went towards the sea and he followed it. The bird flew up into the sky, to where the divinities live and then descended to the earth, still followed by the young man. He kept on going deeper and deeper into the earth and finally entered the Singomalè[171] cave. He went into the Singomalè cave. He descended again and again and suddenly went through something that led to the place where the divinities live, above the sky. He didn't want to descend any longer. The bird Gago'Suro Lekapo no longer existed. In fact, he was the child of a divinity. He went up into the heavens and stayed there. Pemahsuri, however, was pregnant. She was pregnant and the time for delivery approached.

She gave birth to a child, a son named Bosu Sati.[172] This was the name he was given. There were also servants there, a young one and an old one whose names were Sema and Terah.[173] Pemahsuri sent a message into the heavens to inform the shellfish king, who was formerly the ogre. He was now a divinity and the message he received told him to come down. But he didn't want to. He didn't want to descend since he really was very well up above. He was a king among the divinities and he had a son, Bosu Sati, who was growing into an adult.

"What should I do, mother? I would like to go and see what my father left before he went away. In effect, my father left something and it is you who must guard it. He left a rifle, a yellow horse that he had trained, an elephant that he had also trained and a rattan ball game.[174] And there are still other things."

"You can go and see. But come back quickly."

"Don't worry, I will not be long."

And the young boy went to the big field. He went there and knew it well even though he had never been there before. It was there that his father had played the game in the past. He had played chess with the pieces made of gold and brass:[175] *bolé* with pieces of gold and brass; the knucklebone game with gold and brass. This was the very place where he had played with the forty children of the divine servants. Everything was clean. He went to a platform to rest and fell asleep.

"It is midday and we must rest," said Bosu Sati. "Even the birds have stopped singing."

He sat down, then leaned on his side and finally lay down. He suddenly heard the noise of a rifle shot. It came from the fork of the river.

"Go and see what is happening," he said to his servant. "Why has a rifle shot sounded near the fork of the river? Go and ask those who are responsible for this place."

The young servant went off and soon arrived at the place where the rifle shot had come from. He reached a spot where there was an old man. He went closer to him.

"What is this rifle shot all about?" he asked him."

"Ah! The rifle belongs to King Laleng."

"Ah! Good!"

"He is coming along and he took out the old powder from the butt of his rifle. But it has nothing to do with fighting. Why don't you go and see for yourself? I was just about to go when you arrived."

"Good. Then I will go alone."

He went towards the boat of King Laleng.

"Ah! Whose servant are you?"

"I am the servant of Bosu Sati."

"Then come and sit down with us."

He climbed on board, changed his clothes and ate some cakes. He changed his trousers and his shirt.

"That's fine, but where are you going?"

"We are going to the Gunung Berité[176] country."

"And what about the rifle shot?"

"We were only removing the old powder from it. We stopped on the way to the Gunung Berité country. I am going there to become engaged to Dame[177] Jano Mudo. Let's go. We must leave you here. Give my salutations to Bosu Sati and ask him to excuse us for the rifle shot, but it wasn't intended to provoke a war."

The servants went back and related everything that they had learned.

"What!" cried Bosu Sati. "This King Laleng is acting so badly and deceiving us. He has treated me badly because this girl had been promised to me for a long time now. When my mother was pregnant with me, she came to an accord with Dame Jano Mudo's parents, who lived with King Sanyanyo,[178] in the Gunung Berité country. Let's go home, servants."

He [Bosu Sati] went home and put on the sarong of the ogre whose skin was covered with ashes. He was very angry and jealous. But he couldn't convince King Laleng, who finally offered him some opium.

"Do you want to smoke some opium?"

"Ah! I don't smoke."

"Ah! Nevertheless, you should," he answered.

So he carefully prepared some opium and made him smoke it. He was soon drugged. The king took advantage of this to catch hold of him and cut his throat along the road. The three companions, Bosu Sati and his servants, reached the crossing.

During this time, the tree[179] that was in front of the ladder of his house lost a branch. The branch broke near his mother's house, on the side of the ladder. Bosu Sati went to tell his mother. It was a sign and he was troubled.

"If a branch of this tree breaks, it means that I am in danger." His mother then took a betel leaf, so as to transmit a message to the sky.[180] She called the flies and told them to give the message to the divinity Sesewo. This message explained the problem her child was having among men. Even though the flies transmitted the message, Sesewo refused to descend. But, nevertheless, he looked at it.

"Eh! There is a problem at Sangnyayos," he said.

They asked him to descend and put his feet on the earth. Pemahsuri[181] asked him to descend. But he refused to make magic with the betel. He refused. He preferred to make magic with the betel leaf and an areca nut. He threw it all on to the ground, near the ladder. It was the skin[182] of the mother-tiger, a big tiger named Jegila Jerironging.[183] Ah! This is how the spirit[184] appeared. He was a man who transformed himself into a tiger[185] by using the skin of the mother-tiger, the big Jegila Jerironging.

It was dawn and Pemahsuri left to wash her face in the well. She carried the water and then noticed something under the ladder.

"Oh! older one, you didn't descend."

She climbed up so that she could put on a pair of trousers and a shirt and then went down to get the skin of the mother-tiger, the big tiger. She put it on and cried out three times before she went on the road to fight. She was going to the Gunung Berité country to fight. Everyone there was afraid. All the inhabitants of the country took refuge in the citadel while the mother-tiger was there, breaking their hands and feet.

She sent a dream to Dame Jano Mudo in order to awaken her desire for some corn, even though it wasn't the season. Ah! The king didn't know what to do. He called his servants and told them to prepare a dried field. But the tiger devoured them all because the child Bosu Sati had been captured. But there was one couple who remained. The man was old and the woman was still young. They planted corn and peas so that the king could eat them. They cultivated a field in the forest called Baleguo Taro. This was when the divinity Sesuwa came down to rejoin his wife. It is not possible for anyone to remain peaceful if their companion has a problem. Pemahsursi had a child in the forest. The divinity took him away so that he could take care of him in the sky. Night soon fell and the female tiger came near the couple who were preparing the field. She took off her tiger-skin covering and put it behind a tree. This is the way Pemahsuri entered.

"Where are you going, mother?"

"I am taking a walk, old man. Can I remain here tonight, old man?"

"Ha! Of course you can. Climb up then."

She climbed up the ladder and stopped at the entrance to the house.

"Ha! Eat some rice with us, mother."

"I am not hungry," she said.

"But it's not possible, You must eat. Eat with my wife."

"Eat with me," said the wife. "That will be no problem. Eat."

She asked:

"What do you think, mother of this raging tiger who comes from the country of King Sanyanyo?"

They had gone to plant corn and peas for the king's meal, so they prepared the field in the forest called Beleguo Taro.[186]

"Ah! I really pity the inhabitants who take refuge in the royal chambers. Some of them cry and others suffer. As long as the three prisoners are not freed, things will remain the same."

"Ah! Is that what has happened?"

"Yes," she answered.

"But that is not serious, mother. You mustn't be afraid."

"I am not afraid. A tiger goes and looks for his food, that's all."

They ate and then prepared the mats to lie down on.

"We will now go to sleep, mother."

"You will sleep in the middle of the house," said the old man.

"It's fine here."

"But one cannot sleep near the entrance to the house. That's not good."

The old man's wife went out and returned at dawn. She had gone to see the king.

"Ah! What is lacking?" he asked. "Fish, rice, what then?"

"I am not lacking anything. I still have some rice. But I would like to speak to you about something."

"About what?"

"It concern some news that was transmitted to me by the song of the birds.[187] If the three prisoners are not liberated, the tiger will continue to eat all the people of the country."

"Ah! If this is the way things are, we will liberate them today. We mustn't create any problems. We will liberate them."

"Yes. This is nothing."

"Yes, that's true," said the king.

"Yes, it really is, lord."

And this is what was done. The mother tiger was sleeping in the house. She woke up and put her covering back on. Then she went in the direction of the country of Gunung Berité and climbed up to the royal chamber.

"Where is Dame Jereno Mudo of the Sanyanyo country?"

"She is in the citadel."

"You must give her to me; if not, I will go and get her myself. Give her to me or I will go and get her."

"Pardon me, mother tiger, but we can't give you our daughter like this. Everything must be done according to the rules and we must organize a party for the marriage. It is only then, that we can give you our daughter."

"Ah! Alright then."

"Yes, that's how things are done."

The mother tiger had already gone into the royal chamber but the king told her to leave it.

"I forbid you to take her!"

She wanted to take her right away but she finally went out of the royal chamber.

"It is not possible. We must first make a party for the marriage."

"Ah! Alright then. We will organize a party."

"Don't be worried about the party since we have everything we will need for it here." They king's staff prepared the food.

Bosu Sati sent a message to his uncle, the divinity Sati.[188] He asked him for dances, a mask theatre[189] and heavenly ceremonies because he was going to marry Dame Jerano Mudo of the country of Gunung Berité. But the king's children wanted a small party and said that it was not necessary to ask Uncle Sati. But they spoke empty words by wanting just to cut a water container in two or simply sacrifice a skate fish. The message had already been sent and the dance and theatre were included in the party and lasted for three months. At the end of three months, the dancers and actors were sent back home.

"Hey! These children really don't know what they are talking about, half a calabash[190] of water and a small skate fish for a party that will last for three months!" A message was sent to a boat asking for merchandise since they now had to welcome the future wife in Gunung country, where Guo Batu Singa Male was.

"I won't permit you to go along," the uncle said. "You are going to lie to me again. You have already deceived me."

He sent the boat with all the merchandise. The boat was loaded with everything. Dame Jerano Mudo climbed aboard and arrived in the country of Chesing. The welcoming party for the married couple was held on the seashore, with dances and the theatre of masks. It lasted one month. They held a party that lasted one month and Bosu Sati found Pemahsuri once again.

"Ah! This is what happened, my younger one Pemahsuri. My uncle's sons played a trick on us when they said that they wanted half a calabash of water and only one skate fish for a party that would last three months. They wanted to do the same thing for the reception. But we asked for a boat loaded with merchandise."

The uncle remained for one more month, while the party lasted. When it ended he put Dame Jerano Mudo on the boat filled with merchandise and went back to the country of Gunung Berité. Bosu Sati went back to the country of Guo Batu Singa Male and this is where the story ends. He became the king of two countries, the country of Guo Batu Singo Male and the country of Gunung Berité, the one of King Sanyanyo. These two countries belonged to Bosu Sati from that time on. Ah! Here you have the epic of the Shellfish king! And when we give a performance of it with the Moyong, three days aren't enough. In order to perform it well, one needs seven days. From the birth of the Shellfish King to his arrival in the big field, this is only one night for the Moyong. Ha, ha! And we haven't even arrived at the rifle shot yet!

### 3.5. Chémè Chéwè[191]

***(Village of Samoh, Province of Narathiwat, November 1993***
***Narrator: Wo Seng***
***Type of story: bahri)***

This is the story of a rich merchant and a captain/ship-owner, the fathers of Chémè[192] and Chéwè.[193]

They were very rich and sent their children to school. The children went to school and grew up. They went to the same school. One day, Chéwè went towards Chémè; he desired her but she said:

"Who do you think you are? If you want to marry me, you will have to carry my sarong that I use for bathing."

Chéwè's friends heard this and they all said he had to respond to such an insult. They gathered together and Chéwè told them that if he wanted to marry Chémè, he would have to carry her wet sarong from the well to the house.

"Oh! That's not very kind. You absolutely must do something and answer."

So he said to Chémè:

"If I become your husband, the dowry will be ridiculous, a sapec."[194]

Time passed. They went to school together until the fourth level of primary school,[195] since in the past, one could not go any further.

Then came the day when the captain/ship-owner asked the merchant for the hand of his daughter Chémè.

"Yes, this is possible," he said. "We live close to one another and we have enough work to be able to eat and take care of ourselves."

"Well then, that's perfect. But we now have to decide on the day[196] of the marriage."

"Yes, we must find a day and arrange all the details for the future. This day will be the fifteenth of the month, on a Thursday night."

Ché Hawè came with his retinue to his fiancée's house. He arrived and then left, came back and left again. When the marriage ceremony ended, he took his wife to his house. The captain/ship-owner took the fiancée to his house for one night and then took her back to her own house the next night. They continued to go and come. Haa! Yes, this is the way it was. The couple spent one night there, one night at Hawè's house and one night at Chémè's[197] house. This lasted for about a month. They lived together, going from one house to another. Ché Hawè's father spoke. What did he say?

"Who owns the land between our houses? It belongs to both of us, no? Why don't we build a house there?"

"Why not? That's a good idea."

"We must build the house at the same distance away from each household. It must be built in the centre."

So, the land was cleared. They cut down the trees,[198] the "rattan" trees. The land was cleared and each one sharpened his blade so that they could continue to work next day. They went home from time to time in order to eat and then left immediately afterwards. They returned when night was falling. The land was finally ready for the house to be built.

"Go ahead, Chémè. I am going to look for some cakes and water."

Ché Hawè prepared the ground and Chémè followed. They had some cakes, tea and other good things to eat. They sat down in the shadow of the rattans.[199] Only a few trees remained far off. They installed themselves under the branches, put a piece of cloth on the ground, in the shadow of the rattans. Then they went to sleep. But something was moving and their backs began to itch: "nyu, nyu, nyu."

"Hey! What is it?"

They turned over, removed the cloth and saw that the earth moved every time something passed over its surface.

"Hey! What then is this animal,[200] Ché Hawè?"

Ché Hawè started to run away.

"I don't know. It's something that makes a noise 'nyu, nyu, nyu' and undulates under the earth."

He took off the piece of cloth and dug in the earth with a blade. He raised something that was as fat as a mortar for betel.

"What then is this, Ché Hawè"

"I don't know. I never saw anything like it. But it is as fat as the mortar used for the service of betel."

"Haa! They say that it is a golden animal."

Its skin is like that of shells that one cannot remove. It is like a lid that one cannot remove.

"Ha! Let's take it back with us. That would be the best thing to do."

They went back to the captain/ship-owner's house.

"Hey! But this is a golden animal! Guard it preciously since it brings good luck to the house."

The land was soon cleared and everything was prepared to build the house with. It would be built on the same spot where they had found the golden animal.

Ché Hawè[201] went to his parents' and parents-in-law's houses and got all the wood he needed to build it with. But the young people didn't know how to build a house and had to ask for help. The columns were put up first. It took them only one day to do this thanks to Ché Hawè's friends who helped them, as well as all their parent's family connections. The walls and the rest of the house were finished in two days. Ché Hawè was then able to go and look for some animals to slaughter so that the invited guests would have something to eat.

Everyone made invocations and prayed that Ché Hawè would have good fortune in his house. Days passed and the young couple worked so that they would have food to eat. Mother Sari prepared the meals. If anything was needed, one only had to ask

**Fig. 42.** Traditional coastal Malay house. (Ivanoff, 1989)

**Fig. 43.** The *kolè'*, traditional Malay boats that formerly were able to travel on the high seas. (Ivanoff, 1989)

her. She also planted whatever was needed for cooking: eggplants, peas, chilli. Chémè never had to occupy herself with all these things since there was someone to take care of all this for her. As for Ché Hawè, he was a boy and so he didn't have to plant anything. Time passed and the plants grew and fruit appeared on them. Mother Sari went to sell peas in the king's stall and also in the big market place. During this time, Ché Hawè started to think. He went to speak to his father and father-in-law because he wanted to go out to sea and do some trading in order to earn some money.

"That's no problem. You can go out to sea. Take some money and go and ask your father for some, too."

He went home and asked his wife to bring him some purée of *sama*[202] chilli and fish brine, *budu tumih*.[203] This is how things were done in the past. One took along the brine of the *tunih* fish for long voyages and put all of it in hollowed-out coconut. It was then packed and brought along for sea voyages. He went to his parents-in-law's house the next morning at dawn to tell them that he was going to leave and to ask them what the secrets for trading were. The sun was at its height when he returned.

"Is the rice cooked?"

"Yes, it is ready."

"I am hot," he said.

"If you are hot, go and wash yourself."

"Yes, but you come with me to bathe, too."

Chémè took the bowl and a cloth to bathe herself with and change her clothes and then left.

"Take a piece of cloth."

"Yes, I will need one to wash myself with. I am coming."

When Chémè had finished washing herself, she stood up and when Ché Hawè had also finished washing himself, she told him to wring out his cloth and carry it on his shoulder.

"Carry my cloth and the water, also."

Chémè was very shrewd to speak like this. They climbed up the ladder, poured the water into the jar and drank a mouthful, then spat it out.

"One, three, five, seven and it is finished.[204] It is just as I had predicted."

"Predicted what?"

"Do you remember the day, when we were young, and I told you that one day I would order you to carry my cloth to bathe with and that you would take it up the ladder and bring it to the house?"

"Yes, it's true. You have succeeded but, as for myself, not yet."

**Fig. 44.** Fishing is a family activity, essential for the survival of the villages, because the Malays are above all sailors, fishermen and traders. (Ivanoff, 1989)

Time passed and the boat would soon have to be put into the water and loaded with rice and other things. They then needed two sailors. The sail was hoisted and the boat sailed away. It wasn't long before it could no longer be seen.

It was almost night when Chémè noticed that there was no more fuel for the petrol lamp.

"Give me some money and I will go and buy some."

"There is no more money."

She searched everywhere and found a sapec in the betel service. All that was left was one coin with a hole in the centre. It was damaged on the sides. One sapec was worth three satang,[205] in former times. Haa! There was no more money and the situation was serious. But they didn't go to see the parents to ask for some. Mother Sari left with the last coin to buy some fuel. She obtained one dose with it.

"Don't worry about tomorrow," Mother Sari said. "I will gather the peas and other produce from the garden and sell them."

She was going to sell the jasmine flowers. She left at dawn and returned to the house when the sun was at its zenith.[206] She then saw the Sakai who were exchanging a *myno* bird,[207] for rice. There were Sakai here in the past. They came to exchange birds for rice and tobacco.

"Haa! People say that this bird speaks."

"He speaks?"

"Yes, he is able to speak."

"Well then, we must have one. Take this quantity[208] of rice and a pinch of tobacco. One must not give too much rice and tobacco to the Sakai. They don't like that. If you give them too much, they will not come back because they will think that you will be angry with them and hate them."

"What must we do with this bird?"

"You must cut the end of his tongue, then pull on it and pass the gold on the back of the tongue. If you do this, he will be able to speak with his hoarse voice."

He had a forked tongue and so, it had to be cut at the end, pulled and the gold put over it, the gold of the skin of the golden animal because it shed its skin every month. They made his skin fall off and were able to make jewellery with this gold. They passed the gold over his tongue with the skin of gold. One or two months passed like this. They were able to eat thanks to what they had planted. Two months passed.

"Where are you going, mother?"

"It was Gold who said this. Our bird can speak, mother."

"Ha! Can he speak and ask us where we are going?"

"Where are you going, Mother Sari? Where are you going, Mother Sari?"

He kept on repeating this.

"I am going to sell flowers, Gold."

"What flowers?"

"Jasmine flowers."

"Take a great number of them this afternoon. I will go and sell them tomorrow."

"Do you know how to sell?"

"Yes, I can do this. I can. I can."

This is what Gold kept on repeating to Mother Sari. She had to put many flowers into the basket.[209] When the basket was half-full, he flew away and then came back and landed.

"Ha! Close the basket now, Mother Sari. Everyone in the village will want to see what's inside."

Mother Sari put the basket on the top of her head and Gold sat on it.

"Eh! Come here young people and see what Gold is selling. He is selling jasmine flowers, three for one sapec."

**Fig. 45.** Birds and especially turtledoves who sing are highly appreciated by the Malay who raise them. They have them participate in competitions and carve them on their boats. (Ivanoff, 1988)

Many people came to look but no one bought any. They came only to hear the bird speak.

"Three flowers for one sapec. Three flowers for one sapec."

And little by little, the people began to buy the flowers. They were very cheap and soon the basket was half-empty.

"Ha! We now have a great deal of money, no?"

"Let's go and buy some cakes in the king's stall, in the citadel."

"Don't open the basket until we get there."

Mother Sari opened the basket when they reached the stall.

"Do you sell bananas here? Gold would like some to eat."

There were some old people and some youngsters there who had come to see the bird. Gold, who was on the top of the basket, started speaking. Everyone wanted to give him something: bananas, money and chilli.

"I have some chilli but they are not ripe."

**Fig. 46.** Singing turtledove contests are very important throughout Southeast Asia (particularly in Singapore and Hong Kong) and attract many participants and visitors. The criteria for the best singers are based on the register and length of the songs. (Ivanoff, 1995)

And this is the way they were able to buy some cakes.

"We can go home now, Mother Sari."

They gathered everything together and Mother Sari put the basket on her head and Gold went inside it. But he soon started to have a backache and wanted to get out.

"Open the basket, Mother Sari. I am aching all over."

Mother Sari opened the basket and the bird flew out.

"Mother, Gold has come back with many, many cakes."

"We can now eat, Mochè."[210]

This is what he called his mistress. Days passed with going to and from the market when suddenly he had an idea.

"Where is your husband?"

"I don't have one, Gold."

"What do you mean you don't have one? And who made the house? Tell me what happened."

"But I don't have a husband, Gold."

"Where did he go?"

"He went out to sea four years ago."

But he was in prison at King Sanyanyo's place.

"Why did he leave?"

"I don't know why. He went to do some trading and never returned."

"What does he look like?"

"He took two sailors with him, Gold."

"Is your husband rather light or rather dark?"

"He is rather dark."

"And his face? What is it like?"

"He has a great deal of hair but it is bare behind the ears, with a long pony tail."

"And his boat. What does it look like?"

"It is yellow and the top of the broadside of the hull is white, like the prow. The three sailors are about the same height, neither very tall nor very small."

"Don't worry, Mochè. Go and get some bananas for me."

"Ha! Yes, there are some bananas in the house, Gold. I cut them off the day before yesterday. They are very ripe."

"Ha! Go and get them, Mochè. I will carry them in my beak. Seven bananas will be enough food for the voyage."

"And when will you leave, Gold?" said Mother Sari.

"I will leave tomorrow since it is too late to leave today and it will be night before I return."

"And where are you going?"

"I don't know."

"You don't even know where you are going! Who knows if you will come back."

Mother Sari got up the next day and prepared the rice. Then she went to wake up Gold so he could eat something. She had cooked rice for him but it was cold and there were no side dishes, only rice. There was only rice in the plate. So Gold ate, "po, po, po."

"Prepare some water in the washbasin so I can wash myself."

Mother Sari prepared the water and the earthenware dish. He went out and dried himself, since one cannot fly with wet feathers. Finally, he was ready.

"Ha! I want my bananas, the bananas, Mochè. Separate them from their branches so I can carry them. I am going to leave now."

The bananas were put on the top of the ladder. Mochè came to watch him leave.

"Go now, Gold. I will watch you leave."

He took the bananas and flew straight ahead and soon disappeared. He soared and soared and continued to soar. he went over three countries, including the country of King Sanyanyo. He saw other countries before this one. He looked for boats but didn't see any.

"I am going back into another country, the one of King Sanyanyo; where there are many boats. Ha! This is perhaps the place I am looking for but I can't see very well. There they are! Now I see some boats. Yes, they are boats. There is a yellow one with the top of the sides of the hull of a white colour."

He quickly descended and landed on the prow.

"This is no doubt Mochè's husband's boat. It is yellow with a white prow. I am going to look in the king's house to see if he is there."

He no sooner said this than, "pu", he flew until he reached the king's house. There were three men digging there. There were three men there. He watched them attentively, then he flew up and landed on the top of a banana tree. He took his last three bananas; he had already eaten four. Two of the men said:

"Why have you stopped working, Ché Hawè?"

"It's him! It is really him!"

"I am tired," he said.

He noticed the hair in a pony tail wound around his neck and saw that the three men were of the same height. He flew away, "bu, bu, bu," and threw the bananas on to the knees of the three men who were sitting down cross-legged.

"Ha! What is that?"

"It's a bird who is throwing bananas."

"What bananas?"

"Little bananas. He is there and is offering one to each of us."

He called his companions and told them to eat the bananas.

"A bird! But this isn't possible!"

"Nevertheless, it is a bird who threw them to me."

"And how did he do that?"

"Look! One can see the mark of the knife that has separated the bananas from their branches so that the load would be lighter. Perhaps this bird has come from far away. Maybe he even comes from the place where we lived. There is no doubt that he has come to help us. He is sitting behind me and throwing the bananas to me."

"Where do you come from?"

"I come from a country on the other side of the valley, from the land of the Malays. I come from the house of Mochè, whose name is Chémè, the daughter of a trader. I have come looking for Ché Hawè."

"Ha! That's me! How are you able to throw these bananas? Why have you come?"

"And why are you being held prisoner? What did you do?"

"This is what happened, Gold. We came here a long time ago. We had stopped on the way before reaching the fork of the river, not far from here. We had made a fire to announce our presence. King Sanyanyo sent his guards to see what was going on and who had come here and whether the boat was going to remain here for a long time. He then asked: 'What are you selling? What is your name?'

[I replied] 'My name is Ché Hawè."

[The guard said] 'You can sleep here peacefully. There are no bandits. Everyone is good here. There are no cruel people in this place.'"

The sailors went to sleep; they were exhausted after their voyage on the high seas. They slept profoundly. During this time, someone put a golden turtle in the boat by raising the plank where the cooking stove had been put; it was at the front of the boat. They put the turtle inside, "tek." The next morning, the king asked his guard to sound the alarm. Everyone came running.

"The ones who have just arrived must not leave because something belonging to the king has disappeared."

"But we haven't done anything bad! What has the king lost?" Ché Hawè asked. "We never even set foot on this land. We have never gone on to the land."

The king's men started searching and raised the planks of the deck and discovered the turtle there.

"Take it and carry it away! Capture these men and take them to the citadel! Immobilize the boat as well and take everything that is on it."

They were put in prison without anyone telling them what their sentence would be. It is now four years since this happened.

"Don't worry," said Gold. "As long as my wings are not broken, you mustn't worry. I am going to leave now."

"Send my greetings to my wife and parents."

"Don't worry. Eat until you are full and sleep profoundly. Refresh yourself, as well. I will return if my wings don't break."

And, "pung", he disappeared into the sun that was setting behind the mountain. He went straight ahead until he reached the house. Mother Sari said to Mochè:

"He has come back."

"Well then, did you find him?"

"Yes, I found him?"

"And what happened?"

"Let's not talk about this now, Mochè. It would be better to wait until tomorrow."

He had no desire to say anything that night.

"Let's wait until tomorrow. Then we will go and see the parents and speak together with them. If I speak now, what would I be able to say? Nothing."

The next day finally arrived.

"Go and get the parents, Mother Sari."

"Why?" she asked.

"Gold wants to speak to all of us about something."

"Very well then. I will go there."

Mother Sari went to the trader's house.

"Gold has returned."

"And what did he say?"

"I don't know. He is waiting for you to come."

"Let's go to Chémè's house."

"Come here, all of you. Come nearer. I want to talk to all of you. I want to tell you what happened to Ché Hawè."

"Haa! And what happened, Gold?"

"He told me about some bad things that happened to him. There are problems in the country of King Sanyanyo. He has been in prison for four years now. Who knows when he will come out of there? It all depends on the goodwill of the king."

"What are we going to do?"

"Here is what we are going to do. You, father-in-law, do you know the *dika*?"[211]

"Yes, I know it very well. I have even taught it."

"And you, captain/ship-owner, do you know how to play *takro*?"[212]

"Yes, of course I do."

"In that case, you will go and look for some silversmiths, three of them, who come from different countries. As for you, Ché Mudo,[213] you will go and look for some blacksmiths."[214]

"Why?"

"Don't ask me now."

"Should we do something?"

"Yes. Put a great deal of rice and all the musical instruments on a boat and go to the island that is found in the center of the sea. As for you, trader, you must teach Chémè how to play *takro* until she becomes agile, strong and rapid. You, captain/ship-owner, you will show her how to use the *bagayong silat*,[215] to strike with the blade surely and quickly."

"Why, Gold?"

"We are going to look for Ché's husband and bring him back with us. But if you don't do everything I tell you to do, we will not be able to do anything. We won't be able to take him out of prison. He won't get out until we are able to play in a perfect way."

"And the blacksmiths and silversmiths?"

"They must go to the island."

"What will they do there?"

"Don't worry, there will be work for them. But they must wait there."

"What kind of work must they do?"

"I will go and get the silversmiths," said the trader. And I will also teach the *silat*."

Then they left. They left the port and the gongs started to ring out, "gung, gung, gung" and all the musicians went to the island in the centre of the sea. They taught there for one month. Everyone followed Gold's idea and it wasn't long before everyone could use the *silat* and play *takro* perfectly, even Chémè.

"It's finished now, Ché Tuwo, Ché Mudo and you three silversmiths. Mother Sari is now going to become the wife of Chémè."

They went out to sea and navigated for a long time, until they reached the country of King Sanyanyo.

"We have arrived!"

They lowered the sail and entered the port. They made a fire to announce their presence.

"Haa! Guards!" King Sanyanyo said:

"Go and see what kind of merchants they are, what they are selling and why they have stopped here. Don't they have any more water or provisions? Do they need wood?"

The guards left.

"We come from the country on the other side of the valley, from the land of the Malays."

"What is your name?"

"My name is Adé Hawè."

"What are you selling?"

"Balls of rice."

"And where are you going to sell them?"

"There are places where we can sell them. But we have only this one to sell."

"It doesn't matter. You can sleep here since you come from far away. Don't be afraid, there are no bandits here."

This is what the guard said. Then he went back to see the king.

"What are they selling? Where do they come from?"

"They say that they come from the land on the other side of the valley, from the land of the Malays."

"And what are their names?"

"Adé Awè."

"Ah! There are many names like this in the Malay lands. It wasn't long ago that it was someone called Ché Hawè and now it is Adé Awè. The people like these names very much over there. Return and be very careful and prepare everything."

"But everything is already prepared. The rope and hooks have been prepared to carry the [golden] turtle with."

He returned to the boat to look after the sailors. Everything was peaceful on board and they were all snoring, "sohasa, sohasa." Only the bird who was resting on a piece of wood was not asleep. He had come back.

"Well then, what has happened?"

"Everyone is sleeping."

"Good! Go quickly and prepare the turtle."

"Gugè, gigè", they left with the turtle on their shoulders. They were carrying it "geregah" and were going towards the boat. When they arrived there, they raised the second plank of the thwart in order to put the turtle into it, "kukah, kukah, kuka."

"Hurry, hurry!"

They went off quickly until they were far away.

"Ah! Ché Tuwo and Ché Mudo."

"What is it, Gold?"

"Wake up! Wake up! Don't ask any questions. It is not the moment."

"Why?"

"Prepare everything. Turn the boat around towards the sea. Cast off the mooring ropes."

The boat slid gently into the sea and left the port with the sail that was waving in the wind. Before long, the wind filled the sail[216] and then "bero, bero, bero."

"Don't say anything. We mustn't speak yet."

They sailed further away.

"Raise the sails, Chè!"

They soon arrived on the island in the middle of the ocean. Once they were there, they prepared a lever to eject the turtle from the boat, "dung." And Gold said:

"Blacksmith, cut this turtle in half for me. Silversmiths, do your work quietly and make some bracelets and rings for me. Make as many as you like. Don't think about how much you will earn right now. We will take care of this later on. What is most important is that you take as much care of this heavy turtle as big as a van."

Gold said:

"There is still not enough to compensate for the four years Ché Hawè has been in prison. Let's go back as quickly as possible now."

They went back to King Sanyanyo's place, in exactly the same spot, and no one noticed anything there.

"Everyone must be asleep now."

It would soon be morning and when it broke, they heard the alarm bell ring.

"Don't let those who have just arrived get away because something belonging to the king has disappeared. If they escape, I will kill you."

"But what is happening?" said the captain/ship-owner. "We haven't gone anywhere. We haven't moved from here at all."

"Ah! Go and search then."

He said to Chémè, who is called Adé Hawè here:

"Empty everything that you find on the boat. Empty the coconut from the shell and the balls of rice."

[Then] they looked on all the king's boats. They emptied the boat until there was nothing left. They did this on all the king's boats. Everything happened exactly as Gold had said it would. Once everything had been taken off the boats, there was nothing left to look for.

"There was nothing at all there," said Chémè, who knew what it was all about.[217] She turned towards the king and said:

"Pardon me, lord, but I would like to go home."

"No, it is not possible," said the king's son, who had fallen in love with Chémè. She had won his heart. He was someone who loved women. "Come with me to the king's house," he proposed.

"No, it is not the moment to go there. I will come tomorrow. It's the same."

The king's son left. Gold followed him, "pu" and went directly into the hole in the mango tree that was beside the king's house. He leaned over and listened to what was being said.

"Well then, what happened?" asked King Sanyạnyo.

"Ah! I really don't know, father. The turtle that should have been on the boat wasn't there. But I am certain that it is there. I looked everywhere but found nothing and I am afraid that these people left last night."

"This is not what happened last time."

"Ah! Yes, it's true, father. I don't think anyone knows where this group of sailor-merchants come from, the ones led by Adé Hawè, nor where they are going. At the same time though, the boat has remained in the same place. I, myself, went to attach it and it hasn't moved since then."

Oh, yes! The bird did everything very well!

"Anyway, I think the trader is a woman."

"And where have you ever seen a sea trader who is a woman?"

"But how can one be certain today? Anyway, even if she is a girl, she will be perfect for me. She is very pretty, also. And moreover, why can't she be a woman? Maybe she wound her hair around her head and put on tight trousers and a tight shirt. In that case, no one would be able to see her breasts; they would be squeezed in. Yes, she has no doubt put on several shirts in order to hide her breasts."

"Whether a woman or a boy, we will know tomorrow. We will have her come to the palace. You will say to her: 'Come, Mochè, it is the moment to play *takro*. If it is a boy, he will be unable to resist playing since when a boy sees a game of *takro*, it is as irresistible for him as glutinous rice.'"

"Alright then. We will do this. We will invite him to come and play when night falls."

———

"Well then, Gold?"

"Be very careful tomorrow, Mochè. Take good care of your clothes."

"Why, Gold?"

"The king's son will play *takro*. He spoke to his father who told him that if you were really a man, you would come and play."

Mochè remained in a state of shock for a minute. She didn't think that she would know how to play.

"If you go to play, don't take off any of your clothes and put several shirts and pairs of trousers on, so that no one will notice anything. Hoo! Put a turban on very tightly to hide your hair. Put your hair inside it. Be very careful about your trousers, so that no one will be able to see that you are a girl."

The sun went down and someone began to prepare the game.

"Uh! Don't go, Adé, the captain/ship-owner. Come to our palace."

"Ah, yes! I am coming."

She put on the trousers and shirts. They were long trousers and there were two pairs.

"Ah! Hurry up."

"I am coming," she said. She got down on to the land and went to the palace.

"Here I am, father," she said.

She made a salutation to King Sanyanyo, who was staring at her.

"If she is a girl, she is really very pretty."

King Sanyanyo said:

"Stay here. We are going to play *takro*. Will you remain with us?"

"Ah! But I don't know how to play this game. I don't know how to hit with my foot. I don't know how to play very well."

She got up and went to where there were some young men. The king's son hit the ball, twenty, thirty, forty times. He sent the ball to Mochè who caught it and hit with her foot, straight ahead. She hit it with her foot, head, knees, shoulders and elbows almost one hundred and twenty times before she sent the ball back to the king's son.

"Hola! You have really hit the ball very well, young merchant. How did you do this? Eh! I am not as good a player as you are. I can't play with you. The maximum I can reach is fifty."

Chémè was very happy that she had been able to play very well. She hit the ball with her back, head and shoulders, from right to left and it always remained close to her. She played with her head and the ball went straight over her. Then she hit it with the lower part of her back and the ball bounced before she caught it again with her head. The game lasted like this for a long time. She was able to hit the ball one hundred and twenty times before she sent it back to the king's son. His father said:

"Ah! Well, do you still think it is a woman?"

"I am not yet convinced."

"Sleep here, young trader."

"Ah! I can't. I haven't informed my wife and we will quarrel if I don't return."

"It doesn't matter. You can sleep where you want. You play so well! One hundred hits!"

But he still continued thinking it was a woman.

"It must be a woman, father, but I am still not totally convinced."

Dawn approached and the bird came and landed in the hole in the mango tree so that he could hear what the king was saying.

"What will we do now?" the king asked.

"Yes, what are we going to do?"

"I don't know. He plays *takro* very well and very quickly. We have to make him sleep with us so that we can see what kind of sex [organ] he has."

"How will we be able to feel it?"

"If it is a man, his sex will move when one touches it."

"Ah, yes! That's a good idea."

"We will play *takro* again today."

Gold immediately flew off, "puh," and went back to the boat.

"Ah! Moché, you must put two pairs of trousers on and, as for myself, I will put a mouse as fat as a big toe inside. I will attach its two paws to the seam of the trousers on your pelvis. It will have to remain quiet and you will do whatever you can to see that it remains in place. If someone touches it, it will begin to stir. Don't tap too hard if it begins to move. The mouse mustn't die."

"Alright, Gold."

She went to play *takro* and really played very well.

"Let's go into the flower garden."

They went there and the king's son showed her his plants.

"Now we will try to urinate as far as possible, above the well. Can you do this?"

Gold went to look for a hollow bamboo and put it into Moché's pocket.

"Since you are the king's son, you go first."

The king's son raised his sarong, "chooo", but his urine only went as far as the well, "chruuu." He only reached the wall of the well.

"Now it's your turn."

"Alright! But I am ashamed. You are standing too close to me."

She took the bamboo and put it in her hole and went much farther than the well.

"Ah! You are really very strong. You urinate very well."

"When I urinate, lord, I pierce the leaves."

"Ah, yes! You are truly strong."

They returned to the house and on the way saw the bird.[218]

"Here is my father's bird. Catch it."

"Auh! But one cannot be gentle with this bird. One has to jump on top of it. But in that case, he might die."

"Well then, let him die."

They encircled the bird and jumped on it. The bird defecated and then died.

"It doesn't matter. It is my father's bird. Let's go back now since it will soon be night."

"You mustn't sleep too close to me since I have nightmares."

"Ah! It doesn't matter."

They ate and prepared the mats and lay down side by side.

"Don't go to sleep too close to me since I don't know what kind of dreams I will have."

They soon fell asleep and, "piyoh, piyoh", the king's son came closer, "keso", then a bit closer, then, "keso", even closer until he caught hold of Mochè's sex [organ].

"Uh! But what are you doing? You are disturbing me. I am going to go back to my boat to sleep."

They both got up and started to laugh.

"Why doesn't his sex move like a normal sex [organ]? I only just touched it and "nyu, nyu, nyu" it started to stir. Yes, I am asking myself questions. He plays *takro* very well but there is something going on here. I see a bird. He is certainly a spy who tells someone everything we say to each other."

"I don't know."

"Ah! Let's sharpen the branches of a coconut tree and rub some resin on it and some latex. We will put it in his hole."

The next day at dawn, the bird went back into his hole and "peruh", he went inside and "peruh", he went in and fell down.

"Ah! Here he is."

"Keyèh, keyè."

The bird cried "keyèh, keyèh." They removed his feathers and this made him very angry. He soon had no feathers left and was naked. He only had some feathers on his head. The guards came nearer in order to cut his throat. One of them took hold of his legs but the bird dug his claws into the guard's finger, "ka", who let go, "ngah." The bird escaped but he was limping and hid in a pineapple tree.

"Ah! The king is going to be very angry with his servants. We must catch hold of a duck and take off his feathers."

The guards caught a duck, cut his throat and removed all his feathers.

"Now he looks like a bird."

They took off his feathers and cut him into small pieces. They cut off his feet and his beak, too and prepared some salt and saffron. Then the king called to them.

"Is it cooked?"

"Yes, it is cooked."

The guards brought the bird to the king and the king said.

"Why did you cut it into little pieces?"

"Nobody eats the beak."

"And the legs?"

"They don't eat the legs either."

"Ah! In any case, we will be much happier without this bird."

Chémè had a fever and the captain/ship-owner wanted to leave since the bird had disappeared and he had no idea what fate was reserved for them. The boat remained there for seven days. One morning, one of the king's servants was washing the rice. The bird went out of his hiding place with his wings spread so that they could be splashed by the rice water. "Choh, choh, choh." He opened his wings very wide so that they would get completely wet with the water of the rice. Then he went back to his pineapple tree. The first feathers began to sprout three days later and on the fifth day, hairs began to appear; he finally returned to the boat, "Cpuh, cpuh, cpuh."

"Ah! Mochè! Mochè! Mochè! Gold has returned."

Chémè got up, "Gugè! gugè!" She got up immediately and it was as if her heart had started to beat again.

"What is it, Gold? What has happened?"

"Ah! The king's son took off all my feathers. But don't worry, Mochè, we will get our revenge on the son of King Sanyanyo."

"And how will we do this?"

"Wait, Mochè. Wait for another two days. Ah! Mother Sari, prepare some puffed rice, two litres, because I am going to give something to the king's son who tore off all my feathers. Prepare this for me this afternoon."

"It is cooked."

"Ah! Bring it here. Put it in the straw baskets."

The bird went out and threw the grains down as if he was planting them.

"Come! Oh! Rodents, approach all of you who are my servants."

And all the rodents arrived. Some of them were as fat as the wrist and others as fat as the ankle. There were all sorts. All of them arrived.

"Eat my puffed rice and then go and dig a tunnel from the boat to the statue[219] of King Sanyanyo. I must be able to slide until I reach it. When you have finished, come back. It is not worthwhile coming back before then. As for the earth you remove, throw it far away."

All the rodents went to work. They dug without stopping and came back to the boat in the morning.

"Ah! They have finished the work."

"Your hole has been made," said Mochè.

"Give them some more puffed rice so that they can eat again."

They ate two more litres of puffed rice.

"Wait here. I am going to see if it is finished. If it is not finished, they will have to go back there."

He left his hole and reached the statue where an opening had been made at the level of the mouth. Without a hole, it was impossible to speak. No one would dare to go near this statue since it was magic. Two persons passed rapidly by in front of it.

"Eh! Where are you going?"

He tried to speak.

"The king's statue speaks!"

"What is the matter, ancestor?"

"I am asking you where you are going since it will soon be night."

"Ah! We are going to buy some cakes for our children and we must hurry otherwise they will start to cry."

"Go and buy your cakes and come back by the same road."

"Ah, yes! We will come back. We will come back."

But the bird also left and went back to the boat. It was possible to get there thanks to the tunnel which went from the statue to the boat.

"Ah! Mochè."

"Ah! Well then, how was it?"

"I will have to eat tomorrow, otherwise I will die in this statue."

"Ah! Don't worry about that," said Mother Sari.

"I want some hot rice, not cold rice. As for the rest of you, don't say anything while I am away."

He went into the tunnel and climbed into the statue until he reached its mouth. A couple came by with a small baby. The husband was carrying two sacks of rice that he was planning to sell in the market.

"Hey! You who are carrying the sacks!"

They turned their heads.

"Where are you taking your goods?"

"Ah! The king's statue is able to speak."

"Ah! I have wanted to speak for a long time now. Put down your load and go and inform the king."

"But it will soon be night and our child is still very small, great king of the statues."

"It doesn't matter. You can sell your rice later on. Go and see the king now and tell him I want to see him."

"Ah! As for you, look after the rice."

"Don't worry, no one will take any. I will twist the neck of anyone who tries."

"Very well then! Remain here, my wife."

"She will remain here and don't be worried about your baby nor about your rice that you will soon be able to sell."

He ran to the place.

"What's the matter?"

"Wait a minute. I am out of breath."

He was afraid of the king's statue and had hurried. He had to speak quickly because of his fear.

"What do you have to say?"

"The statue of the king, lord, she can speak. She wants the king to come and see her this afternoon, as quickly as possible. Hurry up, since she wants to speak. She wants to say something. As for myself,[220] I must return. But you must make haste otherwise she will be angry with me."[221]

"Ah! Wait a second, we will go together."

They both left.

"Ah! Has the king come?"

"Ah! I am greeting you, statue of the king. I[222] am here."

"Where? Approach, King Sanyanyo. Stand in front of me. If you don't come, I will wring your neck."

Ah, yes! The bird was venomous and was satisfied. And the king kept making salutations to him. The ancestor spoke again.

"Come here, you have really been doing some bad things for a long time now, King Sanyanyo. And I now know everything. You have committed many sins. You captured some men, took everything away from them, lied to them and threw them in prison. What you did is very bad and you must learn to behave differently. You profited from these poor people and took all their goods so that you could sell them. You will now have to pay for all this. You are going to bring me all your riches and all the things you robbed from the men. I want to see you do all this. All those who you have imprisoned you will now liberate. They will come here and take their goods. Each of them will take what belongs to him, so put them correctly here. You have acted very badly with all the captains for a long time now. Go and come back tomorrow. And if you don't bring everything I asked you to bring, I will break your neck. As for your hooligan of a son, he must cut his hair in the form of a cross and spill some salt and saffron on it. And make sure that he does this, otherwise I will be very angry. You don't know anything, you haven't learned anything and you are really stupid. If you do what I have told you to do, half of your errors will be forgiven."

The king went home and held a council.[223] He gathered everyone together.

"You will bring all your goods tomorrow and go and stand in front of the king's statue. I am afraid not to do this. I will die if I don't do what he asked me to do. Ah! As for you, my son,[224] you must shave your head."

"And why must I shave my head?"

"I don't know why. That's the way it is. He told me that you must cut your hair in the form of a cross and put salt and saffron on it because we have sinned greatly. If we don't do this, we will die. Go and cut your hair, my son."

So, he went to cut his hair and cried, "kiyôh, kiyôh" because this made him suffer. He wanted to put a turban on his skull.

"You must come with your head naked. If you hide your head, I will know about it."

He cut his hair in the form of a cross and rolled it in a cloth.

"Let's see your skull."

"Ah! Son of the king, you have done many bad things for a long time now. You understand nothing, you don't know anything and you are stupid. You are sterile earth. Show me all your riches that you have brought so that we can see them and make a selection. If any one of you takes what does not belong to him, I will kill him."

They came nearer but no one dared to take anything. They had been in prison for too long. Each one took what belonged to him but no one dared to take what remained. On the fourth night, the sailors had taken away all their belongings. All the prisoners had recovered their things. Each one left by sea to go back to his own country. Gold returned to the boat on the fourth night.

"Ah! Ché Tuwo and Ché Mudo, come and recover King Sanyanyo's belongings and we will go home."

"What are you talking about, Gold?"

"Everything has been left in front of the king's statue. All the riches that one could want are there."

So, they transported everything on to their boat and soon after, the boat left the port.

"We have made a great deal of profit."

Ché Hawè had gone back with his boat. All the king's boats transported the balls of rice and the coconut fibre. Gold called to the rodents and told them to make holes in the king's boats so that they would sink in the sea.

"Ah! The boat of the king's son has just arrived."

"Ah! Wait for me, young captain/ship-owner."

"Ah! Well then come, lord."

She took off her clothes and one could now see her breasts.

"Ah! It is just what I thought. She is a woman."

She took off her clothes and everyone could see. Chémè was very angry.

"Come here with your boat."

He took a small boat and rowed very quickly. He soon left the port and the boat sank. He swam until he reached the shore and then took another boat, but it also sank. He swam towards the shore and took another boat but it also sank. The sea finally engulfed him and he died. Only King Sanyanyo remained. He was all alone now.

They reached the island in the middle of the ocean and held a party that lasted for seven days and seven nights. They stayed on this island but didn't count the days since they were very rich. They held a party that lasted for seven days and seven nights with *dika* and theatrical performances. The blacksmiths and silversmiths kept trying to dismember the golden turtle and transform it. They were all very rich, the blacksmiths as well as the silversmiths. Everyone was rich. Seven days later, they put all their riches on to the boat and played music and went from the island in the middle of the ocean until they reached home. When they were not far away from their home, they cut down the mast. This is what people do who have had success in maritime commerce. They cut down the mast, "geruuu" and it fell into the sea. They were now free of all their sorrows. They had made a great deal of profit. They transported all their riches. All of them were rich, including the captain/ship-owner and the trader, Ché Hawè. Ah! Ché Hawè then became the king here. He called his subjects and told them to build a new house where everyone would be made welcome, since the couple had now become very rich. The trader and Ché Hawè asked the men to hold a party for Ché Hawè's marriage. Many animals were offered as a sacrifice. They sat down together[225] and were freed[226] from bad fortune. Hawè was now the king.

### 3.6. Hawè Sada

***(Village of Samoh, Province of Narathiwat, November 1991***
***Narrator: Wo Seng***
***Type of story: bahri)***

A story? Yes, it really is a story. It is one about a couple who didn't have any children. A man and a woman lived together without any children and they were beginning to grow old. "We have many good things: cows, buffaloes, land, but no children. What are we going to do with our heritage?

They went to sleep until dawn. The house was close to a river. The woman went to defecate. Not far from where she was going, she noticed a basket[227] that was stuck by some posts. There was a child in the basket whose umbilical cord had not been cut off (someone had thrown it into the water); the placenta was still visible.

"Eh, old man! Come and see."

"What is it?"

"There is a child here."

"How is this possible?"

But they were happy since they didn't have a child.

"He is stuck against one of the posts near the toilets."

The basket was stuck[228] by one of the posts of the toilet.

"We must go and get him."

The woman caught hold of the baby with her hands and carried him in her arms and washed him.

"Go and look for a piece of pointed bamboo so we can cut the umbilical cord." The umbilical cord was not yet cut since they had thrown the child on to the ground like a package. The woman took a pointed bamboo stick and brought it home.

"Go and look for a piece of cloth to tie the cord with."

They cut the cord and rubbed it; the woman knew how to do this.

"Ah! The cord is now cut," she said to the newborn baby.

It was a boy and they called him Hawè Sada and brought him up. The father worked at cutting the stipites of the coconut trees in order to collect the sap. He used it as milk for the baby. In those days, milk was not cooked but they gave it to the child so he could suck. The child grew up and became a Muslim.[229]

"You will go and study, Hawè. You will go to where the king of the waterhole lives. There is a haji there who teaches the twenty roads to wisdom."[230]

"Oh! Alright, father. Don't be worried."

He called him father. Then he left to study. He studied for many days and nights at the house of the king of the waterholes. Who then was this king of the waterholes? He was a great king and he had a daughter whose name was Dame Benjamin. She was engaged to the son of King Battle Flash; he was a seaman.[231] They had been engaged for three years already, but their parents had still not given them permission to marry.

We are going to speak about Dame Benjamin and the son of King Battle Flash.

"Ah! What are we going to do, my older one?"

"What do you want to do?"

They were waiting for permission from their parents to marry. But they had been waiting now for three years.

"What are we going to do, my older one?"

"Ah! I don't know, my younger one."

"We must run away on Monday night. We will leave in the evening, between Monday and Tuesday night."

"Alright then. We will do this. "

They waited for another three days and then called the servant and told her to crush some chilli, prepare some saffron, brine[232] and some cakes. They would need provisions for the voyage since they were going to run away. They still remained for two days. Then they called the guardian.

"Ah! Go and look for the elephant Wash the Ancestors."[233]

This was the elephant's name. It was an old elephant.

"Why should we wash him then? "

"You will wash him without asking any questions."

So, he went to see the elephant who was soon ready. The afternoon was advancing and they told the servant to load all the provisions: rice, brine, chillies, cakes. They took a servant and a guardian with them. Night was falling when they crossed over the waterhole of the king, with the elephant. They went over it with the elephant because Dame Benjamin was running away with King Battle Flash's son. Not long after that, the king's son had a stomach ache and night was falling. He went to defecate. One could barely see that it was a human form from so far away.[234]

"Eh! Older one."

"Ho?"

"Make the elephant sit down, guardian."

The elephant crouched down.

"Come here and mount the elephant. Don't be worried. Everything will be alright."

So, the newcomer mounted the elephant instead of the king's son. They advanced rapidly all through the night.

"Eh, guardian! We must stop for a time to give the elephant something to eat. We have gone very far already. "

"Ah! That's good."

They then unloaded their things.

"Eh, servant."

"What do you want?"

"Bring me the lamp and put it near the older one."

No one knew who he was but he and Dame Benjamin had been amusing themselves all during the journey while they were on the back of the elephant by pinching themselves. They lit the lamp and went near the older one.

"Hum, hum. Is it you, guardian?"

"What do you want?"

"I think that it is Hawè Sada and not my beloved."

"Ha! What shall we do?"

"Ha! This is how things are. We can't do anything about it. If it is Sada, well then, it is Sada. I would be ashamed if I left now."

The servant and the guardian slept together. They boiled some water and prepared the cakes and the other provisions. The elephant also ate something and then they called him so that they could put back the palanquin and load their belongings on to it.

"Ha! Well then, climb up, older one. We are going to the border of the country called Sanyanyo. It is not very far away. "

She ran away from her father's country. They continued travelling and finally reached a platform on the side of the road and unloaded their things. Dawn was breaking.

"Give some bamboo to the elephant to eat. Ask the people of this village, the one over there."

They unloaded their belongings and the elephant waited there. The guardian went off and soon returned.

"Eh! Mistress, there are some old people there who know the king."

So she left and went there.

"Eh! old man!"

"What is it, mistress?"[235]

"I want to ask you for permission to take some bamboos that are in the thicket for my elephant."

The old man made a salutation and said:

"You can take all you want, Dame who comes from far away, since we wanted to get rid of them anyway."

"Ah! Very well. What is this country?"

"It is the country of a great king."

"Where is the border?"

"It is over there, ahead of you."

"And who does this country belong to?"

"It is the country of King Sanyanyo."

"Alright."

"Let your elephant eat, mistress. We were going to destroy the bamboo thicket in order to make a paddy field."

"Ho! Very well then, if that's the way it is."

They all went to sleep but the elephant was not tied up and he had understood. He went on to the road, "broo," in order to break the bamboo, tear off the thin strips and eat them. He ate them not far from Dame Benjamin and nobody dared to disturb him. He kept on eating until midday and everybody woke up.

"Ah! Get up, servant. We must cook the rice and then leave. It is already early afternoon."

They prepared the rice, ate, loaded their provisions on the elephant and left. All the provisions that the elephant carried made him move forward, "hine, hine." They finally arrived at the border.

"Ah! Here we are, guardian, at the border between my father's country and that of King Sanyanyo. We are going into King Sanyanyo's country. Let's go. I will follow you."

They entered the country of Sanyanyo and reached a very big coconut grove. There was no one there. It was a very big grove.

"We must stop here, old man."

He made a salutation.

"Ah! Yes. We really must stop here."

They wanted to ask for some coconut stipites but the owner was not there.[236]

"Go and climb up, Hawè."

Hawè was really very strong and had a powerful body, so he climbed up to cut some branches of the coconut trees, three branches.

"Ah! That's enough, Hawè. Just one of them will be sufficient for me to eat."

So Hawè cut the dead branches and placed them side by side in order to make a shelter with something to lie down on and a mosquito net. Each couple had a shelter, one for the servant and the guardian and one for Hawè and Dame Benjamin. In the centre, there was a fire near where the elephant would rest. A loosely tied chain was attached to his ankle but he was able to move about. He found himself between the two couples. They all slept there. Dame Benjamin woke up so she could spit out her betel but Hawè didn't wake up. It was not long before the roosters started crowing.

"Ah! There must be people not far away."

"Where, mistress?"

"Not too far away. One can hear the roosters crowing."

There were undoubtedly some houses not far from there. They went back to sleep. The dawn came. Ah! "Yala",[237] a Chinese ghost arrived. "Haa, haa!" a Chinese spirit.

"Ah! 'Yala', lord. Why have you come here? Ah! You cannot stay here, my queen; this is my road and I do not allow anyone, even the owner, to go into the coconut tree grove. Go over there, just in front of the kapok tree. The king's houses are over there."

"Ah! Is this true, pè?"[238]

"Yes, it's true. Go then."

"Ha! In any case, it is now daylight."

"We cannot remain here, guardian. The spirit has told us to leave."

So, they loaded their things on to the elephant's back, while he was crouching down. They didn't even wash themselves. The elephant was crouched down and they put all their things, mosquito nets, mats and pillows, on his back. They didn't even remove the chain from the elephant's ankle, who was pulling on it, "krèng krèng." He went ahead and everyone followed behind until they reached the kapok tree.

"Ah! Here is the kapok tree that the Chinese spirit told us about. This is good."

They unloaded their things. The guardian and Hawè cut down some trees to make field-houses since they were far away from everything. There was no one to be seen, so they had to do this. They prepared the forked pillars which the elephant stamped into the ground. There was a house for each couple. Then they went to sleep. They soon heard the cocks crowing again nearby.

"Guardian! Hawè! You must go towards the northwest."

So the guardian accompanied Hawè and went there. How many houses were there? There were six of them. There was an imam, a *kotep* and a *bilah*[239] there. Everything was here. The imam already knew what was happening.

"Ah! You have come to ask our permission to remain here. Let's go and see."

Everyone came back with the guardian.

"Ah! you can't stay in houses like those. We are going to build new ones."

"Build houses? But with what? There is no wood. There is nothing here."

"Of course there is," said a companion. "Each of us can very well find two pillars and all of us will be able to build a house."

They decided to make a roof, walls with bamboo strips. Everything.

"Ah! We will do this tomorrow. It is too late to do this today."

They started working the next day. Some of them went two by two and carried the pillars on their shoulders. Others carried them alone. They brought the ridge beams and everything else that was necessary. They all went to work; there was a great deal to do for five, or even seven men if one counted Hawè and the guardian. They built a house, a house with six pillars. Then they made the floor and then the veranda and finally an extension for the kitchen. There was everything there and the house was soon finished. Then they cooked the glutinous rice in order to hold the ceremony "climb up into the house." The imam read prayers for the married couples. Hawè had married Dame Benjamin and the guardian had married the servant. The house was full of people because the queen was there and everyone thought this to be a good thing. Ho! Yes, it was all very good.

In the past, everyone thought that it was a good thing to receive a king in his village since then everyone could help one another. The kings of the past were magicians. It is not the same thing today. The kings of today are no longer magicians. But the queen came and they had all helped each other to build the house. The house had walls, a roof and a veranda. Those who lived in the four or five other houses had come to help them and since that time the couples live happily together.

We are now going to speak of something else.

"Eh! Imam, is there any free land here? We want to make dry fields."

"Ah, yes! There is plenty."

"To whom does this land belong?"

"To King Sanyanyo, but it is I who am responsible for this region and we can go and speak to the king."

"We want to make dry fields."

"Where?"

"Over there."

"Let's go and see! There is no one there, so take as much as you want."

They prepared some rice and ate the next day.

"Hawè, my older one. Let's go and see the land."

"Let's go!"

They went to see the land and each one carried a machete. They reached a forest through which a river ran.

"Ah! It is good over there. We are going to clear the land."

"Hum! Let's start working," he said.

But Sada didn't know how to do this. Dame Benjamin worked. She began by cutting down four trees that she planted on each side of their land.

As for Sada, he had already begun the work. They could all cut down as many trees as they wanted. So, they started clearing the land and then went home. The next day, they sharpened their machetes and Sada also brought an axe along. They spent all day clearing the land and their hands were full of blisters since they were not accustomed to working so hard. They couldn't even eat because their hands caused them much suffering.

"Eat with a spoon, older one."

They ate and then went to lie down. Dame Benjamin took hold of his hands.

"Ha!" she said. "It is pitiful to see you like that, older one."

"Ha! I am a man. It is not serious. We must continue but I really can't eat with my hands."

"Hup! Go and rest. We will stop working for a moment."

"No! We must not stop. If we don't cut now, when will we do it?"

They went off to continue clearing the land. They both worked. Dame Benjamin worked in the same place where she had started, "hahaha!" and Sada was farther away.

"Hey!" she said. "Listen, you trees, all of you are going to cut yourselves down. I am telling you this according to my desire."

And the trees fell down day and night. The field was soon very well cleared.

"Come back, older one. We will go home now."

"Ah! it is always the same with women: one works and then one has to go back home!"

They went home and shortly afterwards heard a noise, "gruuh"; it was the noise made by the trees as they fell down.

"Ah! What kind of trees are these?" said the imam. "Are there people still working over there."

"I don't know," said Dame Benjamin.

"Perhaps there is still somebody there."

They heard the wood falling, "grung grung." All the trees fell down since Dame Benjamin had commanded[240] them to do so. This was how Dame Benjamin was. Hoo! The land was now a vast field. Hawè Sada wanted to go and see.

"Maybe someone is trying to take away our land?"

"I don't know. Perhaps," said Dame Benjamin.

"Maybe someone is trying to cut down the trees on the side of our land, over there where we began to work."

"Hum! Is it our land or the land of our neighbours?"

"Hum! Maybe they are working on our land and are getting tired for us?"

"This is not very important," said Dame Benjamin.

They remained there for seven days.

"Imam, when can we put fire to the felled trees?"

"Are they dry?"

"Ah! Then go and gather the leaves of the coconut tree, two or three bundles of leaves attached with rattan ties."

"How many leaves are needed, older one?"

"We need to burn many of them if we want to make a fire."

"Eh! Take them, Dame Benjamin."

She took the leaves that were as long as a forearm. Haa! The fire started. She went back to where she had started working. She made a fire in three parts of the field and said:

"Devour everything. Don't stay far away from the trunks of the trees. Don't be lazy or you will have to start all over again."

She put fire to the three parts. Haa! They were ablaze but no one can say how this happened. This lasted for seven days and seven nights. The fire was a big one and illuminated the sky as far as the house of the king. He said:

"Who is making rice paddies?"

"Eh! I heard that it was someone called Hawè Sada. This is his name."

"Ah! He is powerful, Hawè Sada, very strong and he has a beard."

Ha! This is how the fire was put out. They asked their companions to give them some rice seeds. They asked their companions that lived in the five houses. They asked for rice, peas, peppers, string-beans, cucumber seeds, and calabash seeds. They were able to gather more than one hundred sacks. They now had one hundred sacks of rice seeds. Dame Benjamin then asked Hawè Sada to distribute the seeds. They divided the parcel into rows, five rows, since there were five houses. She then asked him to make seed holes. One must make seed holes before doing anything else. After doing this, he divided the parcel into five. She made the seed holes then while making an invocation. Ho! The kings in those days were kings. The rice soon started growing and all the stalks were of the same height. They had all kinds of things there: string-beans, peas, chillies, corn. Ha! This is how it was. The rice was beautiful and so was the corn. The young corn stalks were there. Everything was growing very well. Then they told the servants and guardians to go and harvest the young corn stalks and everything else. They put everything into two big sacks. Dame Benjamin also asked Hawè Sada to go and see the king of these lands and of the country. Hawè Sada went to see the king, carrying the presents on his shoulder.

"Ah! What is all that?" The king asked.

He made a salutation and said:

"They are the young corn stalks, lord. I offer them to you."

In fact, there were all kinds of products: corn, string-beans, chillies, peas, everything.

"Ah! I really appreciate the brine. So it is you who dried this field?"

"Yes. and I greet you, lord."

"Ha! So it is you who works so hard on the land. We saw your fire burning for seven nights."

Ha! Hawè Sada changed and returned home. He went back to the field that was full of beautiful stalks of rice and corn.

"Let's go, guardian and servants! We will gather the vegetables that are in the field."

"Alright! Let's go."

The next day, the servant went to look for the guardian to tell him to come to Hawè Sada's field. One day was hardly enough to go around it.

"Let's go first to Hawè's house."

"Ah! You have come, guardian. Stop for a moment."

Ha! The guardian and the servant had come with the elephant to gather the vegetables and lemons that were in the garden.

"Ah! There are only the two of us here."

They gathered the vegetables day after day. There were two baskets that they loaded on to the elephant. They put the vegetables into brine so that they could sell them. The rice was soon ready.[241]

"We don't have a rice granary, Hawè."

"Eh! I will go into the forest and cut a large amount of wood there."

He sharpened his axe. Sada sharpened it and left for the forest to cut down a piece of wood for the granary. He prepared it and placed it straight up. The pillar was very big and heavy. He made one pillar every day. When he went home, his hands were swollen and red, full of blisters, haha! It was worse than when he had gone to work to clear the field. Dame Benjamin noticed this.

"But you are full of blisters. You must stop, Hawè. And also, it is very long, older one."

"What do you mean long?"

He didn't listen to her but continued to cut and only returned when night was falling. Dame Benjamin came down and took four pillars that she planted in the ground. She made an invocation and a rice granary, as long as twenty arms' lengths, appeared. There was an extension,[242] a door and walls.

"Ah! My wife is a real magician."

He knew that she was a magician. He divided the rice into several rows; he shared the golden rice with the others. Sada divided the rice into five rows, each one corresponding to a house. He divided his field and told each couple to go and harvest the rice. Each couple then went to harvest the rice. They returned with their shoulders loaded.

They thought that they could repay them for the seed, in this way.

"Eh! I didn't tell you to bring them here," said Dame Benjamin. "Take them home with you."

Each couple had three sacks. The woman put one of them on her head and her husband put two on the scale. They went home and left the baskets at Sada's house, under the veranda of the rice granary. These were the ones they didn't want to take home with them. Ha! As for Dame Benjamin, she would take her rice in three days.

Dame Benjamin had gone to light the flame of the lamp during the night. She said: "Come back all of you, the corn with the corn, the peas with the peas, the cucumbers with the cucumbers, the calabash with the calabash."

The guardian and the servant went with the elephant to sell the cucumbers. And how many rials[243] did they earn? Ninety! Ha! At that time, ninety rials was a great deal of money. They took it to Dame Benjamin.

"Ha!" said Hawè Sada. He told her to come.

"Come here. The guardian and servant are here."

She gave the guardian thirty rials and the servant thirty rials and she kept thirty rials for herself. The servant smiled and was very happy.

"I am going to buy a sarong from Java for myself."

When each one had harvested the rice there were five yokes that remained under the veranda of Sada's rice granary. There was a great deal of dust there, because of the enormous quantity of rice. There really was a great deal of dust and also a great quantity of peas, corn and string beans. The rice was brought to the granary; it was twenty arms' lengths. There really was a great deal. It was impossible to open the door as wide as they wanted. And when they went inside, they had to walk on the rice. Ha! One hundred sacks of rice! A field where one can plant one hundred sacks of rice is really impressive.

Ha! We are now going to speak of something else. The guardian and the servant were in their house. Each one was in their house. And here comes the one who raises birds for the king. He is going to catch birds.[244] He is a bird catcher.

"Ah! There seem to be many people near the kapok tree. Ah! And I am thirsty. I am going to go there."

**Fig. 47.** The rice granary, the mother haystack, the soul of rice, an ancient trilogy in the Malay world. (Ivanoff, 1989)

He caught his bird and before going inside, he carried it with him.

"Ah! Is someone here?"

Dame Benjamin answered:

"Yes, there is someone here. Come up then."

"Prepare some cakes, my servant. He is coming up."

The servant prepared a tray with some cakes on it. He ate the cakes and drank some water. But he stood open-mouthed in front of Dame Benjamin since she was very beautiful.

"I greet you, Dame. I will now go back home."

"Come back."

"I know the road now, so don't worry."

Ah! He climbed down the ladder, jumped over the barrier while still carrying his bird and ran so quickly that one could see a cloud of dust behind him.

"Eh!"

"Ah! What's happening?"

"Wait until I get my breath back. . . Eh! Lord, Hawè Sada's wife is really very beautiful."

"How can this be? Hawè Sada's wife is beautiful while Hawè Sada is so ugly."

"Ah! Maybe Hawè Sada is ugly but his wife is beautiful. One cannot compare her to your wives, king."

"Ah! Is that so?"

"Yes."

Ah! It's a good thing that Dame Benjamin loves Hawè Sada because he is very strong.

"Is she really as beautiful as all that?" the guardian asked.

"She is truly very beautiful."

"Well then, I will go and see," said the cruel king.

In effect, he really was a very cruel king. The next day, at dawn, he slid his knife into his sarong and left. He knew the road that led to the kapok tree. The king had still not arrived when Dame Benjamin said to her servant:[245]

"Prepare a tray with some cakes."

She knew that the king was coming. When he arrived, she said:

"Please sit down."[246]

"Ah! Since I am here, I will climb up."

The king looked at the house and said:

"This house is not very pleasant; the wooden ceiling made of sago is fine but the bamboo pillars are not very nice."

Dame Benjamin said:

"The termites have trouble cutting and eating it."

They shot out answers to each other.

"Eat then. There are all kinds of cakes."

He ate and then went home.

"Well then, lord?" the man who raised birds asked.

"She is really very beautiful and she speaks well."[247]

And the king desired her.

"In what way would this be difficult?"

"Ho! What do I have to do?"

"Oh, king! There is a jasmine flower that is found on the Siyé Miyo[248] mountain, the great mountain. No one can pretend to pick this flower because there is a serpent at the foot of this mountain who will attack you immediately. He is the guardian of the mountain."

"Is that true?" said the king.

"Yes, it's true. No one can pick this jasmine flower, nor put his foot on the mountainsides without sliding. This mountain is so tall that if you look up at the summit, your turban falls off and the serpent will then try to catch you. The head of the serpent is at the foot of the mountain but no one knows where his tail is."

"Ah! Very well."

The next day at dawn:

"Guardian."

"Yes?"

"Go and look for Hawè Sada and tell him to come. Something is keeping me from sleeping with closed fists, eating with an appetite; something which causes me to cover myself without getting warm or to bathe without being refreshed. I can't stop thinking about this flower and it is only Sada who can help us."

And the guardian arrived.

"What do you want, guardian?"

"The king wants to see you."

"Ah! Alright then."

"Go there, older one," said Dame Benjamin. "The king wants to ask something of you."

Hawè Sada went off.

"Ah! What's the matter?"

"Something is keeping me from sleeping with closed fists, eating with an appetite: something that when I cover myself I cannot get warm or if I bathe, I am not refreshed. I can't think about anything else. You are the only one, Hawè Sada, who can help us in all confidence."

Hawè Sada went inside.

"Then tell me what is the matter."

"I want you to go and pick the red jasmine flower."

"Where?"

"On the Siyé Miyo mountain."

"Ah! But how do I climb it without slipping?"

"I don't know. Do whatever you feel is best. You are the only one who can do this."

"Ah! I can't tell you for certain that I will be able to pick this jasmine flower or not, lord."

He sighed and went home.

"Well then, older one?"

"The king asked me to go and pick the jasmine flower."

"Hum, but that's perfect. I am satisfied."

"And why then? The jasmine flower is found in the Siyé Miyo mountain. Even flies cannot go there. How then can men do this? How will I be able to do this then?"

"It is possible. I am here."

"Ah! very well. Is it possible?"

"It is possible. When does the king want you to go?"

"He asked me to go tomorrow."

"Very well. You can go there tomorrow."

"Servant, prepare some cigarettes for me."

The servant prepared three cigarettes and put them in a box.[249]

In those days cigarettes were put in a box.

"Older one, you will go until you reach the water at the foot of the mountain and you will stop there. Fill your mouth with water and rinse it. Then chew on a wad of betel and go towards the foot of the mountain. If you hear a noise, that makes a sound as loud as an aeroplane, take the ring with the precious stone and place it on your fontanel."

"What do you mean, younger one?"

"I doesn't matter. You don't have to know why. Go there."

"How can I go there?"

"You go straight to the mountain and do not turn either to the right or to the left. Go straight ahead until you reach the great mountain."

He took to the road. One could go and return in one day. He walked until he reached the pool of water and put some in his mouth; he rinsed his mouth, chewed a wad of betel and strode over the water until he reached the foot of the mountain. He immediately heard a noise, "buuu!" It was exactly what Dame Benjamin had said. He raised his hand over his head. Everything suddenly became dark; it was the serpent who was responsible for this darkness. He was wrapped around himself. But when he saw Hawè, he lowered his head to signify a greeting.

"What do you want? Why have you come?"

"Ah! I would like the jasmine flower."

"Ah! This is possible, master. Wait here and I will go and pick it." The serpent went up to the summit of the mountain to pick the flower. Its perfume could be smelt from far away. It was Dame Flower of Jasmine. Ah! He descended with the flower and the air was filled with its perfume.

"Here, master. Here is the flower. I have been watching over this flower for a long time and I am tired. You[250] can take it. As for myself, I will remain here."

He went home. He chewed on a wad of betel as he walked. The sun was over the mountain.

"Servant, go and get some water that is in the jar at the foot of the ladder. What does he have wrapped in his sarong?"

Hawè Sada went as far as the ladder.

"Ah! You have returned, older one."

"Yes, here I am."

She went down the ladder and caught hold of Hawè Sada's hand. She helped him climb up the ladder and washed his feet that had been put into the bowl. She spread out a white, clean cloth to greet him with. She held his hand and he went into the house. She washed his feet and his hair. Ah! That was how things were done in those days. He went in and put the flower down.

"Go and look for the embers and the incense, servant."

She brought the embers and the incense soon afterwards.

"I am passing the flower over the embers. Go away, younger one," she said.

And Dame[251] Flower of Jasmine appeared.

The next day, at dawn:

"Guardian."

"Here I am."

"Go and see Hawè Sada. Did he go home to sleep yesterday?"

The guardian went to Hawè Sada's house.

"Ah! The older one is sleeping."

He had his head lying on the knees of Dame Benjamin and Dame Flower of Jasmine was massaging it.

"Ah! I am tired from having climbed up that mountain, my younger ones." The guardian stayed there but didn't say anything.

"Well then, guardian, what's the matter?"

"He is over there, master. He is there with a girl who is prettier than Dame Benjamin.

"What do you mean?"

"He is being massaged at this moment. There are two women, one of them has his head on her knees and the new one is massaging him. He said that his hips cause him pain since he climbed up Siyé Miyo mountain, where he went to find the jasmine flower at the summit."

"Ah! So that's what it is all about."

The guardian did not wait any longer.

"You must go, older one. You must go and take the jasmine flower to the king."

The flower had become flesh. Sada went to see the king.

"Ah! Here you are, older one Hawè."

"Yes, here I am."

"Did you succeed?"

"Hum! You had confidence in me and I succeeded."

"Where is she?"

"Here."

He took out the flower and went into the house. The flower was put over the embers and the incense but there was no longer anything inside it. Dame Benjamin had already made the woman come out of it.

"What do we have to do in order to lose Hawè Sada once again?"

"There is something we can do."

"What then?"

"He must go and look for the tusks of Elephant Mino."[252]

"And where are they?"

"I don't really know. It is said that there is an Elephant Mino in the great field, but that he is protected by a white elephant with black tusks and nine heads. Whoever goes to look for this elephant is crushed. We must send Hawè Sada."

"What do you want guardian?"

"Ah! the king wants you to come. I don't know why."

"Ah! Why don't you go there," Dame Flower of Jasmine asked.

"You must go and see what the king wants."

So he went off.

"Ah! You have come, Hawè."

"I have come."

"I want to ask you to do something since I believe in you. Ten other people are not worth one of you. It is really in you that I have confidence."

"What do you want?"

"I want you to go towards the rising sun, without every changing direction and you will encounter Elephant Mino. When can you go there?"

"Tomorrow," he said.

"It doesn't matter, older one. Ah! Prepare some cigarettes, servants and put some betel in the box. Prepare the leaves for the cigarettes and put them in the box."

The servant immediately did all this. She put three wads of betel in the box. Dame Flower of Jasmine took a ring with a precious stone on it and put it on Hawè Sada's finger.

"Follow the rising sun, older one. Don't change your direction."

He left and walked for a long time before he met an elephant who came running towards him, "hoom." He raised the ring and the elephant collapsed.

"Where are you going, master?"

"Ah! I am going towards the ancestor."

"Ah! Climb on to my back, master. I will take you there."

So he climbed on to the elephant's back and they went on the road.

"Where do you want to get down, master?"

"I want to get down when we reach the pond."

When they reached the water, he got down. There was a terrible elephant there, the forty elephants left because elephants cannot remain where the white elephant with black tusks and nine heads lives. He turned his head to the right and to the left but could not see anyone here. There was no elephant there. He was in the water, the white elephant with black tusks and nine heads. He saw Dame Gadèng of the Coconut Tree[253] at the waterhole. She lived on the gadèng coconut tree and had a room and a mosquito net there; there was also a house there. The woman ran down to the bottom of the ladder.

"Come up, older one."

And he climbed up the *gadèng* coconut tree.

"Why have you come here, older one?"

"Ah! I came to look for the tusks of Elephant Mino. My older sister, Dame Flower of Jasmine, asked me to get it."

"Oh! Does she live over there, the older sister?"

"Yes."

"And when must you go back?"

"I would like to go back today since I am afraid of the darkness."

"Ah! But it is not yet night, older one."

Dame Gadèng of the Coconut Tree served Hawè Sada some cakes. She went down.

"Stay here, older one. I am going to see the ancestor."

She clapped her hands three times on the surface of the water.

"Booh" and something rose to the surface, "ooow."

"Go and look for them, ancestor."

"Oow"! He raised his trunk, made a salutation and, "blu", plunged in to look for them. But he didn't find them so Dame Gadèng of the Coconut Tree went back to the great field to look for the terrible elephant Forty. He went looking but didn't find anything either. They continued searching and the water become murky and almost solid. It was no longer possible to see anything and they had to grope their way forward. They finally found the tusks and brought them up to the surface. Dame Gadèng of the Coconut Tree called the elephant and told him to go back with the older one because it would soon be night. Ah! She had the tusks of Elephant Mino. She rose to the surface and gave them to Hawè Sada and called the elephant.

"Hurry up and go with him before night falls."

So, the elephant, "broo broo broo", hurried up.

"Ah! I will get down here, said Sada."

He didn't want the people to see the elephant. He got down while Dame Benjamin was spreading a white cloth at the bottom of the ladder of the house.

"Ah! Go and look for the embers and the incense, servant."

She soon brought the embers and the incense and placed the tusks above them and the young Dame Tusks of Elephant Mino appeared. She was even lovelier than Dame Flower of Jasmine. She was much more beautiful. Hawè Sada slept for three nights. He woke up one morning and Dame Benjamin said:

"Get up, older one. Go and lie down in the big room with your head on my thighs and your feet on the thighs of Dame Flower of Jasmine. Dame Tusks of the Elephant Mino will massage you."

He was tired from having tried to escape from the elephant. He had pains in his muscles from having run so much.

"Guardian, go and see if Hawè Sada has returned."

"He must have been crushed by the elephant," the chief of the district said.

The guardian went to see.

"Ah! I have pains in the calves of my legs and in my legs, after having run away from the elephant, younger ones."

"Ah! They are now three," said the guardian.

He went back to the king.

"Well then, guardian?"

"Hum! Hawè Sada now has three women, lord. They are all different but all of them are beautiful."

"Ah! So he has been successful. Bring the tusks of Elephant Mino."

The guardian then went back to Hawè.

"Ah! You have come back, Hawè Sada."

"Yes, I have returned."

"Where are they?"

"Here."

The king took hold of the tusks of Elephant Mino and went into the house. He placed them over the embers and the incense but they were empty. There was nothing inside. And now he didn't know how he could further mislead Hawè Sade and kill him. There is no longer any sense in trying to find pretexts, the king thought; I will kill him directly.

"Ah! Go and look for Hawè Sada."

So, the guardian went to look for Hawè Sada.

"You are the only person I believe in. I only have confidence in you to dig a well and find water for me."

"This is possible, lord."

"When can you dig the well, Hawè Sada?"

"I would like you to give me seven days, lord, I will come back in seven days."

And he went home.

"What's the matter, Hawè? You seem to be in a very pensive mood since you returned. What then is worrying you so much? Is it me?"

"Of course not, younger one."

"Ah! Then what is the matter?"

"The king has asked me to dig a well since he has confidence in me."

"Hum! The king is really very cruel, older one. He wants to kill you. But it is impossible for you to refuse without giving the impression of being a coward."[254]

"As you wish, younger one. I don't want to die."

"You will not die, older one. When will that be?"

"In seven days."

"Very well."

Dame Benjamin and Dame Flower of Jasmine cut some cloth to make clothes with: a shirt, sarong, a *keffiyeh* and a white turban. But none of them was sewn together. They put them aside. Night fell.

"Servant," said Dame Tusks of the Elephant Mino, "come here."

She prepared some grilled rice and some puffed rice. There was a sackful. Dame Benjamin no longer did any work since there were now two new women in the house. She took the puffed rice, went down the ladder and called the rodents to come. They all came and there were as many of them as there are fleas.

"Come and enjoy all this food. I will ask you something in exchange. Go and dig a tunnel under the house until you reach the king's well. You will do this so that the older one is able to walk there. When you have finished, come back and I will give you something more to eat. Throw the earth that you dig up far away."

So, "gugah, gugah, gugah, ruuu!" they ran under the house. They dug all night long but were unable to finish the work. They reached the king's well the next day. These rodents were really very strong. The tunnel was perfect and one could walk through it standing up. The animal friends finished their work the next morning and went back to see Dame Tusks of the Elephant Mino.

"It is finished."

"Ku kah ku kah", all of them went up. Night was approaching and Dame Tusks said:

"Come here, older one. We are going to go to the king's well."

She took a lamp since it was dark underground. They walked along the tunnel, Dame Tusks of the Elephant Mino and Sada walked behind. They finally arrived.

"Ha! Look well, older one."

"Is this the king's well?"

"Yes, older one. You will climb down into it but don't be worried. When you are at the bottom, the king will take hold of a stone and close the well. You will then count one, two, three and, "puh", you will go into the tunnel and be able to return home."

"Ah! Very well."

Seven days went by.

"Ah! Here you are, Hawè."

He made a salutation and said:

"I have come, lord. You ordered me to come, so I have come."

He spoke very well since he knew what his wife had prepared.

"Yes, I only have confidence in you, Hawè."

The chief of the village and the chief of the district made a salutation.

"Ah! Bring the garment that was woven for Hawè."

It was a new shirt; a new shirt for working.

"Why new clothes?"

"Don't be worried. This is for you. I am giving them to you."

So, he put on the new shirt that had been prepared for him and went down the ladder made of bamboo.

"Ah! Now I will take away the ladder, older one, Hawè."

"Ah! But how do I remove the earth?"

The king removed the ladder.

"Ah! The ladder has been taken away and now I am going to close the well with a stone. Ah, think well, Hawè. You wanted to help me, Hawè and today will be the day you will leave this earth."

"Ah! Pity!"

He asked for pity but, "brooh!" and went into the tunnel.

"Ah! One, two, three."

"Gruuh!" He jumped into the tunnel while the earth was thrown down and stamped on by an elephant. Then young coconut trees were planted. The king went home and fell asleep. The next day arrived.

"Ah! Wake up, older one."

Dame Tusks of the Elephant Mino said to him:

"Take a bath. Wash yourself well."

He then put on his white clothes that had been prepared for him and took some cakes. No one had ever seen such lovely cakes as the ones that had been prepared for him by his wives.

"You will go and take these cakes to the king and tell him that it is his ancestors who are offering them to him and that they send him greetings, to the king and to his wife. You will tell him that his ancestors are going to go away and that they want to see both of them one more time. They are in the Arepoh field."

It was now Hawè's turn to play a trick on the king. Dame Benjamin smiled. She went back home and prepared all kinds of cakes with the help of the other two wives. These cakes were supposed to have been offered to the king by the ancestors as a salutation. He put on the clothes that had not been sewn and left to go and see the king and take him the cakes.

"Your ancestors want you to go to the Arepoh field since they will soon be leaving. If you want to meet them, you must go to the well." A new well had to be dug. Ah! The king was very pensive but he decided to leave.

"What do I have to do, Hawè?"

"First, you must go to the well and climb down. There is a road that you must follow there."

Hawè Sada went home. The rodents closed a part of the tunnel, a big part of the tunnel. The king, on his side, called many of his subjects to come and dig the well. They raised the stone with some ropes and the king went down.

"Ah! There really is a road here."

He climbed up and told his wife to prepare many different sorts of cakes. He was going to see his ancestors.

"Ah! Hurry up?"

They prepared the cakes, other provisions and some flowers and went down the well to meet the ancestors.

"Go," said Hawè Sada. "Go and find your grandparents and parents again. Be happy."

"Ha! Older one, Sada, take good care of my daughter."

Her name was Dame Benjamin.

"I don't know if I will return. Perhaps I will discover some places where it will be good to live. Ha! Chief of the village and chief of the district, put back the stone; as for myself, I will count one, two, three."

One, two, three, "gung" and the king, "bruh", went into the tunnel.

"Throw some earth and stamp it down well with an elephant because the king will not return."

Three days went by and Hawè Sada went to the king's house. His daughter asked him:

"Ah! Where then is my father now?"

"Ah! Maybe he is now in the field of the dead."

He returned seven days later.

"Where is my father,"

"He must have decayed by now."

Ah! He let nine days go by before he returned with Dame Benjamin, Dame Flower of Jasmine and Dame Tusks of the Elephant Mino. Hawè Sada had just married the daughter of the cruel king. He now had four wives.

# Chapter 4

# Mythical Detours

### 4.1. The crocodile-man

***(Village of Samoh, November 1991***
***Narrator: Po' Suloh***
***Type of Story: hikaya')***

Once in the past a woman became pregnant and said:

"Why is my belly so big? The other women don't have such big bellies."

This seemed strange to her and she thought about it day and night. She finally asked her older son:

"What is happening, my son? I have a belly that is not like the ones the other women have."

"I don't know mother. Things will be as the Lord decides. What can we do since all this is happening in your belly?"

The time came for her to give birth. She gave birth, but to what? To a crocodile! Her child was a crocodile!"

"What are we going to do, my son? Your younger brother is a crocodile!"

"You must put him in a clay jar."

The mother thought for a long time and really didn't know what to do. She looked for a big vase made of clay and put her younger child into it. She raised him until he was bigger.

"He is not big enough mother. Leave him in the well."

So they put him in the large well and he stayed there for a long time. Then one day, the mother was invited to a party.[1]

"Are you going to go to the party, mother?"

"Yes, I want to go. But before I go I will have to tell your younger brother. Young one, do you want to go with us?"

The mother was speaking to her son:

"Young man come to the surface."

The crocodile rose to the surface, "booh" in front of his mother.

"I want to tell you something. I am going to a party today."

"If you go to a party, bring me a heart since I really want one."

"Alright," said the mother.

Many people were going to the party. When the mother arrived, she said to the man who had organized it:[2]

"I want to ask you something."

"What is it?"

"My son stayed home but he wants a heart."

"Ah! That's possible."

She asked the person who was preparing the meat for a heart. He cut a piece and gave it to her.

"Where are you going to put it?"

She attached it to some bamboo [in the] forest and went to eat. When she was finished, she went to get her piece of heart.

"Eh! Where is it?"

A dog had eaten it. She started to cry and went home. She was afraid that her crocodile-son would be angry. She spoke to the people who had accompanied her:

"We must order some food and take it to him."

So she went and asked the man who had organized the party for some food and then went home. She said:

"All this is fine, but why does this phrase come into my head? 'You cannot lie to your son'?"

She put the food in the well.

"You can come to the surface now."

"I am happy that you have come back. Did you bring me a heart?"

"Eh! He gave it to me."

"Well then?"

"I left it attached to the bamboo [in the] forest and a dog ate it."

"Mother, you are good for nothing."

He was very angry with his mother.

"Come down to me."

The mother went down and when she was close to him, the crocodile ate her with one gulp. He ate his mother. His older brother waited for a while but couldn't decide to return home. He waited for an hour but did not go. He finally said:

"It is possible that my younger brother has eaten my mother."

He called out to him:

"Younger brother, younger brother, younger brother! Come up to the surface. Why did you eat our mother? I guessed that you ate her when I saw your big belly."

So the crocodile-man came on to the land. His brother took a knife[3] and cut open his belly and his mother came out. He then went to the cemetery and put her there and said:

"I am going to sew up your belly, younger brother."

And that is what he did. He said:

"We can't stay here if you keep on eating people."

So they went to a big river and stayed there for a long time. Then the younger brother wanted a woman and said:

"What do I have to do to have a woman, I am not like other human beings? Nevertheless, I absolutely want the king's daughter."

He only wanted the king's daughter. So when she came to wash herself, he caught hold of her. She was the youngest child. The king then called to the soothsayer and told him to find his daughter. Some of the people who were there felt that even if it were possible, nobody there could do it. Then a man said:

"And why not that man over there; the one who has a young crocodile brother?"

"Go and get him."

So the man went to look for the older brother.

"The king wants you to come to the throne room."

"Why does he want me to go there?"

He went to the meeting hall and asked:

"What's the matter? Why did you want me to come here?"

"I want you to find my youngest daughter who has been eaten by the water spirit or by, I don't know who."

"That's not difficult."

"What do you want then?"

"I want a sack of puffed rice."

He soon got the sack of puffed rice, prayed again then poured the puffed rice into the water. The puffed rice slipped away in the current and he said:

"No one is to come near here!"

He plunged into the water, waited and listened. He called out:

"Younger one, younger one, younger one!"

He listened in the water. After a short time his younger brother answered: "Yo!"

"Come here, younger one. Did you really take the king's daughter?"

"Yes."

"Which one did you take?"

"I took the youngest one."

"And what do you want to do with her?"

"I want to marry her."

"You mustn't do that, younger one. You must let her come back. The king said that the one who brings back his daughter will become a new king. He will divide the country and give half of it to the medium-healer who succeeds."

They spoke like this rapidly together and the younger one went to look for the king's daughter who was in his cave. He took her to the medium-healer who carried her over the water. Then the people made a line of honour up to the king's house. They soon arrived and married. He became the new king since the father had divided his territory and given his half to him. He was happy and said:

"My wife will never be given to anyone else. If you want a woman, younger one, I will make one for you."

With what would he make a woman? He made one from a piece of wood. He called the workers and many of them came to the king's house. He made an image of a woman with eyes and all the rest, than called his younger brother who soon came and sat down near his wife.

"You see, you really have a woman, younger one."

And he prayed:

"As soon as my saliva is salty, I can reunite everything. I will ask for things and things will be: when I want things they appear."

"Here is your wife, younger one. But you must go now into the sea."

He came out to go into the sea but never saw his older brother again. It is wood that gives life.

This is the story of the one who became a crocodile.

### 4.2. The marriage of the Chinese Lim Tô' Khiam (Lin Tao-ch'ien) and the Malay "Beautiful Princess"[4] (collected by I. Besson)

#### 4.2.1. The version of the young sailor madly in love

According to Thai documents, edited by the provincial governor,[5] sultan Mohamad Shah who reigned towards the end of the 17th century, during a period when Patani was a harbour town, and relatively prosperous, had a very beautiful daughter.

The Chinese captain Lim Tô' Khiam had sold all the merchandise in his sampan in Nakhon Si Thammarat and prepared to set sail with his crew to return to his native country (undoubtedly the region of Hokkien in southern China). A rumour of the existence of this marvellous Malay princess[6] reached his ears and the young trader couldn't resist the temptation to go and verify it, or perhaps he also had good reasons to believe that he would be able to fill the empty hold of his boat with new merchandise in Patani. In effect, the captains and crews of Chinese boats generally do not receive a fixed salary but only a small percentage of the merchandise when it is sold and a fraction of the space on a boat is reserved for them for goods that they personally have bought to eventually sell. So, as is the custom, having been authorized to leave the boat in the Muslim town, Lim Tô' Khiam went to pay homage to the sultan and presented him with some gifts. This gave him the chance to catch a glimpse of the beautiful princess and he immediately fell in love with her. So he put off his departure and was rewarded for his audacity by being able to meet the princess. She and her father seemed receptive to his arguments and Lim Tô' Khiam was finally able to marry the princess, but only after being converted to Islam.[7]

Nothing more is known about Lim Tô' Khiam except that he was an excellent artisan whose area of expertise is never specified. He was no doubt very talented in different arts as are the local inshore captains who are, even today, good mechanics. So he was subsequently charged by Mohamad Shah to draw up plans for the construction of the largest mosque in the sultanate, which would be situated very close to the palace. Unfortunately Ko Nieo, Tô' Khiam's young sister, who was inclined to be possessive, came from China to look for her renegade brother, who was busy drawing up construction plans in his adopted society and delighted to be able to undertake such a noble religious task assigned to him by his father-in-law.

It is always said that Tô' Khiam's family consisted only of his mother and his unmarried sister. The impression is given that both of them were very young and rich enough to be able to acquire a quantity of merchandise sufficient to fill a sampan. It is astonishing that no more is known of a family which was apparently so rich but whose members were so few in number. Ko Nieo suddenly became desperate at the thought that she would be unable to accomplish her mission so she hanged herself on a big cashew-nut tree that was growing in front of the mosque, but only after forcefully warning her brother that she hoped that he would never finish his work, though she secretly was convinced that he was perfectly capable of doing so.

The only thing remaining then was to erect the dome of the mosque but a thunderbolt hit the mosque and the sister's fateful vow was realized twice before her brother finally remembered her fatal words. We should not forget that this mosque was undoubtedly the tallest monument in the region. Tô' Khiam then no longer had the courage or desire to commence for the third time the construction of another dome and assure the happiness of his new family. But his wife, who was aware of his refusal to build a new dome, started to eat her heart out when she saw how upset he was. But it was too laté, and the mosque has remained unfinished to this today. The same rumour that had pushed the high-spirited captain to the shores of Patani spread out and everyone was convinced that the Chinese captain was sufficiently strong to triumph over the sultan's will and, though less evident but also implicit in this, to triumph also over Allah.

It is pointless to say that other versions of this story exist, even if the Chinese don't like the way their god could be desecrated.

### 4.2.2. The version of a hard-hearted pirate who conquers the throne of Patani

According to research by a Chinese historian[8] and the local Sino-Thais' oral version of the story recorded by Skinner,[9] Lim Tô' Khiam was in fact one of the most notorious pirates and bandits of southern China during the period 1560 to 1570. It is true that he came from Fujian, but he was perhaps of Teochiu or Hokkien origin.[10] He was pursued and ran away, looking for a hiding place in the "southern seas." It seems that he had an army and made an attack on Patani. The army was sufficiently powerful[11] to enable him to occupy the town and convince the sultan to accept his demand to marry his daughter and inherit his throne.

### 4.2.3. Other versions: the hard-hearted pirate who conquered the throne of Patani by manufacturing a cannon

Skinner also reports that in the "Annals of Patani"[12] Tô' Khiam was described as a simple Hokkien naval foreman who married a Malay woman, settled there and was naturalized. Following the order of the queen, he cast three cannons but was killed while trying to place one of them in the furnace. One of these pieces of artillery, which was later prized by the sultan, is supposedly the one the Siamese carried away during their conquest of Patani at the end of the 17th century. It is displayed today in front of the Ministry of Defence which at that time ruled the southern provinces. The cannons were able to shoot enormous cannon balls having a calibre (diameter) of 9 inches (23 cm). It is also said in the Annals of Patani that the Malays of Kase [Kru Sé in Thai or Gersik in Malay] all say that Lim Tô' Khiam is the ancestor of their family."

It is still possible, finally, according to Hsü, that Lim Tô' Khiam married the sultan's daughter, took over the throne and manufactured cannons until his accidental death. His wife became the first queen of the sultanate (that is, the Green Queen who reigned from 1584 to 1616)! And Skinner concludes that it is not necessary to accept this version. Tô' Khiam had probably lived "like a king so far as he was a cultural hero;" his position was exaggerated in the later narratives.[13] The Chinese version of the Patani story records the failure by Tô' Khiam's sister to persuade him to return to his own country, but not her suicide, nor his construction of the mosque.

According to the official Thai document, her tomb at the foot of the cashew-nut tree was not visited by people who wished to make an invocation in memory of the deceased, such as those who were destitute or who had suffered misfortune or even, for example, people whose cattle had been stolen.. Perhaps the story was made up to explain the good "feng shui" of this place.[14] The legend says that requests made will be granted, and this story continues to this today.

### 4.2.4. Continuation of the legend several hundred years later and the important present-day ceremonies

According to oral tradition, recorded in the same sources,[15] at the end of the 19th century, Malay boatmen discovered, in a waterway entering the bay of Patani, something that they thought at first was a block of blackened wood. They seized it and wanted to cut it up but the first axe-blow released a copious flow of blood. Tan Cu Lai, the second son of Tan Pui and an unofficial leader of the Chinese community in Patani,[16] who suffered an incurable sickness and had no choice but to put himself in the hands of supernatural forces, learned what happened, and ordered someone to bring him the object This was a small statue from the same region of China where Lim Ko Nieo lived. It must have come from a boat where everything had been lost during a shipwreck off the coast of cape Tachi in the mouth of the bay of Patani. Tan Cu Lai placed the relic in his clan temple, the sanctuary of Leng Cu Kieng. His father had built the temple on a large piece of land near the Chinese market. His sons lived nearby, on Anoru Street,[17] where their descendants still live today. He then learned in a roundabout way, that in order to be cured, he would have to carve a statue of Lim Ko Nieo from the wood of the cashew-nut tree in the shade where it had fallen and include it in the family shrine. So, he did this, and since then a big ceremony takes place every year at dawn, following the full moon of the third lunar month (normally at the end of January or in early February). During the ceremony, a light-coloured wooden statue of Lim Ko Nieo, and also those carved in dark wood, are later placed near it. The statues likewise represent less well-known Chinese heroes that have equally marvellous powers. These statues are carried throughout the town of Patani by groups of two or four men. These young men, who have previously temporarily abstained from sexual relations, have to cross the river without drowning and complete a course of more than ten stages through the historic parts of the centre of the town of Patani, the last of which is a long bed of hot coals, prepared the day before, which they have to cross without burning themselves.

This is one of the rare occasions for people of Chinese origin, who had left home to start a new life in distant places, to return, prepare and participate in an annual festival, which is more important than the "trut cin", the Chinese New Year. And even if this reunion is not the occasion for the parents and grandparents to give their children or grandchildren some money that they have hoarded until they became adolescents, it does contribute strongly to the preservation of a common identity. It is also an occasion when donors are generous towards the temple and when enterprising individuals have a chance to engage in a new activity by borrowing the funds needed directly from the shrine consecrated to Lim Ko Nieo, one of the most venerated gods among the population of peninsular Thailand.

### 4.2.5. Relationship with history and sociology

The sultan referred to in the Thai document (Mohamad Shah) does not appear in the list that Mohd Zamberi A. Malek put together.[18] The only name close to it is Muzaffar Syah, the second sultan of the Seri Wangsa dynasty, who was in power from 1530 to 1564 but this is much too early. The period referred to (2200 B.E.), is the period one hundred years after 1660. A sultan bearing this name did, in fact, reign from 1776 to 1786, but this is too late, particularly since in the text an allusion is also made to the Ayutthaya period, which had then just ended.

Although the list may have been incomplete before 1729 and/or the name of the sultan may perhaps be incorrect, it is possible to conclude that the Thai version of these events may have taken place at the end of, or just after the Kelantan dynasty. The decline at the end of the reign, and the need for funds, can perhaps also explain an apparently unusual marriage at this level. This version of the story does not refer to the subjects of the "Celestial Empire", whose place of origin remains unknown,, nor to an inconstant husband, a poor artisan, or a false Muslim. It would seem that inter-ethnic marriages were then a common occurrence and accepted. It is also possible that wealthy rajas and Malay aristocrats ordinarily possessed four wives, perhaps including a Thai or Chinese wife ; the number of royal descendants was certainly numerous.

### 4.3. The true story of the Kru Sé[19] mosque
***(Village of Tanoh Meroh, Province of Patani, February 1993***
***Narrator: Méa***
***Type of Story: torèh)***

We are going to tell the story of the king of Kru Sé; he was the king here. But the king's chief contractor was Chinese. He had come from China with his three brothers and sisters, and it was they who built the mosque. We Malays don't know how to build;[20] at least that is what is said in this story.

It is the elders who told it to us.

These three brothers and sisters were the children of a Chinese king. They had left China and come to this mosque. Is this story of the Malays the same as the one of the Thais?[21] No one knows, but everyone has a different idea about it today. It was the Chinese who built this mosque. It is certain that the king of Kru Sé had hired the Chinese to build the mosque. It was he who asked them to build the mosque. So, the three brothers and sisters who came from China built the mosque. The three of them built it because the king of Kru Sé asked them to build the mosque. They went to work.

The youngest was very beautiful. Yes, she was really very beautiful. Of the three Chinese, she was the most beautiful and the king's son fell madly in love with her. The mosque was built but before it was finished the king's son started flirting with the youngest of the Chinese. They flirted with each other and it wasn't long before lightning and thunder struck the mosque and it collapsed. The mosque was destroyed two times by lightening. It is not a Chinese mosque but one ordered by the Malays and this is why everyone comes here. It is because of the king's son that people come. But the mosque made by the Chinese is the one where the Malays are unable to pray. This is because some very disagreeable things happened there. It is because two people flirted in it that it is no longer pure.[22] This happened a longtime ago, during the reign of this king. No one likes to talk about this since it was the king's son who flirted with a Chinese girl. If anyone spoke, he was killed. The king killed people without asking any questions. Whatever the king wanted took place immediately. It's not the same thing today. One can speak about anything now and it doesn't matter. But a long time ago, it was another story; if one spoke one was killed. That is why one kept everything to oneself. No one dared to speak about this mosque that was left unfinished because of an impure action. No one could pray there. This is why it was never finished.

The story of the temple of Lim Ko Nyao came after the one about the mosque. This is the place where Lim Ko Nyao was abandoned. There is a statue[23] of her here. The king desired her because she was very beautiful. She was Chinese. But she didn't want the king and was afraid that he would kill her. So she hanged herself on a cashew tree, not far from the mosque. This story comes after the one about the mosque, at least, this is what the elders say. She hanged herself from a cashew tree because the king desired her. She was very beautiful. She committed suicide by hanging herself not far from the mosque. It is in this place that she committed suicide. What happened afterwards? The elders tell the following story:

There was a place named "the spot where cannons were forged,"[24] near the mango trees. Hoo! The forge was the one used to make cannons, big cannons; the kings of the past made cannons. They knew how to make important arms. They tried but did not succeed. They tried again but it still did not work. So that the labourers would not run away, the king cut off their feet. He cut off their feet so that they would continue to make cannons. The king was afraid that they would run away. Then the labourers said:

"If it ever happens that the cannon works, we will be used for munitions."

And the cannon worked. So they were put into it and stuffed inside like powder. Then a fire was lit . . . "kup"! and no one ever knew what happened to them. They went in and died. They could no longer walk because their feet had been cut off. They could no longer walk and served as cannon shot for the cannons.

### 4.4. The mouse-deer

**(*Village of Samoh, November 1991*
*Narrator: Po' suloh*
*Type of Story: bahri*)**

Once, at the beginning of the world, a mouse-deer was lying down and thinking:

"Men wanted me to be the first animal in the zodiac.[25] Why did they want such a thing, since I didn't give them anything? I will now have to do something."

Humans made the mouse-deer the first of all animals and he wanted to pay back his debt to men. In those days, and for a long time afterwards, animals spoke with human beings. So, the mouse-deer spoke:

"Hey! What are you doing here, uncle?"

"I am making a yoke."

"Eh! Well then, uncle, you have chosen me to be the first among the animals of the zodiac, so now I will have to do something for you. I must do something now, uncle, so that your descendants will talk about me."

"Eh! What do you want to do?"

"I will organize competitions from today on."

"Competitions? Why not? We can then watch them."

"Wait and see, uncle. We are going to call all the animals of the forest." The mouse-deer jumped on to a mound of earth. He called out:

"Woo! Woo! Woo!"

Then all the animals arrived. First came the elephant and then all the other animals. They all came because the mouse-deer had called them.

"What do you want, mouse-deer? We have answered your call. But what do you want?"

**Fig. 48.** The mouse-deer gathering the animals.

"I have called all you animals of the forest, since I want to do something for men. I must give them pleasure. Human beings have chosen me to be the first of all animals of the zodiac and in turn, I must give them something."

The elephant asked: "And how will you do this?"

"We will begin with the game of hide-and-seek. We are going to make a competition."

This is what he said to all the animals.

"Who will be the first one to close their eyes?" the mouse-deer asked.

"I will begin," said the dog.

So the mouse-deer took a piece of cloth and tied it over the dog's eyes. All the animals went to hide: the chicken went to one side and the elephant to the other; all the animals went to hide. Then the mouse-deer called the dog and told him to go and look for them. The dog started to sniff around and found the elephant and then the chicken. Then the dog said:

"Here you are, elephant! Here you are, chicken!"

He found them thanks to his sense of smell.

"We can't play with the dog because he sniffs."

So the mouse-deer said that they would have to start again.

"I will close my eyes first," said the chicken.

He closed his eyes and all the animals went into hiding, one here and one there. But the mouse-deer was the most cunning and hid himself on a branch. He called the chicken who went to look for him. The chicken searched and searched and finally found himself on the elephant's back. He started pecking at him and the elephant cried out because it hurt.

"Your pecks hurt me."

"I do what I want to do!"

The chicken left and found the centipede. It wasn't long before he found all the animals.

"You are really intelligent, my friend," said the mouse-deer. "Who is going to close his eyes now?"

He said to the elephant: "It is you who will close your eyes now."

"No," said the elephant. "You do it first."

"No. It will be you. Let's go."

The elephant closed his eyes with his ears. The mouse-deer sprang up and went to hide. Not long afterwards, he called to the elephant. The elephant started to walk towards him but his enormous feet crushed the centipede who

**Fig. 49.** The mouse-deer play hide-and-seek.

**Fig. 50.** The trick of the elephant.

died. Then the chicken flew away and all the animals were afraid because the elephant was so big.

"Why are you all running away? I just arrived."

The elephant came close to the mouse-deer who said to him:

"Eh! Come out of hiding all of you."

The mouse-deer took a leaf[26] from the tree and hid under it. The elephant went away, "Gering, gering, gering." He went to lie down with his paws in the air. The mouse-deer went to look for the chicken and the dog and soon found them and all the others. Then he went to look for the elephant but couldn't find him.

"Say something. What kind of game are you playing?"

The elephant was very close.

"This animal remains silent."

The mouse-deer leaped on to the elephant's paws and said:

"Hey! But this is an old pillar of a house. It is also completely destroyed and only the foundations that supports the wooden pillars are left. Eh! Where are you hiding, elephant? Do as you like, elephant but I am getting tired of looking for you. And you don't even bother to answer me."

So then the elephant started speaking:

"How can I call to you if you are perched on top of me, over my feet?"

"But I thought it was the pillars of a house in the field. You are really crazy, elephant! You are very clever!"

The mouse-deer was ashamed and went to look for Master Tou.

"Eh! I lost."

"What do you mean you lost?"

"We were playing hide-and-seek."

"And so?"

"We were playing hide-and-seek and the elephant found us."

"If this is the way things are, men are more stupid than you are since they have chosen you to be first animal."

The mouse-deer became very angry.

"I am leaving. I cannot remain among men. However, I am still the first of all animals."

But at this time, the mouse-deer created even more problems for the elephant.

"Eh! Come to my place tomorrow, elephant."

"Why?"

"I want us to have another competition."

"Alright. I would like to compete with you."

The elephant arrived the next day and said:

"What kind of game will we play?"

"We will have a urinating competition. The one who urinates the for the longest time will win."

"Don't do that! I already pity you. You are going to lose many drops."

"It is not easy to do this in the forest, so we will go to the paddy field tomorrow."

"If this is what you want, we will go to the paddy field."

"I don't want to go into the forest since there is no water there and there is a lot of water in the paddy field, close to the waterhole. I will drink and then urinate."

"Let's go there. Let's have a competition."

They went to the paddy field the next day. The elephant spread his legs and urinated. The mouse-deer did the same, "tera, tera, tera," in the waterhole.

The elephant urinated and they counted the time it took until he had not even one drop left.

"Watch me now. I am going to fill the waterhole."

"You have a lot of strength."

The elephant lost, even though he had completely emptied his bladder. But the mouse-deer was very happy to have won. He went to tell Master Touwa.

**Fig. 51.** The elephant playing against the mouse-deer.

"I won."

"What kind of game did you play?"

"The game of urinating."

"You were able to beat the elephant at this game? I can't believe it."

"I urinated in the waterhole."

"With the elephant?"

"Yes."

"Well then, you really did win. You are really very clever."

The mouse-deer left and met the fresh water turtle.

"What are you doing, turtle?"

"Why?"

"As for me, I walk from morning to night."

"I wish I could do the same thing."

"Where do you want to go?"

"I would like to find some bananas."

"Why then?"

"To plant them."

"I would like to have a competition with you. Which one of us will be the first one to find the fruit?"

"Alright, if you want."

"Let's go then."

The mouse-deer gathered some red flowers from the banana tree and planted them because he wanted to have bananas as quickly as possible. The turtle, though, planted a shoot from the banana tree. When everything was finished they went to see.

"What end of the shoot did you plant?"

"I planted the root end."

"I planted the other end."

Many months passed and a season passed. The turtle's fruit were red and ripe. Those of the mouse-deer were rotten. The turtle went to see the mouse-deer.

"Mouse-deer!"

"What!"

"The bananas are ripe."

"I want two of them."

"But no! You can't eat them. This is a competition."

The mouse-deer went to see the turtle's bananas; they were ripe.

"How will you pick them? How will you be able to get them? Are you able to climb up?"

**Fig. 52.** The turtle tried to climb the tree but each time she fell down.

"I am going to try to climb up."

The turtle tried to climb but each time she fell down.

"You see! Share with me. I will go and pick them and throw them to you. Then we can both eat them."

"That's perfect."

The mouse-deer took a leap and jumped on to the branches. He began eating the fruit of the bananas and let the skin fall down for the turtle.

"Give me the bananas, mouse-deer."

"But I am throwing them down to you each time."

So the turtle ate the skins and the mouse-deer the fruit. He ate everything and then climbed down.

"I am full."

"I am full, also."

"I am really very full because I ate the fruit. I chewed it thoroughly."

"But I also did this with the skin and I am full."

They then separated. The mouse-deer walked for a long time and found a beehive hanging from a branch.

"I am going to play a trick on the tiger. The tiger is bad because every time he meets someone he attacks them. He attacks buffaloes and men."

**Fig. 53.** The mouse-deer makes the tiger beat the so-called "royal gong".

He went to find the tiger who was not far from the beehive.

"What are you doing here, mouse-deer? Do you want me to eat you?"

"Who do you want to eat?"

"You, of course!"

"Hey! You can't eat me."

"And why not ?"

"Because I am the guardian of the royal gong."

The tiger raised his head.

"Yes, it's very nice. The colour shines."

"Yes, but be careful. If you strike the gong, twelve things will appear."

"Ah?"

"Yes, it's really nice but prohibited. If anyone hits the gong, the king will kill me."

"Let me strike it only once."

"But if it is you who strikes it, this will be even worse."

"Let me strike it once. I want so much to hear the sound it makes."

"But I can't let you do this, or the king will kill me. What good would it do me to let you do that and be killed by the king?"

"Just once. Where is the hammer?"

"It is over there. That nice hammer with knots."

"Give it to me."

"But that's impossible. If the king hears the noise, I will be killed."

"Well then! You just have to run away from here; don't stay in this country. I really want to hear the sound of the gong."

"As you wish. But if there isn't any noise, it won't be my fault."

The mouse-deer ran far away, far from the beehive and let the tiger know when he was as far as possible. The tiger then seized the hammer and struck hard. Many bees came flying out of their hive and bit the tiger. His face started to swell.

The mouse-deer was near two branches that were close together and formed a trap. The tiger was furious and went off to look for him.

"Eh! You have tricked me."

"In what way?"

"You told me to hit the gong! But what gong? The bees bit me on my face!"

"What are we now going to play?"

"The only game you are going to see is your death because I am going to devour you today."

"Come! You want to eat me but I am unable to run and you have no pity. Anyway, even if I do run, I will die nevertheless."

"Why?"

"The king told me to take care of his flute."

"Which one?"

"That one. You can listen to it if you want but you must stay below while I climb up the tree so that I can blow it."

"Why don't you stay below?"

"If I do, the sound won't be good. I have to do as men do."

The mouse-deer climbed up a branch. The wind blew and the mouse-deer pretended that it was he who was playing the flute. But in fact the noise came from the wind in the branches.

"Bo! Bo! Bo!" This was the noise the tiger made. The mouse-deer descended.

"That's really a very nice sound," the tiger said.

"Nonetheless, I really don't know how to play very well. But if you blow into it it will make a nice sound."

"Well then, let me blow into it."

"Alright. But don't blow too hard."

"Why?"

"If you blow too hard, the king will hear it and kill me. If I remain here, you will eat me and if I leave, the king will kill me because I abandoned his flute."

The mouse-deer then let the tiger blow into the flute. He said:

"If the wind is too strong, you will have to put your tongue on the wooden fork."

The mouse-deer left and the wind blew. The tiger stuck out his tongue and placed it between the prongs of the wooden fork. It closed up and cut his tongue. The tiger was furious with the mouse-deer because he had tricked him.

The mouse-deer went towards the paddy field where he found some buffalo dung. He separated it into two parts with a piece of wood. During this time, the tiger arrived.

"You are going to die, mouse-deer! You started with the bees and then you cut my tongue. I am going to devour you."

"You can do that if you want, but you won't be satisfied."

"Well then, what must I do to be satisfied?"

"You must eat this cake?"

"But it's buffalo dung!"

"No it isn't! It's a cake. It was cut in two for the king's children. He put it there and no one could take it."

"It looks very good."

"Good or not good, it's a cake that comes from the king."

"Can I have some of it?"

"No, you can't. You can have something else, but this belongs to the king."

"Nevertheless, I want some of it."

"Alright then. I will give you a mouthful of it, but if the king should arrive tell him that I went to look for shellfish in the clear water." The mouse-deer went off and the tiger ate all of the buffalo dung. When he became aware of what he had eaten, he was furious. The mouse-deer had disappeared and he couldn't find him. The mouse-deer had gone to the river to drink some water. He met a shellfish there and asked him:

"Where are you going, shellfish?"

"I am taking a walk."

"Why then? You are going so slowly."

"What do you mean?"

"What I do in one hour, you do in ten hours."

"That's true, but I would like us to hold a competition."

"Alright. But I will give you two months' lead."

"Give me three days to do some training."
"Alright!"
"I am going to do some training."
"If you want. I will leave you one season before the competition."
"Come back in three days."
The mouse-deer went away. The shellfish called all the other shellfish and said to them:
"All of you are going to place yourselves along the route where the race will take place."
"Why?"
"I am going to have a race with the mouse-deer. When he comes, all those who are in front of him will answer his question."
"Alright."
All the shellfish warned their friends. The mouse-deer arrived three days later."
"Here I am, shellfish."
"Let's go."
"Don't you want me to give you a season's lead."
"Don't show off."[27]
"When will we start?"
"Tomorrow."
The mouse-deer arrived the next day.
"Are you ready?"
They got ready to leave, one, two, three. . . he leaped up. A little later, he asked:
"Shellfish?"
"Wo!"
It was the shellfish that was just in front of him who answered. He leaped once again and called out:
"Shellfish!"
"Wo!"
It was the shellfish just in front of him who answered. And the same thing was repeated.
"Let's stop because I am tired."
"You have lost then!"
"You are really very rapid. You run very fast."
"Perhaps I run very fast but the men didn't see me. If the men had seen me, I would be tired."

**Fig. 54.** The mouse-deer lose against the shellfish.

"I lost against you. I am going away alone now."

"Where are you going?"

"I don't ever want to see men again. I don't ever want to meet anyone again. I will remain just as I am. This is my destiny. I am going to sit on a tree stump."[28]

He sat on the stump but some resin came out of it and stuck his bottom to the wood. Then a young girl said:

"You stay there, and your bottom is covered in resin."

Since that time, the mouse-deer has had resin on his bottom.

### 4.5. The birds
***(Karo, District of Patani, December 1992***
***Narrator: Bélo)***

"The bird *ngabo'jamo*[29] is magic like five.[30]
The bird *kuko*[31] is magic like a male buffalo.
The magic of the turtledove[32] is like two kings."

I remember this from when I was a small child.[33] Everyone likes turtledoves.

**Fig. 55.** Chendrawasi, the bird of paradise, is a frequent theme. The story is about a bird that is unable to land and makes magical eggs fall on the earth. They are sometimes considered to be the origin of rice.

## 4.6. Salt

***(Village of Bang Pu, Province of Patani, October 1992***
***Collected by Rusli Wereyeng***
***Narrator: Unknown)***

An old man arrived. One day, a long time ago, the king bought a motor.[34] His name was King Gashew Nut. He bought a motor and told a man to install the motor at the edge of the water. The motor was a big one but it couldn't absorb the water; the water didn't rise. So they had to use bamboo, which in Jawi is called a "mouldboard basket."[35] With the bamboo, they made mouldboard baskets.

[Assistant]: "Then did the king have a motor?"

"Yes, he used to have one but it didn't work."

"Was it in Bang Pu?"

"Yes, in Bang Pu."

"Isn't it true that the motor came from Chere?"[36]

"Yes."

"This is what men did long ago: they poured water with their hands and used windmills."[37]

"No, you are wrong; there were not yet any windmills. People used mouldboard baskets. The handle was made of bamboo and was used for draining and drying. There was a fork at the end of the bamboo. There was a piece of bamboo at the top for pouring the water, raising the mouldboard basket and pouring the water into the reservoirs."

"Did they know that there was a Dame of Salt[38] in the sea? Isn't it said that she is the origin of salt?"

"Yes, that's true. It is no doubt that Dame."

But in order to make salt, it was necessary for the water to rise. You had to wait until the level was high enough, then you waited for the water a second time, a third time and finally a fourth time. When the water reached the fourth level (of the reservoir), the floodgate was opened and the water flowed into the salt paddies. In the past, it was flattened and that is how it is done today. Whatever people know today comes from the past. So, the water was made to flow into the salt paddies but you had to pay attention and see if the Dame was in the water or not. She is salty; she is really very salty, that old woman. And there is no doubt that this Dame was there.

But the earth had to be well prepared and flattened before the floodgates were opened. You have to wait three months before you are able to consume the salt. Haa! Then you can see the water, the rows and traces [of salt]. You see the traces and these are the Dame. You also see moss growing on the side, on the embankments. It's the same as with sugared water, you see traces. Then you have to wait for five days. It is only then that the salt is present and you can collect it. How many times can you make the water go into the salt paddies? Many times. But at the beginning, you have to rake the earth so that it will be light. You do this with a rake. You also have to use buffaloes or do the work in another way. You have to work the soil so that the earth will be beautiful. To do this, you have to flatten the surface once and then a second time, more deeply; this is called *bita*. And you do this so that the earth will be dry. To flatten the soil, you use the trunk of a tree. And when the water arrives, everything is very dry. And when it is dry, you start flattening the soil, if it is not too old. If you can do this, then the field is ready; but if not, then you start to flatten it again. Men today are not tired out like they were in the past.

Sometimes, you did all this for nothing, since with one [downpour of] rain everything was upset and then you had to start all over again. At times, the earth was all ready but the rains destroyed everything. There were years when there was nothing and sometimes, even several years. But it is not the same today. Today, people are happy because there is no rain.

This is what happened a long time ago when king Cashew Nut bought a motor. He had bought it in order to pump the water into the salt paddies but it broke. In the past, people used mouldboard baskets and the windmills. Today, we use motors. In the old days, people knew how to make salt from sea-water. They were also intelligent. This is what they did: they filled big oval pots with salt water and boiled it. What remained was the salt. They put water to boil and when it was evaporated, what remained was salt, crystal salt, like the kind we buy in stores. It is broken into pieces and brittle.

Ban Na and Pare are the places where the first salt paddies were found. But ours is better because the water is not so salty.[39] In those other places, the water is very salty.[40] But on the other hand, things are done more quickly over there. Before we have even finished, they are already collecting the salt. Sometimes there is a time difference of one month.

All this began with king Berabeh. In those days, there was no salt because of disagreements with the king of Patani. It was many generations ago that all this began with the king of Pare.

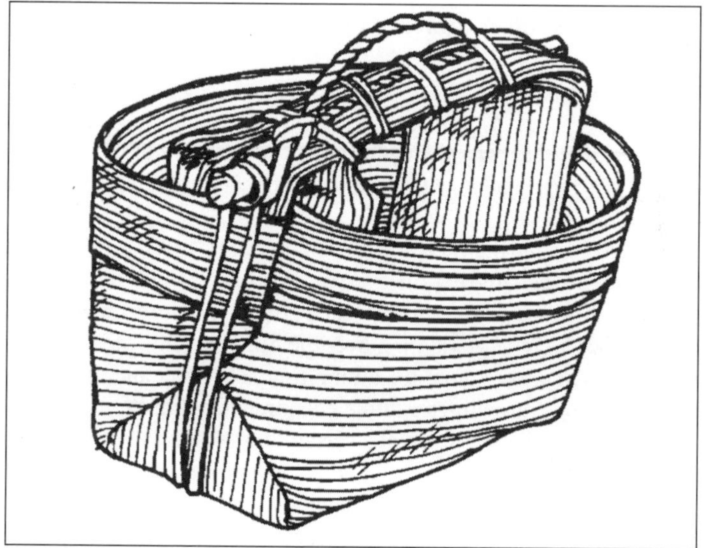

**Fig. 56.** Wicker basket for transporting water.

**Fig. 57.** The Malay house and the well.

### 4.7. The origin of the name of Yaring
***(Village of Tanoh Meroh, Province of Patani, March 1993***
***Narrator: Méa***
***Type of Story: bahri)***

This is the story that tells why the name Jamu[41] became Yaring.[42] This story tells us of the origin of Jamu and its name. And we will also tell you why Taning[43] has this name.

We find ourselves during the time of the ancestors, at the beginning of time, when places were named, during the time of the kings. This is the story of a king who lived a long time ago. He wanted to eat a golden mouse-deer. So he ordered a hunting party; they were to go hunting over the hills, the hills of Nadé, over there, a hunting chase. They were gone for a long time, shouting and driving back the animals with the dogs' growlings and the encouragement of the king, "ju, ju, ju"! During the chase, the king hesitated at a certain moment as to what road to follow. He found himself in the place that is called Nadé.[44] It was in this place that he had to catch the mouse-deer. He continued the chase and soon arrived here where we are, in Jamu. It is here that his *aring*[45] fell down, the hilt of his dagger. His *aring* fell right here. This is why we call this place Yaring. People of today ask:

"What is the name of this district?"

Well then, its name is Yaring. Haa! That's how it once was; it is now almost a province.

The king soon began his chase again. After another hesitation, he decided to go over there, near the beach there,[46] until he reached the province of Patani. It was once an area where weaving was done, there in Bangpu, the "house of the crab."[47] In effect, there were crab holes there. It is like Nibong,[48] which became Yala.[49] It is no longer Nibong. People speak of Nibong because of the forest there. Haa! It was near Nibong. We Malays call this place Nibong. Since then, we prefer to give it the name of a mountain nearby that is called Yalo. There was also a village called Yalo[50] that is some distance away from the centre.[51] We took the name of the mountain for the province. This is what the ancestors said.

There is also a broken mast[52] here. It was attached here. The anchor was thrown down here, where the mast broke, and this place is now called "broken mast."[53] Yes, this is what happened. The mast broke on a day when there was a strong wind. It was in the middle of the sea. This place where we are at this moment (Tanoh Meroh) was once a sea. It was a well and no one could make it work, because it was dirty. It was the sea. It was a swamp and there were many shellfish in it. Men decided to make rice paddies and there were big shellfish there, different shellfish. Yes! This place was once the sea.[54]

# Appendix 1.

# Elements of comparison

As Skeat, 1955 (1961), p. 11, writes, "The tales themselves, as will be obvious to the reader, are the merest gleanings from an extensive harvest-field, and make no pretention whatever to any completeness or finality."

However, it is possible to identify certain elements. One may briefly mention three Moken and Malay tales that have identical mythical themes, each referring to a particular historical period. They point out the value of oral literature and the importance of migratory schemas and ideological constructions. The Moken tale of Awang the Frog (Ivanoff, 2001) and the Malay tale of The Shellfish King have the same images, themes and heroic figures. The tale of Nyonya (Ivanoff, 2001), which recounts the difficulties of a loving and intercultural relationship between a Malay man and Chinese woman, adultery committed by her, and voyages made between kingdoms, empires and even supernatural and human worlds, has exactly the same themes (for example, the poisoned needle) as the Malay tale of Nakhoda Ragam (Skeat, 1955 (1961), p. 62). The epic tales of Awang and Nyonya, marking the passage of one culture to another, are the expressions of values that one should either preserve or abandon. These stories serve as historical markers of traditions and the forms of social structures that have been either abandoned or preserved; they have thus become a safeguard of memory on which the society is built. Of course these transcultural mythical themes and markers of one passage of a social structure to another can be analyzed in different ways since the texts of oral literature are situated on different levels. The story of Nakhoda Ragam, for example, reminds us that sexual relationships are extremely dangerous when one is out at sea.

> "Ship-master Ragam was the master of a Malay merchant-vessel, and one day he sailed from Jering taking with him his beautiful wife Che Siti of whom he was very fond. On the way she was annoyed by her husband's incessant embraces and warned him to be

more careful, reminding him that she was sewing, and remarking how unlucky it was to indulge in such gallantries at sea. Such was his infatuation however that he paid no heed to her warnings, and as he was attempting once more to embrace her, she pricked him to the heart with her needle so that he died." (Skeat, 1955 (1961), p. 62).

The Moken, however, live on their boats with their wives and children. In conformity with their tradition, the young men were obliged to go out to sea alone in order to symbolically wed the spirit of the sea (*cf.* the story of Bisèt in Ivanoff, 2001) before visiting a woman on the land and establishing a convivial loving relationship, while at the same time always giving priority to the spirit of the sea. It is the same with many Malay fishermen who refuse to take their wife on board, preserving their heart and strength for the spirit of the sea. The same is true for men on land who fall prey to the charms of the soul of rice, a beautiful and sensual young girl, of whom the women are jealous. This unassimilated jealousy of Malay women destroys their era of abundance. As far as the Moken are concerned, the primacy of a woman of the sea is accepted and makes relations between men and their environment tolerable.

The sea is thus a sexually marked domain, in which sexuality and love dominate. It symbolizes the conquest of women and the death of men who show them disrespect. Sea and death are thus at the heart of the cycle of metamorphosis, the symbolism of all great religions. The elements are the conquest by women, the encounter with and the acceptance of the female spirit of the sea (who marries Moken men when they are alone on their boat, without their consent) who is the enemy of women and sexual relations, the spirits of Man/Nature, or a female spirit of a tree that grows in the navel of the world and causes the death of all men. The sea is the domain of women and to take a woman on board a boat is risky, according to Malay stories, but this can be a calculated risk, as it is for the Moken, who accept the primacy of women of the sea. This explains why women never do any diving and why Moken boats serve as a socializing vehicle for their nomadic society.

One becomes aware that the moral aspect of images is constantly changing. However, the basic imagery remains the same. Tales about the mouse-deer are also identical, with a common imagery as concerns animals and the moral precepts that men are able to apply to their society. These stories underline the importance of unity, or at least of an animal social structure in relation to a human social structure that is under construction. Here, once again, one discovers epic markers of time in these stories, one stage of the ideological construction of a mythical social foundation. Finally, the story of the battle of cereals (rice) (Skeat, 1955 (1961);

Ivanoff, 2001), which takes place in order to dominate society, is also important for both the Moken and the Malays. The battle carries with it elements of the invasion of traditional societies by the modern world, and represents the last cultural link between the Malay and the Moken. It lies at the crossroads of the epic path. Rice and the epic battle for the domination of men are the true cultural differentials. This is why stories about rice are much more complex in the Malay world than they are among the Moken, who have adopted them in order to preserve a "civilizing" link with their Malay cousins.

## A1.1. Malay Oral Literature (Skeat, 1900 (1965))

### A1.1.1. Skeat, 1900, pp. 8–10

There was once a Selangor man named Haji Batu, or the Petrified Pilgrim, who got this name from the fact that the first joints of all the fingers of one hand had been turned into stone. This happened in the following manner. In the old days when men went voyaging in sailing vessels, he determined to visit Mecca, and accordingly set sail. After sailing for about two months they drifted out of their course for some ten or fifteen days, and then came to a part of the sea where there were floating trunks of trees, together with rice-straw (*batang padi*) and all manner of flotsam. Yet again they drifted for seven days, and upon the seventh night Haji Batu dreamed a dream. In this dream one who wore the pilgrim's garb appeared to him, and warned him to carry on his person a hammer and seven nails, and when he came to a tree which would be the Pauh Janggi he was to drive the first of the nails into its stem and cling thereto. Next day the ship reached the great whirlpool which is called the Navel of the Seas, and while the ship was being sucked into the eddy close to the tree and engulfed, Haji Batu managed to drive the first nail home, and clung to it as the ship went down. After a brief interval he endeavoured to drive in the second nail, somewhat higher up the stem than the first (why Haji Batu could not climb without the aid of nails history does not relate), and drawing himself up by it, drove in the third. Thus progressing, by the time he had driven in all the seven nails he had reached the top of the tree, when he discovered among the branches a nest of young rocs. Here he rested, and having again been advised in a dream, he waited. On the following day, the parent roc had returned and was engaged in feeding its young with an elephant which it had brought for the purpose, he bound himself to its feathers with his girdle, and was carried in this manner many hundreds of miles to the westward, where, upon the roc's nearing the ground, he let himself go, and thus dropping to the earth, fell into a swoon. On recovering consciousness he walked on till he came to a house, where he asked for and obtained some refreshment. On his departure he was advised to go westward, and so proceeded for a long distance until he arrived at a beautifully clear pool in an open plain, around which were to be seen many stone figures of human beings. The appearance of these stone figures rendering him suspicious, he refrained from drinking the water, and dipped into it merely the tips of his fingers, which became immediately petrified. Proceeding he met a vast number of wild animal—pigs, deer, and elephants—which were fleeing from the pursuit of a beast of no great size indeed, but with fiery red fur. He therefore prudently climbed into a tree to allow it to pass. The beast, however, pursued him and commenced to climb the tree, but as it climbed he drove the point of his poniard (*badik*) into its skull, and killed it. He then robbed it of its whiskers, and thereafter, on his reaching a town, everybody fled from him because of the whiskers which had belonged to so fierce a beast. The Raja of that country, begging for one of them, and giving him food, he presented him with one of the whiskers in payment. After paying his way in a similar manner at seven successive villages, the Petrified Pilgrim at length reached Mecca.

### A1.1.2. The saint who was shot out of his own cannon (pp. 58–9)

The Raja of Patani ordered Che Long to cast a couple of cannon. The first one was cast successfully, but the second one at every attempt cracked in pieces. At length the Raja told Che Long (the workman) that if he could not succeed in casting it at the next trial, he should die. Che Long replied, "I will cast it then at lost costs," and in despair of saving his life, he uttered a vow and said, "So my Raja's pleasure be fulfilled, may I take the place of a cannon-ball and be shot out of my own gun." As soon as the words were uttered the casting succeeded and Che Long entering the gun caused it to be fired. The charge was exploded in front of the Palace gate at Grésik and Che Long only fell to earth when he reached the village at Kuala Barat six miles away. Here his remains received burial, and a shrine was built and called by the name of the Saint of the Western River-mouth. Now in the meanwhile the two guns were put on board ship to be conveyed to Bangkok, and on the way they were both discharged, one of them called the Luck of Patani emitting a great roar and enveloping the whole country in smoke. This gun is still to be seen at Bangkok. But the other one fell overboard between Telok Tengar and Sabor, and was lost. And up to this day vows are [made at the Tomb of Che Long, especially for the recovery of lost straying cattle, whose milk when the cattle are recovered is offered at the tomb. And in the case of lost or straying cattle, the Patani folk say, "Fool me not, Grandfather, but point out to me where my cattle are, and if you do so I'll make a pilgrimage to your tomb."

### A1.1.3. The saints whose grave-stones moved (pp. 60–1)

To' Panjang or "Father Lanky" (as he is generally called) was one of the earliest apostles of Islam in the State of Patani and enjoyed a great reputation. At length however Sah Nyaya the Unjust King came to the throne and requested To' Panjang to assist in casting some cannon, the copper being placed in his charge for the purpose. But one day a foreign merchant came to visit him and begged for a portion of the copper, which the Saint gave him, intending no harm thereby. Taxed by the Raja with stealing his copper, To' Panjang admitted his mistake and was condemned to die. A pupil of his own was chosen to execute the sentence, but refused to do so, whereupon both master and pupil were strangled[1] and their bodies thrown into the Patani River, which then escaped to the sea in the neighborhood of Jambu. But when they were thrown into the river the two corpses[2] instead of sinking stood miraculously upright in the water, and in this position travelled continually against the stream, both at flood and ebb. At length however the Raja commanded the remains of both saints to be buried ashore, but as often as the bodies were measured for their shrouds, so often they kept outgrowing them. At length therefore a goat was sacrificed and the shrouds having then been measured again were at last found to be of the correct length. The burial therefore was completed; but up to this day the grave-stones of both saints continue to make miraculous movements in proof of the divine nature of To' Panjang and his pupil.

These two tombs are very potent shrines and they lie about two or three miles along Patani Point. The grave-stones at head and foot are usually found to be about ten feet apart, but it is customary to measure the distance between them twice . . . in order to take omens as to the length of one's future life. The second measurement is always . . . different from the first; but if the second measurement proves to be longer, one's future life will be long in the like proportion.

### A1.1.4. The legend of Patani (pp. 63–4)

There once lived, in the interior of Raman (a province of Patani), a King of the Fairies who had a beautiful daughter named Princess Nang Chayang. This Fairy Princess was first of all born in a cave, but the old astrologer prophesied evil of her and said, "This infant must never be kept ashore, set her adrift on the water." Therefore a feast of purification was held in the land, and the Fairy Princess was thrown into the river to drown. Instead of drowning however she rose to the surface, and floated down the river, resting on a mass of foam. As she floated down she was rescued by Raja Siung, the Tusky Prince. He was called the Tusky Prince because he ate men's flesh till his eye-teeth developed into tusks like those of a cannibal. For once when a follower of his had taken the carcase of a slain goat (which was to be roasted for the Prince) down to the river, to scour it, a vulture flew down while his back was turned, and carried off the goat's heart. The young man feared to take back the flesh without the heart, therefore he slew a boy who was passing by and forced into the goat's carcase the heart of his victim. So the Prince partook of the boy's heart, and when he had eaten it, he rejoiced and said, "This is a better goat's heart than [any] I have tasted. Why is it so much sweeter than that [of] other goats I have eaten?" At first the youth said nothing, but afterwards he confessed that it was the heart of a boy. So the Prince commanded [his servants] to slay a boy daily, in order that he might eat the heart thereof. Wherefore his tusks grew like those of a cannibal, two at the top and two at the bottom.

Now when Raja Siung had rescued Princess Nang Chayang he brought her up in his own palace. And one day when he was hunting in the Jungle he heard the voice of a child, and going to the spot he found a male infant within the hollow stem of a big Bamboo which had been riven open by the wind. This infant he adopted also, and brought up the two children together. And one day when they were sitting on his knees and playing, each of them by accident pulled out a pair of the tusks. And when the Princess grew up, she married Prince Samura, who may not partake of the young Bamboo shoots, because [his] ancestor came out of the Bamboo [before] they entered Islam.

### A1.1.5. Skeat, 1965 (pp. 19–20)

Thus we are told that man was created from the four elements—earth, air, water, and fire—in a way which the following extract, taken from a Selangor charm-book, will explain:

> "God Almighty spake unto Gabriel, saying,
> 'Be not disobedient, O Gabriel,
> But go and get me the Heart of the Earth.'
> But he could not get the Heart of the Hearth.

'I will not give it,' said the Earth.
Then went the Prophet Israfel to get it,
But he could not get the Heart of the Earth.
Then went Michael to get it,
But he could not get the Heart of the Earth.
Then went Azrael to get it,
And at last he got the Heart of the Earth
The empyrean and crystalline sphere shook,
And the whole universe (shook).
When he got the Heart of the Earth he made from it the image of Adam.
But the Heart of the Earth was then too hard;
He mixed Water with it, and it become too soft,
(So) he mixed Fire with it, and at last struck out the image of Adam.
. . .
When they were married (Eve) bore twins every time,
Until she had born forty-four children,
And the children, too, wedded, handsome with handsome, and plain with plain."

The magician who dictated the above account stated that when Azrael stetched forth his hand to take the Heart of the Earth, the Earth-spirit caught hold of his middle finger, which yielded to the strain, and thus became longer than the rest, and received its Malay name of the "Devil's Finger" (*jari hantu*).

### A1.1.6. The fish-man (Skeat, 1965, p. 187)

Thus the *k'ra* (*Macacus cynomolgus*) is believed to develop into a species of fish called *senunggang*, and the fish called *kalul* (*kalui* or *kalue*), Sir W. E. Maxwell writes: "The *ikan kalul* (is believed) to be a monkey transformed. Some specially favoured [observers] have seen monkeys half[-way] through the process of metamorphosis—half-monkey and half-fish." The species of monkey which is believed to turn into the *ikan kalul* is, as I was told in Selangor, the *b'rok* or "cocoa-nut monkey".

### A1.1.7. The crocodile-man ( Skeat, 1965, p. 285)

There was a woman who had a child which had just learnt to sit up, and to which she gave the name of "Sarilang." One day she took the child to the river-side in order to bathe it, but during the latter operation it slipped from her grasp and fell into the river. The mother shrieked and wept, but as she did not know how to dive she had to return home without her child. That night she dreamed a dream, in which her child appeared and said, "Weep no more, mother, I have turned into a crocodile."

## A1.2. Moken Oral Literature (Ivanoff, 2001)

### A1.2.1. The Ancestor Pakèt Goes West

I am going to tell you a story of olden times, the story of a Moken who lived in Burma. During this time, the Burmese had a great king and White Strangers, also. Burmese, White Strangers and Moken one day embarked on several boats with two hundred seamen on board. They were going to the magic lands of amber. They sailed day and night towards the West with sails and oars. They finally reached the land of Télèm during the low tides and started to drift, inexorably penetrating into the land of amber. Then the boat of the White Strangers made a half-turn while the Burmese continued to go deeper into the magic lands. They sailed for a long time, when suddenly gigantic waves struck the boat and they were carried away by the current. They soon reached a cave. It was there that they discovered the Ficus tree which produces all the fruits of the world. They had reached the origin of the amber and the Ficus tree. The Burmese said:

"Eh! There is a lovely girl below. How can we reach her ?"

"Let me be the first one to pass," said the king.

He got off the boat but the girl, who was below, was now perched on top of a tree.

"Eh, king! Are we going to have this girl or not? Let's all go and try to catch her even if we should die in the attempt."

This is what finally happened because every one of them fell down and was devoured by sharks. When there was no longer anyone left, the boat was sucked in by the stern and sank in the dark cave. Only three of the men survived. They threw some hooks on to the tree and the ancestor Man was the first to climb on to it.

"Climb up towards the bird Kedah,"[3] the ancestor Pakèt said.

The three men climbed on to the tree before the boat had been totally sucked under. They stayed there for many days and ate fish and turtles. Every time the bird, who lived on the top of the tree, saw them, he tried to kill them.

"What are we going to do with this bird who only dreams of devouring us? I am going to ask the big fish to come and help us," said the ancestor Pakèt.

The first one to arrive was the mother ray. But as soon as Pakèt put his foot on top of her, he began to sink. The ray left and other fish arrived: sharks, dugongs, etc. But not one of them could support his weight.

"Come and help me mother-fish, named the fish Pakèt."

The fish arrived out of the high seas. The ancestor climbed on to its back three times but did not sink.

"Help me to go back home."

The fish turned over and the ancestor took some matches and put a lighted candle on his fins.

"You will remain on the surface for three days and three nights and then the mainland will appear."

So they left and three days later they caught sight of a child who was walking on the beach.

"Grandmother, grandmother! There is a fish approaching."

"Where do you see a fish? I only see some rocks with a bird on top of it."

The ancestor got down from the fish and left to rejoin his group. But all of them ran away when they saw him coming towards them. So he left and nobody knows where he went.

But here is the story of one of our male ancestors, a Malay. He was sadly walking along the beach. His only desire was to leave this place. As he was returning from hunting for birds, he noticed a boat filled with "black Indians". In order to make them come nearer he invoked the spirits.

"Eh, Atua! I am a human being, so listen to my words and make this boat drift towards me."

His words must have been heard because the boat was coming towards him.

"Climb on board, grandfather," said the captain. "We have three hundred buffaloes on board."

But when the ancestor climbed on board the boat, he was so heavy that it began to lean over and all the buffaloes fell down on top of him. Then they put all the buffaloes on one side and the ancestor on the other side. But the boat soon ran aground and hit the rocks.

"That's nothing," said Man. "The wind will soon take us out of here."

"Are you a divinity who is able to ask the wind for help? Prepare some rice for the grandfather," said the captain.

The grandfather ate and invoked the wind.

"Eh, you hidden divinity! I am closing my eyes and by my words I am asking the boat to get us out of here."

The boat then arrived at its destination in India by a route which none of the seamen knew about. But the captain did not permit the ancestor to get off the boat. He remained for a week and returned to Singapore where he met his group and children again.

Now here is the story of the ancestor Pu. The mother of the bird Bada flew towards the land of Jawa[4] in order to bring some buffaloes to her child. She left one morning very early and the child called out to the ancestor since he was able to speak.

"Grandfather, grandfather, come here! As soon as my mother returns she will smell your odor and eat you. Hide in my thigh and when my mother embraces me you will come out and climb on top of my mother who has lice on her as big as turtles. You will hold fast to her and in this way you will be able to return home."

The mother soon returned. She had a buffalo on her back. She flew all over the land sniffing the odor of human flesh. Then she gave the buffalo to her child and fell asleep, clasping him to her. The ancestor then woke up and held fast to the bird's side, on the part where she could not catch him. The mother left the next day.

"Be careful, mother, while you are flying. If you fly too high, the wind will become stronger."

So the mother flew close to the ground and this is why the lice could not fall off. She came to a large field in Jawa and chased after buffaloes. She continued to fly lower and lower and so the ancestor was finally able to get off her. He ran and took refuge in a Ficus.

The child of this monstrous bird is a human being since he is able to speak. He once was a man but a woman put a spell on him with some bits of termitarium and since then, he has become the spirit of the tree and he makes it possible for the ancestor Pu to go back home. Nobody knows where the ancestor died. Maybe he died in Malaysia and has become a Malay like his children who perhaps remained in Jawa.

### A1.2.2. The mouse-deer

We are going to tell you the story of the mouse-deer. Listen everyone!

One day, the ancestor Buhum took his axe and went off with his son, to cut down a tree, a *Hopea odorata*, in order to make a boat hull. They were sweating blood and water while they hollowed out the tree, when suddenly a mouse-deer appeared and jumped onto the hull.

"No, grandfather! You will never be able to achieve anything if you continue doing things in this way. You are really very ignorant. You made a mistake and you will not succeed, grandfather."

The father and the son tried to catch the mouse-deer, who jumped from the prow to the stern of the boat and then ran off into the forest. He returned the following day and for three days afterwards and insulted the grandfather, who was so angry that he took the shavings of a tree and threw them at the insolent animal.

"Hey! Are you suffering now, mouse-deer?"

Since then, the mouse-deer carry the marks of the shavings on their backs. And if you capture one of them, you must throw away the back because it has a bad smell.

Then the mouse-deer started to play with the tiger, who wanted to eat him. The mouse-deer dragged the tiger into the sea where there are giant clams that nipped at his feet.

"The water is rising! The water is rising," cried the tiger.

"Eh! Well then, tiger, you are going to die."

The tiger called out for help but the water entered his mouth every time he opened it. When the tiger was dead, the mouse-deer went back into the forest and met another tiger.

"Eh! You tricked me and lied to me. So now, you are going to die with me. I am going to devour you."

The mouse-deer fled into the forest and met a python. He played on his reed pipe for him: "Tétété."

"Give me the pipe or I will denounce you to my master."

But the mouse-deer caught the serpent in his mouth and beat him, tore out his eyes and threw them on top of the tiger. He fled into the forest where he met the elephant, who threatened to kill the mouse-deer if he didn't stop playing games with everyone. The mouse-deer insulted him and the elephant went running after him.

"You can't kill me because I can run faster than you. Let's go and look for a tree. We will hit it and the first one who makes it fall down is the winner." They soon found a suitable tree and started bashing away at it. But the elephant had flat feet and this stopped him hitting the tree, so the mouse-deer won the bet. Then he met some men who wanted to exchange some fish for wood. The mouse-deer brought them some branches with big thorns on them. The men put the wood on their shoulders and the thorns jabbed them severely. Then the tiger, the elephant and the men started chasing the mouse-deer. He cried out to the crocodile:

"Oh, crocodile, my friend! Help me to reach the other side."

In this way the mouse-deer was able to cross to the other side of the river, sound in both mind and body. The men had dogs who came towards the mouse-deer and when they reached him, they climbed on to the crocodile and defecated all over him. So the crocodile ate all of them.

### A1.2.3. Awang the frog

Though no reference is made to the nomads in the following tale, nor is it sung, the Moken nevertheless remember it very well and accept the mythic themes as containing the fundamental constructs stored in their collective memory. The incessant quarrels, the fighting and the intervention of supernatural warriors, historical and mythological figures, remain very much alive in their minds. Even though, for example, they themselves do not believe in the existence of any naga or flying weapons, they nonetheless appreciate the different stages of fighting, which they either remember or imagine. The Malay world, with all its imagery, thus occupies a very important place in their hearts. It serves as a source from which they have constructed their identity. Several themes are particularly worth mentioning since they resemble the narratives of Malay storytellers, notably the *dalang*, and their repertory based on Hindu and lunar cosmology, the elephant (which is a sign of royalty) and above all the theme of bathing in golden and silver wells. One cannot help but associate these wells with the sun and the moon, especially since, in Malay tales, the sun is male (as in the Moken myth of *The Sun and the Moon*, *cf.* Ivanoff, 2001) and the moon is female. These images correspond perfectly with what Cuisinier (1936) describes when she refers to the Indian background and to lunar cosmology as underlying all the narratives of the shadow theatre. There are other factors that exist in Moken culture to reinforce this impression. For example, the Moken have kept the knowledge contained in the shadow theatre and certain sacred dances (even if they are simply performed). They have given life to a knowledge that had become rigid in its expression. Thus, there seems to be no doubt that the sacred men, *olang puti*, are descendants of the Malay *orang putri*, the dancers of Malay trances.[5] Dances, knowledge, invocations and mythological themes seem to have emerged from the Malay matrix and became the canvas from which a new form of Moken ritual came into being.

The Moken tale *Awang the Frog* is above all interesting as it offers an explanation for the social differentiation that exists in the Malay world. Here are foreshadowed the first distinctions that appear (littoral/land, rich/poor, sea/land) upon which the first stages of Moken identity will be constructed. In fact, from an external point of view, the Moken do not differ very much from the humble Muslim fishermen of the littoral. Nonetheless, differences do exist and are based on socio-cultural divisions. We have already seen, in the narrative of Nyonya, the appearance of a social distinction between the poor littoral communities and the "rich" land dwellers who engage in rice cultivation. This social division forms the central theme of the tale of Awang, though, thanks to magic, he is able to transcend these social differences. This will be a constant theme in the following narratives: in order to restore the cultural unity present in the epic poem of Nyonya, it will be necessary to resort to magic, or in other words, for the Moken, to chance or to love. A rapprochement will then occur between groups of different cultures and social conditions, but in the end the exploitation of the environment will result in social and cultural differentiation within the population.

Like the Malay hero, Awang is a poor child who has been adopted by a family which earns its livelihood by fishing or by bartering. However, the barter system is already dominant and has led to the existence of a social hierarchy. Those who live in dire poverty, like the adoptive parents of the frog hero, are unable to cultivate rice (perhaps because they lack land) and are obliged to obtain it by bartering fish for rice. Later on, the Moken will defend this barter system to avoid becoming rice cultivators, which inevitably leads to a sedentary life style. The Moken consider the poverty of the Malay to be a virtue because it is an important cultural value for them.

### A1.2.3.1 Extracts from the tale, Awang the Frog

Two poor old people went off one day to go fishing in the river with their casting nets. The grandmother's name was Flower and her husband's name was Chiwang. . . . Every time they threw out their nets, they caught a frog.

"Since we catch a frog[6] each time, let's keep it and raise it."

They put the frog on the doorstep. Grandfather was very tired and went to bathe himself while his wife prepared the meal.

"What kind of frog is this? Maybe it is a magician."

The next morning:

"Eh! We don't have any more rice!"

The grandmother had asked princess Sélopa to look after the rice which had been spread out over seven mats.

"I am afraid the rain will soon come from the east. If it falls, make haste and put the rice in a sheltered place."

"Let's go! We are going to catch fish and then exchange them for rice. We are poor people. If we have something to eat in the morning then we eat in the morning. If we have something to eat in the afternoon, we eat in the afternoon."

They went off and the frog called to the rain, "kang kang". The rain soon fell, "plom plom." Then the wind came with the rain.

"Eh! Chiwang, our rice is soaking wet. Our granddaughter still hasn't done what we told her to do."

They caught many fish in the river and both of them carried the fish on their shoulders. The grandmother strung the fish on to rattan sticks. She put ten of them on each stick and then went to the king of the village. Sélamat, the guardian asked:

"Where are you going?"

"I am going to sell my fish."

The seven princesses arrived and wanted to buy the fish.

"Father and mother, if you really love me, you will ask for the hand of the princess for me."

"Eh! We will do so if this is really what you desire, Awang. But what will the king say? That you don't know how to do anything? That you are not able to carry anything?"

The grandmother wished to respect her son's desire, so three days later she said:

"Grandfather! I am going to speak to the king."

The name of the king of the land of Naradak was Grandfather Busu and his wife's name was Kenu. Their daughters' names were Girl[7] Alama, Elder[8] Chi, Elder Chum, Elder Chilum, Elder Chilama and Elder Chu. The queen said:

"What brings you here, Grandmother Flower?"

"My son, Awang the Frog, is asking for the hand of your daughter."

"Wait a while. I am going to ask her."

The queen spoke to the youngest daughter, as all the others were already married.

"Eh! What do you think of all this, Alama?"

"Who and what are you speaking about?"

"The one who is called Awang the Frog is asking for your hand. What do you think about this?"

"I will do whatever my father wishes."

"Eh! But what does he know about, this Awang Kata?[9] Your six sisters say he is lazy."

"Even so, I will marry him whether you want me to or not."[10]

"In that case, listen carefully to me, Grandmother Flower, and repeat what I say to Awang Kata. If he wants to marry my daughter, he must build a bridge made of gold and a bridge of silver.[11] If he finishes the work in time, I will buy everything necessary and we will celebrate the marriage. If he doesn't, well then, I will kill all of you."

"Tonight is the seventh day. My son is asking you to remain calm because he is going to build the bridge of gold and the bridge of silver. He will also build a house for him and his wife. No matter what kind of noise you hear, whether it comes from the hills or from the mountains, you must remain calm, otherwise you will die. Warn everyone about this."

Grandfather Busu ordered Sélamat to strike the gong.

"If you hear any noise coming from the mountains, remain calm and don't tell any lies."

Sélamat hit the gong, which made the sound: "Mong! Mong!"

"You must remain calm tonight and tell no lies. Awang Kata is going to build the bridges of gold and silver. If you don't listen to what he has said, you will die and be abandoned."

"Everyone has been warned now, Grandmother."

"Very well then, I am going now, Grandfather Busu."

Awang left at midnight while everyone was sleeping. He planted the grains of puffed rice everywhere, even right up to the foot of the ladder of the king's house, and he ate whatever remained on the spot where the house of the future married couple was to be built. He made an invocation to the columns of the bridge:

"Yang Yang Déwata, divinities who caused me to be, listen to my words! Comrade, father of the spirits, help me to build the bridges in this place!"

His comrade, the father and the king of the spirits, appeared.

"What do you want, my friend?"

"Build the bridges of gold and silver for me. Help me, otherwise the king will kill me!"

"Alright."

Sabat, Awang's comrade, was the king of the spirit world. The spirits resemble men in this land. Sabat's wife's name was Tiwi.

"You must have confidence and not be troubled by the terrible noises that you may hear tonight."

The columns of silver and the bridge of gold rose up.

"Look, comrade! I am doing the same thing that people of long ago did."

The roosters crowed as the first dawn broke and Sabat went into the forest.

"Does this suit you, comrade?"

"It's perfect! I hope you will participate in the rejoicing. I hope you will come to my marriage, comrade, king of the spirits, ancestor of former times."

Sabat disappeared and the roosters crowed when the second dawn broke. The little chicks descended to the earth and daylight broke through the night. Grandfather Busu and his wife Kenu woke up, but when they stood up, they fainted.

"Those who are hungry shall eat; those who like to play games will do so and those who like to dance will dance. We have seven days and seven nights to amuse ourselves."

When the seven days were over, the frog spoke:

"Eh! Father, father."

He called to the elephant who came from the river. His name was Nang Taru and he was a white elephant,[12] the frog's grandfather. He stopped in front of the ladder and the people there offered him some bananas. He finished eating in the afternoon and then someone called for Awang. He was to go and get his wife. So he jumped on the elephant's back. Grandmother Flower stayed in the house but Grandfather Chiwang followed the procession. The servants all clapped their hands along the way and Awang threw money to them. The poor people began to fight among themselves for the money. When he arrived at the house of Grandfather Busu, the king, Awang was invited to go into his wife's room. They spoke together in the presence of those who were already gathered there, lit cigarettes and offered them to those who had been invited. They, in turn, put money into a bowl. They filled two bowls with the money. When the ceremony ended, Awang took his wife and went into the big house, which had been built in the middle of the road. The elephant went home.

"Eh! Our sister's husband is really superb. How is it that this frog is so handsome? Is he the magic child of the river?"

Sélamat went to the house in the middle of the road to look for Alama because her brothers-in-law wanted to ask her some questions.

"Eh! Younger sister, come here. We are going to have a talk together. Where is your husband?"

"He has gone to play games at king Rapace's house, in Pinang Kutay."

When her husband returned, he first of all took a bath. Then his servants, his boys, served him a meal. The frog and Alama ate together.

"My older ones told me that I must attach a knife to the end of a string and put it over the door of the house. It will serve as proof of love."

She attached the knife. When her husband arrived, he descended from his horse, came near and pushed the door open.

"Eh! What's this? A knife? I could have killed myself! Why did you do such a thing? Never do it again!"

"My elders say that it is a proof of love. If you love me you will not die."

Seven days later, the king asked Sélama to make the gong resound all over the country.

"Who is going to look for a mouse-deer?"

His wife had a desire to eat the flesh of a mouse-deer, so all the men went off with their dogs to hunt one. Three days later, Alama said to her husband:

"Eh! Awang Kata, everyone has gone off to hunt for a mouse-deer."

"If your mother has such a desire, maybe she is pregnant. I will leave tomorrow morning."

He went on to the top of a high mountain where leaves no longer grow. He made an invocation:

"Yang Yang Déwata! Listen to me, you divinities who caused me to appear! Listen to my prayers and make it possible for all living things to hear me."

All the wild pigs and mouse-deer came to him. Seven days after they had left, the hunters, who were empty-handed, arrived at the top of the high mountain where the ancestor Lumpu Lumpèt lived.

"Eh! Grandfather, what is this golden-coloured shining object? Is it a divinity?"

It was Awang Kata, who was sitting down and his body was shining. The six brothers-in-law and their servants consulted one another to decide what to do.

"Shall we go and see if it is a divinity who has descended from the sky?"

They greeted Awang Kata who said:

"Why are you here? What do you want?"

"Our grandmother has a great desire to eat the flesh of a mouse-deer."

"You will obtain one on one condition."

"What is it, Grandfather?"

"Each of you will give me a piece of your nose."[13]

"And who is it who feels he has the right to ask for a piece of our nose? If we don't accept we will not have a mouse-deer. Alright, Grandfather, take them."

He took a knife and cut a piece of nose from each one and he then gave them a mouse-deer in exchange. They decided to take it back with them after they had cut it into pieces. But the frog had already gone home to his wife.

"Eh! Alama, take this meat to your mother."

"Eh! Your older brothers-in-law still haven't returned."

Someone took the meat to the queen. She had an excellent meal. Then the six brothers-in-law arrived.

"Where have you been? The frog has already arrived."

"We took another road."

"Now that I have eaten all I want of the mouse-deer, go and get me some fish."

She had a desire for fish because she was pregnant. So, the six brothers-in-law prepared the nets and took them on board their boat. They went home and left at dawn the next day. But no matter where they threw out their nets, they were unable to catch anything.

Awang the Frog was there; he was as luminous as is our monkey rock. He called all the fish to come. In the morning, the six brothers-in-law saw him standing on a rock but they didn't recognize him.

"Eh! Is it a divinity or a spirit? Let's go and see. Maybe it's a divinity who has come down from the sky. Maybe it is the genie of this place. Let's go."

They made a salutation to him.[14]

"What are you doing?"

"We are fishing with our nets."

"Why do you want fish?"

"It is our grandmother who wants the fish."

"You can have some on one condition."

"What is it?"

"Each of you will give me a piece of his ear in exchange for the fish."

"Wait, we will think about it! Eh! He wants a piece of our ear! The last time, it was a piece of our nose and now it is our ears! What sort of divinity is this?"

The older brother thought and said:

"Alright."

So, each of them gave the divinity a piece of their ear. In exchange, they were given some fish. They went back with their oars and sails, while the frog went home.

"Your fish are very beautiful!"

Sélamat carried the fish and the boy prepared the meal. The brothers-in-law arrived at that moment but the grandmother had already eaten.

"They were delicious!"

Seven days later the father said:

"Eh! Sélamat, tell my sons-in-law to come here. We will hold a council because I am old and I must now think of my succession. Who is going to be the chief?"

Sélamat hit the gong, which echoed "mong mong." He called the sons-in-law who were scattered all over the country. All of them came to the meeting, which took place in the king's house. They all came to see Grandfather Busu.

"We must choose a successor. Who will become the chief after me?"

The king noticed that pieces of the noses and ears of each of his sons-in-law had been cut off.

"What has happened to all of you? It is only Alama's husband who has a complete nose. Why are yours so different? What has happened?"

"We hit ourselves on the coral while we were diving into the water."

The meeting ended.

"Choose whoever you wish, father."

So, he chose the oldest one, King Moda, Grandfather Nanang, as his successor. The frog arrived the next day at the king's house, with the pieces of ears and noses threaded on to a rattan stick.

"Look! These bits of nose were those given in exchange for the fish."

The king called his six daughters.

"Look at the ears of your husbands! And to think that I detested your young sister so much that you spit on her!"

The kingdom was then taken away from the oldest and given to the last born. The oldest was furious and the king said:

"Don't fight among yourselves because there is no doubt that all this is true."

All the sons-in-law were told of what had happened.

"We can no longer remain. Let us return to our father."

They were referring to King Salty Water.

"Why are you all quarrelling? It is because of your noses?"

They told their father what had happened to them.

"You have acted like idiots! How could you have allowed your noses and ears to be cut off!"

"Eh! Do you think we should have a war with the frog?"

"Do as you wish! We have many servants."

It is true that they really had a great number of servants, thousands and thousands. Everyone made preparations for a war so that they could wash away the affront that had been made to the sons of King Salty Water. Nine days later, their father said:

"Send a message to Awang the Frog if you decide to go into combat with him."

So, they sent a message to him. They dug trenches and sharpened their weapons. On the ninth day, King Salty Water's army started to advance. The guards heard a noise not long afterwards, "pugu pugu." The noise came from the sea. There were bursts of fire; the darts of the blowpipes went flying, the music of the flutes, drums and gongs resounded. The army arrived. The frog made an invocation:

"Yang Yang Déwata! Listen to my words, you divinities who caused me to appear. And you, my comrade, father of the spirits, help me! Send me a naga who will sink their fleet."

A naga, who had been sent by the spirits, arose out of the water. He spat out so much water that the entire fleet sank. Many of the men died but those who survived reached the shore and continued the combat. It lasted for seven days and seven nights. There was blood flowing everywhere. The battle lasted for months on end. Finally, King Moda and his father Salty Water declared:

"We must have some respite so that my men can eat and rest."

A truce was then declared which lasted for seven days. The six brothers went up the mountain, to the edge of the river, so that they could sharpen their weapons, while Awang walked about holding his bow. But even if the six brothers had used an entire mountain, it was impossible for them to sharpen their weapons because the spirits were not on their side. When Awang saw the brothers, he loosed one of his arrows and it hit the testicles of the oldest brother. He jumped up with a start and all six of the brothers went down from the battlefield so that they could eat something. The flags were raised on the seventh day and the drum beaten. The combat began again and continued without ceasing for seven days. They fought with their hands and feet.[15] Then King Salty Water made an invocation:

"Yang Yang Déwata! May a rain of fire descend! Father and mother, who gave life to me, listen to my prayers. Let the rain of fire descend."

And then the frog said:

"Yang Yang Déwata! Listen to my prayers once again. Help me, king of the spirits! Help me to put out this infernal blaze. Eh! Come back, naga, and help us."

So the naga spat water again. There was so much water that the land became completely submerged. Thousands and thousands, tens of thousands and even hundreds of thousands of men perished. Only the six sons-in-law survived.

"Shall we continue the combat?"

"Yes! We will fight until the very end."

The six sons-in-law fought without respite but none of their lances were able to penetrate the frog's body. The frog threw his weapon, which hit his adversaries on the chest. His six rivals fell to the ground.

"Have pity on us! Mercy! Spare our lives!"

"I will allow you to live only if you stop making claims on this land. But the next time, I will kill all of you."

The combat ended and those who had been vanquished said:

"Eh! Younger one, Awang Kata, Awang the Frog! We have lost the battle and we now recognize you as being the king of these lands."

### A1.2.4. Nyonya

This epic poem, which lasts for eleven hours, is entirely sung (except for a short preamble of a few lines) in Malay by the officiants; it takes three days to narrate. The discovery of this narrative gave me the opportunity to address the hypothesis of the cultural proximity, the separation and the reunion of the Malay with the Moken. There are many developments of the epic story which can be analysed and they all have different levels of meaning, but the recurring themes are identical to those of the great Indian epic poems narrated by the Malay *dalang*, master of the shadow theatre:

> "the ethnological themes like those of marriage following a capture, an adoption, or an alliance of the winner of a battle after his victory, by marriage to the daughter or sister of the losing commander, are common both to primitive India and to the Hinduisation of Indonesia." (Cuisinier, 1957, p. 103)

Or further on (1957, p. 116):

> "No combat exists which does not have as its object the conquering of a woman . . . . When he marries his wives' sisters, whether or not he submits to the rule of matrimonial exchange established by the *adat* (custom) . . . , he still remains tender to all of them, with those which custom—or victory in war—gives him."

#### A1.2.4.1 Extracts from the tale of Nyonya

The wind is pushing us along, Jawan Moda. The foam, which we can see in the wake of the boat, shows us that it's moving well. The waves are carrying us, and the sails, which are held by the halyards, are full. I don't know where we are or how long it has been since we left. Tell the coolies, Jawan Moda and Palung Junga, that we have already been sailing for a long time now. Today, we are out on the high sea and can no longer see the coast. Tell the musicians to strike their drums and gongs so that we can make merry. Eat and amuse yourself, Palung Junga."

Jawan Moda! Speak to Palung Junga. It has now been some time since the land disappeared behind us, according to Pang Léma. If the coolies are tired, tell them to play the drum and the gong, to drink and to eat."

Seamen! Coolies! Nyonya has transmitted Pang Léma's words to me. She is afraid that the wind and waves will make you seasick. Pang Léma can no longer see the land from his cabin and we are alone on our boat. If you are tired, play the drum and the gong, eat and drink. Rejoice and make merry, all of you!"

Oh Jawan Moda! Today, I am going to sew the cloth that comes from Pang Léma's home. I will sew it with the big needle. There is a long dress and a batik, which I took from Pang Léma's parents. I will put on my batik and my parents will ask me where such lovely cloth comes from. Pang Léma, I am sewing now but if I sew with my left hand, you push it and if I sew with my right hand you push it also.[16] Don't go far away from me and don't be angry. Put your arms around me and kiss me."

Coolies! Do not make fun of Nyonya and Pang Léma who are kissing and hugging each other in their room. We are servants and must remain quiet, otherwise Pang Léma will be angry with us."

How is the boat going, Nyonya? It is a long time now since we left my parents. I am going to lie down, kiss and embrace you. Oh Nyonya! Lie down and sleep with me. Do not be sad. Let us go to sleep in the room, under the mosquito net."

The last time we left, Nyonya, there wasn't anything either, neither to the right nor to the left, but we found a small island where we anchored. The seamen were able to rest there and the rowers were able to lie down. That island also lay straight ahead. But Nyonya, I am sick. Where will we find a medicine to cure me? I am unhappy because I am unable either to kiss you or put my arms around you."

Jawan Moda! The island where we will stop is just ahead. The sails are full, and we will arrive there very soon now. But I am worried because Pang Léma is sick. He cannot kiss or embrace me.

### A1.2.5. The magic fish

This is a story from Surin, a story told by Unya about a magical fish called Sékot. Unya went off to go fishing in the coral reefs but was unable to catch any.

"The water is too warm here; we will not have any accompaniment for our meal tonight."

Unya went home and prepared his meal by himself, since he was not married. The situation remained the same for a month; he was unable to catch any fish! It was then that Unya had a dream about his father, who advised him to go and fish in deeper waters but above all to avoid fishing during the slack tide. Thanks to this precious advice, Unya went off to look for sand worms on the strand which he was going to use as bait. Then he went with his boat far off out to sea, in a place which was as deep as the vault of heaven.[17] He very soon caught some fish.

"Dawn is about to break and the fish still continue to bite."

It was then that he caught a big fish, whose name was Sékot. The big fish Sékot cried out: "hu hu!" as he fell on to the deck of the boat. Unya didn't have the courage to kill it and took some water from the sea so that it would remain alive. He went back home and prepared a little basin for his fish. That night, he dreamt of the fish he had caught.

"Your fish is a woman."

He was petrified at the idea that his fish might be a magical woman.

"How am I going to be able to love this fish if it is a woman or if this woman is a fish?"

That night he slept deeply and the fish was transformed into a young and pretty girl named Sélopa. They lived together as husband and wife for five months.

Sélopa said that they should begin thinking about planting rice; so Unya did so with the help of all the members of his family. He asked his wife's advice as to what would be the best day[18] to cultivate the earth.

"Wednesday is a good day," she said.

So, on the seventh day, he sharpened his axe and adze[19] and went off to cut down some trees.

"Hurry up," said Sélopa, "because once the trees are cut down and burned[20] they must dry for six months."

They did just that and in the seventh month, the field was clean and covered with ashes.

Unya then wanted to go fishing but the sky was overcast and a storm would soon arrive. Sélopa, who was pregnant, declared nevertheless that the rains would not arrive before the eighth month. In the ninth month, Sélopa began to have her first birth pains and Séliang, Unya's first wife, said:

"What are you going to do about the rice, Unya?"[21]

There had not been much rain this month but, in the tenth month, the rain fell without stopping for seven days and seven nights. So the royal rats went to work in the fields. The woman followed the men who, armed with their tools for making seed-holes, prepared the land. In the tenth month, Sélopa gave birth to a boy who was named Sigama.

"Be careful how you raise this child and do not lie or tell tales, especially not until the rice has been harvested."

In the eleventh month, the rice was finally ripe and the first wife exclaimed to Unya:

"The rice has been born."

"We must now prepare to harvest it," said Unya. "As soon as we reach the third month, we must look after the fields to protect them from the birds and the rodents. Listen, you birds and rodents! Do not eat the rice if you don't want to become sick!"

When the fourth month arrived, all the family came together to harvest the rice. The work lasted for nine[22] days. Unya went home and found his son crying. He took him in his arms but the child continued to cry. He gave him something to eat but this didn't change anything. So, in order to calm him, he told the boy that his mother was going to come, accompanied by his first wife. But when the two of them arrived much later, Sélopa asked her husband why he had lied. She said that Unya no longer loved her since he had lied to their son. She then went to the end of the wharf.

"Take a good look at me, Unya, because you will not see me again. We no longer love each other."

Unya took care of his son for a time and then went off to go fishing. Time passed and his son asked questions about his mother because he wanted to know where she was but nobody was able to give him an answer. It was then that his mother came to speak to him in his dreams.

"Sigama, if you want to find me, you must go very deep into the forest, in an area which is made of fields of flowers."

He remained for some time with his father but when he was able to do so, he went into the forest without his father, who was afraid to follow and complained:

"Who then will help me if you go?"

But Sigama had become a young man; he went off, going through one field after another, climbing one mountain after another. He passed through countries where there was not a soul and through forests filled with all kinds of animals. He finally arrived at an Old Man's house, whose name was Danka, and he stayed with him for three days and ate yams.

"I cultivate bananas and vegetables and I make cuttings of the yams which I sell to the king."

Sigama then left with a full basket of food for King Machiton, whose father was Séladin. His wife was called Diri and she gave him seven measures of rice in exchange for his products. He stayed to eat and sleep at the king's house. His mother came and spoke to him once again during the night.

"Eh! Listen, my son! You must go to the summit of the high mountain called Taratan but in order to do this, you must go through the territory of the ogres."

Sigama remained for some time with Sélamat, the guardian of the king's lands.

"I come from a place called Lujun and I am going to look for my mother," Sigama told him, "because she came to me in my dreams to tell me that her ancestors had called for her to return into a vast stretch of water. She lives there in a lotus."[23]
"Yes, it's true, the place you describe exists and it is guarded by ogres. I am alone now that my children and my wife are dead, so don't be worried, you will not die. Don't be afraid because I am here with you."

"But the ogres know the smell of men and devour them."

"I told you, don't be afraid. You must stay under the wind and as for myself, I know how to make the ogres die."

So Sigama left and shortly after encountered an ogress. Sigama said to her:

"I hate you and those like you. I will make an invocation to the gods whom I have believed in since I was born. I will ask them for magic spears and knives."

The gods heard the words of Sigama because very soon after the knives and spears rained down, cutting the ogress's arm. She fell down and begged for pity. Then he returned to Sélamat.

"Well, what has happened?"

"I won but I didn't want to kill her because it is not good to do such a thing."

But the male ogre was very angry and demanded reparation for what had happened to his wife.

"Yang, Yang. I speak to the gods and ask them to grant my wishes. I want them to give me sharp weapons and victory."

"If you permit me to live, Sigama, I will help you."

The ogre then went back to his wife accompanied by Sigama. They went to the land where the lotus is found. It was then that he saw his mother, arising slowly from the lotus to the surface of the lake. Sigama went towards the residence of the princess Jasmine. He stopped and thought for some time before deciding to go around the lake to try to get closer to his mother and take her away. But the naga was looking after the area of the lake and they saw each other.

"Eh! What are you doing here, young man?"

"Yang, Yang. Through my prayers and my words I ask the gods, whom I have believed in since I was born, to help me. I told the king of the djinns to come and fight."

Out of nowhere, there then came forth a djinn but though he jumped about in all directions, trying to hit him, he was thrown into the water by the naga. Then he invoked the knife to cut the naga's tail into four pieces and the naga died. Sigama grabbed a flower of jasmine which was close by and went back to Sélamat. The king told him to plant the jasmine which he had found in the spot where his mother had sprung up. The next day, he left to try to find his mother again. He went through countless fields and deep forests and was attacked by tigers and serpents. Finally, he arrived close to a river one of the elbows of which formed a small lake on which a lotus was peacefully rising. He reached the house of the queen whose daughter was named White Rat.

"What are you doing here, Sigama?"

"I want to find my mother."

"She is over there, in a house which is far away."

"She told me that if I really loved her I would find her. I came all alone because my father did not want to come with me. I really have to leave now, White Rat."

"I will go with you."

They went off together, going through countless fields and forests hoping that one day they would reach the land of the parents of his stepfather, who was an ogre who had married his mother. There was a naga guarding the region.

"Eh! Don't kill them, my son, because they are human beings. We will be unable to kill them anyway, since the ancestors are helping them. I married an ogre and we had a female child. That child is White Rat."

So Sigama lived at his half-sister White Rat's house for many months. She told him:

"If you want to live here, we will remain. If you want to leave, we will do so and go to where your ancestors live."

"Then let's go to St Matthew Island."

"Alright. But how will we do this? This land is far away and we do not have any money."

"Yang, Yang. You gods whom I have believed in since I was born, listen to my prayer and respect my words."

Spiders then appeared and a bridge was constructed until it reached Davis Island.

"How will we now be able to cross over to reach St Matthew Island?"

"Yang, Yang. Make a naga appear."

A naga appeared and carried them to St Matthew.

"Hey! What fair wind brings you here, grandchild?"

"Nothing special. We have come to live here with White Rat and Tima, the daughter of King Machiton."

They remained there for one year and decided to grow rice. During the fifth month, when Tima was pregnant, Sigama decided to go and see his parents and grandparents, those who eat yams. Moreover, it was the time of the celebration of Spirit Poles, which took place from the seventh to the fifteenth day of the fifth month. It was at that time that all the old men and shamans, Busu, Daya, Sitin, Péran, Madut, Polan, Giya and Molin were reunited. The eldest of the group, Sigama, declared:

"All of you, help me look for alcohol and offerings. Master of ritual, send your men to go and look for a turtle."

So hundreds of Moken boats gathered in the same place, under the direction of the shaman, who was there to greet them. They celebrated the festival until the full moon rose. Then each group left. When the ninth month arrived, Tima felt the first pains of childbirth and Sigama began to be afraid of the spirits.

"Don't be worried. The old Daya and the shaman Sitin are here. And anyway, all women suffer like this when they are about to give birth."

When the tenth month arrived, twelve midwives were called for.

"Eh! It is a girl."

"Oh! I love her already," said Sigama.

He cut the umbilical cord and the child began to cry.

The rains arrived before long, but none of the fields had been prepared. So Sigama decided to build a boat, a notched-out one[24] and an even smaller one because he had to find some food.

"If we don't find some shellfish and sea-slugs soon, we will be forced to eat whatever we find. We must work as much as possible to find the sea-slugs and shellfish. The Siamese are here and can tell us what we must do."[25]

Sigama and his friend Jimunu went off to the island called Indian Frog to look for shellfish and swallows' nests. They soon reached the Siamese territory and when they found an island, they lit a candle, prepared a quid of betel[26] to chase away the sharks and grey slugs, since they were very poor people[27] now and had to dive into the water to find green turbots. But this is another story, the one about Djimunu and Sigama.

# Appendix 2.

# Presentation of the language

This appendix is based on the report of the workshops held at Prince of Songkla University on 6 and 10 July 1995, augmented by more detailed information from Christopher Court. The transcriptions in this book follow French pronunciation, except in the myth presented in Appendix 3. I do not differentiate between the /o/ and the /ɔ/. All the written letters are pronounced (*an* is pronounced *ane*, for example). For proper names I have written /ch/ for /c / (Chéwè, for example).

The correspondence between this transcription and the international phonetic alphabet is as follows: the central (ə) is noted as (*e*); the front (ɛ) is noted as (*è*), the back closed-mid (e) is noted as (*é*), the back closed (u) remains as (*w*) (pronounced (*ou*)), the plosive voiceless palatal consonant (c) is noted as (*tch*), the plosive palatal nasal consonant (ɲ) is noted as (*my*) the plosive nasal velar (ŋ) is noted as (*ng*), the voiceless palatal voiced (ɟ) is noted as (*dj*), the semi-vowel (i) is noted as (*y*), the fricative uvular (ʁ) is noted as (r) and the glottal stop (ʔ) is noted as (ʿ).

The seven rules of transformation from standard Malay to Jawi are as follows:

1. The Malay /r/ becomes /ʁ/.
2. /a/ + /ng/, /n/ or /m/ final, becomes /ɛ/.
3. The final /ak/ becomes /ɔʔ/.
4. /p/, /t/, /k/ in final, become /ʔ/.
5. The /i/ becomes /e/ in the closed syllables.
6. The final /s/ becomes /h/.
7. /n/, /m/, /ng/ become /ŋ/.

## The consonantal[1] system of the Jawi language (according to C. Court)

| | bilabial | labio-dental | dental and alveolar | palatal | velar | glottal |
|---|---|---|---|---|---|---|
| plosive voiceless | p | | t | c | k | ʔ |
| plosive voiced | b | | d | j | g | |
| aspirated | (ph) | | (th) | (ch) | (kh) | |
| nasal | m | | n | ɲ | ŋ | |
| lateral | | | l | | | |
| trill | | | (r) | | | |
| fricative voiceless | | (f) | s | (x) | h | |
| fricative voiced | | | (z) | | ɣ | |
| affricate voiceless | | | | tʃ | | |
| affricate sound | | | | dʒ | | |
| semi-vowel | | | | y | w | |

## The vocalic system of the Jawi language (according to C. Court)

| | | front | central | back |
|---|---|---|---|---|
| high | closed | i ï (ŋ) | | uü (ŋ) |
| medium | closed-mid | e | | |
| | | | ə | o |
| | open-mid | ɛ ɛ̈ | | ɔ ɔ̈ |
| low | open | | | |

# Appendix 3.

# Phonetic transcription of the myth, *The origin of the soul of rice* (version 2) [1]

/ɔʊɛ dulu diyo taʔ dɔʔ
/person/in times past/he, she, it, they/negation/to have/
ɔʊɛ jadi sapo/
people/to be/who/

/toʔ adɛ toʔ hawɔ diyɔ
/lord/Adam/lord/Eve/he, she, it, they
bəʊañɔʔ tube duwɔ duwɔ abih/
/to be born/to go out/two/two/complete, finished/

/kalu gitu tuhɛ waʔ wi adɛ tu adɛ
/if/that one/lord/to do/to give/Adam/that one/Adam/
tu nɔʔ waʔ humɔ/
/this one/to want/to do/slash and burn/

/bənïh taʔ dɔʔ benï taʔ dɔʔ
/seed/negation/to have/seed/negation/to have/
tanɛ apɔ taʔ dɔʔ
/to plant/what/negation/to have/
pahauŋ nɔʔ tanɛ taʔ dɔʔ
/tree/to want (future)/to plant/negation/to have/

/gi waʔ humɔ̈ tu cuci habih/
/to go/to do/slash and burn/this one/to clean/complete/

pəʊoŋ baka cuci habih tu/
/pepare the earth/to burn/to clean/complete, finished/this one/

/diyɔ wi alamã maʊi lah/^

/he, she, it, they/to give/sign/to come/exclamation/

/ŋi-ŋŋiga (gitu)/ tu/

/ to dream / that one/

/suʊoh toʔ adɛ cicɛ

/to command/lord/Adam/to cut up /

añɔʔ diyɔ/

/child/he, she, it, they/

/anɔ̈ʔ diyɔ/

/child/he, she, it, they/

/anɔʔ ttinɔ cicɛ hamba/

/child/girl/to cut up/to scatter the seeds/

/bətɔ hamba tu/

/true/scatter the seeds/this one/

/tumboh jadi paddy/

/to grow/to be/paddy/

/tumboh jadi paddy/

/to grow/to be/paddy/

/hã/

/exclamation/

/pah kalu gitu adɛ pəʊiyɛ makɛ nasiʔ/

/exclamation/if/that one/Adam/moment/to eat/cooked ice/

/pəʊiyɛ makɛ gandoŋ paddy

/moment/to eat/flour of *sali*/paddy/

taʔ dɔʔ lagi

/negation/to have/again/

bəʊah ta? dɔ? lagi makɛ
/husked rice/negation/to have/again/to eat/
gandoŋ makɛ gandoŋ hã/
/corn/to eat/corn/exclamation/

/biniŋ hawɔ hawɔ diyɔ katɔ manɔ anɔ̈? sɔʊɛ
/woman/Eve/Eve/he, she, it, they/to say/where/one + person/
lagi adɛ diyɔ katɔ/
/again/Adam/he, she, it, they/to say/

/anɔ̈ do? dalɛ humɔ̈ diyɔ katɔ/
/child/to remain/in/rai/he, she, it, they/to say/

/pa? wa? paddy pa? tanɛ̈ paddy/
/place/to do/paddy/place/to plant/paddy/

/tumboh dɔh paddy tumboh dɔh/
/to grow/affirmative exclamation/paddy/to grow/affirmative exclamation/

/gɛnɔ̈ diyɔ katɔ aku gi ta? dɔ?/
/why/he, she, it, they/to say/I/to go/negation/to have/

/ta? jjupɔ ta? dɔ? jawa?
/negation/to meet/negation/to have/to answer/
/paŋge/
/to call/

/ta? dɔ? thəmuŋ diyɔ katɔ/
/negation/to have/to meet/he, she, it, they/to say/

/adɛ katɔ/
/Adam/to say/

/gi paŋg o mɛ̈? le?
/to go/to call/exclamation/small girl/to come back/
niŋ jawa?

niŋ jawaʔ
/here/to answer/
leʔ niŋ paŋge leʔ nuŋ jawaʔ laʔ nuŋ/
/to come back/here/to call/to come back/there/to answer/towards/there/

/diyɔ tɔʔ napɔʔ/
/he, she, it, they/negation/to see/

/to die/affirmative exclamation/to die/affirmative exclamation/
/a tu/
/exclamation/this one/

/kalu gitu/
/if/that one/

/buleh makɛ paddy/
/to be able/to eat/paddy/

/paddy tubeʔ buwɔh tu buleh makɛ
/paddy/to come out/fruit/this one/to be able/to eat/
paddy sapa kəla niŋ/
/paddy/until/epoch/here/

/hã tu diyɔ paddy
/exclamation/this one/he, she, it, they/paddy/
a hãh hãh hãh tuhɛ
/exclamation/exclamation (laughing)/lord/
wãʔ paddy wi paddy buleh makɛ
/to do/paddy/to give/paddy/to be able/to eat/
sapa kəla niŋ lah/
/until/epoch/here/exclamation/

/dulu taʔ dɔʔ paddy paddy taʔ dɔʔ
/in times past/negation/to have/paddy/paddy/negation/to have/
makɛ gandoŋ apɔ tu
/to eat/flour of *sali*/which one, what/this one/

lah hãh hãh hãh a tu/
/exclamation/exclamation (laughing)/exclamation/this one/

/pah jadi buleh makɛ paddy sapa kəla niŋ
/place/to be/to be able/to eat/paddy/until/epoch/here/
jadi baɲɔ̈ paddy oʊɛ poŋ kɔhɔ ʊamã ʊamã/
/to be/many/paddy/person/and/too much/many/many/

/a baɲɔ̈/
/exclamation/many/

/baɲɔ̈ anɔ̈? adɛ/
/many/child/Adam/

/sapɔ bəlakɔlah anɔ̈? adɛ bəlakɔ kitɔ
/until/all/exclamation/child/Adam/all/I, we/
ssəmɔ̈ nabi adɛ hãh hãh hãh nabi adɛ
/all/prophet/Adam/exclamation (laughing)/prophet/Adam/
hã adɛ hã nabi adam/
/exclamation/Adam/exclamation/prophet/Adam/

/bəlakɔ lakɔ lah anɔ̈? cucu to? adɛ:
/all/all/exclamation/child/grandchild/lord/Adam/
bəlakɔ hãh hãh hãh ssemɔ̈ jadi ma?nusiyɔ
/behind/exclamation (laughing)/all/to be/human being, humanity/
niŋ jadi ɔʊɛ ɔʊɛ baɲɔ̈ baɲɔ̈/
/here/to be/person/person/many/many/

/ta? dɔ? hɔ? laeŋ ta? dɔ? bəʊañɔ?/
/negation/to have/thing/other/negation/to have/to give birth/

/to? adam ŋã hawɔ bəʊanɔ̈?/
/lord/Adam/with/Eve/to give birth/

/jadi tube? duwɔ duwɔ tube ha? niŋ tube? nïŋ/
/to be/body/two/two/body/exclamation/here/body/here/

/hɔʔ niŋ dəŋã niŋ nikɔh hɔʔ nïŋ nikɔh
/thing/here/with/here/to marry/thing/here/to marry/
hɔʔ nïŋ dəŋã nïŋ ha ha ha taʔ dɔʔ
/thing/here/with/here/exclamation (laughing)/negation/to have/
maʔnusiyɔ taʔ dɔʔ ah
/human being, humanity/negation/to have/exclamation/
manusiyɔ taʔ dɔʔ/
/human being, humanity/negation/to have/

hã buləh makɛ paddy gɔʔ buləh makɛ paddy
/exclamation/to be able/to eat/rice/thing?/to be able/to eat/rice/
lah sapa kəla nïŋ
/exclamation/until/epoch/here/

/ah tu diyɔ yɔ/
/exclamation/this one/he, she, it, they/expression/

/dalɛ hadeh katɔ tu jadi hahaha taʔ dɔʔ ãh/
/in/Adam/to say/this one/to be/exclamation (laughing)/negation/to have/exclamation/

/a dulu lah ɔʊɛ manɔ̈ manɔ̈ waʔ makɛ
/exclamation/in times past/exclamation/person/where/where/to do/to eat/
taʔ taʔ dɔʔ sədaʔ makɛ ggapɔ kali
/negation/negation/to have/tasty/to eat/what/time (classifier)?/
jamɛ̈ 1la niŋ ɔʊɛ ŋaji baɲɔ̈ʔ
/epoch/that one/here/person/to learn/many/
dɛh ambeʔ boh ggɔ tu
/exclamation/to take/to put/thing/this one/
boh ggɔ niŋ sayo ggɔ tu
/to put/thing/that one/I/thing/this one/
sayo ggɔ niŋ makɛ jadi/
/I/to put/this one/to eat/to be/

/jadi sədaʔ jamɛ̈ tu taʔ dɔʔ baka
/to be/tasty/epoch/this one/negation/to have/to burn/

makɛ cicɔh ae gaʊɛ makɛ
/to eat/to taste/water/salt/to eat/
ha ha ha jadi səda?/
/exclamation (laughing)/to be/tasty/

/a ta? dɔ? dulu ta? dɔ?
/exclamation/negation/to have/in times past/negation/to have/
hanã bawɛ̈ ladɔ
/?/onion/chilli/
tɔ? tahu asɛ
/negation/to know, to understand/acid/
poŋ tɔ? tahu baka makɛ
/and/negation/to know/to burn/to eat/
cicɔh ae gaʊɛ ha ha ha kəla niŋ
/to taste/water/salt/exclamation (laughing)/epoch/here/
jamɛ̈ haʊi tu habih tu diyɔ
/epoch/day/this one/complete, finish/this one/he, she, it they/
buləh ʊɔya? habih/
/to be able/to transmit/complete, finished/

# Notes

## Introduction

[1] *Cf.* Jacques Ivanoff, 2004, *Les naufragés de l'histoire. Les jalons épiques de l'histoire moken*. Les Indes Savantes, Paris. This book contains phonological analysis and an account of the linguistic relations between the Moken and the Malays

[2] *Cf.* Thomas I. Parks, 2005, who explains that Satun cannot be mistaken for the Greater Patani of separatists for historical reasons (namely, the fact that local elites did not disappear after the transfer of the region to Siam), for linguistic reasons (the majority of the inhabitants speak Thai) and for reasons related to the border (the frontier is more secure there than on the other side).

[3] Grand Sud with the support of an International Scientific Cooperation Programme between the CNRS (French National Research Council) and Prince of Songkla University, coordinated by Narumon Karchanathat and Jacques Ivanoff. The project was multidisciplinary and had accepted Ph.D. candidates (in agronomy, ethnology, architecture) and training courses for masters students in agronomy. It had developed archaeological research and had worked towards establishing an eco-museum, creating a documentation centre and amassing a collection of books (several thousand titles).

[4] The development project also aimed to undertake deeper studies in some villages, i.e. to study them by techniques other than questionnaires. I chose Lubo Panyang (Lubo Panyè in the local dialect),Yaha District, Yala Province for this investigation.

[5] I refer here to the fact that they do not allow the sub-sets to emerge from reciprocal borrowings, for example. From analogies, I was able to extract some coherent constants which reflect the ethnic composition of the region.

[6] I only mention the Moken when I wish to point out some possible thematic comparisons. They are not very often presented in the comparative analysis of rice since their mythical

and ritual approach is very different from those of the Malays. After having studied the different structures that exist between Austronesian populations, I will now look for factors of convergence.

[7] *Tragulus javanicus* and *Tragulus napu*. See, for example, W. Skeat, 1955, J. Ivanoff, 2001. Skeat (1955, p. 12) says: "It is a small chevrotain called mouse-deer. It is a favorite character in Malayan folk-tales . . . In fact, the place occupied by the Mouse-deer in Malayan Folk-lore is exactly analogous to the place occupied by Reynard the Fox in the folk-tales of Europe." The mouse-deer or chevrotain is the hero of many Malay folktales in which, given the name of Sang Kanchil, he outwits all the other animals (*cf.* H. Bernatzik, 1958, pp. 50, 51). The mouse-deer is the Malay trickster.

[8] With perhaps the exception of Cortez, 1996, who conducted very useful research concerning the fishermen of Patani and who was one of my sources of inspiration in my description of boats in Volume 2.

[9] I am indebted to C. Court, some of whose material is reproduced in the present volume.

## Chapter 1
## Epic literature in Peninsular Thailand: A coveted isthmus

[1] The example of the Moken reveals the value of such study. First, many themes and stories originated from the same cultural background as those of the Malays (*The shellfish king* (see Chapter 3) and *The mouse-deer*(*see* Chapter 4), for example). Secondly, an analysis of their oral tradition has revealed a model of society that is the opposite of reality (e.g. exogamy is held up as the pillar of mobility, though it now hardly exists; the constant presence of symbols of a technology that is less necessary technically but which permits the affirmation of the choice of a nomadic way of life). Other characteristics that have been justified in the texts of oral literature and which have permitted the Moken to build their society inside an exogenous socio-political framework include the incised notches on their boats, the practice of non-accumulation, the cultivation of small gardens the produce of which is not collected and the acceptance of poverty as an identity reference (*cf.* J. Ivanoff, 1999, 2001a, 2001b).

[2] For Moken oral literature *cf.* Ivanoff, 2001b.

[3] All the titles of the articles in the *Encyclopaedia* have been translated and a summary was made with the help of Ratana Supapong, French-language student at Prince of Songkla University.

[4] As described by Josselin de Jong, 1965, p. 290: "We are still justified in asking whether there is a middle road between studies of single cultures on the one hand and 'random', or

apparently random or exploratory comparison on the other. Leaving apart historical and distributionary studies, with which we are not concerned at present, I would suggest that a middle road, straight enough and well paved, is the one which leads along what in Leiden we are accustomed to calling 'ethnological fields of study.'"

[5] Ivanoff and Le Roux, 1991.

[6] Locally known by the name of Taning, Yala "sparrow-hawk net", Nibong "palm tree". The etymology of the name Patani is more complex. For administrative purposes, the name of the province is spelled Pattani, for reasons relating to phonetic Thai transcription, notably the duplication of the intervocalic. This tendency perhaps contains hidden political motives (i.e. the transformation of common names to efface any memory of the past); numerous mythological derivations have been proposed:

(a) *Pata ini* "this beach here", derived from an epic hunter's pursuit of a mouse-deer that had disappeared "on that beach there." According to Court (1995a, 1995b), one says *pantai ni* "this beach" in standard Malay, which in modern dialect gives *jawi pataning*, with a variant pronunciation *pata ning*. Then the initial syllable disappears, and this is followed by the doubling of consonant "*t*": *pataning* becomes *taning*.

(b) *Pak Tani* "the peasant Tani" whom the king encountered while he was pursuing a mouse-deer or an elephant. Court (personal communication) mentions that the "*e*" or "*a*" are interchangeable. For example, there is a Petani village (Trenganu or Kelantan). In standard Malay, *petani* means "farmer" and can also mean *patani* (interchangeable *a* or *e*). The local pronunciation of *patani* or *petani* would be *petani*. In the more modern Jawi dialect one would say *petaning*.

[7] Ivanoff and Rozier, 1990; Teeuw and Wyatt, 1970.

[8] See the results of Janice Stargardt's research (*cf.* Bibliography) and the investigations by Prince of Songkla University (Ivanoff and Sawang Lertrit, 1995).

[9] The Moklen, on the other hand (sedentary coastal nomads who have contact with the Thais) have a tonal language.

We will now refer to the transcription adopted: the transcription of the words used in the Jawi language (local dialect) is adapted by the use or one phonological rules defined by C. Court (1995, "Phonetics transcription", and a word-for-word transcription of *The origin of the soul of rice*, version 2, in Chapter 2). *See* Appendix 2.

[10] Personal communication by C. Court.

[11] My father P. Ivanoff had already begun this study during his missions among the Moken, notably in 1973–4; most of the texts I have collected are transcribed and translated in my doctoral thesis (1989, *cf.* Bibliography).

[12] *Cf.* Court, 1995a and 1995b.

[13] *Cf.* Ivanoff *et al.*, 1991, and report on Lubo Panyang village (Ivanoff, 1990).

[14] Transcribed: Samoh in Thai, corresponding to the Malay standard transcription.

[15] Transcribed: Sudang in Thai, corresponding to the Malay standard transcription.

[16] Transcribed: Lubo Panyang in Thai, corresponding to the Malay standard transcription.

[17] Transcribed: Benang Dalam in Thai, corresponding to the Malay standard transcription.

[18] Transcribed: Petani in Thai, corresponding to the Malay standard transcription.

[19] Term related to the Malay *putrid*, to which I will refer later (*cf.* also glossary in Volume 2).

[20] A development project undertaken by the army had reached these villages during recent years. There is a road under construction which may cause the villagers to be relocated; irrigation projects have disturbed traditional rice culture. Simultaneously, exploitation of the forests continue.

[21] *Khatib*, *bilal*, *imam*, regular staff of older people in charge of the mosque.

[22] In fact there were three storytellers since one of the stories, *The mouse-deer* (in Chapter 4), was narrated by Po' Long, an "occasional" storyteller, quite apart from those of the neighbouring villages (whose names we will give whenever they can be identified) and the Moken storytellers.

[23] His real name is Useng Dereh (pronounced Usèng Dérèh), nicknamed Wo (from *tuwo*, "old man") Seng.

[24] His real name is Samoh Paksuloh, Po', equivalent in Malay to *pak*, "father", a title of respect, and Suloh, his name.

[25] *Kenduri*: Malay festival considered to be religious: a meal which follows is an important event, either religious or considered to be religious.

[26] Magical dance for healing (*cf.* Cuisinier, 1936 and below).

[27] From the Malay *puteri*, a magical dance, *main puteri*. For more information on this word, *cf.* glossary in Volume 2.

[28] The one we participated in lasted for 3 days and 3 nights, during which time Wo Seng held centre-stage continuously, giving the tone with his *rebab* and following the rhythm of the story.

[29] The figure of the naga is different according to the country. They are the lords of the serpents and possess countless magical powers A female naga is a nagi. Representations of the naga exist in India with a human head and the body of a serpent.

[30] The word *baha'ri* in Malay is translated as "fresh, full of youth, spring-like." It is also used to designate the blade of the kris (the Malay knife with a curved blade) of Patani (Wilkinson, 1959, p. 65) and can be understood locally as referring to the beautiful things of the past.

[31] Syukri, 1985; Anderson, 1890.

[32] *Cf.* Ivanoff and Rozier, 1990.

## Chapter 2
## Myths and epics

[1] My assistant helped me to collect all the stories in this book, unless otherwise indicated.

[2] Where it has been possible to identify the type of story, this is indicated.

[3] Slash-and-burn cultivation.

[4] According to another unrecorded version and narrated on 7 September 1992 by the same storyteller, they are twins. Their presence in this myth resembles the Malay version.

[5] Lord is written with a capital L when it refers to the Christian God.

[6] This final paragraph consists of remarks made after the storyteller's narration.

[7] Literally "the beginning of rice", when 7 or 9 plants are put into a parcel so as to welcome the soul of rice, and the ceremony of their return to the rice granary at the beginning of the harvest.

[8] The square brackets [ ] indicates a comment or explanation made by the authors or an external intervention, which is then specified.

[9] *Pulai* in Malay: big tree with whitish sap. *Sepulèh*: *Fagraea racemosa* or *Ophioxylon serpentinum*. According to Skeat (1900 (1965), p. 185, note 3) the *pulai* tree is the Malay substitute for cork, used to make floats for fishing-nets.

[10] *Hilè* (Malay *hulu*) "summit, uphill."

[11] *Aya'* (Malay *ayat* ) "verse, sentence, phrase."

[12] *Ilmung* (Malay *ilmu*) "knowledge, learning." The *bomoh* will explain that the knowledge of rice is *rasoh* (or *asoh*) *paddy*.

[13] *Auzu billahi* "god is my refuge."

[14] *Saito* (Malay *setan* or *syaitan*) "Satan."

[15] *Ro* (Malay *roh*) "spirit, breath."

[16] "In god's name."

[17] *Rohani* "spiritual."

[18] *Jémalè* (Malay *jembalang*: "evil spirit of the soil"). It is linked to rice and should be chased away from the paddy fields at the time of transplanting. It is then that a small area is arranged for it. This evil spirit can take different forms. He remains close to men and divinities without being either the one or the other.

[19] This seems to mean the cardinal points.

[20] This could refer to Jémalè; this bad spirit of the soil can neither stay in the soil nor go up to the sky, so it is neither a human being nor a divinity.

[21] The animals.

[22] Rattan *tawa* (*Costus speciosus*).

[23] *Krama'* (Malay *kramat*) "sacred, miraculous" and by extension, capable of doing extraordinary things, therefore a magician.

[24] *Cf.* preceding note.

[25] A plant used by the *bomoh* during rituals, notably those intended to chase away the evil spirit of the paddy fields (Indonesian *bolong, alpinia malacansis*, a *zingiberaco* of the same species as the big galangal).

[26] It is probable that Jémalè is, in this case, plural but the term "you" is too ambiguous to be certain.

[27] Refers to *képèng*: "sapec."

[28] *mé*: appellation for young girls.

[29] *hawè*: appellation for young boys.

[30] *Seri*: "charm." Notion of three or triptych (resembling the trilogy of Hindu divinities).

[31] *Imo*: girl.

[32] *Jaki*: boy.

[33] Soleiman: here described as the leader of the rodents.

[34] The narrator added during a conversation: "water is your nourishment. The herbs are your toys."

[35] *Ganong* "flour for bread and *rotis*", according to the informant.

[36] Sometimes pronounced *héni* "Hindustan"(?) According to the informant the inhabitants there have dark skins and are smaller than Indians and this country is close to Burma.

[37] *Genoh berah*, (*berah* "husked rice"), a fired clay vessel, a kind of *pasu* but larger and taller. Its shape varies according to the location. It is used as a container for various substances and people refer to it in terms of the contents (e.g. a fish container).

[38] *Selèng.*

[39] *Halo berah.*

[40] *Chupo* (Malay *chupak*) "half of a coconut."

[41] Not identified. During our conversation with the narrator he said that one needed three branches of three different trees (*fagraea, racemosa* or *ophioxylon serpentinum* and *setawa desoriphere*, the name for *costus speciosus*). The narrator also said that when one plants the branches of a tree, by association this causes the rice to grow as high as the branches.

[42] Rattan *tawa* (*Costus speciosus).*

[43] The word *baloh* is employed.

[44] This version is somewhat different from the preceding one, but narrated by the same person.

[45] *Hennu* "Hindustani"(?)

[46] This is not explicit but it always refers to a soul, that can take many different forms. As in other tales it seems to be a hermaphrodite. In this tale a boy's name is used, Hawè.

[47] *No*: an Arab word meaning "luminous, light," *seri* "charm", the notion of "three" or "triple" (a reminder of the trilogy of Hindu gods).

[48] The word used here is *dato* and not *wo*.

[49] *Genoh*: a kind of *pasu* "baked clay dish".

[50] The word used to describe their arrival is *jatoh* "to fall" which implies that they were flying, according to our assistant who compares them to the goddess *nang tabung*, who is able to fly.

[51] *Ngedèng*: plant which causes itching.

[52] *Huba' riyo'* (Malay *ubat*) "remedy": *riok, timonius penducularis,* perhaps also from the Malay *siur* (*xanthophyllum lanceotum).*

[53] *Antistiris gigantea* or the *media villosa*.

[54] *Semo* (Malay *semah*) "sacrifice."

[55] *Bola*, ritual plant, *cf.* glossary in Volume 2.

[56] *Dao* "prayer, incantation."

[57] *Kerama* (Malay *keramat* "sacred", "miraculous").

[58] Female spirit who flies. She has long hair and a breast on her back.

[59] Refers to teachers, religious teachers in Koranic schools or to the *pono* (Malay *pondok*) "cabin", religious school and cabin for students.

[60] Verse used to "calm the earth", in other words to frighten the spirits.

[61] *Karim*, merciful.

[62] *Laha* "a prayer made before noon"; *lohor* "a prayer of the middle of the day."

[63] *Tamahul* "tolerance."

[64] *Musa* "Moses."

[65] *La*: "it is not."

[66] Not identified, *ma muy* in Thai.

[67] Not identified.

[68] *Bambusa vulgaris*.

[69] "Evil spirit of the ground."

[70] *Pujo* (Malay *puja*) "pray to the idols."

[71] Once in the granary, the soul of rice multiplies.

[72] *Siloh*, not as ancient a story as a *hikayat*. This is why the word *bérito* is used in this story. However, it is considered as being as true a story as a *hikayat*.

[73] The narrator uses here the term *bérito* "new."

[74] *Kenuwo cino*: according to the narrator, a country under the sun.

[75] Promise to make many offerings to her.

[76] *Chi*: polite form of address.

[77] *Ibu paddy* "mother rice."

[78] See Skeat, 1900 (1965), p. 240 who describes the ten prayers that are made in silence while holding one's breath: "The first is God, the second is Mohamed, the third, Holy water of the five Hours of Prayer by Day and Night. The fourth is Pancha Indra, the fifth, the Open Door of Daily Bread. The sixth, the Seven Stories of the Palace-Tower. The seventh, the Open Door of the Rice-sifting platform. The eighth, the open Door of Paradise. The ninth is the Child in its Mother's womb. The tenth is the Child created by God, the reason of its creation being our lord. "

[79] *Mé jabut*: the term used is the name of the hero of the story of the soul of rice, Hawè Jabut

[80] *Panyong* "umbrella."

[81] An ancient village.

[82] *Siri*' "non-Muslim beliefs."

[83] *Pujo* (Malay *puja*) "pray to the idols."

[84] Ancient Thai currency which became the rial (Spanish dollar) that was formerly used. It may refer here to Thai money.

[85] *Anging* (Malay *angan*) "thought, idea, imagination"(?).

[86] *Napsu* "feelings", but not always good ones.

[87] *Maléaka* (Malay *malaikat*) "angels." These angels can be replaced by the more ancient divinities and are very important in local myths. For more details, *see* Volume 2, as well as Skeat, 1900 (1965), p. 98.

[88] *Gata* (Malay *gantang*), equal to 4 *cupoh* (Malay *cupak*), which is half of a coconut for each one. It will be translated by "sack" in this book.

89 We should point out that, in the beginning, rice was considered as a wild plant that grew in the swamps. Certain theories corroborate these beliefs.

[90] An action that reminds one of the *mula paddy* "beginning of rice."

[91] *Zaka* (Malay *zakat*), a tax the proceeds of which are to be shared with the poor.

[92] The narrator pronounced the name Awè rather than Hawè; but we noticed that the presence or absence of the *h* has no phonological relevance.

[93] A skin disease, *krapudahu*. Hawè has an ugly appearance because he has still not been husked; and like the pod of the rice grains, he is full of wrinkles.

[94] *Akirat* "next life, next world."

[95] *Nipi* (Malay *nimpi*) "dream", which implies communication with another reality and notably with the supernatural.

[96] Refers to Hawè Jabut. He creates or causes the creation of everything he needs for his growth.

[97] *Nyawa* (locally pronounced *nyawo*) "breath, soul, life."

[98] The original narrator used male and female pronouns interchangeably when referring to the soul of rice.

[99] *Supah* "anger"; this term implies here that her anger ceases by magical means (usually by a judgment that is heard in the spiritual world).

[100] *Pawoh* (Malay *pawa*) "share half of production."

[101] *Berka* (Malay *berkat*) "blessed."

[102] Several terms are used: (1) *nazar, nyany* "promise;" and (2) *keraman*.

[103] *Tuwoh* (Malay *tuwah*) "chance."

[104] There is a ceremony called *b(e)lo mulut* "split the mouth open" that consists of giving some glutinous rice to a baby, so that he or she will be able to speak. This takes place 30 or 40 days after birth.

[105] The narrator told us that this is why all rice stalks today have a broken or bent stem.

[106] *Belanyo* "price of the fiancée" or dowry.

[107] *Hikma'* (Malay *hikmat*) "wisdom, magic."

[108] Local brine.

[109] Malay term, *sambai*, Malaysian spice, a paste made of shrimps mixed with some chilli.

[110] We find the same situation in the themes of oral literature in continental Southeast Asia, where the "burning seat" of the Buddhist and Hindu divinities made them aware of the very special action of men.

[111] *Hatu* (Malay *hantu*) "ghost."

[112] *Selawat*: prayer, invoke God's blessing.

[113] *Baco* (Malay *baca*) here "invocations", "prayers", eventually from the Koran. They are the sacred words (magic?) that make charms possible.

[114] From where, according to the narrator, originates the "split the mouth open" ritual. But as we have seen in the story, Hawè Jabut passed a leaf of glutinous rice across the mouth of the guardian in order to wake him up.

[115] *Keramat*: *kerama* "sacred", "miraculous."

[116] Jémalè (Malay *Jembalang*) "bad spirit of the soil" (*cf.* Volume 2).

[117] *Guru* "teacher."

[118] *Pono* (Malay *pondok*) "cabin", religious school and cabin for students.

[119] *Ano'murè* (Malay *anak murid*) "child, student."

[120] *Hibleh,* among the *hantu* that we can call the first degree; those who are able to transform themselves into humans. This desire to learn about religion recalls the story of

the naga who wanted to be a monk but could not because the Buddha reserved his teaching for men.

[121] *Melek'a* (Malay *malaikat*) "angel."

[122] *Jinn* "spirit, genie."

[123] *Kita* (Malay *kitab*) "writing, all kinds of books."

[124] *Jatuk*.

[125] This is how the rubber tree succeeded in playing the evil role that the spirit willed: giving life but taking away knowledge, giving money but killing understanding in order to better enslave the population.

[126] The word should be transcribed *mo'yong* but since this refers to a proper name that is written in various ways in the literature, we have simplified it.

[127] An ocean in Hindu mythology.

[128] This might come from the Malay *telaga* "well."

[129] Refers to Jibrael.

[130] Refers to the middle finger.

[131] *Bada* (Malay *bandar*) "port, city"; *lamo* (Malay *lama*) "old," literally "old country."

[132] *Permaisura*: queen of an inferior rank than her husband; *permai*: in Malay "pretty, handsome."

[133] *Rebab* (this instrument is one of the most important as it permits communication with the spirits; people have the means but not the knowledge).

[134] As a general rule, all ritual theatrical performances and particularly the Moyong are performed outside.

[135] The Malays recognize that there are seven stages of curves before one touches the earth. It is the third one that is referred to here.

[136] This can be translated as "black sole of the foot."

[137] A provisional resting place, one surmounted by a roof, must always be erected in order to perform the Moyong dance. It is also one of the particularities of the Nora dance, executed by the southern Thais.

[138] *Nèn* "novice" in Thai.

[139] He is still sleeping but his dream is the Moyong's reality.

[140] In fact, he is dreaming and thinks he is a king.

[141] The first song is *lagu* "word, song"; *peré* (Malay *lagu perang*) "war, fight"; in this context, "lieutenant," *khaba* (Malay *kaba*) "story, legend"(?).

[142] *Teri bosu* is translated as "Dame Benjamin."

[143] Name of a tree, not identified.

[144] *Angin mo'yong* literally "wind of the Moyong."

[145] It should be noted that the Moyong had a principal actress who plays the masculine role of the king.

## Chapter 3
## The cycle of Hawè

[1] The term used is Hawè Malah (Malay *awang malas*) "lazy companion." Tales about people who are lazy and finally rewarded are common (recalling a lost paradise when men did not have to labour?) Such people are often those who are chosen by the divinities. Our assistant remembers having heard many stories about lazy men and especially the one about the man who was so lazy that he waited until a fruit fell down into his mouth (a theme one finds also in Thai stories). One day, a bear approached him and put some gold into his mouth.

[2] *Bolepah keré*: a bed of bamboo strips which were used, among other things, for young women about to give birth. The bed is raised and placed near the fire.

[3] *Bujang*: young, unmarried (even if old), divorced.

[4] In Malay *kemala*: "luminous bezoar;" (a bezoar is an intestinal obstruction, at one time reputed to be an antidote for poisons).

[5] *Chèka*: age when children become independent.

[6] *Kito*: "I" or "we."

[7] The beloved, husbands or lovers, are called the elder ones and the beloved, women or lovers, are called younger ones among the Moken and many other populations of Southeast Asia.

[8] *Po'su*: a term normally reserved for those people who are older than oneself

[9] *Serayo* (*shorea curtisii* tree).

[10] He represents the exact opposite of the soul of rice. Men have to work hard to get her in their fields.

[11] *Baya*, here "to give"; it means the benefits you have received in another form than the capital you invested.

[12] There is no indication in the text of the currency referred to here. I have therefore decided to use the baht, the present Thai currency.

[13] Chinese intermediary, trader, patron-entrepreneur, the word employed in the text.

[14] In fact "oldest girl:" *ka'cik*.

[15] *Dekoh*: to give because of one's merits.

[16] *Jetong*: measure, equivalent to a carton of condensed milk.

[17] *Tengku*: polite term used towards a superior.

[18] *Baya hutè*: "to pay back with interest."

[19] *Baya hargo susu*: "reimburse the price of milk (education)."

[20] A belief which is one of the pillars of Islamic faith.

[21] *Pa krama*: "sarong", Thai word.

[22] *Derako kemo*: cause suffering; to strike, an action which goes against the moral religious code.

[23] *Beman* (Malay *glohidium sericeum* tree).

[24] This in fact refers to *piko* (Malay *pikul*).

[25] Always refers to the *serayo* tree, a *shorea curtisii* in this story.

[26] *Balasoh*: smaller than the *surao* (Thai word), which is smaller than the mosque.

[27] *Phèk*: "strange" in Thai.

[28] *Yon*: Thai word.

[29] Unknown measure.

[30] The term employed more specifically means "defecate", *bèrok*.

[31] Same name as the cruel king in the tale of *Chémè Chéwè* (below).

[32] *Jagè* (in Malay *jagal*) "to look after"; *kapa* (Malay *kapal*) "boat."

[33] *Bayaré*: "to buy."

[34] *Ngakè*: "to buy in one place and sell in another."

[35] In other words, intelligent.

[36] *Do'o* (Malay *doa*) "to pray, invocation. "

[37] *Sékzi* (Malay *saksi*) "witness" or *sakti*, supernatural powers of Hindu gods.

[38] This refers to a *pisa raho.*

[39] Apparently a speciality made with tea leaves.

[40] *Guri*: "small clay jar."

[41] *Guri tu kumè*: "clay jar used for water."

[42] *Payè*: "large jar for water."

[43] Refers to a trader.

[44] *Lenyo*: made with rattan and used to carry or suspend things with.

[45] Refers to a *pasu*: "a receptacle made of clay with a wide neck."

[46] The hour of the afternoon prayer. The hours, in this text, are counted according to the times of the five daily prayers.

[47] The king does not specify what it is. It would seem that the pronunciations *maato* "precious stone" and *mato* "eye" by the ship-owner are easily confused because our assistant made a point of explaining that he used the word *maato*, which is a classification for precious stones, rather that *mato* "eye." Moreover, the narrator clearly states: "He says *maato* (precious stone), yes *maato* and not *mato* (eye)." In another version, a play on words is used between *mato ikè* "eye of the fish" and *maato ikè* "precious stone".

[48] *Dari:* refers to women who have an important official post.

[49] *Jeramo prahu*: the small hold on the boat under the plank of the prow deck.

[50] Refers to the bird *tuto (tutu(?))* turtle dove *Streptopelia chinensis tigrina* and not *burung tité Geopalia striata* L. Very much in fashion locally.

[51] *Jepako daning* (Malay *jépak*), unidentified plant, *daning*(?); Jasmine is called *melo* (Malay *melur*) in other tales. But the narrator considers it to be the same plant.

[52] *Lala' langa, lalat*: "fly"; Malay *langa* is perhaps *langau*: a fly that bites, of the *Stomoxydae* species. But for the narrator it is a magic fly, perhaps equivalent to Malay *langah*: "open, wide open."

[53] This is reminiscent of the story of "Lady White Blood" mentioned by Gesik (1995, pp. 84–7) in which a princess makes her appearance from a bamboo which the elephants found.

[54] In other words, Dame Benjamin and the prince.

[55] *Nawa* comes from *tawa, tawar* in Malay "without any taste, insipid", by extension "without force." Insipid water which has undergone a magic treatment becomes energetic and becomes *nawa*. Skeat called it the "neutralizing" rice-paste (*tepong tawar*) "neutralizing" being used almost in a chemical sense, "sterilizing" the active element of poisons, or destroying the active potentialities of evil spirits. The rite itself consists in the application of a thin paste made by mixing rice-flour with water: this is taken up in a brush or "bouquet" of leaves and applied to the objects which the "neutralization" is intended to protect or neutralize, whether they be the post of a house, the projecting ends of a boat's ribs (*tajok prahu'*), the seaward post of fishing-stakes (*puci kelong*), or the forehead and back of the hands of the bride and bridegroom (Skeat, 1965, pp. 77–8).

[56] Expression one finds elsewhere in southern Thailand and which means to abuse something or someone.

[57] Here 'rai' refers, not to the size of the plot, but to the land after slash and burn has been carried out

[58] The child is three years old in this sequence.

[59] The themes of the crocodile who saves the child or the child who becomes a crocodile are equivalent. They give a human nature to the crocodile. The association of crocodile and tiger (Skeat, 1965, p. 286) reminds one of the sacred Moken hybrid (Ivanoff, 2004) tiger/turtle, symbol of the union of the sea and land, men's choice. For the Malays the turtle is replaced by the crocodile since men live not far from the rivers and estuaries.

[60] *Jaka*: "wood, leave. . ." heaped up to protect the crocodile's cavern. *Daré* (Malay *darang*) "underwater cave."

[61] *Nik*: royal "I."

[62] The term employed is *pa'ju*, which is an appellative for old people who are not related to the family or for those that one should respect, for example a teacher.

[63] *Nénèk*: term designating, in effect, an ancestor.

[64] *Nawa*: "soul, breath."

[65] *Geligo*: "bezoar."

[66] *Keretah* (Malay *kertas*) "paper."

[67] 'Six years' is what the narrator said, but if ten years had passed, the boy would now be 13 years old.

[68] The term used is *zeroh* (Malay *ziarah*) "visit a sacred place."

[69] *Muning jatè* (Malay *jatek*) "Elaeocarpus jackianus."

[70] *Sedaro*: collateral, synonym of *wogé* (distant relatives, whether geographically or genealogically close) according to our assistant.

[71] *Pudi* (Malay *puding* ) "*Codiaeum variegatum*"; *puding* is also the leaves of mint.

[72] This theme resembles the Moken story of Pakèt and the Moklen story of the ancestor Sampan. During his voyage towards the navel of the world, he is saved by the garuda's daughter who lives at the top (Ivanoff, 2001, 2004).

[73] She had a human form.

[74] *Bab nikoh* (Malay *bab*: "chapter, scene"; *nikah*: "marriage").

[75] *Temat*: "to take"; *remat* (Malay *remaja*) refers to the period of negotiation for a marriage. It is also a local term used to refer to an agreement that is less sacred than an oath or a promise.

[76] *Nanoé*.

[77] *Saksi*: "witness." Here a witness to a marriage.

[78] *Baso sara'* (Malay *basa*) "ceremonial, observance of traditions", to be understood as meaning to accomplish what is necessary.

[79] *Torèh*: "repetition of a former act."

[80] *Pusa tasè'*: "navel of the sea"; one sometimes finds associated with this *paoh jangi*: "wild mango tree." Most of the Austronesian people know of this tree which is found in the middle of the sea and whose roots are in the underworld of the naga and whose summit is in the sky, where the garuda lives.

[81] The ogre here is called *gasi*.

[82] *Belaso*: "small mask."

[83] *Gah*: "ancient measure."

[84] *Lèdè* or *lègè*: "ancient measure."

[85] Given that the ogress supposedly cannot speak or think, this dialogue cannot be explained.

[86] The word *doso*: "sin" (Malay *doda*) is used here.

[87] The ogre seems to have become a garuda.

[88] In fact we could say that the flower represents the Buddha and the forgotten link between man and plant (they have the same origin). The symbolism of the colours comes from Indian

beliefs and the tree is a reminder of the magical world that existed before the arrival of Hinduism and Buddhism. The trees in the oral stories of continental Southeast Asia are always related to men and indicate their state of mind, first of all because the tree protected the enlightenment of the Buddha; and secondly because the tree is the axis of the universe. It establishes the relationship between plants, animals, human beings, spirits, divinities. The tree is thus a means used by heroes to put into context what is too distant in time or space.

[89] *Wa' anging*: "make wind."

[90] *Pedè* (Malay *pedang*: "sword, scythe."

[91] *Jè'* or *jègu*, respectful form of address.

[92] The narrator speaks of the green flower further on.

[93] At roof level, *berèpè layè*.

[94] *Anging* "wind" but also someone who participates in something and *sako* "to be attracted to."

[95] Associated with the *Moyong* and with the *bagè*, to treat those who are sick. It must refer to *puteri*, a magic dance (*cf.* Cuisinier, 1936). For more information *cf.* Volume 2.

[96] *Diké*, similar to the *diké hulu*: musical ceremony (song in the form of questions and responses accompanied by music).

[97] *Buku*: "problem."

[98] *Mo ano*: "mother, child."

[99] See the story of *Hawè the lazy man*, where one finds the same theme.

[100] In fact, three.

[101] Malay *Musoh*: "enemy."

[102] The story can be narrated within a non-linear time framework. The time of the myths and the different epochs which the hero sees and travels in are reminders of his role as a uniting element for the Malays and their broken history.

[103] The Thai word *sanya* is used here.

[104] In fact, two.

[105] *Kècè angin*: "to speak wind."

[106] *Lagho*: insects that bite cattle.

[107] *Juwal kècè nelè*: "to sell, to speak, to wring without breaking."

[108] The image used is *balé kurong*: "basket to collect rice with."

[109] *Putu*: "to break"; *rohim*: from Malay *roh*, "breath, spiritual"(?).

[110] Social means of showing one's success in Muslim countries.

[111] Seven is the magic number in the world of magic, which existed before Islam.

[112] *Hanumè*: the monkey Hanuman of the Ramayana.

[113] *Pusa tasè'*: "Navel of the sea"; one sometimes finds associated with it *paoh jangi*: "wild mango tree." Most of the Austronesian people know of this tree which is found in the middle

of the sea and whose roots are in the underworld of the naga and whose summit is in the sky, where the garuda lives.

[114] Several terms are used in this story to express this relationship: *wogé*, *kawè*, *adè*, *béradè*, *budok*, distant relatives (geographically) and close relatives (genealogically), companion, younger, older, child.

[115] The narrator is speaking of three *boko*, that is to say the third degree of "magnetic variation." One is at a right angle to the seventh one. After this one leans towards the earth.

[116] *Seru* and not *pangè*: "to call", which signifies that one knows the name of the person (Malay *seru*: "to call someone loudly").

[117] Exactly the same theme is found in the Moken story of Pakèt (*cf.* Ivanoff, 2001, 2004).

[118] *Bujè*: "bachelor" (Malay *bujang*). Name of a country only inhabited by females.

[119] *Hukong mè* (Malay *hukuman*) "right, law."

[120] *Hukong mè atah sakè*: "right over the Sakai."

[121] *Kero*: macaque with a long tail or macaque who eats crabs, *Macaca fascicularis*.

[122] *Bero'* (Malay *beruk*) macaque with a pig's tail or macaque of the coconut tree, *Macaca nemestrina*.

[123] Refers to a *Dolium*. There are many tales in Moken oral literature centred on shellfish. One of them (in Moken) tells the story of the transformation of a shellfish into a monkey. Another one, also in Moken, speaks of a female shellfish (conch); yet another, narrated in Malay, explains how the shellfish became a man. Thailand has the *Sangthong* story.

[124] *Senoh* or *cenoh*, name of a tree that produces yellow flowers (Malay *cenok*). Also vegetable oil obtained from the *Diplocnemia sebifera*, or a species of bird *Rhopodytes* and *Rhinortha*. *Paga*: "enclosure." *Riyoh*: "happiness." According to the narrator Wo Seng, when questioned about the meaning of this word, it refers to the third eye, in the middle of the forehead. It also means "us", "ourselves", "in us."

[125] Note the resemblance to Turas, comic personage of the Panji Cycle. He is a servant, like our hero.

[126] As in continental Southeast Asia there is a belief that plants and humans have the same origin; the fruit-man is an important and casual spirit, an association of the two realms, vegetal and human, made into one. This reminds us of the world of the "unfixed" substances of the mythical world (*cf.* Ivanoff, 1993).

[127] *Dewo*, from the Sanskrit *dewa*, "half god, divinity."

[128] *Pako*: Malay *paku,* generic name of the "*Filices*"; *biru*: the "green" colour of the sea.

[129] An indication of the naga being a female animal; nonetheless the naga is also king of the underworld, the world under the sea; he is also warrior on land and in most case male. But the naga is an ambiguous animal, bad and good (some protect the Buddha, others were allied to

bad spirits), male and female, aquatic and living on land. The naga is the personification of the unclear boundary between the elements, substances and genders of the mythical world (*cf.* Court and Ivanoff, 2001).

[130] *Tuka satiyè* (the same word is used to define something that is *krama'*: "magical"). The magic stick is perhaps like the one belonging to Hanuman, the monkey of the Ramayana. *Tuka* (perhaps from the Malay *tiukak*), a measure of length; *sati* in Malay designates the queen (a corruption of *sakti*), *yang* (the Malay pronunciation of *yè*) divinity.

[131] The "head" of a pole *humi*, that raises men and the other extremity *hujung* that knocks them down.

[132] Eclipse or rainbow.

[133] *Chepako* (Malay *chempaka* ) "flower of the frangipani tree (*Plumiera acutifolia*)."

[134] Refers to a *dato'*, but according to our assistant, it is rather the head of a religious order.

[135] *Kayèngè*: "celestial residence" according to the narrator; one finds the word *yè* in Malay *yang*: "divinity"; *ka* (a locative prefix); *atah langit*: "above the sky," the narrator says by way of explanation.

[136] The first 'my': *teku*; the second *patè*.

[137] *Nujong*: soothsayer.

[138] The white elephant symbolizes royalty almost everywhere in Southeast Asia.

[139] *Pakè*: expert in religion but poor in material wealth. Refers to a man who devotes himself to the study of religion (Malay *pakeh*).

[140] Pillar, support (Malay *jeneng* or *jenang*), principal assistant to a king.

[141] *Pisa raho'*: traditional knife (*see* note 3, p.316).

[142] *Jenoh*: wide-mouthed earthenware container: *jenoh*, also "full", "sufficient" in Malay: *jenok*: "red rice" in Malay.

[143] Local brine.

[144] *Tegiri*: "fish, Scomberomous."

[145] The term used to define the divinity here is *kereso*, indissociable from the number forty; Malay *keresok* "dense"; "stick", or "noise of something that is torn."

[146] *Nguca* (prayer, in Arabic, according to our assistant) *dua kelimoh sada'*.

[147] *Beting*: "sloping sand beach"; *timo* (Malay *timur*) "east."

[148] Refers here to a *kolè'*, a traditional fishing boat of the Malay fishermen of southern Thailand, also found in Kelantan (*cf.* Coatelen, 1982, *cf.* Volume 2).

[149] *Pako*: "filices"; Malay *hijau*: "green."

[150] Previously this referred to *gasi*. It now indicates a *bato'*: the *bato'* is an ogre who resembles men except that he has a tail. The *gasi* is the equivalent of the Thai *yak*, a giant ogre.

[151] The theme of the bottle that contains magic substances exists elsewhere, *cf.* Geddes, 1991, p. 103: "Early in the morning, when the Dragon-chief was yawning just after getting up, Silanting Kuning grabbed the bottle of his mouth."
[152] *Nyawo*: "breath, soul, life."
[153] *Semilah*: "invocation of the name of god"; *leka*: "to attach." See Cuisinier (1936) for the formulas for untying and binding.
[154] *Belano*: Malay *belanak*: *Mugil sp.*
[155] Refers to a net attached to the end of a pole (Malay *jail*).
[156] This theme is found in Moken tale of Awang the frog (*cf.* Ivanoff, 2001, 2004).
[157] Traps, *jahè* and *buhè* (see drawings).
[158] *Mugil sp.*
[159] *Tehè jera'.*
[160] *Tehè jahè.*
[161] *Jera'iring*: "rope with slipknot at the extremity of a pole."
[162] *Ju'* (Malay *jut*) conical trap; the *lopong* (Malay *lopong*) is mentioned later as "wide-mouthed, open mouth."
[163] Refers here to a *guwo.*
[164] *Sèsen*, perhaps the place for an enthronement, described in the following note.
[165] Refers to a raised seat like those used during marriages and which are used for the enthronement of new kings. They are placed near the gods who decide whether to accept them or not.
[166] Literally: *gua*: "cave"; *batu* "stone"; *singo*: "lion"; *manèng*(?).
[167] *Suri*: "queen."
[168] Not identified, divine bird, in Malay *gagah*: "dominant, coercive force"(?); in Malay *sura*: heroes, send a message, an order(?); *lekapo*(?) (*lek*: "divination"; *kapo*: "to embrace", a tree, for example, to climb(?)).
[169] *Baju panah*: "warm shirt": refers to a shirt with a Mao collar that people formerly wore.
[170] *Cf.* note 168.
[171] Literally: the "lion of night."
[172] For the youngest child, the old woman of Goné (the shellfish king), one added *teri*, translated as Dame. Here, it is a boy and one adds *sati*: "sermon, sacred word."
[173] A comic personage found in ceremonies.
[174] *Takro*: a popular game and in former times a ritual in the Malay world. A rattan ball is propelled over a net. The players try to prevent the ball from touching the ground; the players must not use their hands, feet or head.
[175] *Pero*: according to our assistant, a mixture of pure gold and "red gold", perhaps "silver" (Malay *perak*: "silver").

[176] *Gunung*: "Mountain"; *berité*: "shimmering."

[177] The word used here is not *teri* but *peteri* (Malay): soldier or more likely *puteri*: "princess and a dancer for magical ceremonies", *cf.* Cuisinier, 1936.

[178] *Sang*: honorific term for Hindu gods, kings, heroes or animals in folklore.

[179] *Pudi* (Malay *puding*) "*Codiaeum variegatum*"; *puding* is also the leaves of mint.

[180] As everywhere in Southeast Asia, betel is the messenger of men and of gods. It takes the symbolic form here of a letter addressed to the gods, like a prayer.

[181] Refers to her husband, Gonè.

[182] *Suri*, from the Sanskrit: "Queen"; *permasuri*: "her majesty the queen."

[183] *Jeringing* in Malay: "to scold", "bare one's teeth."

[184] *Beluyè* (Malay *belian*) "a spirit, a ceremony"; *cf.* Cuisinier, 1936.

[185] *Halo*: "were tiger."

[186] There are different pronunciations, *sangnyanyo*, *sahnyanyo*, but they are identical for the narrator.

[187] *Khaba burung beriya*: literally "new bird man." Refers to an expression that signifies "from one mouth to another" and is based on the fact that when a large wild animal (elephant, tiger. . .) is close by, the birds begin to cheep.

[188] *Sati*: "sermon, sacred word."

[189] *Royè topèng*: "mask theatre."

[190] *Ludoh aè*: "calabash."

[191] Their names should be written like this: *Chémè' Ché'wè*. But since they are proper names, we have simplified the spelling.

[192] *Mè*: appellation for little girl.

[193] *Wè*: appellation for little boys, diminutive of Hawè.

[194] The narrator specifies that one *képèng* is worth three *satang*. One Thai baht is worth one hundred *satang* today. In former times the *képèng* was a sapec.

[195] *Po si* (in Thai): fourth level of primary school.

[196] *Pocho hari*: literally "to plant the day", in other words, to find a good day.

[197] The same residential instability of young married couples that exists among the Moken. The rule will be, as with the Moken, one of uxorilocality.

[198] *Kedudo* (Malay *kedudok*): "Malay Rhododendron, *Malastoma sp*."

[199] Malay *kemunting*: "Daemonosops geniculatus."

[200] An animal that resembles a small serpent or a large worm. The term used to define it, *ibu*, covers a wide semantic field. The same is true among the Moken who use the term *énong*, mother. Eventually, that which gives life, a superior power in the animal realm but that possesses the same characteristics. Its refers here to something that produces gold.

[201] From the time of his marriage Chéwè becomes Ché Hawè, which is really his full name. Hawè signifies "young boy." The term Ché is a polite form of address used for those with a kinship relationship or people who have socio-economic ties to another (household labour for example).

[202] Brine, the *sambal* of the Malays.

[203] Local brine, fermented fish sauce to which oil, garlic, etc are added.

[204] See Cuisinier, 1936, p. 217 translated as "untie." These words are, for the author, a part of the formula for untying.

[205] In the Thai currency, 100 satang = 1 baht.

[206] To know the time during the day, one counts in relation to the solar axis; Midday: *mato hari bediri* "upright sun, standing up"; *mato hari nyama tah bukè* "going to the other side of the mountain"; *lècho* "leaning (afternoon)."

[207] In Malay *burong tiyong*: praying mantis *Gracula religiosa.*

[208] *Chupo*, container for measuring rice but also used for other things. *Chupak* in Malay is a way of classifying (weight measure for rice: 1/4 *gantang* = 0.78 kg): Labrousse, 1984, p. 168.

[209] *Bako*: wide woven basket (of bamboo strips) (Malay *Bakul*) "braided bamboo basket for rice and dishes."

[210] A polite form of address used for mothers, whether as a classification or real. This may be a contraction of *mo*: "mother" and *ché* (or *chi*) a polite form of address. According to Labrousse, 1984, pp. 140 and 155, it is an abbreviation for *encik* and *cé*, *cèk*, *encik*, a name used for a Chinese person.

[211] *Silat* or *dika* in Patani: a form of martial art.

[212] The Thai name (now internationally accepted) of a popular game, formerly a ritual game in the Malay world. One must throw a ball made of rattan and ensure that it does not touch the ground. The players can use neither their hands, feet nor head.

[213] Character that is not specific. It may refer to a father, father-in-law, mother or mother-in-law.

[214] In fact, a metal worker.

[215] *Begayong*: literally small container for drinking water from, a jar, for example; also a particular type of fighting.

[216] *Makè khela*: literally "to eat bitter."

[217] *Ano kayu*: literally "child wood," expression which means that one knowingly lies, or that a plan goes as predicted and that something will happen afterwards.

[218] *Puyoh* (Malay *puyoh*) *Turnix taigoor.*

[219] *Beralo*: it is worth noting that the statue and the cross (erected later for the king's son) are anathema to Islam.

[220] *Meteku*: polite form of I before a king(?)

[221] The term used is *paté*.

[222] The term *paté* is also used here. In Malay *patik* is a form of address (a term of humility when speaking of oneself), Labrousse, 1984, p. 671.

[223] *Raya saka*. *Ra'yat* (Malay: "people", Labrousse, 1984, p. 671; *saka*: column of maternal ancestors, Labrousse, 1984, p. 707).

[224] *Ni* is the term used.

[225] *Pelatô*: in fact, everything that is in good order: the sequence 1, 2, 3, 4 is *pelatô* but 1, 3, 2, 4 is not *pelatô*.

[226] *Pelepah*: "untied, freed, released."

[227] Container in the form of a small boat made of the same leaf as the one used to make a *timo* (water container).

[228] *Sada*: "to step, block, get stuck." This will be the name of the child.

[229] *Maso jawi*: "to enter jawi": *jawi* here means the Muslims of Southeast Asia.

[230] *Sipa-sipa duo putoh apo*: according to our narrator, this refers to religious teachings, each of which has a symbol (breath, what one sees, what the heart does, etc.).

[231] *Orè laut*: "man of the sea."

[232] *Budu*: local brine.

[233] The exact term is *nené*: "grandparents, ancestors."

[234] Refers to Hawè Sada.

[235] In fact, lord.

[236] A system for marking out the land, or of possession, exists, with "interdiction crosses" (*kayè*) permitting communication with an absent proprietor. It is often dangerous not to indicate that one is using the land since the *baca*, buried magical runes, can make ghosts appear and cause robbers to get lost. *Cf.* Besson and Ivanoff, 1996.

[237] A Chinese expression marking the beginning of a sentence, according to our assistant.

[238] A Chinese expression, according to our assistant.

[239] People employed and living in the mosque.

[240] *Turoh*: "to command"; *sa'ti*: "oath, sacred word."

[241] The word chosen is *putéh*: "white." One normally says that the rice is red when it is mature.

[242] *Serami*: roof or extension of the roof used to cover a veranda or a kitchen, for example.

[243] *Rial*: literally, it is the "real", the Spanish dollar, but understood here as being equivalent to the *rieng*, a currency (small change, today; *rieng baht*: "money" in Thai).

[244] *Tuto*: bird of the same species as the turtledove but much bigger.

[245] *Tepong*: snack to be taken in the evening (Malay *tepung*: "flour").

[246] The term used is *sèlo*, you sit down cross-legged; this is an invitation.

[247] *Koho*: "gently, to speak in a polite way."
[248] *Siang* (Malay pronunciation *siyé*): "daylight"; *Miur* is the Malay equivalent to *mir* (*mior* in Kedah): "emir."
[249] This container is called *kopi* (like the Moken word). It is a container made with a Nestlé brand milk can.
[250] She uses a respectful term and one of modesty, *patè,* when she speaks of her and uses the term *teku* when speaking of Hawè, another term of respect.
[251] The term used is not *teri* but *tuè*: "master" (Malay *tuanin*).
[252] *Gajoh mino* (Malay *gajah mina*); cetacean, seal, sea lion. It is considered here as being the exact replica of the land elephant. Let us note that a creature who is half-elephant and half-fish exists in Thailand. Certain beliefs are associated with this animal, for example that if the tusks touch a tree, the leaves will fall with the animal's tusks.
[253] *Gadèng*: "tusks" but also a species of coconut tree (Malay *nior gading*) "coconut tree with nuts (fruit) of an ivory colour."
[254] Literally, being seen as not a man.

## Chapter 4
## Mythical Detours

[1] *Pulo*: literally "sticky rice" and thus "festival" as the sticky rice is an important offering.

[2] The term use is *tuwè*: "owner."

[3] *Pisa raho'*: traditional knife. The blade of this particular knife is shaped like the leaf of the *Licuala*.

[4] In this story, note the irreproachable attitude of the young sister of Lim Tô' Khiam (Lin Ku-niang). The Chinese personal names are transliterated according to the official pinyin and, in parenthesis, according to the simplified of Wade-Giles system (as given by Skinner, 1957, pp. 4–5,.

[5] *Memento published on the occasion of the inauguration of the offices of the province of Patani*, Patani, September 1965 (edited and annotated by Suwit Khananurak, pp. 75–77, *in* Prayundet Khananurak *et al., The descendant Luang Samret. . .* , Luang Samrejkitjakornjangwang Association, Patani, 1996).

[6] Only her gracefulness has passed into posterity since her name has been forgotten. This explains the presence of her appellation in the title.

[7] There is a suggestion in the oral version the brother was called on to return to the bed of his sick mother but we have been unable to find any written traces of this version.

[8] Hsü Yün-ch'iao, who had the same idea as Yü Yung-ho, *Hai-shang chi-lüeh* (no source given) and see "Po-ni chuan (Annals of Brunei)", in *Ming shih [History of the Ming]*,

vol. 325; the latter refers to Patani according to Yü since "Po-ni" and "Ta-ni" were used interchangeably in Chinese literature (Skinner, 1957, p. 384, n. 25). In the following notes "Po-ni chuan" will be cited as "Annals of Patani."

[9] *Chinese society in Thailand: An analytical history* (1957, pp. 4–5 and p. 384, notes 25–29).

[10] In the north of the province of Guangdong (Canton) or south of Fujian.

[11] "More than 2000 men" according to the *History of the Ming* and a "great army" according to local history recorded in the *History of the Ming* and "a large army" (Skinner, 1957, p. 4).

[12] "Annals of Patani" (p. 5). The author does give the source, either in the notes or in the general bibliography (pp. 421–38). According to Skinner's text, it is not possible to know if these annals exist in written form or if they were only reported orally to Hsü Yün-ch'iao, the same author who recorded the preceding version of the story.

[13] "It is not necessary to accept this rather contrived interpretation, however. Lin probably 'lived like a king' as chieftain of his men and their families at Kase, and, as something of a cultural hero; his position has been exaggerated in more recent accounts" (Skinner, p. 5) and p. 384, n. 28: "One Teochiu version, in fact, has Lin Tao-ch'ien going to Ayutthaya and marrying the King's daughter, but this cannot be taken seriously." See Hsü, 1947, p. 118.

[14] Chinese traditional geomancy, which must be studied in order that a site chosen will not disturb the flow of celestial energy. For the construction of a tomb the entire environment in which it will be placed must be considered.

[15] "This version ['Annals of Patani'] goes on to state that the Malays in Kase all say that Lim To Khiam (Lin Tao-ch'ien] was the ancestor of their family" (p. 5) and p. 384, n. 27; Hsü 1947, 120.

[16] *Memento . . . of Pattani* (1996), pp. 75–77.

[17] *Ano' ru* in Malay literally "descendant of the *ru* tree", *Casuarina sp.*. Anoru is also the name of one of the districts in Patani.

[18] *Memento . . . of Patani* (1996).

[19] Locally pronounced *keresé*. This is a small place about 7 km. from Patani, where there is a ruined mosque. It is adjacent to a Chinese temple, which is also very well known and is the tomb of Dame Lim Ko Nyao. A big festival is held for her every year by the Chinese community. There are two storiesabout this important unfinished Muslim mosque. The official version that was adopted by Bangkok speaks of the love of a sister for her Chinese brother who did not want to return to China and committed suicide. The story that we recorded speaks of the forbidden act of adultery and fornication between a Chinese woman and a Muslim prince.

[20] In many of the stories, it is often the Chinese who not only play the role of merchants and intermediaries but are local specialists in the construction of forges. The important

role played by the Chinese community because of their technical knowledge, seems to be confirmed by archaeological explorations that continue to this day (e.g. workshops where pottery was made by the Chinese).

[21] The Thais have, effectively, a different version of this.

[22] *Zina* (Malay *zinah*) "fornication, adultery."

[23] *To'kong*: "statue"; *me*: appellation for a woman (*pè'* for a man).

[24] Refers to a place situated in the historical heart of Patani, a city that was razed by the Siamese in the 17th century. There are still traces of these cannon forges, which are well known, in the region. One of the cannons is to be found in the park of the Ministry of Defence in Bangkok.

[25] *Umi tahon*: refers to a local zodiac. Thierry (1991, p. 231) records that at the beginning of a new year "there are games everywhere, food, festivities and dances, especially those of the *trott* where they mimic the putting to death of a deer celebrating the new zodiacal sign and the beginning of the civil year."

[26] *Terah*: not identified.

[27] *Jengè kèjè angin*: "don't talk wind."

[28] *Kuwing*: not identified.

[29] In Thai *jamo*: "crest."

[30] Half of ten, or in other words, very little.

[31] Bigger than a *burung tité*.

[32] *Burung tite*: "turtledove."

[33] The expression is "when I was naked."

[34] To pump water with.

[35] See Le Roux (1994) who made use of this story.

[36] Name of a place close to the village of Bangpu (District of Yaring).

[37] According to our assistant, *kipah and baling* are dialectical variations with the same meaning and are interchangeable..

[38] *Ibu garé*: "mother, salted." Salt is a living thing and appears thanks to magical alchemy of which the Dame of Salt is the symbol. In salt paddies, the appearance of salt on the surface is a sign that the Dame of Salt has arrived. This gives us a description of one of the stages in the process of salinization in salt paddies.

[39] *Mudo*: "young", and so not very salty.

[40] *Tuwoh*: "old", and so, salty.

[41] *Jamu*: "cashew."

[42] Actual district in Patani province.

[43] Local name of the city of Patani. Narathiwat is called Nago and Yala Nibong.

[44] In other words, "almost caught", *no'bulè=dza dè*: "almost to wish."

[45] *Aring*: to make an opening with the blade of the dagger situated under the hilt.

[46] *Pata nung, pata tani*, from which is derived the name of Patani, *pata ni*, "this beach", the "official" origin of the name of the city (*cf.* Ivanoff and Rozier , 1990).

[47] Village in Yaring district.

[48] *Oncosperma tigillera*, the name known to the inhabitants.

[49] Capital of the province of the same name.

[50] *Yalo* also means "fishing with a casting net," the official origin of the name of the city.

[51] In other words, the city of Yala.

[52] *Cf.* following note.

[53] Not far from there, just outside of the ancient city of Patani, is *kota cina* "the city of the Chinese," where ceramic ovens were discovered (*cf.* Lertrit 1995). This site is beside a canal that goes to the city of Langasuka, a religious centre where a monument was discovered in the seaward waters of this canal and is the reason why the area adjacent to it gained its character. One should also note that it was a tradition for ship-owners whose trading activities had been successful to cut down their boat's mast and throw it away, as a mark of their success; in this way, they proved that they no longer needed to go out to sea.

[54] The retreat of the sea from the shores of Patani is very important; several kilometres of sea were thus transformed into land over the course of several centuries.

## Appendix 1.
## Elements of comparison

[1] According to another version, they were both beheaded.

[2] According to another version it was the granite grave-stones which miraculously floated and which ever since have continued to move (by way of mute protest, it may be supposed, against the high-handed action of the Unjust King), even when set at rest ashore.

[3] A garuda.

[4] This refers to a mythical place for the Moken which could very well be Sumatra or Java.

[5] The *main Putri* was a rite for cleansing Kelantan, in which a magician or shaman (male or female) took the part of Shiva's Sakti. It was a survival of a Tantric ceremony in which union with the divine was achieved through a nude woman worshipped as a goddess.

[6] The frog represents water.

[7] *Siti*: a title of women of high rank in Malay society. The Moken use the term for sacred dancers and singers.

[8] This is the word *kaka'*: elder sister in Malay.

[9] *Katak*: toad in Malay.

[10] See the story of *Ringkitan and the cuscus* (Alibasah, *Indonesian Folk Tales*, 1986, pp. 40–8) in which it is the youngest child who accepts the animal, which all the sisters reject.

[11] This reminds us of the excessive demands made by the future in-laws among the Moken (in the tale *The Ancestor Man*). It is a theme also found in Indonesia in the story of *Loro Jonggrang* (Alibasah, *Indonesian Folk Tales*, 1986, pp. 16–19) where the fiancé must build a town in one night. It is the same for Nyonya who builds a town in order to please her husband. The parents make a request, which the future husband is incapable of satisfying. It is the means used to refuse a request for marriage but it also implies a disturbance in the classic way a marriage is arranged and calls for the universal networks to be activated. The fiancé, when faced with an impossible situation, provoked by the excessive demands of his about-to-be father-in-law, is obliged to use magic in order to ensure success. Magic and the power of the word have a direct relationship.

[12] The white elephant is a symbol of royalty in Southeast Asia.

[13] It is worth noting that cutting off pieces of noses or ears was also practised in the Arab world. It was a privilege of those who were victorious after a battle to cut pieces of the protuberances off the faces of the vanquished to affirm their victory.

[14] The same term is used for praying and offering a greeting. In both cases, the position is identical: hands joined above the head, as a sign of submission.

[15] In the text the word used is *silat*, traditional Malay combat, a combination of knife fighting and kick boxing.

[16] The narrator later says that Pang Léma pricked himself with the needle and was poisoned.

[17] The celestial vault and the depth of the sea are called by the same name.

[18] The equivalent of *chari hari*, "search for the day", of the Malays of southern Thailand: a divination ceremony intended to determine the most propitious dates for farming operations, a different value being given to each day of the week.

[19] The two most important tools used by the Moken. However, they have transformed the Malay *belium* into a tool, *adjay*, which has multiple uses (as adze, axe, chip-adze).

[20] The rai, *koma* in Moken, was the principal method of rice culture used by the shifting cultivators of the coastal population.

[21] Rice is related to women pregnancy and to the heroines of the tales. In effect rice is a plant which the Moken called "mother" which for them is a giver of life. This reminds me certain symbolic conceptions from the Malay world (and elsewhere) where one sometimes says the rice is "pregnant".

[22] The number seven, which is omnipresent in our tales, is a sign of multiplicity. It is the most important number in epic poems.

The number nine is also a sign of multiplicity but above all, it symbolises the nine months of pregnancy.

[23] "The theme of the encounter of the monk and water flowers also has a Buddhist symbolism . . . and these flowers are so beautiful that he has a strong desire to pick them so he can breathe in their perfume. These resplendent flowers no doubt symbolise all desires and pleasures" (Suthawadee Numbhakdi, 1991, p. 113). The lotus, sometimes substituted for jasmine, floats on the surface of the water and protects human beings. This theme seems to be an Indian influence. This theme is also in Indonesian legends (e.g. *The River Bannyuwangi*, in: Alibasah, *Indonesian Folk Tales*, 1996, pp. 24–8) and quite often in Indian-influenced epic poems. The sacred tree (Ficus) is also a Buddhist theme because it was under such a tree that the Buddha was enlightened. Another Buddhist theme, that of renunciation, concerns the ogre which sacrifices itself to give its skin to the hero,.

[24] A Moken identity reference whose mythical origins will be revealed in the epic poem of Gaman.

[25] An intermediary is necessary for the exchanges. Products must be collected in order to be exchanged.

[26] One of the main means of communication with the divine.

[27] Poverty, which was the social characteristic of coastal communities in contrast to sedentary land dwellers, will become an identity reference.

## Appendix 2.
## Presentation of the language

[1] In this table the consonants between parenthesis do not exist in standard Malay. Court thinks that these consonants are phonologic. According to him, the /f/ is a mixture of several dialects and the /x/ corresponds to three phonemes. [This transcription is made according to French transcription without the phonetic characters.]

## Appendix 3.
## Phonetic transcription of the myth, *The origin of the soul of rice* (version 2)

[1] The myth was collected by myself and transcribed phonetically by C. Court, assisted by Azip Samuyama. It has served as the basis for an analysis of the Jawi language, but the system of transcription has not yet been finalized. I am therefore presenting the text phonetically.

# Bibliography

Aeusrivongse, Nidhi, 2004, "Building Popular Participation: Sustainability of Democracy in Thailand," in: Michael H. Nelson, ed., *Thai Politics: Global and Local Perspective*, Nonthaburi, Prajadhipok Institute, pp. 1–24.

———, 2005, "Understanding the situation in the south as a millenarian revolt," University of Kyoto, *Kyoto Review of South East Asia*, 6 March (URL: http//kyotoreview.cseas.kyoto-u.ac.jp/index.html), 24 pp.

Alibasah, Margaret Muth, 1990, *Folk Tales from Bali and Lombok*, Jakarta, Djambatan (3rd edn), 85 pp., map, illustrations.

———, 1994, *Indonesian Mouse Deer Fables*, Jakarta, Djambatan (3rd edn), 62 pp., ill., word list.

———, 1998, *Indonesian Folk Tales*, Jakarta, Djambatan (7th edn), 99 pp., ill., word list.

Anderson, John, 1890, *English Intercourse with Siam in the Seventeenth Century*, London, Kegan Paul, Trench, Trubner & Co., 390 pp.

Annandale, Nelson, 1904, *Religion and Magic among the Malays of the Patani States*, in *Fasciculi Malayenses*, Anthropology, Part II(a), University of Liverpool, pp. 21–7.

Annandale, Nelson and Herbert C. Robinson, 1903a, "The coastal people of Trang," *Fasciculi Malayenses: Anthropological and zoological results of an expedition to Perak and the Siamese Malay States, 1901–1902*, London, University of Liverpool Press, pp. 63–5.

———, 1903b, *Fasciculi Malayenses: Anthropological and zoological results of an expedition to Perak and the Siamese Malay States, 1901–1902*, Part II, London, University of Liverpool Press, 116 pp.

Barnard, Timothy P. (ed.), 2003, *Contesting Malayness: Malay identity across boundaries*, Singapore, Singapore University Press, 318 pp.

Bernatzik, Hugo Adolf, 1958, *The Spirits of the Yellow Leaves*, trans. E. W. Dickers, London, Robert Hale.

Besson, Igor, 2002, "Le développement de l'hévéaculture en Thaïlande péninsulaire. Essai de synthèse des caractères originaux de la production de caoutchouc à partir de l'étude de la dynamique agraire d'un village malais de la province de Pattani à l'extrême-sud du pays," Ph.D thesis in Comparative and Agriculture and Agricultural Development (INA-PG) 4 vol., 850 pp.

Besson, Igor and Jacques Ivanoff, 1996, "Friches, Biodiversité et tradition. Etude d'un système légalo-rituel d'appropriation temporaire d'une production naturelle dans l'extrême-sud de la Thaïlande," *JATBA (Journal d'Agronomie Tropicale et de Botanique Appliquée)* vol. 38(1), pp. 105–29, 2 photos, 1 map.

______, 1997, *Archaeology in Southern Thailand. A selective bibliography*, roneo.

Boegehold, Betty Virginia Doyle, 1977, *Small Deer's magic tricks*, New York, Coward, McCann & Geoghegan.

Boutry, Maxime, 2007, "L'archipel Mergui, Croisée des Mondes. Dynamiques d'appropriation du territoire et expression identitaire des pêcheurs birmans," Ph.D thesis, Ecole des Hautes Etudes en Sciences Sociales, Paris, 453 pp.

Boutry, Maxime and Jacques Ivanoff, 2008, "De la segmentation sociale à l'ethnicité dans les suds péninsulaires ? Réflexions sur les constructions identitaires et les jalons ethniques à partir de l'exemple des pêcheurs birmans du Tenasserim", Aséanie, Sciences humaines en Asie du Sud-Est, éditions du Centre d'Anthropologie Sirindhorn, Bangkok, décembre 2008, pp. 11-46.

Bradell, Roland, Sir, 1890, "Ancient Times in the Malay Peninsula," *JRASMB*, 13(2); 14(3); 17(1); (21)1; 20, 22.

______, 1980, *Most ancient Kedah, in the Bujang Valley*, Malaysian Historical Society, Lembah Bujang = the Bujang Valley, Kuala Lumpur, Persatuan Malaysia, Paperback, 88 p., 1st edited 1917

______, 1980, *A study of ancient times in the Malay Peninsula and the Straits of Malacca and notes on ancient times in Malaya*. Kuala Lumpur, Malaysian Branch of the Royal Asiatic Society, pp. 103, 416 (MBRAS reprint, 7).

Clifford, Hugh, 2006, *In Court and Kampong: Being Tales and Sketches of Native Life in the Malay Peninsula*, London, Kessinger Publishing (1st edn 1897), 272 pp.

Coatalen, Paul J., 1982, *The Decorated Boats of Kelantan. An Essay on Symbolism*, Penang, Penerbit Universiti Sains Malaysia for School of Social Sciences, 167 pp.

Cœdes, Georges, 1964, *Les Etats Hindouisés d'Indochine et d'Indonésie*, Paris, Ed. de Boccard, (1st edn 1948), 494 pp., index, maps, table.

Cortez, Georges, 1996, *Enquêtes sur les pêcheurs jawi de Patani et Narathiwat (Thaïlande du Sud)*, Great Southern Project, Prince of Songkla University/CNRS, 229 pp., roneo.

Council for Education and Knowledge (peuypedoy kana kamakan faiwijakan), 1989, *Nangsu ti laluk kop lok 370* [Book of souvenirs of 370 years], Masajid Wadi Al Usen (Talo Mano) [Wadi Al Usen mosque], pin ti long prin withaphap patani [printed by Withaphap of Patani], 23 pp.

Court, Christopher, 1995a, *Workshop on the Phonology of Patani Malay*, Patani, Prince of Songkla University, January (8 pp.), app. (30 pp.), 1995, roneo

——, 1995b, *Second Workshop on the Phonology of Patani Malay*, Patani, Prince of Songkla University, July (27 pp.), roneo

Court, Christopher and Jacques Ivanoff, 2001, "Approches linguistiques et iconographiques du bestiaire marin thaï et malais," pp. 121-145, in: Aliette Geistdoerfer, J. Ivanoff and I. Leblic (eds) *Imagi*-mer. *Créations fantastiques et créations mythiques*, Anthropologie maritime, Kétos series, 54 photos, ills., maps, bib., 418 pp.

Cuisinier, Jeanne, 1936, *Danses magiques de Kelantan*, Paris, Institut d'Ethnologie, Université de Paris, ("Travaux et Mémoires de l'Institut d'Ethnologie" series, 22), 206 pp.

——, 1957, *Théâtre d'Ombres A Kelantan*, Paris, Gallimard. Preface by Jean Filliozat. Black and white illustrations, 250 pp, bibliography.

*Cultural Encyclopaedia of Southern Thailand (Sa:ra:nuklom wattanatham pha:k tai)*, 1986, Songkhla, Taksin Khadai Study Institute, Srinakharin Wirod University (with the support of the Toyota and Taksin Khadai Study Foundations), 10 vol., 4389 pp., fig., table, maps, ill. [in Thai].

Dournes, Jacques, 1981a, "Médiateurs et intermédiaires. Leurs fonctions et leurs moyens chez les autochtones indochinois," in: Yves Bonnefoy (dir.), *Dictionnaire des mythologies et des religions des sociétés traditionnelles et du monde antique*, pp. 80–2, Paris, Flammarion, vol. I: 618 pp., vol. II: 585 pp.

——, 1981b, "Sept. Le chiffre sept, le pair et l'impair, chez les autochtones indochinois," in: Yves Bonnefoy (dir.), *Dictionnaire des mythologies et des religions des sociétés traditionnelles et du monde antique*, pp. 429–31, Paris, Flammarion, vol. I: 618 pp., vol. II: 585 pp.

——, 1987, "Entre histoire et rêve: le mythe épique. Un imaginaire indochinois étendu ailleurs," in: Albin Michel, ed., *Colloque de Cerisy, Le mythe et le mythique*, ( "Cahiers de l'Hermétisme" series), pp. 111–24.

Endicott, Kirk Michael, 1970, *An Analysis of Malay Magic*, Singapore, Oxford University Press, Oxford in Asia Paperbacks, reprinted 1985, 188 pp.

——, 1979, "The impact of economic modernization on the Orang Asli (Aborigines) of Northern Peninsular Malaysia," in: J. C. Jackson and M. Rudner, eds, *Issues in Malaysian Development*, Singapore, Heinemann, pp. 167–204.

Fraser, Thomas M. Jr., 1962, *Rusembilan: A Malay Fishing Village in Southern Thailand*, Ithaca, New York, Cornell University Press, Cornell Studies in Anthropology, 281 pp. (1st edn: 1960).

———, 1966, *Fishermen of South Thailand. The Malay Villagers*, New York, Holt, Rinehart and Winston, 110 pp.

Frey, Edward, *The Kris. Mystic Weapon of the Malay World*, Singapore, Oxford University Press, *Images of Asia*, reprinted 1988 74 pp., photos, bib., index.

Geddes, W. R., 1991, *Nine Dayak Nights. The Story of a Dayak Folk Hero*, Singapore, Oxford University Press, *Oxford in Asia Paperbacks*, (1st edn, 1957), 144 pp., index, photos.

Gesik, Lorraine M., 1995, *In the Land of Lady White Blood. Southern Thailand and the Meaning of History*, Cornell University, Ithaca, New York, *Southeast Asia Program*, (Studies on Southeast Asia, No. 18), 98 pp., app., index, bib., map.

Hall, D. G. E., 1968, *A History of South-East Asia*, Basingstoke, Macmillan Education, 1070 pp., 4th edn: 1981, 43 ill., 11 maps, index.

Herriman, Michael, "Language, Ethnicity, Culture and the Conflict in Southern Thailand," *NUCB JLCC*, 7(1), pp. 15-30

Hill, A. H., 1951, "Kelantan paddy planting," *JMBRAS (Journal of the Malayan Branch of the Royal Asiatic Society)*, 24(1), pp. 56–6.

———, 1956, "The Keris and other Malay Weapons. (Keris Types and Terms by Geoffrey Hodgson)," *JMBRAS (Journal of the Malayan Branch of the Royal Asiatic Society*, 29(4), pp. 7–98 (reprinted 1970).

Horstmann, Alexander, 2000a, "The Making of a New Middle Class: Social Space and the Production and Consumption of Cultural Images in Southern Thailand." Ph.D. dissertation, Faculty of Sociology, University of Bielefeld (277 pp.).

———, 2000b, "Re-Negotiating Cultural Spaces for Muslims in Patani/Southern Thailand," *Yearbook of the Sociology of Islam* (Investigating the South-South Dimension of Modernity and Islam. Circulating Visions and Ideas, Intellectual Figures, Locations), pp. 191–211.

———, 2002a, (ed. with Ryoko Nishii) *First Inter-Dialogue Conference: Imagining Southern Thailand: Current Transformations from a People's Perspective*, Prince of Songkla University, Pattani Campus, hosted by Harvard University.

———, 2002b, *Trapped Ethnic Minorities and Local Reworking of Citizenship at the Thailand-Malaysian Border*, Working Paper, Center for Border Studies, Belfast, Queens University of Belfast.

———, 2002c, *Class, Culture and Space: The Construction and Shaping of Communal Space in Southern Thailand*. Southeast Asian Regional/Cultural Studies, Research

Institute for Languages and Cultures of Asia and Africa (ILCAA), Tokyo University of Foreign Studies, Proceedings of the Conference on Identity Politics in South Thailand,.

______, 2004, "Ethnohistorical Perspectives on Buddhist-Muslim Relations and Coexistence in Southern Thailand: From Shared Cosmos to the Emergence of Hatred," in: *SOJOURN, Journal of Social Issues in Southeast Asia*, 19(1), April.

______, "States, Peoples, and Borders in Southeast Asia," *Articles. Kyoto Review of Southeast Asia*, 7, pp. 1–9.

______, 2007, "Violence, Subversion and Creativity in the Thai-Malaysian Borderland," in: *Borderscapes, Hidden Geographies and Politics at Territory's Edge* (Prem Kumar Rajaram and Carl Grundy-Warr, eds), Minneapolis, University of Minnesota Press.

Hsü Yün-ch'iao, 1947, "Notes on Tan-tan", *JMBRAS*, 20(1), pp. 47--63.

Ivanoff, Jacques, 1989, "Moken: les naufragés de l'histoire. Une société de nomades marins de l'archipel des Mergui," Ph.D thesis, "Nouveau Régime," Paris, Ecole des Hautes Etudes en Sciences Sociales, 4 vol., 1966 pp., maps, ill., photos, gloss., index, bib.

______, 1990a, *Lubo Panyang. Evolution culturale et dynamique agraire d'un village de la province de Yala*. Report of the IRCA-PSU-EHESS investigation of small-scale rubber planters, 262 pp., photos, maps, roneo

______, 1990b, (with Christine Rozier) "De Mergui à Patani. D'une mer à l'autre, d'une histoire à l'autre", *ASEMI*, 14(3–4, 1983), N.S. in collaboration with SERIA: *Rôles et représentations de la mer*, pp. 69–96.

______, 1991, (with Igor Besson, Noparat Bamroongrugsa, *et. al.*) *The Golden Forests. Report of an Anthropological, Socio-economic and Technical Survey on Rubber Plantations in the Provinces of Patani, Yala, Narathiwat and Songkla (Southern Thailand). April 1988–December 1989*, 3 vol, Part 1, 152 pp., *General Report*, Parts 2 & 3, 697 pp., *Results of a Daily Technical Survey*, Patani, Prince of Songkla University-IRCA-CeDRASEMI.

______, 1991, (with Pierre Le Roux) "Le phénomène identitaire jawi. Ou l'appropriation d'un référent", *Identités Sud. . . Regard sur trois minorités de Thaïlande*, ed. Bangkok, Prince of Songkla University & ECASE ("Carnets du SERIA" series, 1), pp. 22–38.

______, 1993, "Vers une ethnologie des substances," in: P. Le Roux and J. Ivanoff (eds): *Le Sel de la vie en Asie du Sud-Est*, Patani, Prince of Songkla University-CNRS ("Grand Sud" series, 4), 438 pp., ill., photos, pp. 389–431.

______, 1995, (with Sawang Lertrit) "The Archæological Study of an Ancient Kiln Site in Pattani Province, Southern Thailand", *Arts & Culture*, Prince of Songkla University, pp. 60–1.

______, 1999, *The Moken Boat: Symbolic Technology*, White Lotus, 171 pp., index, app., gloss., 3 maps, 84 b. & w. and 59 col. ill., 32 drawings.

———, 2001, *Rings of Coral. Moken Folktales*, White Lotus Press, translated by Francine Nicolle, 490 pp., 11 col. and 20 b. & w. ill. by Luca Gansser, gloss., bib., index, 10 maps and tables.

———, 2001, (with Aliette Geistdoerfer and Isabelle Leblic, eds) *Imagi*-mer. *Créations fantastiques et créations mythiques*, Anthropologie maritime, Kétos series, 54 photos, ills., maps, bib., 418 pp.

———, 2004, *Les naufragés de l'histoire. Les jalons épiques de l'identité moken*, *Les Indes Savantes*, Paris, preface by Georges Condominas, 593 pp., 5 indexes, gloss., 13 app., bib., 10 maps, 2 tables, 21 figs, 15 b. & w. and 111 col. photos.

Josselin De Jong, P. E. De, 1965, "An interpretation of Agricultural Rites in Southeast Asia, with a Demonstration of Use of Data from both Continental and Insular Areas", reprinted from the *Journal of Asian Studies*, 24(2), pp. 283–91.

Khananurak, Prayundet, Khananurak, Panthep and Watthanayakon, Phanrit, *Tha:ya:t Luang Samrejkitjakornca:ngwa:ng (The descendant of Luang Samrejkitjakornca:ngwa:ng)*, Patani,, Luang Samrejkitjakornjangwang Association.

Labrousse, Pierre, 1984, *Dictionnaire Général Indonésien–Français,* Paris, Archipel ("Cahiers d'Archipel" series, 15), 934 pp.

Leyden, John, 1821, *Malay Annals*, London.

Le Roux, Pierre, 1994, "L'Éléphant Blanc aux Défenses Noires. Mythes et identité chez les Jawi, Malais de Patani (Thaïlande du Sud)," Ph.D thesis, Paris, Ecole des Hautes Etudes en Sciences Sociales, 2 vol., 841 pp., maps, index, bib., ill., photos.

Lertrit, Sawang, Excavation report of the project "Recherches archéologiques en Thaïlande péninsulaire: réinterprétation de l'histoire de Patani et sauvegarde des ressources archéologique," directed by S. Lertrit and J. Ivanoff.

Leeuw, Adele de, 1961, *Indonesian Legends and Folktales*, Thomas Nelson & Sons, Universal Digital Library, 177 pp.

Leeuw, Hendrik de, 1956, *Java Jungle Tales*, introduction by Hendrik Willem van Loon, illustrated by Kurt Wiese, London, Arco Publishers, 304 pp.

Leyden, John (trans.), 1821, *Malay Annals*, introduction by D. Th. Stamford Rafles, London, Longman.

Maxwell, W. E., 1881, "Two Malay Myths: The Princess of Foam, and the Raja of the Bamboo", *JRAS* 13, N.S., pp. 493–523.

Nathalang Siraporn, 2004a, "Conflict and Compromise between the Indigenous Beliefs and Buddhism as Reflected in Tai Rice Myths," in: Nathalang Siraporn (ed.), *Thai Folkore Insights Into Thai Culture*, pp. 99–113, Center for Thai Studies, Faculty of Arts, Chulalongkorn University, Chulalongkorn University Press, 233 pp.

———, 2004b, "Different Family Roles, Different Interpretations of Thai Folktales", in: Nathalang Siraporn (ed.), *Thai Folkore Insights Into Thai Culture*, pp. 1–25, Center for Thai Studies, Faculty of Arts, Chulalongkorn University, Chulalongkorn University Press, 233 pp. (Originally published in *Asian Folklore Studies* 48 (1989), pp. 5–20).

———, 2004c, "Tai Creation Myths: Reflections of Tai Relations and Tai Cultures", in: Nathalang Siraporn (ed.), *Thai Folkore Insights Into Thai Culture*, pp. 81–98, Center for Thai Studies, Faculty of Arts, Chulalongkorn University, Chulalongkorn University Press, 233 pp. (Originally published in *Tai Culture* 2 (June 1977), pp. 56–66).

Newbold, T. J., 1839, *Political and statistical account of the British settlements—With a history of the Malayan States of the Peninsula in the Straits of Malacca*, London, John Murray, 2 vols.

Numbhakdi, Suthawadee, 1991, "Le mythe du nom de Nak na:ù nâk dans l'ordination des moines bouddhistes chez les Phouan", *Inter-Monde*, Rhamkhamaeng University, Bangkok, 2(1), (3), pp. 108–19.

Parks, Thomas, I., 2005, *Maintaining Peace in a Neighborhood Torn by Separatism,* Southeast Asia Studies, Johns Hopkins University, Washington DC.

Pitsuwan, Surin, 1985, *Islam and Malay Nationalism: A case study of the Malay-Muslims of Southern Thailand*, Bangkok, Thai Khadi Research Institute, Thammasat University, 297 pp.

Reid Antony, 1988, *Southeast Asia in the age of commerce 1450–1680.* Volume one: *The lands below the winds*, New Haven, Conn., Yale University Press, 275 pp.

———, 1993, *Southeast Asia in the age of commerce 1450–1680.* Volume two: *Expansion and crises*, New Haven, Conn., Yale University Press, 390 pp.

———, 2001, "Understanding Melayu (Malay) as a source of diverse modern identity", *Journal of Southeast Asian Studies*, 32(3), pp. 295–313.

Revel, Nicole (collector), 1992, *Chants alternés Asie du Sud-Est, Hommage à Jacques Dournes*, Sudestasie Bibliothèque, Paris, 275 pp.

Roseman, Marina, 2003, "Malay and Orang Asli Interactions: View from Legendary History," unpub. Paper, Cornell Univiersity.

Satha-Anand, Chaiwat, 1983, *Islam and Violence. A Case Study of Violent Events in the Four Southern Provinces, Thailand, 1976–1981*, Bangkok, Thai Khadai Research Institute, Human Rights Research Project, Monograph series, 19–21 August.

———, 1987, *Islam and Violence: a case study of violent events in the four southern provinces, Thailand, 1976-1981*, Tampa, Fla.: Dept. of Religious Studies, University of South Florida.

———, 1992, "Pattani in the 1980s: academic literature and political stories", *Sojourn*, 7(1), pp. 1–38.

______, 2004, "Facing the Demon Within: Fighting Violence in Southern Thailand with Peace Cultures", in: *Seeds of Peace*, 6 February.

______, 2005, *The life of this world: Negotiated Muslim lives in Thai society*, Singapore, Marshall Cavendish.

______, 2007, "The Silence of the Bullet Monument: Violence and 'Truth Management,' Dusun-nyor 1948, and Kru-Ze 2004", in: *Rethinking Thailand's Southern Violence*, pp. 11–34, Singapore, National University of Singapore Press, 225 pp.

Skeat, Walter William, 1961, *Fables and Folk Tales from an Eastern Forest (illustrated by F. H. Townsend)*, Malayan Heritage Series 7, Singapore, Eastern Universities Press, (1st edn 1955), 87 pp.

______, 1965, *Malay Magic, being An Introduction to the Folklore and Popular Religion of the Malay Peninsula*, with a Foreword by Charles Otto Blagden, London, Macmillan (1st edn, 1900), 685 pp.

Skeat, Walter William and Charles Otto Blagden, 1906, *Pagan Races of the Malay Peninsula*, 1906, 2 vols, London, Macmillan.

Skinner, William G., 1957, *Chinese Society in Thailand: an Analytical History*, Ithaca, New York, Cornell University Press.

Stargardt, Janice, 1973, "The Srivijayan civilization in Southern Thailand", *Antiquity*, 67(187), pp. 225–9.

______, 1973 "Southern Thai waterways: archaeological evidence on agriculture, shipping and trade in the S'ri'vijayan period", *Man*, N.S., 8(1), pp. 5–29: notes, bib., 18 figs, 3 tables.

______, 1976, "Man's impact on the ancient environment of the Sathing Phra peninsula, South Thailand. I: The natural environment and natural change", *Journal of Biogeography*, 3, pp. 221–8.

______, 1977, "Man's impact on the ancient environment of the Sathing Phra peninsula, South Thailand. II: Ancient agriculture", *Journal of Biogeography*, 4, pp. 35–50.

______, 1979, "L'Isthme de la péninsule malaise dans les navigations au Long Cours. Nouvelles données archéologiques", *Archipel, Etudes Interdisciplinaires sur le Monde Insulindien*, 18, "Commerces et navires dans les mers du Sud", pp. 15–39.

Syukri, Ibrahim, 1985, *History of the Malay Kingdom of Patani*, Athens, Ohio, Ohio University, Center for International Studies, ("Monographs in International Studies", Southeast Asia Series, 68), trans. Conner Bailey and John N. Miksic, 90 pp.

Teeuw, Andries and Wyatt, David K., 1970, *Hikayat Patani. The Story of Patani*, The Hague, Martinus Nijhoff, Koninklijk Instituut, Voor Taal-, Land- en Volkenkunde ("Bibliotheca Indonesica"), 2 vol., 330 pp.

Terada, Alice M., 1994, *The Magic Crocodile and Other Folk Tales from Indonesia*, Collection of fairy tales, Honolulu, Hawaii: University of Hawaii Press.

Thierry, Solange, 1988, *De la rizière à la forêt. Contes khmers*, L'Harmattan ("La légende des mondes" series), 254 pp., gloss.

———, 1991, "Mythes et croyances du Cambodge", in: André Akoun, dir., *L'Asie. Mythes et traditions*, Brepols ("Mythes et croyances du monde entier" series), pp. 224–34, 492 pp.

Weatley, Paul, 1980, *The Golden Khersonese. Studies in the historical geography of the Malay Peninsula before A.D. 1500*, Kuala Lumpur, Penerbit University Malaya, 388 pp.

Wilkinson, R. J., 1959, *A Malay–English Dictionary (Romanised)*, London, Macmillan & Co., 2 vol., 1291 pp.

Wyatt, David K., 1984, *Thailand. A short history*, New Haven, Conn., Yale University Press and Chiang Mai, Thailand, Trasvin Publications, 351 pp.

———, 1994, *Studies in Thai history. Collected essays*, Chiang Mai, Thailand, Silkworm Books, 288 pp.

———, 1975, (trans.) *The Crystal Sands. The chronicles of Nagara Sri Dharmaja*, Ithaca, Cornell University, Southeast Asia Programme, Data paper, 98.